Emerging Electrical and Computer Technologies for Smart Cities

This text discusses smart grid technologies including home energy management systems, demand management systems, source-side management systems and communication technologies for power supply management, and supervisory control and data acquisition. It further covers applications of rooftop solar PV panels, rooftop solar heating systems, solar streetlights, solar traffic signal systems, and electrical demand management for smart cities.

This book:

- Includes design and implementation of intelligent and smart techniques using artificial intelligence, the Internet of Things, and machine learning for the development of smart cities.
- Covers important topics including smart grid power supply, energy management, smart transport system, smart buildings, and traffic management.
- Provides smart solutions for waste management, traffic, parking, energy, and healthcare systems.
- Highlights renewable energy applications including rooftop solar PV panels, rooftop solar heating systems, solar traffic signal systems, and electrical demand management.
- Presents MATLAB-based simulations and results for smart cities solutions.

It will serve as an ideal reference text for graduate students and academic researchers in the fields of electrical engineering, electronics and communication engineering, computer engineering, civil engineering, and environmental engineering.

Emerging Electrical and Computer Technologies for Smart Cities

Modelling, Solution Techniques and Applications

Edited by Om Prakash Mahela,
Baseem Khan and Puneet Kumar Jain

CRC Press
Taylor & Francis Group
Boca Raton London New York

CRC Press is an imprint of the
Taylor & Francis Group, an informa business

Designed cover image: Shutterstock

MATLAB® and Simulink® are trademarks of The MathWorks, Inc. and are used with permission. The MathWorks does not warrant the accuracy of the text or exercises in this book. This book's use or discussion of MATLAB® or Simulink® software or related products does not constitute endorsement or sponsorship by The MathWorks of a particular pedagogical approach or particular use of the MATLAB® and Simulink® software.

First edition published 2024
by CRC Press
2385 NW Executive Center Drive, Suite 320, Boca Raton FL 33431

and by CRC Press
4 Park Square, Milton Park, Abingdon, Oxon, OX14 4RN

CRC Press is an imprint of Taylor & Francis Group, LLC

© 2024 selection and editorial matter, Om Prakash Mahela, Baseem Khan and Puneet Kumar Jain; individual chapters, the contributors

Library of Congress Cataloging-in-Publication Data
Names: Mahela, Om Prakash, 1977– editor. | Khan, Baseem, 1987– editor. | Jain, Puneet Kumar, editor.
Title: Emerging electrical and computer technologies for smart cities : modelling, solution techniques
   and applications / Om Prakash Mahela, Baseem Khan, Puneet Kumar Jain.
Description: First edition. | Boca Raton, FL : CRC Press, 2024. | Includes bibliographical references
   and index. | Contents: Overview of recent practices of smart city projects / Baseem Khan and
   Ahmed Ali.
Identifiers: LCCN 2024006797 (print) | LCCN 2024006798 (ebook) | ISBN 9781032392813 (hbk) |
   ISBN 9781032782379 (pbk) | ISBN 9781003486930 (ebk)
Subjects: LCSH: Smart cities—Technological innovations. | Electric power distribution—Data
   processing. | Medical care—Data processing.
Classification: LCC TD159.4 .E44 2024 (print) | LCC TD159.4 (ebook) |
   DDC 307.1/416—dc23/eng/20240315
LC record available at https://lccn.loc.gov/2024006797
LC ebook record available at https://lccn.loc.gov/2024006798

ISBN: 978-1-032-39281-3 (hbk)
ISBN: 978-1-032-78237-9 (pbk)
ISBN: 978-1-003-48693-0 (ebk)

DOI: 10.1201/9781003486930

Typeset in Times New Roman
by Apex CoVantage, LLC

Contents

SECTION 3
Artificial Intelligence Applications for Smart Cities   49

5 Recent Trends in Artificial Intelligence Applications for Smart Cities: A Review   51

LOPAMUDRA HOTA, BIRAJA PRASAD NAYAK,
PUNEET KUMAR JAIN, AND ARUN KUMAR

6 VANETs for Smart Cities: Opportunities and Upcoming Research Directions   69

ARADHANA BEHURA, PUNEET KUMAR JAIN, AND ARUN KUMAR

SECTION 4
Internet of Things for Smart Cities

9 Traffic Control Using IoT Technologies and LoRaWAN for Smart Cities

J. UMA MAHESH AND JUDHISTIR MAHAPATRO

10 Using the Internet of Medical Things to Self-Monitor Vital Parameters

AISHWARYA

SECTION 5
Smart Grid Technologies and Renewable Energy

11 Renewable Energy Technologies in Smart Cities

RAM NIWASH MAHIA, HEMANT KAUSHIK,
RAGHAWENDRA MISHRA AND OM PRAKASH MAHELA

SECTION 6
Transmission and Distribution of Electrical Power in Smart Cities

14 Comprehensive Overview of Utility Network Technologies for Smart Cities

PRAMOD KUMAR, ATUL KULSHRESTHA,
SANJANA CHUGH AND OM PRAKASH MAHELA

15 Smart Power Quality Monitoring System for Smart Cities   267

EKATA SHARMA AND OM PRAKASH MAHELA

16 A Smart Protection Scheme for Smart City Transmission Feeders Using K-Means Clustering   289

EKATA SHARMA AND RAJENDRA MAHLA

SECTION 7
Recent Advancements in Healthcare Systems   311

17 Time–Frequency Features for the Cardiovascular System   313

RAVI RAJ CHOUDHARY, MAMTA RANI
AND PUNEET KUMAR JAIN

18 Multidomain Features for Emotion Recognition Using EEG Signals 326

SHREYAN SAHA AND PUNEET KUMAR JAIN

About the Editors

Om Prakash Mahela received a bachelor of engineering degree from the College of Technology and Engineering, Udaipur, India, in 2002, a master of technology degree from Jagannath University, Jaipur, India, in 2013, and a Ph.D. from the Indian Institute of Technology Jodhpur, India, in 2018, all in electrical engineering. He received a master of business administration (human resource management) from the Indira Gandhi National Open University, New Delhi, India in 2021. He completed school education from PM Shree Jawahar Navodaya Vidyalaya, Kuchaman City, India. From 2002 to 2004, he was an assistant professor with the Rajasthan Institute of Engineering and Technology, Jaipur, India.

From 2004 to 2014, he was a junior engineer with Rajasthan Rajya Vidyut Prasaran Nigam Ltd., India, then assistant engineer from February 2014 to February 2023 and executive engineer since March 2023 with the same organization. He has authored more than 260 research publications in top-tier journals and conferences and edited five books. He performed more than 300 reviews for the prestigious journals of IEEE, Elsevier, Springer, Wiley and Taylor & Francis.

His research interests include power quality, power system planning, grid integration of renewable energy sources, FACTS devices, transmission line protection, electric vehicles and condition monitoring. He was a recipient of the University rank certificate in 2002, Gold Medal in 2013, Best Research Paper Award in 2018, C.V. Raman Gold Medal in 2019, Senior Professional Engineer Award in 2021 and State-level merit Certificate in 2023 for meritorious performance in the Department. He has been included in the top 2% Scientists worldwide in 2021 and 2022 in the list published by Stanford University, USA. He also received certificates of outstanding contribution from *Computer & Electrical Engineering, International Journal of Electrical Power & Energy Systems, Measurement,* and *Renewable & Sustainable Energy Reviews.* He is a Senior Member of the IEEE.

Baseem Khan received his bachelor of engineering degree in electrical engineering from the Rajiv Gandhi Technological University, Bhopal, India in 2008.

He received his master of technology and doctor of philosophy degrees in electrical engineering from the Maulana Azad National Institute of Technology, Bhopal, India, in 2010 and 2014, respectively. Currently, he is working as an assistant professor in the School of Electrical and Computer Engineering, Hawassa University Institute of Technology, Hawassa University, Hawassa, Ethiopia. His research interests include power system restructuring, power system planning, smart grid technologies, meta-heuristic optimisation techniques, reliability analysis of renewable energy system, power quality analysis and renewable energy integration. He has published five edited books and more than 100 research publications in top-tier journals and conferences. He is also a member of IEEE and IEEE PES.

Puneet Kumar Jain received a bachelor of engineering degree in computer science and engineering from Engineering College Bikaner, India, in 2009; a master of technology degree in information technology from Delhi Technological University, Delhi, India, in 2011; and a PhD in Centre for Information and Communication Technology from Indian Institute of Technology Jodhpur in 2018. He is currently working as an assistant professor in the Department of Computer Science and Engineering at National Institute of Technology Rourkela, Odisha, since 2020.

Before that, he served as an assistant professor at the LNM Institute of Technology, Jaipur and Jaypee University of Information Technology, Solan (H.P). He has research interest in the field of biomedical engineering, where his research focuses on healthcare technology and algorithm development, aiming to advance patient diagnosis, assessment and treatment. His areas of research interest also include image processing, time–frequency analysis, and machine learning.

He has published his research work in peer-reviewed and SCI-indexed international journals and conferences. He is also a reviewer for various renowned international journals including *Biomedical Signal Processing and Control* (Elsevier), *Computers in Biology and Medicine* (Elsevier), *Health and Policy* (Elsevier), and various international conferences. He also received certificates of outstanding contribution in reviewing from *Biomedical Signal Processing and Control*. He has served as a member of organising committees and as session chairs at the international conferences I3CS-2021, PDGC-2016, ISPCC-2017, and ICIIP-2017 and at the international workshops IWMA-2019 and IWMA-2020.

Contributors

Ahmed Ali
Department of Electrical Engineering
Technology
University of Johannesburg
Johannesburg, South Africa

Aishwarya
Department of Computer Science and
Engineering
National Institute of Technology
Rourkela, Odisha, India

Anil Kumar Sharma
Department of Electrical Engineering
Jaipur Institute of Technology—Group
of Institutions
Jaipur, Rajasthan, India

Aradhana Behura
Department of Computer Science and
Engineering
National Institute of Technology
Rourkela, Odisha, India

Arun Kumar
Department of Computer Science and
Engineering
National Institute of Technology
Rourkela, Odisha, India

Atul Kulshrestha
Department of Electrical Engineering
Arya Institute of Engineering and
Technology
Kukas, Jaipur, India

Avinash Sharma
Department of Electrical Engineering
Jaipur Institute of Technology—Group
of Institutions
Jaipur, Rajasthan, India

Baseem Khan
Department of Electrical Engineering
Hawassa University
Awasa, Ethiopia

Biraja Prasad Nayak
Department of Computer Science and
Engineering
National Institute of Technology
Rourkela, Odisha, India

Chandresh Bakliwal
Department of Computer Science and
Engineering
Nirwan University
Bassi, Rajasthan, India

Earu Banoth
Department of Biotechnology and Medical Engineering
National Institute of Technology
Rourkela, Odisha, India

Ekata Sharma
Department of Electrical Engineering
Poornima College of Engineering
Jaipur, Rajasthan, India

Harsh Sonwani
Department of Computer Science and Engineering
National Institute of Technology
Rourkela, Odisha, India

Hemant Kaushik
Department of Electrical Engineering
Poornima College of Engineering
Jaipur, Rajasthan, India

J. Uma Mahesh
Department of Computer Science and Engineering
National Institute of Technology
Rourkela, Odisha, India

Jitendra Kumar Jangid
Department of Electrical Engineering
Jaipur Institute of Technology—Group of Institutions
Jaipur, Rajasthan, India

Judhistir Mahapatro
Department of Computer Science and Engineering
National Institute of Technology
Rourkela, Odisha, India

Lopamudra Hota
Department of Computer Science and Engineering
National Institute of Technology
Rourkela, Odisha, India

Mamta Rani
Computer Science, Central University of Rajasthan Rajasthan
Bandar Sindari, Rajasthan, India

Nisha Jain
Department of Computer Science
S.S. Jain Subodh P.G. Mahila Mahavidyalaya University, University of Rajasthan
Jaipur, Rajasthan, India

Om Prakash Mahela
Power System Planning Division
Rajasthan Rajya Vidyut Prasaran Nigam Limited
Jaipur, Rajasthan, India

Pramod Kumar
Department of Electrical Engineering
Suresh Gyan Vihar University
Jaipur, Rajasthan, India

Prashant Saxena
Rajasthan Rajya Vidyut Prasaran Nigam Limited
Jaipur, Rajasthan, India

Puneet Kumar Jain
Department of Computer Science and Engineering
National Institute of Technology
Rourkela, Odisha, India

Raghawendra Mishra
Department of Mathematics
S.B.S. Government P.G. College
Rudrapur (U.S. Nagar), Uttarakhand, India

Rajendra Mahla
Department of Electrical Engineering
Malviya National Institute of Technology
Jaipur, Rajasthan, India

Rajiv Goyal
Department of Electrical Engineering
Jaipur Institute of Technology—Group
   of Institutions
Jaipur, Rajasthan, India

Ram Niwash Mahia
Department of Electrical Engineering
National Institute of Technology
   Hamirpur
Hamirpur, Himachal Pradesh, India

Ravi Raj Choudhary
Computer Science
Central University of Rajasthan Rajasthan
Bandar Sindari, Rajasthan, India

Sanjana Chugh
Department of Chemistry
Anand International College of
   Engineering
Jaipur, Rajasthan, India

Shalabh Gupta
Department of Botany
S.B.S. Government P.G. College
Rudrapur (U.S. Nagar), Uttarakhand,
   India

Shreyan Saha
Department of Computer Science and
   Engineering
National Institute of Technology
Rourkela, Odisha, India

Suchismita Chinara
Department of Computer Science and
   Engineering
National Institute of Technology
Rourkela, Odisha, India

Sumanta Pyne
Department of Computer Science and
   Engineering
National Institute of Technology
Rourkela, Odisha, India

Susmita Mohapatra
Department of Computer Science and
   Engineering
National Institute of Technology
Rourkela, Odisha, India

Vipul Singh Negi
Department of Computer Science and
   Engineering
National Institute of Technology
Rourkela, Odisha, India

Section 1

General Overview

Chapter 1

Introduction

Baseem Khan and Ahmed Ali

1.1 THE SMART CITY CONCEPT

The idea of a "smart city" first surfaced in the United States during the New Urbanism trend in the 1980s [1]. Information technology was introduced alongside this movement, and the phrase smart city was first popularized in the media in the 1990s [2]. The idea of "Smart Earth," which sought to actualize a "sense, connect, and intelligence" fundamental concept, was put forth by IBM CEO M.S. Peng in 2009, and it greatly increased the appeal of smart cities across the globe [3, 4].

Due to disparities in economic, geographic, environmental, and cultural factors, different nations and regions have diverse definitions of smart cities, which has left the academic world without a consensus. While many academics have tried to define the features of smart cities, concentrating on management, communication, technology, long-term viability transportation, and surroundings, such definitions frequently contain flaws and are not widely accepted. To guide their real creation, provide objective and practical criteria for evaluation, and foster consensus, it is imperative to actually define smart cities.

Reaching a clear understanding is particularly important for dealing with the problems that come with the processes of global urbanization. Scholars from a variety of fields, including public health, information technology, computer science, sociology, and urban studies, have published more than thirty definitions, underscoring the need for additional clarification [5]. Caragliu et al. gave a thorough and impartial definition of smart cities [6]: Smart cities invest in human and social capital, as well as in traditional and contemporary communication infrastructure, and participate in participatory governance to advance sustainable social and economic growth, enhance the standard of living for their populace, and accomplish effective oversight of natural resources.

1.2 CHARACTERISTICS OF SMART CITIES

The material and artistic evolution of a city's exterior look is referred to as urban morphology. A city's distinct form is shaped over time by a variety of factors, including the availability of resources, the initial stage of development, the

DOI: 10.1201/9781003486930-2

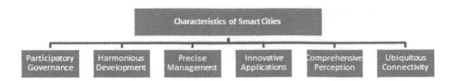

Figure 1.1 Smart grid charecteristics.

external environment, the economic structure, the level of technology, way of life, national the field of psychology, and cultural traits. These elements give a city its changing, varied, structured multifaceted and structural features. Figure 1.1 illustrates the essential characteristics of the smart city, a sophisticated type of urban development [1].

1.3 EVALUATION INDEX OF SMART CITY DEVELOPMENT

The building of smart cities advances when it is guided by reliable assessment indicators. Applications for cross-sectoral integration and the realization of huge multisource heterogeneous data are made possible by a uniform evaluation index system, and technical components need to be built with evaluation criteria in mind. Numerous assessment metric systems are currently being proposed globally from various angles.

For example, IBM's smart city encompasses three primary systems, each with three subsystems: infrastructural services, human services, and management and planning services [7]. Similarly, to evaluate European smart city initiatives, Giffinger and Gudrun established six evaluation dimensions: the economy, government, surroundings, individuals, flexibility, and life; 31 elements; and 74 indicators [8]. Marsal-Llacuna et al. claimed that real-time data-based indicators for monitoring are necessary to track the progress of smart city building and suggested utilizing principal component analysis to create a final synthesized index [9]. China's smart city designation system consists of 101 branches, 16 technological fields, and 5 primary types of criteria split into 4 levels [10]. Certain academics have developed systems for evaluating city development based on government services, infrastructure fields, industrial fields, and cultural traits by utilizing specific examples of city construction [11, 12].

Furthermore, the particular stage of the city's development should be taken into account when building the evaluation index system. Certain cities suggest incorporating specialized assessment frameworks that are tailored to their unique features and phases of development. For example, the European Smart Cities website presents a European smart city model that is divided into sub-models that represent major, small, and medium-sized cities, based on the analysis of indicators taken from over 90 smart city projects in Europe [13].

Additionally, based on six essential components, Cohen [14] proposed a set of 18 indicators for measurement and 46 sub-indicators. This is one of the most thorough classification schemes in the relevant literature because all the important components of smart city indices are covered by these categories. With the investigation and collection of pertinent knowledge, assessment has gradually improved as investigation into smart cities has advanced. The assessment of current smart cities comprises a number of methodical and scientific evaluation indicators that allow for the quantitative computation and analysis of the outcomes of smart city construction [1].

1.4 THE CONSTRUCTION AND INSPIRATION OF SMART CITIES AROUND THE WORLD

To obtain a thorough grasp of the current state of smart city development, we searched the Web of Science, Scopus, and Engineering Villages databases using the terms *smart cities* and *smart city*, and the official government website was consulted for pertinent documents and work reports. The primary goal of the IMD Smart City Index is to examine urban intelligence's reach and effects from the viewpoint of the citizenry [1]. We chose these cities to serve as examples of the most developed smart cities now implemented worldwide. We carried out a comparative study of the aforementioned cities as well as a few other well-known city instances, with an emphasis on the development of the economy, surroundings, flexibility, administration, and standard of life as well as public participation and experience [1].

1.4.1 Smart City Construction Worldwide

The increasing number of people living in cities across the globe is creating problems for infrastructure and services. Because of this, conventional approaches to urban development are insufficient, and in an effort to improve the lives of its residents, numerous cities have started smart city development initiatives. London, Stockholm, Dubai, New York, Barcelona, Hong Kong, Amsterdam, Singapore, Tokyo, Paris, and Copenhagen are a few examples of these cities. However, because every city has different resource, governance, and environmental challenges, there are discrepancies in the definitions of smart cities. Certain conceptions of smart cities stress the structure of data or a company, others emphasize sustainability or democracy, while yet others concentrate on smart transportation or infrastructure [1].

For instance, intelligent living, smart economic benefits, intelligent governance, smart atmosphere, smart electricity, smart communication, and smart transport are frequently the focal points of smart cities in other nations. Building smart cities has been given national strategic priority in the US, which has invested in smart grids and infrastructure. Europe, meanwhile, has put more of an emphasis on increasing energy efficiency. The objective of Japan's i-Japan strategy is to produce digital cities led by citizens that promote trust and vitality. Meanwhile, Singapore's Smart Nation 2015 plan has initiated multiple projects aimed at developing a smarter future city [1].

Many developing nations are also heavily engaged in the subject of exploring and building smart cities; these endeavors are not exclusive to industrialized nations. Developing nations deal with more pressing infrastructural issues and increased rates of urbanization. For instance, India declared in 2014 that it intended to build more than 100 smart towns equipped with advanced technological communication systems [1]. South Korea's National Strategic Smart City Program (NSSP) built a new technology ecosystem and standards for smart cities. NSSP services aim to increase the industrial landscape of smart cities by utilizing data structures and 5G telecommunication technologies. Yang et al. compared the smart city services provided by 15 smart cities in Europe, Asia, and North America with those provided by the NSSP by [15].

Many academics have examined the global growth of smart cities from various angles. In addition to identifying the benefits and drawbacks of each smart city development strategy, Angelidou also offered recommendations [16]. An empirical study by Lee et al. on the development of smart cities in Seoul and San Francisco revealed that management and people must dynamically coordinate on an open innovation platform in order for smart cities to be sustainable. Additionally, they noted the necessity of complimentary connections between different players, which ought to be modified in accordance with the degree of urban growth, social culture, and ability for governance [17].

Countries commonly use two main ways to construct smart cities: a top-down technology-led approach for constructing new cities, and a bottom-up and top-down approach that integrates both methods to promote innovative services in existing cities, taking into account pertinent development requirements [1]. For example, the UAE's Masdar Smart City project, which was started in 2006, aims to use solar technology to build a smart, sustainable, zero-carbon home for 50,000 people, 1500 clean technology companies, and 60,000 jobs every day. The city's operational and financial viability has not been adequately addressed, despite the implementation of certain conventional and intelligent technical solutions including shade connections, smart wind turbines, and shade shelters.

The high expense of living that comes with this urban building paradigm prevents inhabitants from integrating socially, and the highly invested autonomous bus system is insufficient to meet their daily transportation demands [1]. Furthermore, local problems with sand and dust have a negative impact on solar panel efficiency. As a result, one of the biggest problems with Masdar's smart city initiative is its lack of sustainability.

The 2008 Sustainability Award went to South Korea's Songdo smart city project, which was recognized as the most sophisticated new large-scale smart city development project. It did, however, depart from the culturally understood start-ing point by using a top-down, supply-oriented building approach that placed more emphasis on tangible hardware and industrial benefits [1]. This resulted in significant financial outlays and elevated risk associated with investments for the public sector. The lack of public participation, disregard for the demands of the local community, and growing ecological imprint raised possible issues for future development [1].

However, rather than being technology-led, the 2009-started Amsterdam Smart City project promotes the deployment of cutting-edge technologies by a variety of actors, which in turn motivates end users to modify their behavior. In order to deliver remedies to the city and its citizens, it highlights quadruple-helix collabo-ration between business, government, academia, and community. Local commu-nities are involved in a bottom-up strategy via the Smart City Living Lab, which ultimately combines economics and technology with social and environmental development goals. Similar to this, Brisbane, Australia, has improved public trans-portation to the city core and established a knowledge corridor with success [1].

All things considered, smart city development remains in its early stages, and technology cannot build and run a smart city from scratch. It is imperative to make astute choices and implement policies that incorporate the growth of smart cities into a framework for sustainable urban development that considers the quadruple bottom line of financial, social, ecological, and governance. Enhancing the effec-tiveness of cities also requires the knowledge of communities and residents [1].

1.5 CONCLUSION

A number of essential components are included in the notion of a smart city, such as topics, goals, methods, frameworks, settings, safety measures, and support sys-tems. Through their interactions, these components create a complicated metro-politan system with shared features in three overlapping layers: virtual, social, and physical space. The stages at which smart cities are developing also have an impact on these traits. Metropolitan systems of operation, systems of organization, and institutional systems have all undergone radical transformation as a result of the introduction of novel computer technologies and the dramatic changes they have brought about in information transmission. In the end, these modifications have an impact on people's interactions with one another, with the city, with envi-ronment, and with the worthwhile offerings of urban growth.

REFERENCES

[1] Liu, Z.; Wu, J. A review of the theory and practice of smart city construction in China. Sustainability 2023, 15, 7161.
[2] Bibri, S.E.; Krogstie, J. Smart sustainable cities of the future: An extensive interdis-ciplinary literature review. Sustain. Citi. Soc. 2017, 31, 183–212.

[3] Harrison, C.; Eckman, B.; Hamilton, R.; Hartswick, P.; Kalagnanam, J.; Para-szczak, J.; Williams, P. Foundations for smarter cities. IBM J. Res. Dev. Policy Rev. 2010, 54, 1–16.

[4] Palmisano, S. Smarter Planet. Available online: www.ibm.com/ibm/history/ibm100/us/en/icons/smarterplanet/words/ (accessed on 5 December 2022).

[5] Ramaprasad, A.; Sánchez-Ortiz, A.; Syn, T. A unified definition of a smart city. In Proceedings of the Electronic Government: 16th IFIP WG 8.5 International Confer-ence, EGOV 2017, St. Petersburg, 4–7 September 2017; pp. 13–24.

[6] Caragliu, A.; Del Bo, C.; Nijkamp, P. Smart cities in Europe. J. Urban Tech-nol. 2011, 18, 65–82.

[7] Rodrigues, M.; Monteiro, V.; Fernandes, B.; Silva, F.; Analide, C.; Santos, R. A gamification framework for getting residents closer to public institutions. J. Ambient. Intell. Humaniz. Comput. 2020, 11, 4569–4581.

[8] Giffinger, R.; Gudrun, H. Smart cities ranking: An effective instrument for the posi-tioning of the cities? ACE Archit. City Environ. 2010, 4, 7–26.

[9] Marsal-Llacuna, M.-L.; Colomer-Llinàs, J.; Meléndez-Frigola, J. Lessons in urban monitoring taken from sustainable and livable cities to better address the Smart Cit-ies initiative. Technol. Forecast. Soc. Change 2015, 90, 611–622.

[10] Guo, L.Q. The Research Report on Standards System of China Smart City; China Architecture & Building Press: Beijing, 2013.

[11] Chen, M.; Wang, Q.C.; Zhang, X.H.; Zhang, X.W. Study on the system of evalua-tion for Wisdom city construction-Nanjing as the case. Urban Stud. 2011, 18, 84–89.

[12] Zhang, Z.Q.Y.; Zou, K.; Xiang, S.; Mao, T.T. Model construction and empirical study on smart city construction ability assessment. Sci. Technol. Manag. Res. 2017, 37, 73–76.

[13] Giffinger, R.; Kramar, H. Benchmarking, profiling, and ranking of cities: The "European smart cities" approach. In Performance Metrics for Sustainable Cities; Routledge: London, 2021; pp. 35–52.

[14] Shah, M.N.; Nagargoje, S.; Shah, C. Assessment of Ahmedabad (India) and Shang-hai (China) on smart city parameters applying the Boyd Cohen smart city wheel. In Proceedings of the 20th International Symposium on Advancement of Construction Management and Real Estate, Melbourne, VIC, 20–23 November 2017; Springer: Singapore, 2017; pp. 111–127.

[15] Yang, J.; Kwon, Y.; Kim, D. Regional smart city development focus: The South Korean national strategic smart city program. IEEE Access 2020, 9, 7193–7210.

[16] Angelidou, M. Smart city planning and development shortcomings. TeMA J. Land Use Mobil. Environ. 2017, 10, 77–94.

[17] Lee, J.H.; Hancock, M.G.; Hu, M.-C. Towards an effective framework for build-ing smart cities: Lessons from Seoul and San Francisco. Technol. Forecast. Soc. Change 2014, 89, 80–99.

Chapter 2

Overview of Recent Smart City Practices

Baseem Khan, Ahmed Ali,
and Om Prakash Mahela

2.1 INTRODUCTION

The customs, social features, economic bases, and other attributes of various cities vary, so it is difficult to suggest a general theory or specific remedy for the development of smart cities that takes into account the various construction scenarios in various locations [1]. Moreover, there is still a dearth of information regarding the possible drawbacks and problems connected to the expansion of smart cities. In contrast with developed nations, developing countries experience rapid urban population growth, low average education levels, stressful lives, and difficulty implementing many sophisticated management initiatives that call for cooperation or popular participation. These factors present challenges for the construction of smart cities [2].

The current body of study on smart cities has concentrated on the construction effects, policy implications, technology applications, and development path [3, 4]. Large-scale, concentrated urbanization, rapid growth, and the urban–rural dual structure, among other factors, have received less attention [5, 6]. Significant public dangers have also brought attention to the need for improved response to emergencies and resiliency for subsequent smart cities, including the recent pandemic. It is evident that the progress of industrialization has a major influence on the creation of smart cities, and methods and approaches for resolving the particular problems that cities face must change correspondingly.

2.2 SMART CITY: CONNOTATION AND CONCEPT

Three categories have been established for the notion and meaning of smart cities.

2.2.1 Smart City 1.0

The primary goal of the first phase of smart cities, which focused on technology, was to improve operational models and urban development [1, 7]. The initial concept of smart cities revolved around the idea of leveraging new-generation

DOI: 10.1201/9781003486930-3

information technologies to support smart urban design, construction, management, and services. These technologies included cloud computing, big data, Internet of Things (IoT) infrastructure, and geospatial information integration. These approaches concentrate on how technology is advancing urban construction and development [8].

Most hypotheses now in circulation concur that major technology companies such as IBM Corp. [9], Songdo of the Republic of Korea [10–13], Portugal's PlanIT Valley [13, 14], and China's Unicom [15, 16] typically take the lead in building smart cities at this point. The goals of the smart city operating model are to modernize industry, increase productivity, and safeguard livelihoods. It is based on data, intelligent technology, and IT assistance. Writers in [17] offered the typical perspective in view of this level of development, stating that a smart city is essentially an intelligent metropolitan governance and operation machinery that is observable, quantifiable, apparent measurable, and manageable. An IoT-enabled intelligent digital city is referred to as a smart city. The system is put in place by fully digitizing the city's networks, sensors, and computer resources as well as by using a city database management and decision-making framework that has real-time data analysis capabilities [18].

From this theoretical perspective, the emergence of smart cities has exposed a number of issues. For example, Songdo, a new technological city, has incorporated a number of sustainable features, such as green public spaces, effective transportation, buildings that are energy-efficient, sewage reuse and recycling, and waste disposal systems. However, in spite of these initiatives, the city's residents' quality of life is still subpar, living expenses are high, and social and economic sustainability is still far off. The present-day population of the town is only approximately 70,000, a significant decrease from the approximately 300,000 that was originally planned.

Another illustration of the flaws in the first-generation smart city concept is Matsushima, which ignored the humanistic component of urban design in favor of high-tech hardware. What was formerly meant to be a business district, Matsushima, is now more of an upscale international residential neighborhood that doesn't quite reach the goals that were set forth. Therefore, for long-term sustainable growth, it is equally necessary to prioritize humanistic components of city planning as it is to give high-tech hardware top priority.

2.2.2 Smart City 2.0

The second wave of smart cities takes a more comprehensive approach to urban planning, emphasizing idea and vision above technology alone [1, 7]. This strategy is frequently primarily driven by governments. The governing bodies of second-generation smart cities employ high-tech tools, platforms, and software to solve urban issues and improve the lives of their constituents, in contrast to the first-generation smart cities, which placed a strong emphasis on technological advancement.

To keep technology from taking over urban life and decision-making, they carefully restrict how it is used [19]. Certain features of second-generation smart cities—including addressing social concerns, enhancing citizen well-being, maximizing government services, and addressing citizen needs—that are not always technology-related have been addressed by academics like Trencher [20]. Barcelona, Spain, is a prime example here [21–24], where expansion has prioritized sustainable, livable, and green features.

According to experts on smart cities, the main goal of developing a smart city is to improve the standard of living for its citizens by resolving the imbalance among demand and supply that governs a city's many operations [25]. The writers of [26] contended that the fundamental tools and components of urban growth are the environmental wisdom, technological intelligence, and the intellectualization of city dwellers. In contrast, authors in [27, 28] view the smart city as a whole approach to urban development, combining public services, industrial growth, urban operation and administration, and administrative efficacy to create a high-end example of contemporary urban development.

Additionally, academics emphasize that sustainable development ought to come first in smart cities [29]. The authors of [30] argued that in order to meet the needs of urbanization, modern smart cities should place a high priority on sustainability and effective transportation, electricity, healthcare, and governance. The ultimate aim and long-term objective of the development of smart cities in China, according to authors in [31], should be to achieve extensive and feasible social, economic, and ecological progress in order to ultimately meet the needs of the general public for safety and happiness in life. The authors also proposed a pyramid-star structured smart city framework.

Next-generation development is key to the popular conception of a smart city. The Worldwide Organization for Standardization defines a smart city as "an interconnected architecture that efficiently combines physical, electronic, and human factors to offer its citizens with a secure, equitable, and prosperous future" [32]. A smart sustainable city is an innovative urban center that uses technology for communication and information alongside additional materials to enhance the standard of living, maximizes urban operations and services, increases the city's competitiveness, and meets the needs of present and future generations in terms of economics, social issues, the environment, and culture [33]. The International Telecommunication Union's Telecommunication Standardization Sector emphasizes sustainable development, and the New Type of Smart City Assessment Index serves as the central government of China's recognized description of a smart city.

According to this index, a smart city is a forward-thinking urban hub that uses technology for communication and information to integrate various urban management systems seamlessly, encourage sharing of resources and data and business collaboration, encourage smart urban area management and services, improve urban operations and public services, increase city residents' happiness and contentment, and accomplish sustainable development [34]. This description emphasizes precisely the goals and instruments of developing smart cities, gives new technologies like ICT priority, stresses teamwork and resource sharing, and highlights development objectives like fulfillment and equitable growth for the general public's benefit.

In conclusion, there are similarities and parallels in the fundamental idea of a smart city system, even though different academics, organizations, businesses, and cities may have different interpretations of what smart cities are. Individuals, information and data, digital technology (ICT), and mechanical structures make up the fundamental idea [35]. Utilizing information technology to improve judgment in urban administration and services is the fundamental idea behind a smart city.

The main components of a smart city include innovative infrastructure, services for the public, manufacturing processes, integrating resources, security, and humanistic development. These are all intended to promote scientific advancement, effective management, and improved citizen quality of life [36]. In the end, optimizing urban growth patterns, improving urban quality, and addressing or mitigating the numerous problems associated with urban growth are the main objectives of the progress of smart cities [37].

The Smart City 1.0 concept emphasizes how important it is for new technologies to support smart city growth, which is a critical tool for creating smart cities. Smart City 2.0, in contrast, seeks to set itself apart from its predecessor by giving more attention to resolving urban issues, boosting public services, and enhancing citizen well-being. Building on the principles of Smart City 1.0, this version acknowledges the distinctions between the objectives and instruments of smart city development and seeks to encourage a more all-encompassing and comprehensive method of smart city progress.

2.2.3 Smart City 3.0

Smart City 3.0, which relies on the Smart City 2.0 principle, aims to optimize the organization of urban groups. It emphasizes the necessity of building smart cities through paths that prioritize participatory governance, activate and harness the power and wisdom of the people, and integrate top-down and bottom-up approaches [1, 7]. While admitting Smart City 2.0's faults in terms of significant community feedback, this version aims to promote increased citizen involvement in addressing urban challenges and shaping their towns' futures. Smart City 3.0 places a strong emphasis on the value of inclusive decision-making procedures where people may voice their concerns and work together to identify workable solutions to the governance, social, and environmental problems associated with urban development.

Cocreation is a concept that recognizes the vital roles that innovation and entrepreneurship play in advancing the development of smart cities, and it is essential to the accomplishment of Smart City 3.0 [1, 7]. Building a Smart City 3.0 necessitates the active involvement of urban subjects in order to support inclusion, create an inventive atmosphere, and include residents in the process of solving development-related problems. It is imperative that people make the transition from being passive consumers of services to active partners in determining their own level of life. The creation of smart cities should take into account local demographics, geography, history, and culture while maintaining a problem-oriented approach. High-tech and widespread innovation are the primary forces behind these developments.

Numerous academics have attempted to comprehend smart cities from a system theory standpoint. According to system theory scholars, modern cities are part of an open class of huge open systems, and the management of these systems has characteristics of dynamic, nonlinear complex giant connections with several levels, dimensions, structures, and subsystems that are highly interconnected [38]. Specialists in this domain hold that a smart city is an emerging urban ecosystem that influences inhabitants, businesses, and governance through the use of developing technology.

These cities involve managing complex systems digitally through networks such as urban geography, supplies, ecology, surroundings, population, finances, and society, as well as digitizing and informatizing every aspect of urban facilities and life development based on the information system's decision-making capabilities. According to the writers in [39], contemporary cities are intricate systems that combine cyber, physical, and social systems. They define the "wisdom" of smart cities as the convergence between urban information technology, competence, innovative towns, equitable growth, and environmental livability. This description emphasizes the significance of the interconnections between the various systems, going beyond the viewpoint of information and communication technology [40].

The definition of a smart city has shifted from being tool-driven to emphasizing pathways for vision and realization. Academics have expanded their knowledge and comprehension of smart cities by taking into account different viewpoints, such as partial system theory. The features of smart cities have been more apparent as the idea has been examined and refined throughout time.

2.3 CONCLUSION

Three generations of the evolution of smart cities are postulated and described theoretically. Smart City 1.0 aims to achieve prominent understanding, connectivity of all things, and complete intelligence by laying the groundwork for the digitization of information and dramatically increasing the rapidity, length, and precision of information dissemination. This is made possible by the swift advancement of new information technologies.

Building from this, Smart City 2.0 eliminates departmental barriers to data, integrates and applies large amounts of heterogeneous, multisource data widely, and encourages the upgrading and intelligent transformation of numerous fields, offering limitless potential for industrial and economic transformation. Urban civilization paradigm innovation is aided by the growth of intelligent cities. Building on the successes of Smart City 2.0, Smart City 3.0 stresses the involvement of the public in urban governance, goes back to the core objective of enhancing people's lives in cities, and genuinely accomplishes the objectives of balance, living standards, and smart.

2.4 ACKNOWLEDGMENT

This research work is supported by Innovader Research Labs, Innovader IITian Padhaiwala LearnLab Pvt. Ltd., Jaipur, India.

REFERENCES

[1] Liu, Z.; Wu, J. A Review of the theory and practice of smart city construction in China. Sustainability 2023, 15, 7161.

[2] Shen, L.; Huang, Z.; Wong, S.W.; Liao, S.; Lou, Y. A holistic evaluation of smart city performance in the context of China. J. Clean. Prod. 2018, 200, 667–679.

[3] Li, C.; Liu, X.; Dai, Z.; Zhao, Z. Smart city: A shareable framework and its applications in China. Sustainability 2019, 11, 4346.

[4] Li, C.; Dai, Z.; Liu, X.; Sun, W. Evaluation system: Evaluation of smart city shareable framework and its applications in China. Sustainability 2020, 12, 2957.

[5] Li, X.; Fong, P.S.; Dai, S.; Li, Y. Towards sustainable smart cities: An empirical comparative assessment and development pattern optimization in China. J. Clean. Prod. 2019, 215, 730–743.

[6] Wu, Y.; Zhang, W.; Shen, J.; Mo, Z.; Peng, Y. Smart city with Chinese characteristics against the background of big data: Idea, action and risk. J. Clean. Prod. 2018, 173, 60–66.

[7] Caragliu, A.; Del Bo, C.; Nijkamp, P. Smart cities in Europe. J. Urban Technol. 2011, 18, 65–82.

[8] Tahir, Z.; Malek, J.A. Main criteria in the development of smart cities determined using analytical method. Plan. Malays. 2016, 14, 1–14.

[9] Harrison, C.; Eckman, B.; Hamilton, R.; Hartswick, P.; Kalagnanam, J.; Paraszczak, J.; Williams, P. Foundations for smarter cities. IBM J. Res. Dev. Policy Rev. 2010, 54, 1–16.

[10] Carrera, B.; Peyrard, S.; Kim, K. Meta-regression framework for energy consumption prediction in a smart city: A case study of Songdo in South Korea. Sustain. Cities Soc. 2021, 72, 103025.

[11] Patel, M.; Padhya, H. A Smart city development concept: The Songdo experiences. Int. J. Res. Eng. Sci. 2021, 9, 7–10.

[12] Kovalev, Y.; Burnasov, A.; Ilyushkina, M.; Stepanov, A. Political models of smart cities and the role of network actors in their implementation (the case of Vienna, Lyon, and New Songdo in Seoul). In Proceedings of the AIP Conference Proceedings, I International Conference ASE-I-2021: Applied Science and Engineering: ASE-I, Grozny 25 June 2021; AIP Publishing: Woodbury, NY; p. 050002.

[13] Thomas, R.M. Inside smart cities: Place, politics and urban innovation, by Karvonen, Andrew, Federico Cugurullo, and Federico Caprotti. J. Plan. Educ. Res. 2022, 42, 497–498.

[14] Correia, D.; Teixeira, L.; Marques, J.L. Reviewing the state-of-the-art of smart cities in Portugal: Evidence based on content analysis of a Portuguese Magazine. Publications 2021, 9, 49.

[15] Shen, Z.; Guo, Z.; Shen, Q.; Guo, Z.; Sun, L. Promoting China's high-quality development with smart cities. Inf. China 2022, 353, 92–94.

[16] Wang, Y. Rearch on the business development strategy of China Unicom's smart city. Master's Thesis, Shandong University, Jinan, 2020.

[17] Li, D.; Shao, Z. Research on physical city, digital city and smart city. Geospat. Inf. 2018, 16, 1–4.

[18] Li, D.; Yuan, Y.; Shao, Z. The concept, supporting technologies and applications of smart city. J. Eng. Stud. 2012, 4, 313–323.

[19] Etezadzadeh, C. The city of the future. In Smart City—Future City? Smart City 2.0 as a Livable City and Future Market; Springer Fachmedien Wiesbaden: Wiesbaden, 2016; pp. 47–55.

[20] Trencher, G. Towards the smart city 2.0: Empirical evidence of using smartness as a tool for tackling social challenges. Technol. Forecast. Soc. Change 2019, 142, 117–128.

[21] Gascó-Hernandez, M. Building a smart city: Lessons from Barcelona. Commun. ACM 2018, 61, 50–57.

[22] Capdevila, I.; Zarlenga, M.I. Smart city or smart citizens? The Barcelona case. J. Strategy Manag. Res. Pract. 2015, 8, 266–282.

[23] Angelidou, M. Smart city policies: A spatial approach. Cities 2014, 41, S3–S11.

[24] Bakıcı, T.; Almirall, E.; Wareham, J. A smart city initiative: The case of Barcelona. J. Knowl. Econ. 2013, 4, 135–148

[25] Brous, P.; Janssen, M.; Herder, P. The dual effects of the Internet of Things (IoT): A systematic review of the benefits and risks of IoT adoption by organizations. Int. J. Inf. Manag. 2020, 51, 101952.

[26] Li, C. Research on the connotation, characteristic and development of smart city: A case study of smart city construction in Beijing. Modern Urban Res. 2015, 5, 79–83.

[27] Myeong, S.; Jung, Y.; Lee, E. A study on determinant factors in smart city development: An analytic hierarchy process analysis. Sustainability 2018, 10, 2606.

[28] Vukovic, N.; Rzhavtsev, A.; Shmyrev, V. Smart city: The case study of Saint-Peterburg 2019. Int. Rev. 2019, 15–20.

[29] Pira, M. A novel taxonomy of smart sustainable city indicators. Human. Soc. Sci. Commun. 2021, 8, 197.

[30] Souza, J. T. D.; Francisco, A. C. D.; Piekarski, C. M.; Prado, G. F. D. Data mining and machine learning to promote smart cities: A systematic review from 2000 to 2018. Sustainability 2019, 11, 1077.

[31] Xu, Q.; Wu, Z.; Chen, Z. The vision, architecture and research models of smart city. J. Ind. Eng. Eng. Manag. 2012, 26, 1–7.

[32] 30182:2017; Smart City Concept Model—Guidance for Establishing a Model for Data Interoperability; ISO/IEC: Geneva, 2017.

[33] Y.4900/L.1600(06/2016); Overview of Key Performance Indicators in Smart Sustainable Cities; ITU-T: Geneva, 2016.

[34] GB/T33356–2022; Evaluation Indicators for New-Type Smart Cities; State Administration for Market Regulation: Beijing, China, 2022.

[35] Song, Y.; An, X. Analysis on the concepts and conceptual systems of smart city in international standards based on terminology definitions of ISO, ITU-T and IEC. Stand. Sci. 2018, 1, 127–132.

[36] Zhao, D. The research on the construction of the smart city in China. Ph.D. Thesis, Jilin University, Changchun, 2013.

[37] Xiao, H.; Wang, Z. Systemic thinking on smart cities. China Soft Sci. Mag. 2017, 7, 66–80.

[38] Sheth, A.; Anantharam, P.; Henson, C. Physical-cyber-social computing: An early 21st century approach. IEEE Intell. Syst. 2013, 28, 78–82.

[39] Gang, S.; Qiang, T. Modern urban management: An open complex giant system. Urban Stud. 2007, 14, 66–70.

[40] Wang, F. The emergence of intelligent enterprises: From CPS to CPSS. IEEE Intell. Syst. 2010, 25, 85–88.

Section 2

Strategic Development of Cybersecurity for Smart Cities

Chapter 3

Cybersecurity for Smart Cities

Om Prakash Mahela, Nisha Jain, Chandresh Bakliwal, and Baseem Khan

3.1 INTRODUCTION

Smart cities have revolutionized people's lives with technology, but their implementation brings unexplored challenges related to cybersecurity, such as data leaks and malicious cyberattacks [1]. Complex cyberattacks can paralyze industrial control systems, causing adverse consequences. For individuals, cyberattacks usually involve a hijacking of communication systems or mobile ransomware that steals consumer data and personal identity information (PII) [2].

Different researchers have identified potential remedial actions against cyberattacks to minimize losses in smart cities. In [3], the authors presented a framework for data authentication and confidentiality to improve security in smart city communication networks. A shared session key was established between smart meters and control rooms for securing a two-way communication channel.

In [4], the authors designed a security model that installed wireless sensor networks in smart homes and buildings. The system the authors constructed used minimal sensor nodes at high coverage rate for smart buildings. In [5], the authors presented a detailed study of the security issues related to smart city infrastructure and proposed a method for analyzing threats and improving the data security.

In [6], the authors discussed smart cities and the different types of attacks that can occur as well as various initiatives started by the Government of India to safeguard smart cities from different attacks. In [7], the authors presented a big-data method to detect smart city cyberattacks in addition to discussing their types and impacts. They used their big data dataset to effectively identify and predict smart city cyberattacks. The authors in [8] analyzed security threat incidents involving smart city architecture of smart city and identified the possible scenarios of cyberattacks on the service infrastructure and operations of smart city.

This detailed analysis of the literature indicates that cyberattacks have increased in smart city infrastructures, and immediate actions and technology are required to provide security to smart city networks against cyberattacks. For this chapter, we analyzed cybersecurity and possible cyberattacks on different parts of the smart city infrastructure; we critically reviewed a total of 68 research papers and categorized them into six groups:

DOI: 10.1201/9781003486930-5

(i)   Basic concepts of smart cities and cybersecurity [1–8].
(ii)   A detailed study of cybersecurity [9–19].
(iii) IoT sensor applications in smart city networks [20–29].
(iv)   Smart cities, the cloud, and possible threats to smart city infrastructure [30–36].
(v)   Cybersecurity in smart cities including smart power network; smart buildings; and transportation, healthcare and communication systems [37–65].
(vi)   Challenges of cybersecurity in smart cities [66–68].

3.2 CYBERSECURITY

In the present era, in which we depend on connectivity and technology, cyber-security (CS) has emerge as a proactive safeguard of digital systems, networks, and data against malevolent attacks, unauthorized entry and potential hazards. Amid this interconnected landscape, CS assumes a pivotal position in upholding the privacy, trustworthiness, and accessibility of valuable information and digital resources [8, 9]. Following are key issues of CS [11–14]:

- **Digital Threat Landscape**: Proliferation of interconnected devices and the rise of sophisticated cyber threats pose significant challenges to CS. Malware, phishing attacks, ransomware, and data breaches are just a few examples of the threats that organizations and individuals face.
- **Importance of CS**: CS is essential to safeguarding sensitive data, main-taining trust in digital interactions, and protecting critical infrastructure. Breaches can lead to financial losses, reputation damage, and potential legal and regulatory consequences.
- **Protection Measures**: Effective CS involves a combination of technical, organizational, and human-centric measures. These can include firewalls, encryption, multifactor authentication, regular software updates, employee training, and incident response planning.
- **Continuous Monitoring**: Cyber threats evolve rapidly, requiring con-tinuous monitoring and adaptive security measures. Regular vulnerability assessments, penetration testing, and threat intelligence are crucial for stay-ing ahead of potential risks.
- **Collaboration and Regulation**: CS is a shared responsibility involv-ing governments, businesses, and individuals. Regulatory frameworks and industry standards help establish best practices and accountability for CS.
- **Balancing Convenience and Security**: Striking a balance between user convenience and robust security is a key challenge. While stringent security measures are necessary, they should not hinder user experience or impede innovation.

Smart city systems transfer sensitive information, and CS protects this information, its processing, and its storage with a combination of hardware and software [15]. Increased data size and complexity now have pronounced implications for CS in smart cities. CS protects systems, networks, and programs from digital attacks [16]. It protects mobile phones, computers, servers and all electronic devices from attacks of malicious nature, safeguarding users' information and identities [17]. CS helps organizations defend against data breaches and hacking attacks. Main categories of CS are cybercrime (targets systems to monetize), cyberattacks (purposeful gathering of information), and cyberterrorism (destroy electronic systems) [18]. Smart city CS is threatened by malware, phishing, SQL injection, denial-of-service and man-in the-middle (MITM) attacks, and social engineering [19].

3.3 SMART CITY SENSORS

Smart city services cover domains like the environment, transportation, tourism, health, energy management systems (EMS) for homes and buildings, safety and security. The U.S. National Institute of Standards and Technology (NIST) offers a commonly used smart city model with six categories: smart mobility, environment, governance, economy, people, and living [20, 21].

Smart cities require many Internet of Things (IoT) sensors to monitor services for smart parking, noise mapping in real time, structural health awareness, smart street lighting, traffic level monitoring and route optimization, etc. IoT is used as enabling technology for these services and Cloud is used for centralized data storage. IoT sensors play a pivotal role in collecting, transmitting, and analyzing data to enable informed decision-making and optimize city operations. These tiny, interconnected devices serve as the eyes and ears of a smart city, providing valuable insights into a wide range of urban systems and services [22].

IoT sensors measure a plethora of parameters like temperature, humidity, air quality, noise levels, light intensity, motion, and more and transmit the data over the Internet. They are formulated to be low-power and cost-effective, making it feasible to deploy them on a large scale throughout a city's infrastructure [23]. The term IoT refers to the connecting of these sensors and their smart devices across the Internet. Different natures of IoT sensors for smart city monitoring are presented in Table 3.1 [24].

3.3.1 Applications of IoT Sensors in Smart Cities

Some of the major applications of IoT data sensors in smart cities follow [25–27]:

- **Environmental Monitoring:** IoT sensors are used to monitor air and water quality, pollution levels, and waste management. This data helps authorities

Table 3.1 Challenges for Deployment of IoT Sensors in Smart Cities

S. No.	Challenges	Description
1	Data Privacy and Security	Collecting and transmitting high quanta of data reduce privacy and security. Ensuring data encryption, secure communication protocols, and robust access controls is essential.
2	Interoperability	As smart city deployments involve multiple vendors and technologies, ensuring interoperability between different IoT devices and systems can be complex.
3	Scalability	The sheer number of sensors required in a smart city can pose scalability challenges. Cities must plan for the deployment, maintenance, and management of a large sensor network.
4	Energy Efficiency	Many IoT sensors are battery-powered, which raises questions about energy efficiency and the environmental impact of battery disposal.

respond quickly to potential hazards, implement pollution control measures, and ensure a healthier environment for residents.

- **Traffic Management:** Smart traffic lights, parking sensors, and vehicle tracking systems utilize IoT technology for optimizing the traffic flow, reduction in congestion, and improvement in overall transportation efficiency.
- **Energy Management:** IoT sensors enable monitoring energy consumption in buildings and streetlights in real time. This data aids in identifying energy-saving opportunities, optimizing energy distribution, and reducing the city's carbon footprint.
- **Public Safety:** IoT sensors can be deployed to detect and respond to incidents such as accidents, fires, and criminal activities. They provide real-time information to emergency services, helping them respond more effectively.
- **Waste Management:** Smart waste bins fitted with sensors are effective for notifying collection services when they are full, leading to efficient garbage collection routes and reduced litter.
- **Water Management:** Sensors in water distribution systems monitor water pressure, leak detection, and quality, helping prevent wastage and ensuring a stable water supply.
- **Urban Planning:** IoT data assists city planners in understanding population movements, land use patterns, and resource utilization, aiding in the development of more sustainable and well-designed urban spaces.
- **Healthcare and Well-being:** Wearable IoT devices and health monitoring systems can help gather health-related data to improve healthcare services and enable early intervention.
- **Agriculture and Green Spaces:** IoT sensors can be used in urban farming and gardening to monitor soil moisture, plant health, and optimize irrigation, promoting green spaces within the city.

IoT sensors face multiple challenges pertaining to data security, privacy, interoperability and energy efficiency that were briefly described in Table 3.1 [28, 29].

3.4 SMART CITIES AND THE CLOUD

Smart cities store data in the cloud, making it accessible to all authorized stakeholders. However, any threat to an individual smart city component can affect the security of the relevant devices, software, and data stored in the cloud. This creates uncertainty of data accuracy and also reduces the admissibility of data as forensic evidence [30–32]. Table 3.2 presents major threats to smart city data stored in the cloud [33–36].

Table 3.2 Threats to Smart City Data Stored in the Cloud

S. No.	Type of threat	Description
I	Data leakage	Data control is relinquished when data are moving from resources to cloud. Data might be hosted on a multitenant environment. Data may be potentially accessed by third parties.
2	Insecure APIs	The APIs used to interact with cloud services must ensure secure communication that can be authenticated along with access control, encryption, and activity logging and monitoring.
3	Malicious insider threats	Many providers of cloud services do not disclose their clearance and screening methods. The procedures to give client organizations access to their resources are also not disclosed.
4	Denial of service attacks	Outside person who host the services on cloud are the easy target for the adversary to steal information related to smart city infrastructure. This may make data publicly accessible.
5	Malware	Middleware platforms are used by most of the host web applications of the cloud providers. When web applications and servers are not secure and configured, the adversary may leverage this opportunity to carry out malicious scripting attacks.
6	System and application vulnerabilities	Technology and applications are managed by third-party service providers and cloud provide. Therefore, cities do not control their data management and security. Cloud service providers must be trustworthy for providing secure services.
7	Boundaries for data locations and regulation	Smart cities must not have access to stored data.

3.5 CYBERSECURITY IN SMART CITIES

Smart cities are deploying advance smart technologies, but these are increasing the risks of cyberattacks. As an example, attackers may modify or forge the data related to communication between traffic control systems and traffic lights [37]. We next describe CS requirements and possible solutions in the different components of smart cities.

3.5.1 Smart Power Networks

The complex networks used to control and monitor power networks is exposed to possible vulnerabilities pertaining to control, communications as well as equipment. Cyberattacks on smart networks can attack different components of infrastructure [37]. Malicious intrusions on smart networks lead to consequences such as failure of generators, tripping of lines, equipment failure, massive network outage, leakage of customer information, and incorrect readings of consumer meters [39]. Smart power networks use hardware, software, and SCADA (supervisory control and data acquisition) systems for controlling various operations. Cyberattacks on SCADA systems can lead to heavy losses to power networks, as can major vulnerabilities to control systems [40]. A brief description of major threats to smart city power grid is included in Table 3.3. The specifications and purposes of high-level smart city power network requirements are elaborated in Figure 3.1.

3.5.2 Smart Buildings

Privacy breaches and attacks on building automation systems (BAS) are the main security challenges to smart buildings. BAS manage the automatic control

Table 3.3 Security Threats to Smart City Power Networks

S. No.	Type of threat	Description
1	Denial of service	SCADA center control activities are disrupted by traffic flood attacks. Computing resources and bandwidth are consumed to disrupt the smart network.
2	Identify forgery	Attackers disrupt the identification of control and monitoring devices.
3	Delay	Attackers can delay the exchange of messages in the transmission and distribution parts of network.
4	Message distortion	Messages sent to control room are distorted to indicate incorrect views of the grid, which disrupts normal grid operations.
5	Eavesdropping	Eavesdropping gives attackers unauthorized access to information and control, resulting in repetitive attacks on the system.

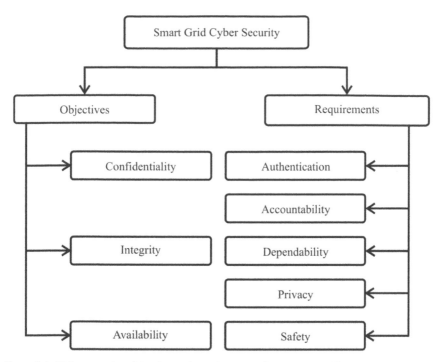

Figure 3.1 Cybersecurity objective and requirements for a smart grid.

of smart buildings' heating, ventilation, air conditioning, fire safety, and lighting systems. This maintains comfort for occupants, enhances the energy efficiency of buildings and reduces their energy consumption, improves demand flexibility, and enhances the life span of building equipment [41]. BAS architecture and communications are divided into three levels: management, automation, and field [42]. Cyberattacks on BAS can be categorized as unintentional attacks, international attacks, and malfunctions. [43, 44]. Common cyberattacks on BAS are elaborated in Table 3.4 [45, 46].

Cyberattacks on BAS target three main components: the management devices that are run on the information technology (IT) network, the interface between IT and operational technology (OT), and the field devices that run on the OT network [47]. Cyberattacks on BAS result in signal corruption, signal blocking and signal delaying [48]. They are commonly detected using approaches like rule-based and data-driven detection and visualization [49]. The field-level defenses against cyberattacks aim to protect privacy and verify devices. Protection at the management and automation levels includes hardening protocols, constructing network firewalls, and normalizing traffic [50]. A cybersecurity framework designed by the National Institute of Standards and Technology (NIST) for BAS is elaborated in Figure 3.2 [51].

Table 3.4 Cyberattacks on BAS

S. No.	Type of Attack	Description
1	Cross-Site Scripting	Malicious scripts are injected in the benign and trusted websites for accessing the cookies and session tokens.
2	Denial-of-Service	These attacks shut down a machine or network and make it inaccessible to the intended users.
3	Electromagnetic	Side-channel attacks are based on the measurement of the electromagnetic radiation generated from a device.
4	Fuzzing	Applications can be infiltrated using an automated process.
5	Man-In-The-Middle	A third party takes over communication control in stealth.
6	Password Brute-Force	Passwords are identified by systematically considering every possible combination of letters, numbers, and symbols until arriving at the correct password.
7	Replay	Valid data transmission is maliciously or fraudulently repeated or delayed.
8	Sniffing	Packet sniffers are used to capture network traffic and steal or intercept data.
9	Snooping	Intruders listen to the network traffic.
10	Spoofing	A person or program successfully falsifies data to gain illegitimate advantage.
11	Structured Query Language	Uses malicious SQL code to manipulate back-end databases and gain access to private information.

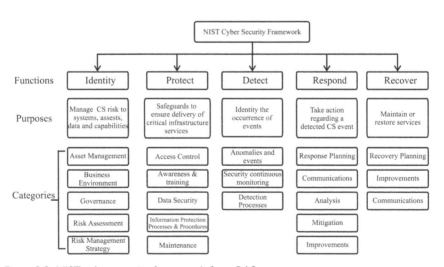

Figure 3.2 NIST cybersecurity framework for a BAS.

3.5.3 Smart Transportation

Smart transportation systems (STS) are an emerging field in smart city design categorized by complex data models, dynamics, and strict time assessment. Cybersecurity to maintain the safety and efficacy of transportation systems is a complex task [52]. Common cyberattacks on the STS of smart cities are vehicular ad hoc networks (VANETs) and man-in-the-middle, routing, timing, spoofing, denial-of-service, internal vehicle network, identity attack, eavesdropping, fog, and artificial intelligence (AI) attacks [53]. STS are a subset of IoT technologies. Figure 3.3 shows a basic IoT-supported architecture used for an STS [54].

The perception layer in an STS features smartphones, sensors, and infrastructure devices. The network layer is a complex alloy that uses wired and wireless technologies, and cybersecurity is provided by authenticating VANET nodes. In the application layer, the device interacts with the user to provide information, give warnings, and even activate vehicle systems. STS architecture, possible cyberattacks, and security approaches are elaborated in Table 3.5 [55, 56].

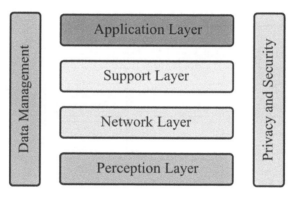

Figure 3.3 Basic architecture used for an STS.

Table 3.5 BAS Security Measures against Cyberattacks

S. No.	Layer	Security issue	Cyberattack	Security method
I	Perception	Devices are configured and initialized. Internal vehicular network is designed.	DoS and Spoofing	Security is ensured by contract and fusion of sensors.
2	Network	Undesired authentication in VANET	Sybil, DoS, MITM, eavesdropping, and routing	Blockchain, reputation-supported models, bloom filter combined with auxiliary techniques and game approach

(Continued)

Table 3.5 (Continued)

S. No.	Layer	Security issue	Cyberattack	Security method
3	Support	Fog defense	Fog defense	Authentication, encryption, management, and regular auditing
4	Application	Complicated data model, AI defense	Data poisoning, environmental perturbations, and policy manipulation	Blockchain, AI, machine learning, ontology, and game theory

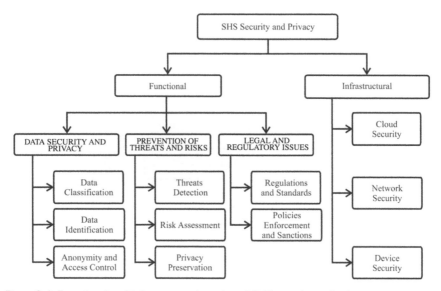

Figure 3.4 Functional and infrastructural modes of SHS security and privacy.

3.5.4 Smart Healthcare Systems

Smart healthcare systems (SHS) use sensors, actuators, and personal medical devices (PMDs) to effectively monitor patient health remotely and relay information to authorized healthcare providers [57]. The major cyberattacks in SHS are routing and location attacks. Location-based attacks include denial-of-service (DoS), fingers and eavesdropping threats, and sensor-based snooping [58]. SHS use private electronic patient information, so cyberattacks pose a critical threat and cybersecurity is a top priority for SHS. Figure 3.4 elaborates safety and confidentiality applications of SHS [59].

A detailed study of smart health applications and associated security and privacy aspects is presented in [60], and more detail on SHS security requirements is given in [61], including challenges to smart city SHS. A detailed study of the security threats to the IoT based SHS is elaborated in [62].

3.5.5 Smart Communication Systems

The innovation of information and communication technologies (ICT) has resulted in new economic and social opportunities in smart cities that help to improve life for citizens and societies. Communication systems play an important role in smart city functioning, and therefore, it is essential to secure smart city communication networks. Cybersecurity has thus become important in adopting smart city ICT systems to ensure information availability, integrity, and confidentiality [63]. Cyberattackers include individuals, nation states, and cybercrime organizations, and web servers, web application servers, personal computers, mobile phones, and stored information have been targeted in the attacks [64, 65].

3.6 CYBERSECURITY CHALLENGES IN SMART CITIES

Advanced technologies like ICT, IoT, AI, machine learning, blockchain, and cloud computing have resulted in cybersecurity risks, compromising the confidentiality, integrity, and availability of individuals' personal information [66]. Major cybersecurity challenges faced by smart cities include the following [67, 68]:

- variety and number of devices
- connectivity, communication, and security vulnerabilities
- addressing residents' data privacy and transparency concerns
- need for efficient and effective data processing and analytics
- data breaches and data loss
- risks arising from security and surveillance systems
- risks from complex network interconnectivity

3.7 CONCLUSION

This chapter presented a comprehensive overview of cybersecurity issues related to smart cities after establishing that it is an important issue for the advancement of smart cities. Cybersecurity is essential for safeguarding sensitive data, maintaining trust in digital interactions, and protecting critical infrastructure. IoT sensors play an important role in cybersecurity for smart cities. Environmental monitoring, traffic management, energy management, public safety, waste management, water management, urban planning, healthcare and well-being, agriculture, and green spaces are key applications of IoT sensors. Smart city sensor data are stored in the cloud for access by authorized stakeholders.

Smart city clouds face different types of threats such as leakage of data, insecure APIs, malicious insider threats, DoS, and malware. Cybersecurity is required for smooth operations of smart power networks, smart buildings, smart transportation, smart healthcare systems, and smart communication systems, and this chapter presents a review of 68 research studies related to critical cybersecurity challenges to functional smart cities. These findings should be helpful for engineers, scientists, and academicians working in the cybersecurity field to develop secure smart city infrastructure.

3.8 ACKNOWLEDGMENT

This research work is supported by Innovader Research Labs, Innovader IITian Padhaiwala LearnLab Pvt. Ltd., Jaipur, India.

REFERENCES

[1] D. Chen, P. Wawrzynski, Z. Lv. "Cyber security in smart cities: A review of deep learning-based applications and case studies." Sustainable Cities and Society, 66, 102655, 2021. https://doi.org/10.1016/j.scs.2020.102655.

[2] Z. Szabó. "Cybersecurity issues in industrial control systems." In 2018 IEEE 16th International Symposium on Intelligent Systems and Informatics (SISY), pp. 000231–000234, IEEE, 2018.

[3] F. A. Alfouzan, K. Kim, and N. M. Alzahrani. "An efficient framework for securing the smart city communication networks." Sensors, 22(8), 3053, 2022. https://doi.org/10.3390/s22083053

[4] G. Dinc and O. K. Sahingoz. "Smart home security with the use of WSNs on future intelligent cities." In 2019 7th International Istanbul Smart Grids and Cities Congress and Fair (ICSG), Istanbul, pp. 164–168, 2019. https://doi.org/10.1109/SGCF.2019.8782396.

[5] P. Wang, A. Ali and W. Kelly. "Data security and threat modeling for smart city infrastructure." In 2015 International Conference on Cyber Security of Smart Cities, Industrial Control System and Communications (SSIC), Shanghai, pp. 1–6, 2015. doi: 10.1109/SSIC.2015.7245322.

[6] M. A. Jabbar, K. M. V. V. Prasad and R. Aluvalu, "Future challenges for cyber-security in a smart city environment in Indian context." In 3rd Smart Cities Symposium (SCS 2020), Online Conference, pp. 359–364, 2020. doi: 10.1049/icp.2021.0904.

[7] F. Hajamohideen and S. Karthikeyan, "Cyber threats detection in the smart city using bigdata analytics." In 3rd Smart Cities Symposium (SCS 2020), Online Conference, pp. 233–238, 2020. doi: 10.1049/icp.2021.0872.

[8] J. Lee, J. Kim and J. Seo, "Cyber attack scenarios on smart city and their ripple effects." In 2019 International Conference on Platform Technology and Service (PlatCon), Jeju, Korea (South), pp. 1–5, 2019. doi: 10.1109/PlatCon.2019.8669431.

[9] F. Abdullayeva. "Cyber resilience and cyber security issues of intelligent cloud computing systems." Results in Control and Optimization, 12, 100268, 2023. https://doi.org/10.1016/j.rico.2023.100268.

[10] M. Lang, S. Dowling and R. G. Lennon. "The current state of cyber security in Ireland." 2022 Cyber Research Conference—Ireland (Cyber-RCI), Galway, pp. 1–2, 2022. doi: 10.1109/Cyber-RCI55324.2022.10032682.

[11] N. Ahmad, U. A. Mokhtar, W. Fariza Paizi Fauzi, Z. A. Othman, Y. Hakim Yeop and S. N. Huda Sheikh Abdullah. "Cyber security situational awareness among parents." In 2018 Cyber Resilience Conference (CRC), Putrajaya, pp. 1–3, 2018. doi: 10.1109/CR.2018.8626830.

[12] B. Craggs and A. Rashid. "Smart cyber-physical systems: Beyond usable security to security ergonomics by design." In 2017 IEEE/ACM 3rd International Workshop on Software Engineering for Smart Cyber-Physical Systems (SEsCPS), Buenos Aires, pp. 22–25, 2017. doi: 10.1109/SEsCPS.2017.5.

[13] A. Cartwright, E. Cartwright, E. S. Edun. "Cascading information on best practice: Cyber security risk management in UK micro and small businesses and the role of IT companies." Computers & Security, 131, 103288, 2023. https://doi.org/10.1016/j.cose.2023.103288.

[14] H. A. Chattha, M. M. U. Rehman, G. Mustafa, A. Q. Khan, M. Abid and E. U. Haq. "Implementation of cyber-physical systems with modbus communication for security studies." In 2021 International Conference on Cyber Warfare and Security (ICCWS), Islamabad, pp. 45–50, 2021. doi: 10.1109/ICCWS53234.2021.9702959.

[15] T. Tam, A. Rao and J. Hall. The good, the bad and the missing: A Narrative review of cyber-security implications for australian small businesses." Computers & Security, 109, 102385, 2021. https://doi.org/10.1016/j.cose.2021.102385.

[16] S. Hasan, M. Ali, S. Kurnia and R. Thurasamy. "Evaluating the cyber security readiness of organizations and its influence on performance." Journal of Information Security and Applications, 58, 102726, 2021. https://doi.org/10.1016/j.jisa.2020.102726.

[17] B. Uchendu, J. R. C. Nurse, M. Bada and S. Furnell. "Developing a cyber security culture: Current practices and future needs." Computers & Security, 109, 102387, 2021. https://doi.org/10.1016/j.cose.2021.102387.

[18] B. Gunes, G. Kayisoglu and P. Bolat. "Cyber security risk assessment for seaports: A case study of a container port." Computers & Security, 103, 102196, 2021. https://doi.org/10.1016/j.cose.2021.102196.

[19] J. Huang, D. W.C. Ho, F. Li, W. Yang and Y. Tang. "Secure remote state estimation against linear man-in-the-middle attacks using watermarking." Automatica, 121, 109182, 2020. https://doi.org/10.1016/j.automatica.2020.109182.

[20] H. Mansor, K. Markantonakis, R. N. Akram, K. Mayes and I. Gurulian. "Log your car: The non-invasive vehicle forensics." In 2016 IEEE Trustcom/BigDataSE/ISPA, Tianjin, pp. 974–982, 2016. doi: 10.1109/TrustCom.2016.0164.

[21] J.-Y. Byun, A. Nasridinov and Y.-H. Park. "Internet of things for smart crime detection." Contemporary Engineering Sciences, 7(15), 749–754, 2014. http://dx.doi.org/10.12988/ces.2014.4685.

[22] Z. A. Baig, P. Szewczyk, C. Valli, P. Rabadia, P. Hannay, M. Chernyshev, M. Johnstone, P. Kerai, A. Ibrahim, K. Sansurooah, N. Syed, M. Peacock. "Future challenges for smart cities: Cyber-security and digital forensics." Digital Investigation, 22, 3–13, 2017. https://doi.org/10.1016/j.diin.2017.06.015.

[23] P. Yadav and S. Vishwakarma, "Application of internet of things and big data towards a smart city." In 2018 3rd International Conference on Internet of Things: Smart Innovation and Usages (IoT-SIU), Bhimtal, pp. 1–5, 2018. doi: 10.1109/IoT-SIU.2018.8519920.

[24] E. Oriwoh and M. Conrad. Presence detection from smart home motion sensor datasets: A model. In E. Kyriacou, S. Christofides and C. Pattichis (eds) XIV Mediterranean Conference on Medical and Biological Engineering and Computing 2016. IFMBE Proceedings, vol 57. Springer, Cham, 2018. https://doi.org/10.1007/978-3-319-32703-7_240

[25] A. Alkhamisi, M. S. H. Nazmudeen and S. M. Buhari. "A cross-layer framework for sensor data aggregation for IoT applications in smart cities." In 2016 IEEE International Smart Cities Conference (ISC2), Trento, pp. 1–6, 2016. doi: 10.1109/ISC2.2016.7580853.

[26] P. Yadav and S. Vishwakarma. "Application of internet of things and big data towards a smart city." In 2018 3rd International Conference On Internet of Things: Smart Innovation and Usages (IoT-SIU), Bhimtal, pp. 1–5, 2018. doi: 10.1109/IoT-SIU.2018.8519920.

[27] K. L. Keung, C. K. M. Lee, K. K. H. Ng and C. K. Yeung. "Smart city application and analysis: Real-time urban drainage monitoring by IoT sensors: A case study of Hong Kong." In 2018 IEEE International Conference on Industrial Engineering and Engineering Management (IEEM), Bangkok, pp. 521–525, 2018. doi: 10.1109/IEEM.2018.8607303.

[28] M. Ilyas. "IoT applications in Smart Cities." In 2021 International Conference on Electronic Communications, Internet of Things and Big Data (ICEIB), Yilan County, pp. 44–47, 2021. doi: 10.1109/ICEIB53692.2021.9686400.

[29] W. Wang, S. De, Y. Zhou, X. Huang and K. Moessner. "Distributed sensor data computing in smart city applications." In 2017 IEEE 18th International Symposium on A World of Wireless, Mobile and Multimedia Networks (WoWMoM), Macau, pp. 1–5, 2017. doi: 10.1109/WoWMoM.2017.7974338.

[30] W. Guo, M. Zhu and D. Qi. "A general cloud service architecture of smart city based on component assembling." In 2021 3rd International Symposium on Smart and Healthy Cities (ISHC), Toronto, pp. 41–46, 2021. doi: 10.1109/ISHC54333.2021.00016.

[31] L. F. Herrera-Quintero, J. Vega-Alfonso, D. Bermúdez, L. A. Marentes and K. Banse. "ITS for smart parking systems, towards the creation of smart city services using IoT and cloud approaches." In 2019 Smart City Symposium Prague (SCSP), Prague, pp. 1–7, 2019. doi: 10.1109/SCSP.2019.8805705.

[32] M. Avalos, P. Salazar, V. M. Larios and H. Durán-Limón. "Smart health methodology and services powered by leading edge cognitive services consumed in the cloud." In 2016 IEEE International Smart Cities Conference (ISC2), Trento, pp. 1–6, 2016. doi: 10.1109/ISC2.2016.7580862.

[33] N. Mohamed, J. Al-Jaroodi, S. Lazarova-Molnar, I. Jawhar and S. Mahmoud. "A service-oriented middleware for cloud of things and fog computing supporting smart city applications." In 2017 IEEE SmartWorld, Ubiquitous Intelligence & Computing, Advanced & Trusted Computed, Scalable Computing & Communications, Cloud & Big Data Computing, Internet of People and Smart City Innovation (SmartWorld/SCALCOM/UIC/ATC/CBDCom/IOP/SCI), San Francisco, CA, pp. 1–7, 2017. doi: 10.1109/UIC-ATC.2017.8397564.

[34] P. Wang, L. T. Yang and J. Li. "An edge cloud-assisted CPSS framework for smart city. IEEE Cloud Computing, 5(5), 37–46, 2018. doi: 10.1109/MCC.2018.053711665.

[35] F. Sabahi. "Cloud computing security threats and responses." In 2011 IEEE 3rd International Conference on Communication Software and Networks, Xi'an, pp. 245–249, 2011. doi: 10.1109/ICCSN.2011.6014715.

[36] A. Behl. "Emerging security challenges in cloud computing: An insight to cloud security challenges and their mitigation." In 2011 World Congress on Information and Communication Technologies, Mumbai, pp. 217–222, 2011. doi: 10.1109/WICT.2011.6141247.

[37] M. Tabaa, F. Monteiro, H. Bensag, A. Dandache. "Green Industrial Internet of Things from a smart industry perspectives." Energy Reports, 6(Suppl. 6), 430–446, 2020. https://doi.org/10.1016/j.egyr.2020.09.022.

[38] S. B. Slama. "Prosumer in smart grids based on intelligent edge computing: A review on Artificial Intelligence Scheduling Techniques. Ain Shams Engineering Journal, 13(1), 101504, 2022.

[39] P. Singh, M. Masud, M. Shamim Hossain, A. Kaur. "Blockchain and homomorphic encryption-based privacy-preserving data aggregation model in smart grid." Computers & Electrical Engineering, 93, 107209, 2021. https://doi.org/10.1016/j.compeleceng.2021.107209.

[40] Z. Masood, R. Samar, M. A. Zahoor Raja. "Design of a mathematical model for the Stuxnet virus in a network of critical control infrastructure." Computers & Security, 87, 101565, 2019. https://doi.org/10.1016/j.cose.2019.07.002.

[41] T. I. Salsbury. "A survey of control technologies in the building automation industry." IFAC Proceedings Volumes, 38(1), 90–100, 2005. https://doi.org/10.3182/20050703-6-CZ-1902.01397.

[42] L. Martirano and M. Mitolo. "Building automation and control systems (bacs): A review." In 2020 IEEE International Conference on Environment and Electrical Engineering and 2020 IEEE Industrial and Commercial Power Systems Europe (EEEIC/I&CPS Europe). IEEE, 2020.

[43] Y. Liu, Z. Pang, G. Dán, D. Lan and S. Gong. "A taxonomy for the security assessment of IP-based building automation systems: The case of thread." IEEE Transactions on Industrial Informatics, 14(9), 4113–4123, 2018. doi: 10.1109/TII.2018.2844955.

[44] T. Mundt and P. Wickboldt. "Security in building automation systems—A first analysis." In 2016 International Conference on Cyber Security and Protection of Digital Services (Cyber Security), London, pp. 1–8, 2016. doi: 10.1109/CyberSecPODS.2016.7502336.

[45] B. Pingle, A. Mairaj and A. Y. Javaid. "Real-world man-in-the-middle (MITM) attack implementation using open source tools for instructional use." In 2018 IEEE International Conference on Electro/Information Technology (EIT), Rochester, MI, pp. 0192–0197, 2018. doi: 10.1109/EIT.2018.8500082.

[46] S. Gupta and B. Bhooshan Gupta. "Cross-Site Scripting (XSS) attacks and defense mechanisms: classification and state-of-the-art." International Journal of System Assurance Engineering and Management, 8, 512–530, 2017.

[47] W. Granzer, F. Praus and W. Kastner, "Security in building automation systems." IEEE Transactions on Industrial Electronics, 57(11), 3622–3630, 2010, doi: 10.1109/TIE.2009.2036033.

[48] I. Kotenko and A. Chechulin. "A cyber attack modeling and impact assessment framework." In 2013 5th International Conference on Cyber Conflict (CYCON 2013), Tallinn, pp. 1–24, 2013.

[49] G. Li, Z. Yang, Y. Fu, L. Ren, Z. O'Neill and C. Parikh. Development of a hardware-In-the-Loop (HIL) testbed for cyber-physical security in smart buildings. arXiv preprint arXiv:2210.11234, 2022.

[50] P. K. Manadhata and J. M. Wing. "An attack surface metric." IEEE Transactions on Software Engineering, 37(3), 371–386, 2011. doi: 10.1109/TSE.2010.60.

[51] M. Barrett. Framework for Improving Critical Infrastructure Cybersecurity Version 1.1, NIST Cybersecurity Framework, 2018. https://doi.org/10.6028/NIST. CSWP.04162018, www.nist.gov/cyberframework (Accessed August 11, 2023).

[52] P. Coppola and F. Silvestri. "Autonomous vehicles and future mobility solutions,: In Autonomous Vehicles and Future Mobility; AET Series; Elsevier: Amsterdam, 2019.

[53] T. Mecheva and N. Kakanakov. "Cybersecurity in intelligent transportation systems." Computers, 9(4), 83, 2020. https://doi.org/10.3390/computers9040083

[54] L. Cui, G. Xie, Y. Qu, L. Gao and Y. Yang. "Security and privacy in smart cities: Challenges and opportunities." IEEE Access, 6, 46134–46145, 2018.

[55] M.A.A. Careem, A. Dutta. "Reputation based routing in MANET using blockchain." In Proceedings of the 2020 International Conference on COMmunication Systems & NETworkS (COMSNETS), Bengaluru, pp. 1–6, 7–11 January 2020.

[56] V. Deshpande, T. Das, H. Badis and L. George. "SEBS: A secure element and blockchain stratagem for securing IoT." In 2019 Global Information Infrastructure and Networking Symposium (GIIS), Paris, pp. 1–7, 2019. doi: 10.1109/ GIIS48668.2019.9044957.

[57] N. Dey, A.S. Ashour, F. Shi, S.J. Fong and R.S. Sherratt. "Developing residential wireless sensor networks for ECG healthcare monitoring." In IEEE Transactions on Consumer Electronics, 63(4), art. no. 8246822; 442–449, 2017. DOI: 10.1109/ TCE.2017.015063

[58] K. Watson and D. M. Payne. "Ethical practice in sharing and mining medical data." Journal of Information, Communication and Ethics in Society, 19(1), 1–19, 2021.

[59] H. A. El Zouka and M. M. Hosni. "Secure IoT communications for smart healthcare monitoring system." Internet of Things, 13, 100036, 2021.

[60] D. Ding, M. Conti and A. Solanas, "A smart health application and its related privacy issues," 2016 Smart City Security and Privacy Workshop (SCSP-W), Vienna, Austria, 2016, pp. 1–5, doi: 10.1109/SCSPW.2016.7509558.

[61] A. Rabii, S. Assoul and O. Roudies. "Security requirements elicitation: A smart health case." In 2020 Fourth World Conference on Smart Trends in Systems, Security and Sustainability (WorldS4), London, pp. 776–781, 2020. doi: 10.1109/ WorldS450073.2020.9210330.

[62] S. A. Butt, J. L. Diaz-Martinez, T. Jamal, A. Ali, E. De-La-Hoz-Franco and M. Shoaib. "IoT smart health security threats." In 2019 19th International Conference on Computational Science and Its Applications (ICCSA), St. Petersburg, pp. 26–31, 2019. doi: 10.1109/ICCSA.2019.000-8.

[63] A. Ghosal and M. Conti. "Key management systems for smart grid advanced metering infrastructure: A survey." In IEEE Communications Surveys & Tutorials, 21(3), 2831–2848, thirdquarter 2019. doi: 10.1109/COMST.2019.2907650.

[64] K. Kyounggon, J. Seok Kim, S. Jeong, J.-H. Park, H. Kang Kim. "Cybersecurity for autonomous vehicles: Review of attacks and defense." Computers & Security, 103, 102150, 2021. https://doi.org/10.1016/j.cose.2020.102150.

[65] K. Kim, K. Cho, J. Lim, Y. Ho Jung, M. Seok Sung, S. Beom Kim, H. Kang Kim. "What's your protocol: Vulnerabilities and security threats related to Z-Wave protocol." Pervasive and Mobile Computing, 66, 101211, 2020. https://doi.org/10.1016/j. pmcj.2020.101211.

[66] A. S. Elmaghraby and M. M. Losavio. "Cyber security challenges in Smart Cities: Safety, security and privacy." Journal of Advanced Research, 5(4), 491–497, 2014. https://doi.org/10.1016/j.jare.2014.02.006.

[67] M. Chen. "Smart city and cyber-security; technologies used, leading challenges and future recommendations." Energy Reports, 7, 7999–8012, 2021. https://doi.org/10.1016/j.egyr.2021.08.124.

[68] M. Vitunskaite, Y. He, T. Brandstetter and H. Janicke. "Smart cities and cyber security: Are we there yet? A comparative study on the role of standards, third party risk management and security ownership." Computers & Security, 83, 313–331, 2019.

Chapter 4

Cybersecurity Issues and Solutions for Smart Power Networks

Prashant Saxena

4.1 INTRODUCTION

The power sector is experiencing several simultaneous changes, culminating in an evolved energy system that I describe in this chapter. The initial analysis focuses on the interplay of shifting toward more unpredictable renewable energy, cyber susceptibility, and climate impact on electric security. Additionally, I delve into the relevance of emergent technologies, responses from the demand side, and the electrification of increasing sectors. Examples and case studies from actual power grids depict these transformations, offering insights and best practices to aid policy makers in navigating the fluctuating energy landscape. Given this ubiquitous reliance on electricity, it is of utmost importance to ensure a steady, uninterrupted supply. Any disruption can have severe impacts, leading to business downtime, financial loss, and even threats to human life. The energy sector is currently facing numerous challenges that threaten the reliability of electricity supply. Decarbonization efforts are leading to a shift away from traditional, carbon-intensive energy sources toward variable renewable sources, like wind and solar power. While beneficial for the environment, these sources are less predictable and depend on weather conditions, thereby introducing volatility to the power grid [1].

Ensuring a stable and dependable electricity supply is paramount to societal advancement and the smooth functioning of a 24/7 digital economy. The recent Covid-19 pandemic has reinforced the indispensable role of electricity in every aspect of life, from ensuring the functionality of healthcare equipment and IT systems to enabling remote work and video communication. It is imperative for each country to prioritize the sustenance of a secure and reliable electricity grid. Looking ahead, electricity is expected to play an amplified role in a range of digitally integrated sectors such as heating, cooling, transportation, communication, banking, and healthcare. To maintain the operation of modern economies, rigorous electricity security protocols are necessary. Thus, guaranteeing reliable access to electricity has emerged as a top concern in energy policy [2].

The energy sector has witnessed considerable shifts, transitioning from a stage dominated by centralized, vertically integrated systems utilizing a handful of large, dispatchable thermal power plants to a market teeming with diverse power

DOI: 10.1201/9781003486930-6

producers, many employing variable renewable resources. Concurrently, digital tools' influence is burgeoning at an impressive pace. Although emerging digital technologies unlock new potential for economic development and simplify the management of these complex systems, they also expose the power grid to cyber threats. While government and corporate entities work toward mitigating greenhouse gas emissions, adapting the electrical system infrastructure to climate change repercussions is paramount for maintaining the system's strength and resilience [3].

4.2 CYBERSECURITY ISSUES IN THE POWER SECTOR

In the era of digital transformation, the power sector is increasingly reliant on advanced technologies and networked systems for grid management and control, which opens up a new spectrum of cybersecurity vulnerabilities. One of the major issues is the risk of cyberattacks targeting supervisory control and data acquisition systems, which are crucial for the operation of power grids. These systems gather and analyze real-time data, allowing operators to control equipment remotely. Any successful infiltration can disrupt the grid operation, leading to blackouts or even physical damage to the infrastructure [4].

The growing integration of renewable energy sources, such as wind and solar, is another aspect that increases the complexity of the grid, making it a larger target for potential cyber threats. These distributed energy resources often use Internet of Things (IoT) devices for monitoring and control, which can be vulnerable to attacks if not properly secured. Smart grid technologies including smart meters and digital substations, while offering numerous benefits like efficiency and better demand response, also introduce new potential entry points for cybercriminals. The enormous amount of data generated and transmitted by these devices needs rigorous protection measures. Moreover, the power sector often relies on legacy systems that were not designed with current cybersecurity threats in mind. Upgrading these systems without disrupting the service is a significant challenge.

Lastly, there's the risk of state-sponsored cyberattacks aimed at crippling a country's critical infrastructure, of which power systems are a part. These attacks could be politically motivated and have wide-ranging implications for national security. To mitigate these issues, the power sector needs to implement robust cybersecurity measures that include secure network design, regular vulnerability assessments, advanced threat detection mechanisms, employee training, and incident response strategies. Collaborative efforts between governments, regulatory bodies, and private entities are also crucial to stay ahead of emerging cyber threats.

4.3 INCREASING CYBER-PHYSICAL SYSTEMS

Cyber-physical systems (CPS) are integrations of computation, networking, and physical processes in which embedded computers and networks monitor and control the physical processes with a feedback loop. The increasing prevalence of these systems across industries like healthcare, transportation, and energy introduces new potential risks and challenges, some of which include [5]:

- **Data Security and Privacy**: CPS often deal with sensitive data that, if breached, could have serious consequences. For instance, healthcare systems might deal with private patient information, or transportation systems could potentially reveal a user's location. Ensuring data privacy and security is a critical concern.
- **Physical Harm**: Unlike purely digital systems, CPS can cause physical harm if compromised. A compromised industrial control system could lead to equipment damage, environmental harm, or even human injuries.
- **Complexity**: CPS are typically complex systems with many interconnected elements. This complexity makes it difficult to predict and mitigate potential points of failure, increasing the risk of successful attacks.
- **Real-Time Operations**: Many CPS operate in real time, meaning that a delay or disruption could have immediate physical consequences. This increases the need for robust, fail-safe cyber protection measures.
- **Reliability and Availability**: CPS are often critical systems that need to operate reliably and continuously. Attacks that affect their availability, such as distributed denial-of-service (DDoS) attacks, can have significant impacts.
- **Interoperability**: CPS often need to interface with a variety of other systems, which can introduce additional security vulnerabilities.
- **Legacy Systems and Equipment**: Many CPS incorporate or interface with older, legacy systems and equipment that might not have been designed with modern cybersecurity threats in mind.
- **Insider Threats**: Given the potential impact of CPS, they can be a prime target for insider threats, where individuals with authorized access to the system cause damage intentionally or inadvertently.

To address these risks, it's essential to have comprehensive cybersecurity strategies that include regular system updates, vulnerability assessments, intrusion detection systems, encryption, employee training, and incident response plans. Collaborative efforts between technology providers, operators, and regulatory bodies can also help in effectively managing the cybersecurity risks associated with CPS.

4.4 PRESENT-DAY CYBERSECURITY STANDARDS IN THE ELECTRICITY INDUSTRY

The importance of cybersecurity in the electricity industry cannot be understated, given the essential nature of power services and the increasingly digital nature of power infrastructure. In this section, I aim to elucidate the current cybersecurity protocols being implemented within the electricity sector.

One of the significant frameworks guiding the power sector, especially in the United States, is the North American Electric Reliability Corporation's Critical Infrastructure Protection (NERC CIP). These standards were designed explicitly for the electricity industry and are focused on securing the critical assets needed to operate the bulk electric system in North America. NERC CIP provides a range of requirements, from physical security of assets to information protection, recovery plans in the event of a security incident, and personnel training. Adherence to these standards is enforced through rigorous audits, and noncompliance can result in substantial penalties, highlighting the seriousness of these cybersecurity protocols [6].

In the global context, the ISO/IEC 27000 series has gained widespread recognition. This series provides a robust framework for managing information security. It provides guidance on assessing and treating risk, implementing and maintaining controls, and continuously improving the organization's information security. While it is not specific to the power sector, it is sufficiently adaptable to be applied in a wide range of industries, including the electricity industry.

Another essential standard that is increasingly gaining traction in the power sector is IEC (International Electrotechnical Commission) 62443. This standard is geared toward industrial control systems (ICS), which are integral to the operation of power networks. IEC 62443 provides a detailed and practical guide for designing, implementing, and maintaining secure ICS. It covers the entire life cycle of ICS, from initial concept through to decommissioning, providing comprehensive guidance for the power sector.

In the United States, the National Institute of Standards and Technology Framework for Improving Critical Infrastructure Cybersecurity is another crucial resource for the power sector. This framework provides a flexible and risk-based approach for managing cybersecurity risks. It draws on existing standards, guidelines, and practices to help organizations understand their current cybersecurity position, define their target state, identify and prioritize opportunities for improvement, assess progress, and communicate among internal and external stakeholders about cybersecurity risks. Lastly, the ISA99/IEC 62443 Industrial Automation and Control Systems Security standard, developed by the International Society of Automation and the IEC, provides a secure framework for industrial automation and control systems. The standard, designed with a robust structure, offers comprehensive guidance to organizations on establishing and implementing effective cybersecurity protocols.

These standards and protocols have proven instrumental in protecting the critical infrastructure within the electricity sector. However, due to the constantly evolving nature of cyber threats, continual vigilance, regular system updates, and proactive risk management are necessary to maintain effective cybersecurity within the sector. The commitment to these principles at all levels of an organization is fundamental to the overall security of the power sector.

4.5 ELEVATED SIGNIFICANCE OF CYBERSECURITY IN THE ELECTRICITY INDUSTRY RELATIVE TO OTHER SECTORS

The increased emphasis on cybersecurity in the power sector, in comparison with other sectors, is influenced by a unique blend of factors that underscores the critical nature of power systems. The power sector is not just any industry—it is a complex, vital, and interconnected system that society fundamentally depends on. As one delves deeper into the factors enhancing the importance of cybersecurity in the power sector, it becomes evident why safeguarding these systems is crucial [7].

4.5.1 Fundamental Critical Infrastructure

First, the power sector represents a critical infrastructure upon which nearly all other sectors rely. From healthcare and telecommunications to finance, transportation, and even the functioning of homes: All depend on the continuous and reliable supply of electricity. A cyberattack on power supply has the potential to send shockwaves through society, disrupting everyday life and economic activities. For instance, emergency services could be paralyzed, transportation could come to a standstill, and essential communication networks could fail. This ripple effect, caused by a single point of disruption, distinguishes the power sector from most others. In comparison, a cyberattack on sectors such as retail or hospitality, while damaging, would likely not have such a profound or widespread impact on society.

4.5.2 Public Safety Risks

Next, public safety risks related to cyberattacks in the power sector significantly enhance the importance of cybersecurity. Unlike a data breach in, say, a social media company, a successful cyberattack on a power grid could lead to severe physical consequences. From endangering human lives due to power outages in hospitals or traffic management systems, to causing potential industrial accidents, the risk is real and significant. Thus, cybersecurity in the power sector transcends beyond data protection to ensuring the safety and well-being of individuals.

4.5.3 Large-Scale, Interconnected Systems

The power sector operates on a large scale, with highly interconnected systems often spanning geographic boundaries. A cyberattack on one part of the grid can spread and potentially compromise the entire power system. This "domino effect" is unique and particularly relevant to the power sector due to its interconnected nature. For instance, a problem in a single, local substation can potentially escalate into a widespread blackout if not managed correctly.

4.5.4 Real-Time Operational Requirements

Another key factor is the real-time operational needs of the power sector. Power systems require a precise balance between electricity supply and demand. Even minor discrepancies or disruptions can trigger significant consequences like blackouts or equipment damage. Cyberattacks aimed at disrupting this delicate balance, such as injecting false data into control systems, pose significant threats. This strict need for real-time operation distinguishes the power sector from many other industries.

4.5.5 Transition to Smart Grids and IoT

As the power sector embraces digital transformation with the advent of smart grids and the IoT, it also increases its cyber vulnerability. With numerous interconnected devices monitoring and controlling electricity flow, the attack surface for cyber threats significantly expands. While this digital transformation brings substantial benefits, including better grid management and efficiency, it also emphasizes the need for robust cybersecurity measures.

4.5.6 Legacy Systems and Interoperability Challenges

The power sector often includes legacy systems that were not designed considering modern-day cyber threats. Many of these older systems lack the security features that current systems possess, leaving them vulnerable to cyberattacks. Upgrading these systems can be challenging due to continuous operational needs and interoperability issues with newer technology. This situation necessitates a well-thought-out approach for integrating advanced cybersecurity measures while maintaining system functionality.

4.5.7 Regulatory Compliance

Finally, regulatory and compliance requirements further emphasize the importance of cybersecurity in the power sector. Regulatory bodies often impose stringent rules and standards to ensure that power companies invest adequately in cybersecurity measures. Noncompliance can result in substantial penalties, adding a financial impetus to the safety and operational incentives for maintaining strong cybersecurity practices.

The power sector's critical nature, potential safety risks, and operational requirements and the ongoing digital transformation significantly elevate the importance of cybersecurity in comparison with other sectors. It requires a proactive and comprehensive approach involving risk assessment, continuous monitoring, incident response planning, employee training, and regular system upgrades to safeguard against evolving cyber threats. The focus should not just be on resilience, being able to bounce back from an attack, but also on resistance, preventing successful attacks in the first place. The investments made today in securing our power systems will pay dividends in ensuring a safe, reliable power supply for the future, upon which all of society depends.

4.6 CYBERTHREAT-RESILIENT POWER SYSTEMS

Creating a cyber-resilient power system involves implementing robust defense measures, preparing for possible incidents, and ensuring the ability to recover swiftly in the face of potential cyberattacks. A comprehensive and proactive approach to cyber-resilience includes strategies that span people, processes, and technology [8].

From the human perspective, fostering a culture of cybersecurity awareness is paramount. It involves regular training and awareness programs for employees at all levels to ensure that they understand the cyber risks and their role in mitigating them. This effort should not be a one-time initiative but a continuous process that evolves with the changing threat landscape. Properly designed and enforced operational processes can significantly contribute to cyber-resilience. These processes should include, but not be limited to, access controls, data protection, risk management, incident response, and disaster recovery.

Access controls, for instance, should be strict enough to prevent unauthorized access but flexible enough to not impede crucial operational activities. Data protection should address not only the confidentiality of sensitive information but also its integrity and availability. Risk management should be a continuous process that involves identifying, assessing, mitigating, and monitoring cyber risks. Incident response and disaster recovery plans should be well-documented and regularly tested to ensure the power system can recover quickly after a cyberattack.

On the technological front, multiple layers of defense should be implemented, known as defense in depth. This strategy implies having several defensive measures in place, so if one fails or is breached, others are there to prevent further intrusion. Measures can include firewalls, intrusion detection systems, encryption for data in transit and at rest, secure system configurations, regular system patching, and redundancy for critical system components. Given the growing interconnection and digitalization of power systems, cybersecurity measures should also address the challenges brought about by the IoT and smart grids. Devices connected to a network should be securely configured and monitored, ensuring that they do not become the weak link in the chain. Furthermore, as power systems increasingly rely on data for operational decision-making, data integrity should be prioritized, ensuring that false data injection attacks do not lead to adverse operational outcomes.

Cyber-resilience also involves engaging with external stakeholders, such as other utilities, regulatory bodies, cybersecurity firms, and law enforcement agencies. Sharing information about threats and best practices can significantly improve the overall cybersecurity posture of the power sector. Regular audits and regulatory compliance checks should also be seen not as burdens but as opportunities to identify and address potential vulnerabilities.

One crucial element in building a cyber-resilient power system is preparing for the worst-case scenario. This preparation includes simulations and drills to test and improve the organization's incident response and disaster recovery plans. By simulating a cyberattack, the power system can assess its readiness, identify gaps, and improve its resilience.

Lastly, cybersecurity is not a one-time effort but a continuous endeavor. The threat landscape continuously evolves, and so should the power system's cyber-resilience strategies. Regular assessments, system updates, and employee training are all crucial elements in maintaining a resilient power system in the face of growing and evolving cyber threats.

Building a cyber-resilient power system involves a multi-faceted approach that addresses people, processes, and technology. It requires a strong commitment from top management and participation from all employees. It demands robust defense measures, sound operational processes, technological upgrades, continuous monitoring, and timely incident response. It's a challenging yet vital task for ensuring the reliable functioning of the power sector and, by extension, all the sectors of society that it supports.

4.7 THREE-DIMENSIONAL MODEL FOR ORGANIZATION CYBERSECURITY MATURITY

An effective cybersecurity strategy requires a mature approach that encapsulates three critical dimensions: hunting, detection, and response. These three aspects offer a comprehensive perspective on threat management, enabling organizations to stay one step ahead of potential cyber threats. Each dimension represents a critical stage in managing cyber threats and should be addressed with equal emphasis [9]. These dimensions are elaborated in Table 4.1.

Table 4.1 Dimensions in Maturity Modeling

Dimension	Definition	Key Activities	Tools/Technologies
Hunting	Proactive search for threats before they manifest.	• Behavioral analysis • Anomaly detection • Deep dive investigations	• Threat intelligence platforms • Endpoint detection & response • User and entity behavior analytics

(Continued)

Table 4.1 (Continued)

Dimension	Definition	Key Activities	Tools/Technologies
Detection	Identify and validate potential threats in real-time.	• Real-time monitoring • Signatures & heuristics • Correlation rules	• Intrusion detection systems • Security information & event management • Network traffic analysis
Response	Act upon and mitigate identified threats.	• Incident triage • Forensics • Remediation strategies	• Incident response platforms • Forensic tools • Automation & orchestration platforms

4.7.1 Hunting

The hunting dimension represents proactive measures taken to identify potential vulnerabilities and threats before they manifest into actual cyber incidents. Cyber threat hunting involves a continuous and iterative approach to searching, identifying, and understanding the cyber threat landscape. The main goal of hunting is to discover unknown threats in the network that traditional detection measures might miss.

An organization with a mature approach to hunting invests in advanced threat intelligence tools and techniques to understand the evolving threat landscape. It also cultivates a team of skilled cybersecurity professionals who can interpret threat data, predict potential attack vectors, and proactively mitigate risks. Regular penetration testing, vulnerability assessments, and red team exercises are typical activities in this dimension.

4.7.2 Detection

The detection dimension focuses on the ability to identify real-time cyber incidents promptly. This phase involves continuous monitoring of network activity, employing advanced detection tools such as intrusion detection systems, security information and event management systems, and anomaly detection algorithms.

A mature approach to detection involves developing sophisticated capabilities to distinguish between normal and abnormal network behavior accurately. Organizations should implement machine learning algorithms and artificial intelligence to sift through vast amounts of network data and detect potential security breaches. Additionally, ensuring full visibility across all systems and networks is crucial to enhance detection capabilities. Figure 4.1 presents a simulation of this three-dimensional model of cybersecurity maturity.

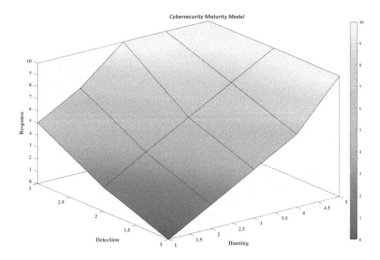

Figure 4.1 Simulated 3D model of organization cybersecurity maturity.

4.7.3 Response

The response dimension addresses an organization's ability to react promptly and effectively once a cyber threat is detected. This includes having a well-structured and practiced incident response plan in place, detailing steps to contain the threat, eliminate the risk, and recover systems to their normal state. In cybersecurity, the relationship between hunting, detection, and response can be better described qualitatively rather than through precise mathematical equations, as I elaborate on.

4.7.3.1 Dependency and Overlap

- Hunting may be seen as a proactive subset of detection, where threats are sought out before they become active.
- Response relies on effective detection, including both the proactive (hunting) and reactive aspects.

4.7.3.2 Continuous Feedback Loop

In the continuous feedback loop, hunting (H) feeds into detection (D), which then informs response (R), and the lessons learned from responding to incidents can, in turn, improve future H:

$$H \rightarrow D \rightarrow R \rightarrow H \tag{1}$$

4.7.3.3 Weighted Importance

It may be required to allocate resources across these dimensions. Let's say you divide your efforts into H, D, and R with weights ω_1, ω_2 and ω_3, respectively, and you want the total effort to be normalized. Then the relationship is

$$\omega_1 \times H + \omega_2 \times D + \omega_3 \times R = 1 \qquad (2)$$

The weights ω_1 ω_2 and ω_3 can be adjusted based on organizational priorities and threat landscapes.

4.7.3.4 Effectiveness Relationship

The effectiveness of the overall cybersecurity strategy might be a function of the effectiveness of each of these three dimensions. You could consider a simple linear relationship or more complex models:

$$E = \alpha \times H + \beta \times H + \gamma \times R \qquad (3)$$

where (α, β, γ) are constants that represent the impact of each dimension on the overall effectiveness (E) of the cybersecurity strategy.

Maturity in response means that the organization can quickly contain a threat, minimizing the potential damage. Moreover, it should have robust disaster recovery and business continuity plans to ensure minimal disruption to operations. Post-incident analysis is also crucial for understanding the root causes of breaches, learning from incidents, and improving future response efforts.

The three-dimensional approach to cybersecurity maturity encompasses a proactive stance (hunting), efficient real-time surveillance (detection), and swift and effective mitigation efforts (response). Each dimension is equally important, and organizations should strive for maturity in all three areas to fortify their cybersecurity posture. This holistic approach ensures that organizations are prepared for cyber threats at all times, from anticipating potential attacks and detecting them promptly when they occur to responding effectively to minimize damage and recover swiftly.

4.8 CONCLUSION

I conclude that the growing integration of digital technology and the rapid advancement of cyber threats significantly elevate the importance of cybersecurity in the power sector. The significance of electricity in our lives and the transition to a more interconnected power system heighten the power sector's vulnerability to cyber threats. As such, it is crucial to recognize the enhanced importance of cybersecurity in the power sector relative to other sectors.

The interconnected nature of power systems, their status as critical infrastructure, and their capacity to influence many aspects of daily life underscore the need for a robust and comprehensive approach to cybersecurity. The potential impact of cyber threats extends beyond data loss or financial damage; it also includes the potential disruption of essential services and risks to public safety.

In response to these threats, the power sector has begun to implement current standards and protocols for cybersecurity. Adherence to these standards helps to protect power systems from various cyber threats, including those that specifically target industrial control systems. However, these standards alone are not enough. They must be complemented by continuous risk assessment, employee training, and regular updates of system defenses to address the evolving threat landscape.

The three-dimensional approach to cybersecurity—hunting, detection, and response—represents a comprehensive strategy for managing cyber threats. By proactively seeking out potential vulnerabilities (hunting), efficiently identifying real-time cyber incidents (detection), and quickly reacting to minimize damage (response), power utilities can significantly enhance their cyber-resilience. However, achieving maturity in all three dimensions requires consistent commitment, investment, and a culture that values cybersecurity.

Given the complexities of modern power systems and the rapidly evolving threat landscape, building a cyber-resilient power system remains a challenging task. Nevertheless, it is an essential task considering the potential consequences of successful cyberattacks. Power utilities must view cybersecurity not as a necessary evil but as a fundamental aspect of their operations.

This perspective requires moving beyond mere compliance with regulations to actively managing cyber risks. To achieve this, power utilities should cultivate a culture of cybersecurity awareness, foster a strong commitment to cybersecurity at all organizational levels, and continually invest in the latest cybersecurity technologies and practices. The complexities of modern power systems, the evolving threat landscape, and the increasing importance of electricity in all aspects of daily life all underscore the need for a comprehensive, proactive approach to cybersecurity.

In a world where the power sector's criticality continues to rise, and the cyber threat landscape continues to evolve, it is clear that cybersecurity can no longer be an afterthought. It must be at the forefront of strategic planning and operational decision-making. The power sector has a crucial role to play in fostering a safer, more resilient digital world. The steps taken today to strengthen cybersecurity measures will not only protect power utilities from potential threats but also ensure the continuous, reliable supply of electricity on which modern society so heavily relies.

REFERENCES

[1] Mueller, F., Bhattacharya, S., & Zimmer, C. (2009, July). Cyber security for power grids. In Workshop on Cyber-physical Systems Security. NC State University. https://arcb.csc.ncsu.edu/~mueller/ftp/pub/mueller/papers/cpssec09.pdf

[2]   Mishra, P. K., & Tiwari, P. (2020). Cyber security in smart grid. International Research Journal on Advanced Science Hub, 2(6), 26–30.

[3]   Hasan, M. K., Habib, A. A., Shukur, Z., Ibrahim, F., Islam, S., & Razzaque, M. A. (2022). Review on cyber-physical and cyber-security system in smart grid: Standards, protocols, constraints, and recommendations. Journal of Network and Computer Applications, 103540.

[4]   Wang, W., & Lu, Z. (2013). Cyber security in the smart grid: Survey and challenges. Computer Networks, 57(5), 1344–1371.

[5]   El Mrabet, Z., Kaabouch, N., El Ghazi, H., & El Ghazi, H. (2018). Cyber-security in smart grid: Survey and challenges. Computers & Electrical Engineering, 67, 469–482.

[6]   Al Mughairi, B. M., Al Hajri, H. H., Karim, A. M., & Hossain, M. I. (2019). An innovative cyber security based approach for national infrastructure resiliency for Sultanate of Oman. International Journal of Academic Research in Business and Social Sciences, 9(3), 1180–1195.

[7]   Venkatachary, S. K., Prasad, J., & Samikannu, R. (2017). Economic impacts of cyber security in energy sector: A review. International Journal of Energy Economics and Policy, 7(5), 250.

[8]   Amin, S. M. (2010, July). Electricity infrastructure security: Toward reliable, resilient and secure cyber-physical power and energy systems. In IEEE PES General Meeting (pp. 1–5). IEEE.

[9]   Pamnani, G. D., & Saxena, P. (2023). "Cyber security"-Backbone for a resilient power sector. Water and Energy International, 66(2), 29–32.

Section 3

Artificial Intelligence Applications for Smart Cities

Chapter 5

Recent Trends in Artificial Intelligence Applications for Smart Cities

A Review

Lopamudra Hota, Biraja Prasad Nayak,
Puneet Kumar Jain, and Arun Kumar

5.1 INTRODUCTION

Cities across the globe are not only expanding but also striving to restructure themselves for a sustainable future that prioritises a better standard of living for all inhabitants. According to the United Nations Department of Economic and Social Affairs, urbanisation is anticipated to increase to encompass 68% of the global population by 2050. In 2016, there were roughly 512 cities with a population of one million and 31 megacities with a population of more than 10 million. About 662 city areas and 41 megacities are anticipated by 2030, most of which will be concentrated primarily in developing countries [1].

Modern smart cities use a range of technology and support innovations that help cities realise their socioeconomic prospects and long-term goals. Numerous studies have shown that various smart city initiatives are being implemented at different geographic locations, creating a rich tapestry of urban visions [2]. Implementing artificial intelligence (AI) for smart city viability has several advantages, including advanced waste management, energy management, and reduced traffic congestion, noise, and pollution.

Most smart city initiatives and innovations have centred on gathering data and learning more about the dynamics and intricacy of a city [3, 4]. AI has revolutionised cities by enabling city managers to utilise real-time generated data and smart technologies to support decision-making. By 2025, AI will initiate over 30% of smart city applications, including urban transit options, potentially enhancing urban social welfare, vitality, and resilience [5].

Due to the swift acceptance of AI-based smart city initiatives, policy makers, researchers, and practitioners continually look for the latest findings and techniques for developing smart cities. However, according to [6], while smart city AI applications have advantages like providing efficacy and automation, they also raise ethical, legal, and regulatory concerns like discrimination in the delivery of services. It's important to look into AI algorithms' benefits, drawbacks, and impacts on smart cities.

DOI: 10.1201/9781003486930-8

AI in smart cities entails maximises energy efficiency, utilises renewable energy sources to their full potential, and expands electric modes of transportation at an unprecedented scale [7]. The reduction of the AI and machine learning (ML) can reduce the carbon footprints of energy, food, transportation, and industrial manufacturing at our homes, offices, and cities. Net-zero emissions are only theoretically feasible because of renewable energy sources like the sun, wind, biofuels, and renewable-based hydrogen. However, to operate continuously, solar and wind facilities need sophisticated grid management and real-time responsiveness because their output changes with the seasons, weather, and time of day [8].

Smart grids that use data analytics can function effectively with large amounts of energy generated by solar and wind, but significant strides are needed for storing energy using higher-capacity batteries such as for powering electric vehicles. With autonomous vehicles, smart cities can significantly reduce carbon emissions, but these technologies need to advance before people can trust them for their mundane activities [9]. Because smart cities are implementing recent technologies to diversify their capacity for innovation, scholarly attention on technological advances in cities has increased and will increase in the future.

By integrating contemporary digital technologies, organisations have realised the performance and processes for innovation and competitive improvement. AI is a digital technology that enables smart cities to develop and grow in the digital age, which impacts cities to re-innovate and respond to domestic needs [10]. The application of AI to handle various challenges in the contemporary smart city is examined in this chapter.

The rest of this chapter is arranged as follows: Section 2 presents the pertinent details on smart cities and AI. In Section 3, the incorporation of AI in smart cities is covered. Section 4 provides a detailed study of use cases of AI incorporated in various countries. Section 5 addresses all the potential unresolved issues, challenges, and future research directions. Finally, Section 6 summarises the chapter.

5.2 BACKGROUND STUDY ON SMART CITIES AND AI

In this section, we review the work on emerging smart cities and applications of AI in smart cities. "As cities become smarter, they are becoming more livable and responsive, but this is just the beginning of the advancement in technology contributing towards cities in the future." Investments in digital transformation and smart cities are progressively expanding [11]. According to the Smart City Index 2021 [12], Singapore, Zurich, Oslo, Taipei City, and Lausanne are the top-ranked smart cities nationwide.

The development of Internet technology and several other networks and communication channels has led to the Internet of Things (IoT) becoming one of the most vital infrastructures in smart cities. In 2017, the number of IoT components and devices deployed in smart cities increased by 39% from 2015. It is estimated that 3.3 billion IoT devices and parts were used in 2018 [13]. Additionally, in 2017 and 2018, the number of IoT devices and components increased by 42% and 43%, respectively. The proliferation of smart cities has been facilitated by the development of smart components and IoT-based solutions [14].

Home appliances such as refrigerators, ovens, washing machines, and dishwashers can be smart enabled. For convenience and effectiveness, these appliances include remote control, energy monitoring, and automation functions [15]. Identifying the most precise and effective course of action while working with vast amounts of complex data may be challenging. Sophisticated methods like AI, DRL, and ML can be used to analyse vast amounts of data to arrive at the best possible denouement.

John McCarthy, a computer scientist, first coined the term "artificial intelligence" in 1979 and later gave it the definition "the science and engineering of making intelligent machines" [16]. AI instructs machines to emulate human thought patterns and actions. Brynjolfsson and McAfee contend in their book *The Race Against the Machine* that significant progress in AI and ML will prevent modern society from supporting anything resembling full employment [17].

According to a MarketsandMarkets research report, the size of the global AI market is projected to rise at a compound annual growth rate of 36.2% over the next few years, from USD 86.9 billion in 2022 to USD 407.0 billion in 2027 [18]. Recently, AI has been used in research and practises related to smart cities, and academics have observed its growth in significance for smart urbanisation. AI has the potential to boost productivity and ease the livelihood in future smart cities by incorporating cutting-edge machine vision, natural language processing (NLP), ML, robotics, and other technologies with vast resource pools.

ML, a subfield of AI, enables computer programs to improve at forecasting without being explicitly trained. The forecasting is based on historical data taken as input. NLP, another subfield of AI, is concerned with interacting computer systems with human languages by algorithms that comprehend the contextual form. Robotics is the process of building machines capable of performing activities without individual interaction. In contrast, AI technology creates systems that imitate the individual's brain in making decisions and learning processes.

In this chapter, we examine AI and its application in contemporary smart cities. The conceptualisation of AI utilised in smart cities is seen in Figure 5.1. A theoretical framework for the application of AI in smart cities is presented, including AI applications, AI ML algorithms, big data concepts for storage and analysis, and IoT sensors for data collection.

5.3 AI ADOPTION IN SMART CITIES

The adoption of AI in smart cities is gaining momentum as cities worldwide increasingly turn to this technology to improve efficiency, enhance sustainability, and provide better services to their populations. AI has the potential to transform the way cities are managed and operated, making them more responsive, resilient,

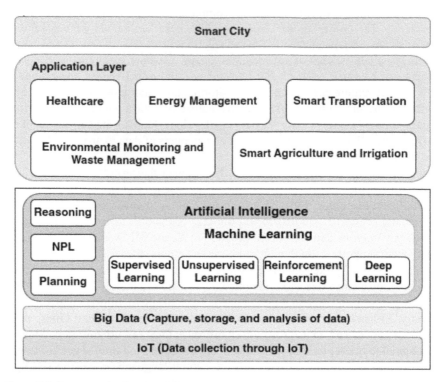

Figure 5.1 Framework of a smart city.

and sustainable. Collaboration between various stakeholders, including city officials, tech companies, and residents, is necessary for adopting AI in smart cities. City leaders must ensure that AI is used in a way that is ethical, accessible, and aware of people's privacy rights. They must also invest in the necessary infrastructure and training to support developing and deploying AI-powered systems [19]. Figure 5.2 gives a pictorial representation of how smart cities employ AI. Some of the scopes of AI in smart cities include:

a. **Transportation:** AI can improve public transportation services by optimising traffic flow and reducing congestion [20]. For example, AI can analyse traffic patterns to provide drivers with alternative routes and real-time traffic updates.

b. **Energy Management:** In smart cities, AI can optimise energy use and increase the effectiveness of energy generation and delivery [21]. AI, for instance, can examine patterns of energy use to forecast demand and modify energy production accordingly.

c. **Public Safety:** AI can enhance population control in public areas, identify and prevent crime, and manage emergency response management [22]. AI,

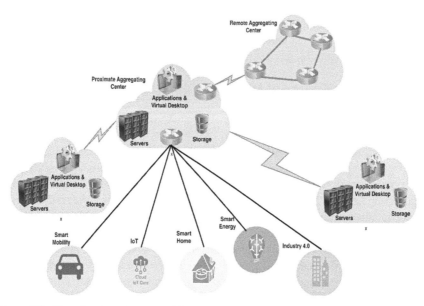

Figure 5.2 AI applications in smart cities.

for instance, can examine video feeds to detect suspicions and notify law enforcement.

d. **Environmental Monitoring:** AI can monitor air and water quality, identify the origins of pollution, and foresee environmental risks [23] in smart cities. It can analyse data from cameras and sensors to identify incidents, dispatch emergency services, or reroute traffic quickly [23]. AI can also evaluate sensor data to find pollutants and issue early alerts for potential environmental dangers.

e. **Healthcare:** AI can optimise healthcare delivery in smart cities and enhance disease diagnostics and disease outbreak prediction [24]. AI, for instance, can review patient records to identify high-risk patients and recommend precautions.

f. **Waste Management:** In smart cities, AI can improve waste collection, lower waste creation, and encourage recycling. Using garbage disposal trends, AI can pinpoint places where recycling efforts might be strengthened [25].

g. **Smart Buildings:** AI-driven systems can optimise functioning in a building and reduce expenses and energy use [26].

h. **Effective Resource Management:** AI has made it possible for smart cities to handle resources like transportation, water, and electricity more effectively [27]. For instance, AI-powered smart grids can optimise energy use and cut waste.

i. **Predictive Road Maintenance:** By evaluating data from sensors and cameras to detect operational wear and tear, AI can be utilised to optimise road repairs. It can suggest maintenance tasks and forecast when roads are predicted for damage [28].

Next we describe applications of AI in smart cities in various fields.

5.3.1 Transportation

AI-powered traffic management systems use data analytics and ML algorithms to improvise the public transportation. For example, in Singapore, an AI-assisted traffic management system uses real-time data analytics to forecast traffic flow and ease congestion [29]. AI has the potential to significantly improve traffic management in smart cities by optimising traffic flow, improving public transportation, and managing incidents more efficiently.

AI can be used to develop intelligent transportation systems that predict traffic congestion and accidents and provide real-time recommendations to drivers on the best routes to take. It can also optimise public transportation schedules and routes to reduce waiting times and improve efficiency. Intelligent traffic management integrates AI-based decision-making in safe driving [20, 30]. AI can also optimise smart parking by analysing data from sensors and cameras to identify available parking spots and direct drivers to them as well as predicting parking demand and adjusting pricing accordingly to incentivise the use of public transportation or other alternatives [31].

ML, AI, and DRL approaches are crucial for efficiently tracking and analysing real-time data based on traffic management and are essential in next-generation smart transportation management. The authors of [32] highlighted AI's role in intelligent logistics, traffic management, manufacturing, and public transit. They applied cutting-edge deep NLP principles to create a technique for learning about employee engagement in a logistics organisation. One of the most important and challenging study areas for modern intelligent transport systems is processing vehicular surveillance video in heavy-traffic states. Given the quick development of transport networks, the continued expansion of surveillance infrastructure on the street generates vast amounts of traffic data, which is a major challenge for data analysis. To prevent traffic congestion, the research group in [29] created a vehicle redirection system that uses a deep learning model to anticipate real-time traffic in future conditions.

Over the years, there has been an increase in the use of AI for mobility-related decision-making and rerouting. Some researchers have built AI-based models to identify safety concerns, including distracted driving from cell phones, dangerous pedestrian situations, human-centred dangers, etc. Using a new technique, the authors of [33] proposed a mechanism for identifying distracted drivers. They employed a deep learning convolutional neural network (CNN) and a wide-angle camera positioned on the ceiling to find these careless drivers.

Using video data gathered by traffic security cameras installed at road crossings, the authors of [34] proposed a unique mechanism for detecting potential pedestrian occurrences. A Grassmann manifold-based neural network was proposed by the authors of [35] to analyse video data for traffic monitoring and surveillance. They contended that their method was more accurate at traffic congestion prediction than traditional approaches.

5.3.2 Energy Management

AI can help optimise the management of electricity grids by predicting demand and adjusting supply accordingly [36]. This can help reduce waste and enhance efficiency. AI can analyse data from sensors and meters to monitor energy consumption in real time, identifying areas of waste and opportunities for improvement, predicting when maintenance is required, reducing downtime, and improving reliability. AI can significantly improve the sustainability of energy management in smart cities, reducing costs and environmental impacts while improving citizens' reliability and quality of life.

For example, an AI-powered energy management system in California implements real-time data to predict demand and adjust energy production accordingly. There is a significant surge in global energy consumption and carbon footprint due to population growth and rising comfort standards, and smart energy models were created to integrate AI into the conventional energy sector. Creating completely automated smart energy grids calls for a reliable mechanism for anticipating electric load. AI-enabled energy forecasting techniques are essential because most smart city applications demand more energy. An energy consumption forecast model must be trained using ML techniques [37].

Owing to the development of AI technologies, end users with controllers and smart meter monitoring can optimise consumption costs by selecting from a range of price plans offered by various retail energy estimation systems. To facilitate the selection of electricity price plans, authors in [38] proposed a reinforcement learning (RL)-based decision system to minimise power consumption and charge dissatisfaction. Electric vehicles and charging infrastructure are prone to failure and inefficient charging, and the authors in [39] examined the integration of blockchain and AI with the EV charging infrastructure in response. The IoT, AI-based analytics, blockchain, and energy architecture have all contributed to improving key aspects of smart grid services like sustainability, stability, availability, resilience, security, and dependability.

5.3.3 Healthcare

AI has numerous applications in the health sector in smart cities. It has the potential to significantly improve healthcare in smart cities by providing personalised medicine, detecting and preventing diseases, optimising resource allocation, analysing medical imaging data, and enhancing telemedicine services. By combining traditional technology and equipment with AI-integrated solutions, many traditional towns aim to emulate smart city healthcare.

Healthcare systems have significantly benefited from IoT with AI integration. AI-based devices detect and prevent diseases in smart cities by analysing data from wearable devices, medical records, and other sources. It can identify early warning signs of diseases and provide recommendations to individuals to prevent or manage them.

Authors in [40] proposed a diabetes and heart disease detection system using AI and IoT convergence methods. The recommended technique uses a cuckoo search optimisation-LSTM (long short-term memory) model to diagnose illnesses. By fusing fog computing, AI, and smart health, the authors of [41] created a trustworthy platform for early thyroid infection identification. AI can be used to optimise healthcare resource allocation by analysing data on population demographics, disease prevalence, and other factors. It can identify areas where healthcare resources are most needed and allocate resources accordingly, such as by opening new clinics or hospitals in high-demand areas.

An LSTM neural network was utilised by the authors in [42] to forecast patient health status, with a focus on diabetes. The research demonstrated that vital signs and clinical factors helped predict hospital readmissions [43]. AI can be used to process medical imaging data such as MRIs, X-rays, and CT scans to diagnose diseases and detect abnormalities. It can identify subtle differences that may not be easily noticeable to humans, improving diagnostic accuracy and reducing the need for invasive procedures.

The authors in [44] suggested a voice pathology detection system as a component of a smart healthcare framework. Researchers have created healthcare assistance systems using social media and imaging data. For instance, to assess satellite images and maps of rural communities for better planning and healthcare, the authors of [45] proposed ML and DL algorithms.

AI can be used to improve telemedicine services in smart cities by analysing data from remote consultations and providing recommendations to healthcare professionals. It can also help to streamline administrative tasks such as appointment scheduling and billing. Hospitals have introduced a web-based chatbot for frequently asked questions [46].

5.3.4 Environmental Monitoring and Waste Management

AI has numerous applications and potential in waste management in smart cities by optimising waste collection, sorting, and recycling, detecting and preventing illegal dumping, optimising landfill management, and improving waste-to-energy conversion. It is crucial to know the efficiency of smart cities in handling environmental and waste management issues. Trash production has increased globally due to urbanisation, population expansion, and economic development.

According to the World Bank 2018 data, 2.0 billion tonnes of municipal solid waste were created in 2016, which is anticipated to increase to 3.4 billion tonnes by 2050 [47]. AI-powered environmental monitoring and waste management systems [22] use sensors and data analytics to monitor air and water quality, detect pollution sources, and predict environmental risks. For example, an AI-powered environmental monitoring system in Barcelona uses sensor data to detect pollutants and provide early warnings of potential environmental hazards.

Reverse vending machine garbage categorisation using a dual image-based CNN ensemble model was suggested by the authors of [48]. AI can be used to sort waste and identify recyclable materials more efficiently [49]. It can also be used to optimise waste-to-energy conversion by analysing data on waste composition and energy demand and identify the most efficient ways to convert waste into energy and optimise energy generation from waste. AI can suggest ways to reduce waste generation and landfill use, such as recycling and composting [50].

5.3.5 Smart Irrigation and Agriculture

AI significantly improves the efficiency and sustainability of agriculture and irrigation in smart cities, increasing yield and profitability while reducing waste, water usage, and environmental impact. Agriculture has a significant economic impact on both people and nations as a whole. Automation in agriculture is a blooming topic and a significant source of concern worldwide [51].

As the population of the world increases, traditional farming methods are going to be insufficient to meet food demand. With AI, new automated procedures have been created that have revolutionised agriculture. The recent technological enhancement safeguards agricultural production against various threats, including labour shortages, climatic changes, problems with food security, and population growth. Researchers in [51, 52] studied the impact of AI on smart agricultural development, and the authors of [53] thoroughly analysed the rise of smart digital technologies, including robots, IoT, Big Data, AI, and blockchain in agriculture.

AI can also help farmers select the best crops to plant based on soil quality, weather patterns, and market trends to maximise yield and profitability [54] and help monitor crop health and identify pests and diseases early, enabling farmers to take corrective action before they spread. The authors of [55] demonstrated a smart garden for irrigation integrated with existing smart house control systems. At the master station, they used a fuzzy logic irrigation algorithm that adhered to the guidelines to water the trees and grass.

AI can help farmers adapt to changing weather patterns and climate conditions by analysing historical data and predicting future patterns to inform planting decisions and optimise irrigation practices [56]. The authors of [57] presented an AI sensor-based method for smart agriculture using Agrobot. AI can help optimise water usage in agriculture by monitoring soil moisture levels, weather conditions, and water usage to suggest optimal irrigation schedules and reduce water waste. It can also help farmers track livestock's health and behavioural patterns, identify issues early, and optimise feed and nutrition for improved productivity [58].

5.4 TEN COUNTRIES IMPLEMENTING AI FOR THEIR CITY DEVELOPMENT

The case studies presented in this section demonstrate AI implementation in smart city development worldwide, focusing on optimising traffic flow, energy consumption, waste management, and public safety. AI superpowers aren't simply strengthening economies and advancing society [7]. AI may be utilised as a potent military tool to change the balance of power in the world and launch new enterprises. We must hope that AI is used to build a strong and united world if AI capabilities increase exponentially.

Future developments in artificial intelligence will drastically alter all facets of life. For improved future opportunities, all nations—developed, developing, and underdeveloped—are working on embracing AI. AI has the potential to identify faces, produce better internet results, drive autonomous vehicles, and boost business across a variety of industries. Automation and digitalisation are the focus of AI, and these have drastically altered global structures and processes.

a. **India**: Regarding software and AI, Indians are regarded as having exceptional knowledge. More than 20–30% of the startups in Silicon Valley, California, home to both startups and large international technology corporations, are run by Indians. India is making significant investments in the AI industry. India attracted foreign direct investment from AI companies totalling USD 100 million in 2017. According to news sources, an Indian Institute of Science student from Bangalore has created software to help identify fake news, which will significantly impact the future because fake news is currently disseminated widely on social media. Scientists in Pune developed an AI-powered traffic management system that uses data analytics to optimise the flow of traffic on roads and reduce congestion. India has also implemented an AI-powered water management system that uses data to detect leaks and predict equipment failures. India, at its full potential, is adopting AI for the country's technological development [59].

b. **Singapore**: Singapore is one of the richest and most developed nations in Asia. With a 97% literacy rate, it has the best educational system in the world, and Singapore has been a leader in the use of AI in smart city development; the administration is attempting to fully integrate robotics and AI into the nation. It has implemented an AI-powered traffic management system that uses real-time data to optimise traffic flow, reduce congestion, and improve public transportation. Singapore has also used AI in its water management system to detect leaks and predict equipment failures, and AI is now being used for indoor farming as well. Singapore is a true example for the rest of the globe because despite having limited resources and space, it makes the greatest use of what it has and is far ahead of nations like the US or the UK [60].

c. **United Kingdom:** As we all know, the UK controlled 20–30% of the world's landmass when the first Industrial Revolution began. With 121 AI-enabled businesses, the UK is an undisputed leader in Europe. Tech companies in the UK raised USD 8.6 billion in private investment in 2017. It represents roughly 38% of all venture capital investments made in the UK in that particular year. The UK government also revealed USD 78 million in funding for robotics and AI businesses and research initiatives that same year [61].

d. **Germany:** Germany has implemented AI applications in its smart city development. The city of Hamburg developed an AI-powered traffic management system that uses data to optimise traffic flow and reduce overcrowding on roads. Additionally, Germany has built a data-driven AI-powered trash management system that optimises waste collection and encourages recycling [62].

e. **United Arab Emirates:** AI is a key component of the numerous initiatives the UAE is embarking on to develop smart cities. Dubai operates a real-time, data-driven AI-powered traffic control system to reduce congestion. The UAE has also incorporated AI into its energy management system to reduce waste and maximise energy utilisation [63].

f. **United States:** The United States has included AI technology in creating its smart cities. For instance, San Diego operates a streetlight system powered by AI that uses sensors to monitor vehicle and pedestrian traffic and change the lights when necessary [64]. Chicago has built a predictive maintenance system powered by AI for its water management infrastructure.

g. **Japan:** Japan is the most developed country in Asia, boasting the best education system in the world and a literacy rate of over 95%. By 2030, the Japanese government hopes to have fully incorporated AI. For instance, Tokyo operates a traffic control system powered by AI to improve traffic flow and lessen congestion. City leaders have also introduced a disaster management system powered by AI that analyses data to anticipate and address natural catastrophes [65]. The Japanese government wants AI and robots to mimic humans. Japan is far ahead of other countries in this regard as they have already started working on it. Japan is poised to lead AI in the future as well.

h. **South Korea:** The city of Seoul, in South Korea, has implemented a real-time data-driven AI-powered traffic management system that optimises traffic flow and lowers congestion as a part of smart city development. Additionally, South Korea has implemented an AI-driven energy management system that uses data to optimise energy use and cut waste [66].

i. **Canada:** Canada has applied AI in multiple cities to manage the traffic flow based on generated data, and Toronto has implemented an AI-powered energy management system that uses data to optimise energy consumption and reduce waste [62].

j. **Australia:** Australia has implemented AI applications in its smart city development. For example, the city of Sydney has implemented an AI-powered traffic service to redirect traffic flows and reduce traffic jams. Australia has also implemented an AI-powered energy management system that uses data to reduce energy consumption and efficiently manage waste [67].

5.5 CHALLENGES AND FUTURE SCOPE

AI in the future aims to enhance knowledge, skills, and useful tools. Additionally, it will make it possible for decision-makers and important stakeholders to promote AI adoption for inclusive and long-term social and economic developments. Today's developing cities face a variety of issues, such as those involving energy usage, venerable infrastructure, healthcare, privacy and security, and the environment. While the potential benefits of AI in smart cities are significant, several challenges need to be addressed for its successful implementation [68]. Some of the challenges include:

a. **Data Privacy and Security:** AI relies predominantly on data, and there are worries regarding the privacy and security of this data. Gaining the public's trust in AI applications requires securing and protecting personal information [69].

b. **Integration with Legacy Systems:** Many smart cities rely on antiquated legacy systems that might not work with AI technology. Integrating AI can be a complex procedure that requires careful preparation and execution.

c. **Governance and Regulation:** AI in smart cities is a relatively new topic, and there's a lack of rules or standards to direct its creation and application. Building trust and acceptability among citizens depends on ensuring that AI is used morally and for the benefit of the public [70].

d. **Skills and Expertise:** Integrating AI into practice and controlling it in smart cities demands particular knowledge and skills that might not be easily accessible. Training and education programs are required to create a trained workforce capable of installing and managing AI systems.

e. **Digital Divide:** AI has the potential to widen the gap in access to technology between users having an approach and those who do not. Building smart cities that benefit everyone requires ensuring that AI is applied inclusively and fairly [71].

AI has the potential to assist in making cities more effective, sustainable, and liveable as technology develops and more data becomes available. AI can help cities use energy more efficiently, cut waste, increase public safety, and give citizens better services [72]. Additionally, it can enhance all citizens' living standards and assist communities in adapting to changing climatic conditions. With proper planning and implementation, AI in smart cities has a bright future and the ability to transform work and way of life in urban areas.

5.6 CONCLUSION

Cities have seen a significant transformation in recent years due to the accelerated innovation and widespread use of various innovative technology. Two key technologies, AI and the IoT, have revolutionised cities into sustainable smart cities. In this chapter, we discussed AI adoption in the key sectors of smart cities, including transportation, agriculture and irrigation, healthcare, waste management, and the environment.

However, some regulatory challenges exist, such as privacy, moral and legal issues, and discrimination in service delivery. In addition, we acknowledged that impediments and challenges to AI deployment in smart cities include data accessibility, lack of people with the necessary skills, expense and duration of AI efforts, and a high unemployment rate. Nonetheless, with careful planning and implementation, AI revolutionises the ways of life in both urban and rural areas, making it more sustainable and efficient. The main focus of this chapter is the use of AI technologies across a broad spectrum of industries for the development of smart cities. The application of AI in smart cities has enormous prospects to transform urban living from traffic management to energy management, public safety to healthcare, waste management to smart building management, and waste management. As technology advances and data availability increases, AI's potential applications in smart cities become perpetual.

REFERENCES

[1] Population Division, Department of Economic and Social Affairs, United Nations. The World's Cities in 2016. *Data Booklet*, 2016.

[2] Francesco Paolo Appio, Marcos Lima, and Sotirios Paroutis. Understanding Smart Cities: Innovation Ecosystems, Technological Advancements, and Societal Challenges. *Technological Forecasting and Social Change*, 142:1–14, 2019.

[3] Navaljit Kapoor, Nadeem Ahmad, Subrat Kumar Nayak, Surya Prakash Singh, P Vigneswara Ilavarasan, and Prasanna Ramamoorthy. Identifying Infrastructural Gap Areas for Smart and Sustainable Tribal Village Development: A Data Science Approach from India. *International Journal of Information Management Data Insights*, 1(2):100041, 2021.

[4] Chai K Toh, Julio A Sanguesa, Juan C Cano, and Francisco J Martinez. Advances in Smart Roads for Future Smart Cities. *Proceedings of the Royal Society A*, 476(2233):20190439, 2020.

[5] Federico Cugurullo. Urban Artificial Intelligence: From Automation to Autonomy in the Smart City. *Frontiers in Sustainable Cities*, 2:38, 2020.

[6] Ya Zhou and Atreyi Kankanhalli. AI Regulation for Smart Cities: Challenges and Principles. *Smart Cities and Smart Governance: Towards the 22nd Century Sustainable City*, 101–118, 2021.

[7] Oleg Golubchikov and Mary Thornbush. Artificial Intelligence and Robotics in Smart City Strategies and Planned Smart Development. *Smart Cities*, 3(4), 2020.

[8] Marianne Rose Kjendseth Wiik, Kristin Fjellheim, Camille Vandervaeren, Synne Krekling Lien, Solveig Meland, Tobias Nordstr¨om, Caroline Y Cheng, Helge Brattebø, and Thomas Kringlebotn Thiis. Zero Emission Neighbourhoods in Smart Cities. *ZEN Report*, 45:30, 2022. https://hdl.handle.net/11250/3054311

[9] Nacer Eddine Bezai, Benachir Medjdoub, Amin Al-Habaibeh, Moulay Larbi Chalal, and Fodil Fadli. Future Cities and Autonomous Vehicles: Analysis of the Barriers to Full Adoption. *Energy and Built Environment*, 2(1):65–81, 2021.

[10] Daniel Luckey, Henrieke Fritz, Dmitrii Legatiuk, Kosmas Dragos, and Kay Smarsly. Artificial Intelligence Techniques for Smart City Applications. In *Proceedings of the 18th International Conference on Computing in Civil and Building Engineering: ICCCBE 2020*, 3–15. Springer, 2021.

[11] Ingrid Vasiliu Feltes. Emerging Technologies and Smart Cities. www.forbes.com/sites/forbesbusinesscouncil/2021/12/17/emerging-technologies-and- smart-cities/?sh= 744ce8a6a8d4, 2021. [Online; accessed 18th May 2023].

[12] Smart City Observatory. www.imd.org/smart-city-observatory/home/, 2023. [Online; accessed 18th May 2023].

[13] Eunil Park, Angel P Del Pobil, and Sang Jib Kwon. The Role of Internet of Things (IoT) in Smart Cities: Technology Roadmap-Oriented Approaches. *Sustainability*, 10(5):1388, 2018.

[14] Minhaj Ahmad Khan and Khaled Salah. IoT Security: Review, Blockchain Solutions, and Open Challenges. *Future Generation Computer Systems*, 82:395–411, 2018.

[15] Min Li, Wenbin Gu, Wei Chen, Yeshen He, Yannian Wu, and Yiying Zhang. Smart Home: Architecture, Technologies, and Systems. *Procedia Computer Science*, 131:393–400, 2018.

[16] Shubham Mathur and Uma Shankar Modani. Smart City-A Gateway for Artificial Intelligence in India. In *2016 IEEE Students' Conference on Electrical, Electronics and Computer Science (SCEECS)*, pp. 1–3. IEEE, 2016.

[17] Klaus Prettner and Holger Strulik. Innovation, Automation, and Inequality: Policy Challenges in the Race Against the Machine. *Journal of Monetary Economics*, 116:249–265, 2020.

[18] Artificial Intelligence (AI) Market. www.marketsandmarkets.com/PressReleases/artificial- intelligence. asp, 2023. [Online; accessed 18th May 2023].

[19] Arash Heidari, Nima Jafari Navimipour, and Mehmet Unal. Applications of ML/DL in the Management of Smart Cities and Societies based on New Trends in Information Technologies: A systematic literature review. *Sustainable Cities and Society*, p. 104089, 2022.

[20] Asma Ait Ouallane, Ayoub Bahnasse, Assia Bakali, and Mohamed Talea. Overview of Road Traffic Management Solutions based on IoT and AI. *Procedia Computer Science*, 198:518–523, 2022.

[21] Md Shafiullah, Saidur Rahman, Binash Imteyaz, Mohamed Kheireddine Aroua, Md Ismail Hossain, and Syed Masiur Rahman. Review of Smart City Energy Modeling in Southeast Asia. *Smart Cities*, 6(1):72–99, 2023.

[22] Baozhen Yao, Ankun Ma, Rui Feng, Xiaopeng Shen, Mingheng Zhang, and Yansheng Yao. A Deep Learning Framework about Traffic Flow Forecasting for Urban Traffic Emission Monitoring Systems. *Frontiers in Public Health*, 9:2233, 2022.

[23] Siddharth Seshan, Dirk Vries, Maarten van Duren, Alex van der Helm, and Johann Poinapen. AI-based Validation of Wastewater Treatment Plant Sensor Data using an

Open Data Exchange Architecture. In *IOP Conference Series: Earth and Environmental Science*, 1136, p. 012055. IOP Publishing, 2023.

[24] AS Albahri, Ali M Duhaim, Mohammed A Fadhel, Alhamzah Alnoor, Noor S Baqer, Laith Alzubaidi, OS Albahri, AH Alamoodi, Jinshuai Bai, Asma Salhi, et al. A systematic review of Trustworthy and Explainable Artificial Intelligence in Healthcare: Assessment of Quality, Bias Risk, and Data Fusion. *Information Fusion*, 96:156–191, 2023. https://doi.org/10.1016/j.inffus.2023.03.008.

[25] Lynda Andeobu, Santoso Wibowo, and Srimannarayana Grandhi. Artificial Intelligence Applications for Sustainable Solid Waste Management Practices in Australia: A Systematic Review. *Science of The Total Environment*, 155389, 2022.

[26] Sharnil Pandya, Gautam Srivastava, Rutvij Jhaveri, M Rajasekhara Babu, Sweta Bhattacharya, Praveen Kumar Reddy Maddikunta, Spyridon Mastorakis, Md Jalil Piran, and Thippa Reddy Gadekallu. Federated Learning for Smart Cities: A Comprehensive Survey. *Sustainable Energy Technologies and Assessments*, 55:102987, 2023.

[27] Joshua O Ighalo, Adewale George Adeniyi, and Gonçalo Marques. Artificial Intelligence for Surface Water Quality Monitoring and Assessment: A Systematic Literature Analysis. *Modeling Earth Systems and Environment*, 7(2):669–681, 2021.

[28] Elahe Sherafat, Bilal Farooq, Amir Hossein Karbasi, and Seyedehsan Seyedabrishami. Attention- LSTM for Multivariate Traffic State Prediction on Rural Roads. arXiv preprint arXiv:2301.02731, 2023.

[29] Pedro Perez-Murueta, Alfonso Gómez-Espinosa, Cesar Cardenas, and Miguel Gonzalez-Mendoza Jr. Deep Learning System for Vehicular Re-Routing and Congestion Avoidance. *Applied Sciences*, 9(13):2717, 2019.

[30] Jagendra Singh, Mohammad Sajid, Suneet Kumar Gupta, and Raza Abbas Haidri. Artificial Intelligence and Blockchain Technologies for Smart City. *Intelligent Green Technologies for Sustainable Smart Cities*, 317–330, 2022.

[31] H Alqahtani. Smart Parking and Smart Transportation with AI-based Parking and Driving. *Big Data and Computing Visions*, 2(2):95–100, 2022.

[32] Rachit Garg, Arvind W Kiwelekar, Laxman D Netak, and Akshay Ghodake. I-Pulse: A NLP-based Novel Approach for Employee Engagement in Logistics Organization. *International Journal of Information Management Data Insights*, 1(1):100011, 2021.

[33] José María Celaya-Padilla, Carlos Eric Galván-Tejada, Joyce Selene Anaid Lozano-Aguilar, Laura Alejandra Zanella-Calzada, Huizilopoztli Luna-García, Jorge Issac Galván-Tejada, Nadia Ka- rina Gamboa-Rosales, Alberto Velez Rodriguez, and Hamurabi Gamboa-Rosales. "Texting & Driving" Detection using Deep Convolutional Neural Networks. *Applied Sciences*, 9(15):2962, 2019.

[34] Byeongjoon Noh, Wonjun No, Jaehong Lee, and David Lee. Vision-based Potential Pedestrian Risk Analysis on Unsignalized Crosswalk using Data Mining Techniques. *Applied Sciences*, 10(3):1057, 2020.

[35] Peng Qin, Yong Zhang, Boyue Wang, and Yongli Hu. Grassmann Manifold-based State Analysis Method of Traffic Surveillance Video. *Applied Sciences*, 9(7):1319, 2019.

[36] Tehseen Mazhar, Hafiz Muhammad Irfan, Inayatul Haq, Inam Ullah, Madiha Ashraf, Tamara Al Shloul, Yazeed Yasin Ghadi, and Dalia H Elkamchouchi. Analysis of Challenges and Solutions of IoT in Smart Grids using AI and Machine Learning Techniques: A review. *Electronics*, 12(1):242, 2023.

[37] Azadeh Sadeghi, Roohollah Younes Sinaki, William A Young, and Gary R Weck-man. An Intelligent Model to Predict Energy Performances of Residential Buildings based on Deep Neural Networks. *Energies*, 13(3):571, 2020.

[38] Tianguang Lu, Xinyu Chen, Michael B McElroy, Chris P Nielsen, Qiuwei Wu, and Qian Ai. A Reinforcement Learning-based Decision System for Electricity Pricing Plan Selection by Smart Grid End Users. *IEEE Transactions on Smart Grid*, 12(3):2176–2187, 2020.

[39] Hossam ElHusseini, Chadi Assi, Bassam Moussa, Ribal Attallah, and Ali Ghrayeb. Blockchain, AI and Smart Grids: The Three Musketeers to a Decentralised EV Charging Infrastructure. *IEEE Internet of Things Magazine*, 3(2):24–29, 2020.

[40] Romany Fouad Mansour, Adnen El Amraoui, Issam Nouaouri, Vicente Garċıa Díaz, Deepak Gupta, and Sachin Kumar. Artificial Intelligence and Internet of Things Enabled Disease Diagnosis Model for Smart Healthcare Systems. *IEEE Access*, 9:45137–45146, 2021.

[41] Prabh Deep Singh, Gaurav Dhiman, and Rohit Sharma. Internet of Things for Sus-taining a Smart and Secure Healthcare System. *Sustainable Computing: Informatics and Systems*, 33:100622, 2022.

[42] Alessandro Massaro, Vincenzo Maritati, Daniele Giannone, Daniele Convertini, and Angelo Galiano. LSTM DSS Automatism and Dataset Optimization for Diabetes Prediction. *Applied Sciences*, 9(17):3532, 2019.

[43] Mohy Uddin and Shabbir Syed-Abdul. Data Analytics and Applications of the Wearable Sensors in Healthcare: An Overview. *Sensors*, 20(5):1379, 2020.

[44] Ghulam Muhammad and Musaed Alhussein. Convergence of Artificial Intelligence and Internet of Things in Smart Healthcare: A Case Study of Voice Pathology Detec-tion. *IEEE Access*, 9:89198–89209, 2021.

[45] Emilie Bruzelius, Matthew Le, Avi Kenny, Jordan Downey, Matteo Danieletto, Aaron Baum, Patrick Doupe, Bruno Silva, Philip J Landrigan, and Prabhjot Singh. Satellite Images and Machine Learning can Identify Remote Communities to Facili-tate Access to Health Services. *Journal of the American Medical Informatics Asso-ciation*, 26(8–9):806–812, 2019.

[46] Mamta Mittal, Gopi Battineni, Dharmendra Singh, Thakursingh Nagarwal, and Prabhakar Yadav. Web-based Chatbot for Frequently Asked Queries (FAQ) in Hos-pitals. *Journal of Taibah University Medical Sciences*, 16(5):740–746, 2021.

[47] WHAT A WASTE 2.0 A Global Snapshot of Solid Waste Management to 2050. https://datatopics.worldbank.org/what-a-waste/. [Online; accessed 18th May 2023].

[48] Taeyoung Yoo, Seongjae Lee, and Taehyoun Kim. Dual Image-based CNN Ensem-ble Model for Waste Classification in Reverse Vending Machine. *Applied Sciences*, 11(22):11051, 2021.

[49] Shanaka Kristombu Baduge, Sadeep Thilakarathna, Jude Shalitha Perera, Mehrdad Arashpour, Pejman Sharafi, Bertrand Teodosio, Amkit Shringi, and Priyan Men-dis. Artificial Intelligence and Smart Vision for Building and Construction 4.0: Machine and Deep Learning Methods and Applications. *Automation in Construc-tion*, 141:104440, 2022.

[50] T Fidowaty, L Wulantika, and Agus Mulyana. Waste Management based on Smart City Management by using Internet of Things (IoT) and Artificial Intelligence (AI) Technology. *ABDIMAS: Journal Pengabdian Masyarakat*, 5(1):1756–1762, 2022.

[51] Mohamed Abdelaty Habila, Mohamed Ouladsmane, and Zeid Abdullah Alothman. Role of Artificial Intelligence in Environmental Sustainability. In *Visualisation*

Techniques for Climate Change with Machine Learning and Artificial Intelligence, pp. 449–469. Elsevier, 2023.

[52] Manas Wakchaure, BK Patle, and AK Mahindrakar. Application of AI Techniques and Robotics in Agriculture: A Review. *Artificial intelligence in the Life Sciences,* 100057, 2023.

[53] Antonio Manuel Ciruela-Lorenzo, Ana Rosa Del-Aguila-Obra, Antonio Padilla-Meĺendez, and Juan José Plaza-Angulo. Digitalisation of Agri-Cooperatives in the Smart Agriculture Context. Proposal of a Digital Diagnosis Tool. *Sustainability,* 12(4):1325, 2020.

[54] Yaganteeswarudu Akkem, Saroj Kumar Biswas, and Aruna Varanasi. Smart Farming using Artificial Intelligence: A Review. *Engineering Applications of Artificial Intelligence,* 120:105899, 2023.

[55] Abdul-Rahman Al-Ali, Murad Qasaimeh, Mamoun Al-Mardini, Suresh Radder, and Imran A Zualk- ernan. Zigbee-based Irrigation System for Home Gardens. In *2015 International Conference on Communications, Signal Processing, and their Applications (ICCSPA'15),* pp. 1–5. IEEE, 2015.

[56] Mohd Javaid, Abid Haleem, Ibrahim Haleem Khan, and Rajiv Suman. Understanding the Potential Applications of Artificial Intelligence in Agriculture Sector. *Advanced Agrochem,* 2(1):15–30, 2023.

[57] B Ragavi, L Pavithra, P Sandhiyadevi, GK Mohanapriya, and S Harikirubha. Smart Agriculture with AI Sensor by using Agrobot. In *2020 Fourth International Conference on Computing Methodologies and Communication (ICCMC),* pp. 1–4. IEEE, 2020.

[58] Elsayed Said Mohamed, AA Belal, Sameh Kotb Abd-Elmabod, Mohammed A El-Shirbeny, A Gad, and Mohamed B Zahran. Smart Farming for Improving Agricultural Management. *The Egyptian Journal of Remote Sensing and Space Science,* 24(3):971–981, 2021.

[59] Sudhir Kumar Rajput, Tanupriya Choudhury, Hitesh Kumar Sharma, and Hussain Falih Mahdi. Smart City Driven by AI and Data Mining: The Need of Urbanization. In Emerging *Technologies in Data Mining and Information Security: Proceedings of IEMIS 2022, Volume 2,* pp. 139–151. Springer, 2022.

[60] Tan Yigitcanlar, Rashid Mehmood, and Juan M Corchado. Green Artificial Intelligence: Towards an Efficient, Sustainable and Equitable Technology for Smart Cities and Futures. *Sustainability,* 13(16):8952, 2021.

[61] J Bughin, L Herring, H Mayhew, J Seong, and T Allas. Artificial *Intelligence in the United Kingdom: Prospects and Challenges.* McKinsey Global Institute, 2019.

[62] Anabel Ortega-Ferńandez, Rodrigo Martın-Rojas, and Víctor Jesús Garćıa-Morales. Artificial Intelligence in the Urban Environment: Smart Cities as Models for Developing Innovation and Sustainability. *Sustainability,* 12(19):7860, 2020.

[63] Christopher Grant Kirwan and Fu Zhiyong. *Smart Cities and Artificial Intelligence: Convergent Systems for Planning, Design, and Operations.* Elsevier, 2020.

[64] Maria Enrica Zamponi and Enrico Barbierato. The Dual Role of Artificial Intelligence in Developing Smart Cities. *Smart Cities,* 5(2):728–755, 2022.

[65] Zaib Ullah, Fadi Al-Turjman, Leonardo Mostarda, and Roberto Gagliardi. Applications of Artificial Intelligence and Machine Learning in Smart Cities. *Computer Communications,* 154:313–323, 2020.

[66] Syed Asad A Bokhari and Seunghwan Myeong. Use of Artificial Intelligence in Smart Cities for Smart Decision-Making: Λ Social Innovation Perspective. *Sustainability,* 14(2):620, 2022.

[67] Tan Yigitcanlar, Nayomi Kankanamge, Massimo Regona, Andres Ruiz Maldonado, Bridget Rowan, Alex Ryu, Kevin C Desouza, Juan M Corchado, Rashid Mehmood, and Rita Yi Man Li. Artificial Intelligence Technologies and related Urban Planning and Development Concepts: How are they Perceived and Utilised in Australia? *Journal of Open Innovation: Technology, Market, and Complexity*, 6(4):187, 2020.

[68] Abdul Rehman Javed, Faisal Shahzad, Saif ur Rehman, Yousaf Bin Zikria, Imran Razzak, Zunera Jalil, and Guandong Xu. Future Smart Cities Requirements, Emerging Technologies, Applications, Challenges, and Future Aspects. *Cities*, 129:103794, 2022.

[69] Mujaheed Abdullahi, Yahia Baashar, Hitham Alhussian, Ayed Alwadain, Norshakirah Aziz, Luiz Fernando Capretz, and Said Jadid Abdulkadir. Detecting Cybersecurity Attacks in Internet of Things using Artificial Intelligence Methods: A Systematic Literature Review. *Electronics*, 11(2):198, 2022.

[70] Emma Carmel and Regine Paul. Peace and Prosperity for the Digital Age? the Colonial Political Economy of European AI Governance. *IEEE Technology and Society Magazine*, 41(2):94–104, 2022.

[71] Irene Kitsara. Artificial Intelligence and the Digital Divide: From an Innovation Perspective. In *Platforms and Artificial Intelligence: The Next Generation of Competences*, pp. 245–265. Springer, 2022.

[72] Kashif Ahmad, Majdi Maabreh, Mohamed Ghaly, Khalil Khan, Junaid Qadir, and Ala Al-Fuqaha. Developing Future Human-Centered Smart Cities: Critical Analysis of Smart City Security, Data Management, and Ethical Challenges. *Computer Science Review*, 43:100452, 2022.

Chapter 6

VANETs for Smart Cities
Opportunities and Upcoming
Research Directions

Aradhana Behura, Puneet Kumar Jain,
and Arun Kumar

6.1 INTRODUCTION

The main aims of intelligent transport systems are minimizing fuel consumption and travel times and controlling road accidents, in addition to general smart city traffic management. New cutting-edge technologies (cloud-fog-edge computing, blockchain, quantum computing, green computing, federated learning (FL), Internet of Things [IoT], machine learning (ML), deep learning (DL), 5G, 6G, big data, game theory, and graph theory) are presently being used in many domains to enhance performance [1–3].

Vehicular ad hoc networks (VANETs) are an emerging field in smart transportation that support vehicle-to-vehicle (V2V), vehicle-to-pedestrian (V2P), vehicle-to-road (V2R), and vehicle-to-infrastructure (V2I) communication. VANETs are used in rural areas, in cities, and on highways. Here, we discuss applications, challenges, and how innovative technology provides better security, smarter resource allocation, reliability, driver activity monitoring, high mobility, coverage optimization, fault tolerance, shortest path, task scheduling, resource management, handling link breakage, and less delay and congestion. Modern technologies are used to improve performance or quality of service (QoS) in terms of packet delivery rate (multi-hop data transmission increases network efficiency), link quality, channel allocation, link failure rate, channel utilization, enhanced network lifetime, task offloading, throughput, delay, and energy consumption [5–9].

6.1.1 Application

VANETs are applied for entertainment, comfort, and safety. Comfort applications include weather forecasting and identifying nearby hotels. Safety applications of VANETs manage intersection collision avoidance, blind spot detection, post-crash warning, sign extension, vehicle diagnostics, and maintenance.

DOI: 10.1201/9781003486930-9

6.1.2 Architecture

VANETs are autonomous and self-configurable wireless ad hoc networks. They use vehicles as mobile nodes to create a network and help decrease traffic deaths and improve travel comfort by increasing inter-vehicle coordination. The most commonly considered applications are related to public safety and traffic coordination. The procedure of sending data to several users at the same time in a computer network, i.e., the sender has the choice of sending the data to some users. Mainly due to the real-time mobility feature of a node (vehicle) VANET network, it is difficult to harness the data at that point in time. Moreover, connectivity between nodes and infrastructure forms the major basis for the exchange of information and taking the required action based on the data. Therefore, routing is the major issue in any ad hoc network. Thus accordingly, we need to have a suitable routing protocol that can receive or send messages with certainty from a source node to one or many destination nodes. To tackle some of the situations mentioned above, we implement multicast routing. This is so because multicast routing can effectively organize the resources, and reduce congestion and workload in a network, thereby reducing the power consumption, transmission overhead, and control overhead by sending multiple copies of messages to various vehicles simultaneously. Figure 6.1 depicts various vehicular communication strategies.

The different communication paths include vehicle to vehicle, vehicle to everything, intra-infrastructure, vehicle to infrastructure, vehicle to sensor, vehicle to personal device, vehicle to pedestrian, vehicle to cellular network, and cellular vehicle to everything.

Bajracharya [10] proposed a dynamic price procedure (vehicular communication using an unlicensed band) to maximize profit and utility for 6G to choose

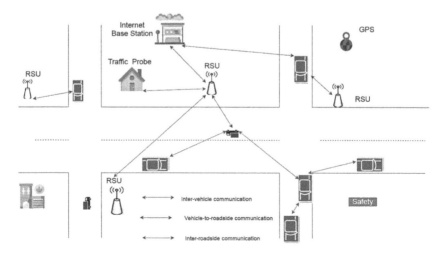

Figure 6.1 VANET architecture.

high-paying customers. They used various pricing domains: no pricing, fixed TS pricing, variable TS pricing, and Nash bargaining. Many charging policies are based upon various factors such as interference, power and time. Bandit optimization is used in reinforcement learning to reduce exploit–explore issues and optimize the cumulative reward.

LTE on unlicensed spectrum, licensed assisted access, LTE WLAN aggregation, and voice over new radio are unlicensed bands; we can compare each band with respect to standardization, aggregated bandwidth, the technology used, delays, deployment strategies, carrier dimension, operational bands, and duplexing mode. Stackelberg game-based 6G decision-making not only helps to maximize revenue, duty cycle allocation, spectrum scheduling, efficient resource allocation, and power control but also provides reduced communication collisions, channel assignment, low power consumption, manage traffic and maximizes efficient channel scheduling. Figure 6.2 describes how 6G can be helpful in the dynamic pricing model.

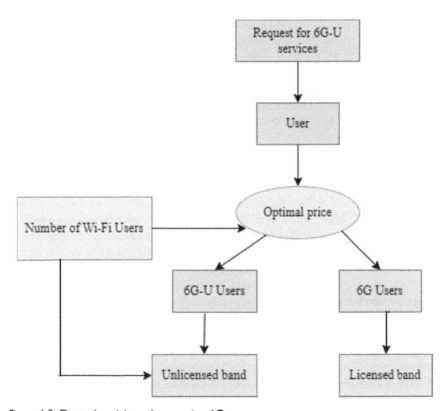

Figure 6.2 Dynamic pricing scheme using 6G.

6.1.3 Characteristics and Issues

VANETs support safe driving, improve passenger comfort, and enhance traffic efficiency. Some significant characteristics are their high mobility, high computational ability, no power constraints, large scale, and variable network density. The unbounded network size means the geographical positions of VANETs are not at all constant; we can increase or decrease the zone according to our convenience.

In VANETs, information is exchanged among vehicles and roadside units (RSUs) frequently and dynamically as nodes gather and exchange data wirelessly. The network density varies according to traffic density, being high in heavy traffic and low in light traffic. VANETs face various challenges, including signal fading, delays, bandwidth limitations, connectivity and channel communication issues, small effective diameter, congestion detection and control, energy efficiency, load balancing, task scheduling, and security and privacy concerns in routing protocols. The main motivation behind VANET development is to enhance traffic security and safety, as the costs incurred due to traffic collisions are significant, and current safety applications are underdeveloped. Research in VANETs is rapidly growing, exploring a wide range of applications for both rural and urban scenarios, making travel safer and more enjoyable. VANETs offer new possibilities for reaching destinations and obtaining help more easily through wireless communication and data-sharing capabilities among interconnected vehicles.

In VANETs, data transmission occurs in a multi-hop fashion, which necessitates the use of a routing protocol. Multicast routing protocols are particularly useful, as they enable messages to be sent from a single sender to a group of interested nodes that act as the destination nodes. These protocols offer an efficient way to address some of the challenges mentioned earlier in the dynamic environment of VANETs.

Because of the rapid movement of vehicles in VANETs, the routing path between the source and destination nodes must be constantly updated and reconstructed. This updating process takes into account the current positions of the nodes to ensure an accurate and reliable routing path in the network. Due to the mobility and frequent changes in the topology of VANETs, multicast routing protocols have become a prominent area of research to ensure efficient and effective data delivery within this dynamic environment. Some of the QoS routing parameters in VANETs are path length, packet loss ratio, bandwidth delay, delay jitter, size of the network (or number of nodes), queue capacity, and transmitter and receiver power.

However, QoS-constrained multicast routing is an NP-complete problem in that only heuristic algorithms can be used to solve them because the solution to this is in danger of falling into the local optimal space instead of the optimal global space, thereby making this one of the major challenges for finding the globally optimal path in multicast routing. Nature-inspired algorithms help to minimize exploitation and exploration in the algorithm [11]. Table 6.1 presents various recent protocols with their techniques, advantages, and disadvantages.

Table 6.1 Various Protocols Used in VANET Applications

Paper	Category	Protocol name	Technique	Advantages	Disadvantages
Rajpoot et al., 2021 [12]	VANET	Independent recurrent neural network-LEACH (low-energy adaptive clustering)	Mean & recurrent neural network	Reduce data redundancy problem, provides scalability	Vulnerable to various attack, high power consumption, direct communication between cluster head (CH) & base station (BS)
Tang et al., 2022 [13]	Vehicular Edge Computing	Dynamic framing offloading algorithm based on double deep Q-network	Deep reinforcement learning used for framing offloading	Mobility of vehicles, offloading decisions, minimization of delay	Complexity increases
Sajedi et al., 2021 [14]	Healthcare sector	Fuzzy LEACH	Fuzzy logic	Optimized residual energy, packet delivery ratio, maximize the life span of the network	Fuzzy logic will produce quantitative data, not qualitative.
Gupta et al., 2021 [15]	VANET, Internet of military vehicles (IoMV) on an autonomous ad hoc network	Blockchain IoMV	Blockchain-based Onion routing	Secure, D2D communication using 5G, improved traceability & trust, better bandwidth utilization, communication latency, data immutability, low latency, & low information storage cost	Frequent link breaks, high data cost because it is ethereum based, and low latency due to 4G and 5G. Performance will improve with the use of 6G.
Yazici et al., 2014 [16]	Ad hoc network	MRSBC	Capacitated arc routing using modified Ulusoy algorithm	Multirobot sensor-based shortest path calculation, minimal cost for tour, minimal redundant sensor node visits if sensor node increases and energy decreases	Maximum node used to give coverage task

(Continued)

Table 6.1 (Continued)

Paper	Category	Protocol name	Technique	Advantages	Disadvantages
Haghighi et al., 2019 [17]	VANET	Anonymous onion routing (used to provide security)	Transmits the same packet after the completion of three retransmissions. The source node would know that a middle vehicular node has gone off. In this case, the source node would choose three new vehicular node & ran the procedure or algorithm again.	Parallel path selection, high packet delivery ratio, robust due to multipath forwarding and dynamic route maintenance through heuristic clustering	Link break, due to high cost, slow sensor node deployment, retransmission decreases when group size increases
Sakai et al., 2017 [18]	Battlefield communications	Delay-tolerant onion routing network	Data encryption using onion routing.	Predict node & path anonymity; if onion size increases, then packet delivery rate increases	Throughput decreases, path anonymity, delivery rate, & traceable rate
Wang et al., 2021 [19]	IoV (Internet of vehicles)	Privacy-aware 5G-enabled routing	Federated reinforcement learning used	Privacy preservation	Low latency, load balancing
Omar et al., 2015 [20]	IoV	Gateway Placement & Packet Routing	Multichannel scheme using time-division multiple access	queueing system	Packet delay
Guo et al., 2018 [21]	VANET	Estimating travel time	Dynamic route planning	Less redundancy, lower traffic congestion, efficient packet delivery, and low complexity	Can't predict sudden road accidents
Behura et al., 2022 [22]	VANET	Giraffe kicking-based routing algorithm	Cluster-based routing algorithm	Intra-cluster problem is resolved.	Inter-cluster distance is not minimized.

Abboud & Zhuang, 2014 [23]	VANET	Single hop-based communication link	Markov chain model used for long-lasting link between sensor node	Mesoscopic mobility model	Communication among the hop length rises & the lifetime of link losses with an upturn in the density of the vehicles.
Gayathri et al., 2018 [24]	VANET	Certificateless security integrating batch verification	Elliptic curve algorithm used to provide security	Provides repudiation, authentication, revocation integrity, anonymity, privacy, & non- traceability	Not more secure
Bi et al., 2015 [25]	VANET	Urban multi-hop broadcast protocol	Forwarding-based node selection, mini-slot, broadcast interframe space, and contention window are used in order to avoid propagation delay and interruption in data sending & to eliminate collision	Reduces transmission delay, less redundant message, data propagation speed, & data reception rate	Lack of central coordination & less secure
Ahmad et al., 2021 [26]	IoV	NOTRINO	Hybrid secure scheme, V2V,V2I, & V2P communication	Secure transportation, authentic, malicious packet prediction, detect attackers	Delay, data sparsity & biased selection of the CH if majority node found to be dishonest
Li et al., 2022 [27]	Vehicular fog-edge computing	Game theory-based efficient resource allocation algorithm	Contract-Stackelberg method, joint offloading decision	Efficient resource allocation, low energy consumption, task offloading, & decision analytics	Not secure

(Continued)

Table 6.1 (Continued)

Paper	Category	Protocol name	Technique	Advantages	Disadvantages
Rahman et al., 2022	VANET	Vehicle health monitoring system	Busy tone algorithm is used in IEEE 802.af & IEEE 802.22. Used TVWS band. Slepian wolf coding is used for efficient communication. Blockchain is used for data encryption.	Minimizes interference, high scalability, interoperability, low energy consumption, achieves safety for passenger & pedestrian	Data preprocessing procedure is missing
Kumar et al., 2020 [28]	SIOV	Two-way particle swarm optimization	Green computing & SDN inspired scheme	Traffic safety, multicast clustering	Delay in message transmissions

In this review, we outline both problem-specific and architectural factors in addressing issues. It will help to design a link between smart technology and transportation communities, illuminating upcoming areas and aspects.

6.2 ARTIFICIAL INTELLIGENCE IN VANETs

In this section, we discuss various ML, DL, 5G, and 6G technologies for designing efficient protocols for smart vehicle networks. Rahman et al. [29] describe the role of big data and ML in the field of vehicle networks using the Internet of Everything. Cognitive radio is used for energy estimation, feature selection, spectrum sensing, expectation maximization, backhaul management, and cache management. By incorporating ML with software-defined networks (SDNs), network function virtualization, and mobile edge computing (MEC), the developed protocol outperforms inefficient load distribution, resource allocation & network virtualization. A convolution neural network (NN) is used for vehicle license plate recognition, traffic sign detection, traffic light recognition, etc. [29].

The optimized decision model (ODM) is used for spectrum sensing, channel estimation, radio resource allocation, network traffic control, and routing. Several issues in wireless communication are modulation classification, jamming resistance, physical coding, interference alignment, and link evaluation, and these problems can be resolved using various ML and DL techniques. The 5G technique is used to minimize interference in the network. Slepian wolf coding is used in cloud servers, and it is not only secure but also effective in terms of computation cost, storage, and communication.

Hidden Markov models (HMMs) are very useful critical ML tools for statistical analysis of data sets. This optimization predicts unsuccessful packet transmission and successful data transmission, detects idle states, and handles multi-hop communication, lack of cluster coordination, hidden–exposed terminal issues, rapid topology changes, and saturated & non-saturated traffic conditions [1–4]. Figure 6.3 describes how data analytics is helpful in a cloud platform; this protocol deals with massive redundant vehicular data sets. Figure 6.4 presents a protocol for identifying defective vehicle parts.

Three problems can be solved efficiently. The first problem focuses on the likelihood of a sequence and is solved using a forward, backward procedure. The second problem addressed in the context is about determining the optimal state sequence, and it is resolved using the Viterbi algorithm. The third problem involves re-estimation and can be solved using either the Baum–Welch algorithm or the forward-backward algorithm.

The likelihood of a sequence is referred to as the probability of the observation sequence. To compute the probability of the state sequence, the best possible state sequence is obtained from the observation sequence. The "best possible" sequence is defined as the one with the highest probability, given the observation sequence. The third problem aims to find the transition and

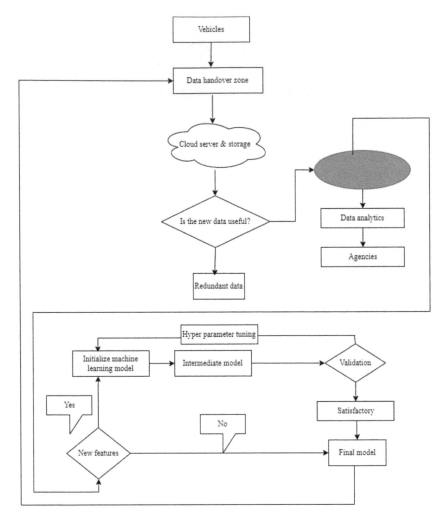

Figure 6.3 Data analytics in a cloud platform.

observation probabilities, which are the parameters of the HMM. This is done based on the output sequence or observation sequences that are either accepted by or generated by the machine. Yao et al. proposed a protocol called PRHMM routing that utilizes the forward-backward algorithm. This protocol not only provides mobility patterns but also enhances the data transmission rate, making it faster and more efficient [7, 30].

The algorithm's primary drawback is the random cluster head selection during each round. To address this, a fuzzy-based clustering system called distributed load balancing with unequal clustering using a fuzzy approach that utilizes the residual energy and node degree from each round to make informed decisions

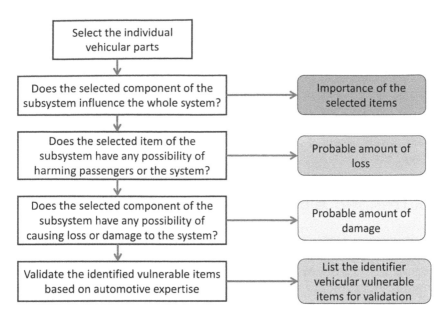

Figure 6.4 Identifying vulnerable vehicle parts with AI.

regarding cluster head selection and clustering degrees. Selecting the cluster head in each round maximizes energy consumption, a disadvantage of this method [31].

A number of researchers work on driver assistant systems and driver monitoring systems, the key features required to maintain intelligent transportation systems [2, 75–78]. Fuzzy logic is helpful for energy-efficient schemes in VANETs. Here, researchers explained that all the other devices (nodes) and roadside units are static. The Euclidean method is used for calculating the distance. The roadside units receive messages from any sensor nodes that are deployed in the area. The fuzzy membership function is used to provide efficient communication, data aggregation, and data retrieval [6]. The support vector machine is an efficient machine learning algorithm used to train the vehicular dataset; when training is completed, the system can use blockchain technology to provide security, but it consumes a great deal of time. The final aim of vehicle networks is to deliver the ever-present connection between the vehicle drivers and passengers on the urban road [5].

Today, traffic congestion is growing globally, and traffic supervision systems are needed to analyze this issue. A smart city needs effective traffic management and complex data handling by integrating IoT with ML. The authors of review analyze a smart traffic management protocol to maximize the total number of automobiles while balancing traffic signals and road intersections using a reinforcement algorithm [34].

Here, we discuss VANET representation learning for recommendations in IoT. Based on link uncertainty and transportation networks, we can frame the research issues as follows. Generally, depending on the vehicular trajectory information, we may build a vehicle network GG = {VV, EE, LL}, where VV signifies the group of automobiles or drivers, EE represents the communication links among the drivers, and LL indicates the uncertainty regarding the communication links. Given the networks, our aim is to vouch for a possible associate for any vehicle driver who depends on their information similarity. Thus, the similarity of the network can be measured precisely by analyzing the whole vehicular network topology [35].

6.3 AUTONOMOUS DRIVING

Here, we investigate the recent cutting-edge technology related to safe driver assistance systems. Our research also highlights recent challenges regarding safe driver assistance, with many research references focused on the improvement of cutting-edge technologies in ad hoc networks, with QoS as their principal requirement. We balance our literature review investigation with empirical outcomes of different architectural designs for many safety-related responsibilities, which shed light on the various prototypes. Figure 6.5 depicts a roadmap of autonomous driving.

Deep learning for autonomous driving performs pedestrian detection, drowsiness detection, collision avoidance, traffic sign detection, road detection, lane detection, and vehicle detection. DL provides QoS-based services such as vehicle driving style prediction for driver assistance, pedestrian interaction with autonomous vehicles, and traffic sign recognition.

6.4 GAME-THEORY-BASED APPLICATIONS IN VANETs

Game theoretic methodologies have been prevalent for demonstrating and swotting pricing decision issues in the fields of business, economics, smart cities, etc. Game theory is divided into two types, cooperative and noncooperative. Hedonic

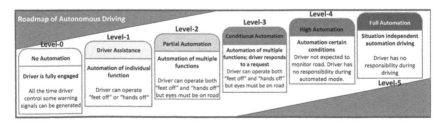

Figure 6.5 Roadmap of autonomous driving.

games of coalition formation, Nash bargaining, and potential games fall under cooperative game theory; differential games, prospect games, n player normal games, Bayesian games, submodular game, and potential games fall under noncooperative game theory.

Game theory helps to optimize energy consumption, link failure rate, delays in data transmission, channel utilization, throughput, ratio of packet delivery, and network life span. It delivers scientific, quantitative approaches to identifying optimal policies and objectives. The Stackelberg game theory-based efficient resource allocation algorithm was used in a vehicular fog-edge computing framework; here, an MEC server was used for high computational efficiency with less communication delay [74]. This protocol follows three stages:

- This is a contract based setup to stimulate vehicles to share their resources.
- Because of the complicated interactions among the RSUs and the vehicles, it is a tedious task to coordinate all of the transactions to ensure that all entities receive profits.
- Stackelberg game theory is used to enhance the pricing strategies to maximize the profit and utilities. The MEC server, vehicles, and RSUs are the three components used. The RSU recruits the computing resources and then establishes communication with the MEC server and the users.

This protocol performs better in terms of energy consumption, task offloading, vehicle compatibility, and decision analysis. Researchers formulated a best connected path data transmission scheme that integrated graph and signaling game analysis and that outperformed a heterogeneous VANET. The utility function of the signaling game depends on both players. The players hinge on the signal created by the leading player and the route of the other player. Table 6.2 presents the various game theory concepts that are applied in VANETs.

Table 6.2 Game Theory Concepts Applied in VANETs

Name of game	Concept of the game	Application Area
Hedonic game coalitions	Maintain agreement and cooperation	Data collection and network monitoring
Zero-sum pursuit	Evasion differential game	Channel optimization, handling attack & jammer
N-player normal form game	Players perform action without bothering the performance of other participants.	Load balancing, maximizing throughput
Submodular game	If one person handles lower action, then others must be taken off lower action.	Maximizing beaconing period

(Continued)

Table 6.2 (Continued)

Name of game	Concept of the game	Application Area
Noncooperative game	Finding suitable individual strategy to maximize one's own payoff	Helps to maximize coverage area
Population game theory	User adopts own method & learns from own error; supports group communication	Useful in data communication
Bayesian game	Learn from associated information	Safety-oriented service
Nash bargaining game	Demands resources. If resources are limited & both players are demanding the same resource, then both will receive nothing.	Maximizes encounter rate
Anticoordination game	Both players can benefit if they select different procedures.	Helps to minimize inference with efficient channel assignment in D2D communication
Prospect game	Players make decisions under any risks and any uncertainty	Transmit power on wireless channels to handle attacks
Potential game	Individual players have own payoff function that depends upon the chosen strategy	Offload task in cloud or fog server

6.5 SECURITY AND PRIVACY PRESERVATION

Privacy preservation is a challenging task; confidentiality, integrity, availability, non-repudiation, authentication, and authorization are the important factor. Mershad et al. [37] proposed the SURFER protocol, which provided intermittent connectivity, low delay, and a secure SDN routing scheme for Internet of Vehicles (IoV) [38–39]. Malicious nodes can be detected by taking the number of detected malicious nodes divided by the total number of malicious sensor nodes. In 5G vehicle networks, blockchain provides better security [39] and better preserves privacy. An artificial intelligence (AI)-based routing algorithm was used in a wireless ad hoc network for an intelligent transportation system [40]. Prateek et al. described how quantum computing [75] helps to provide effective security in terms of decision sequence and interconversion rule. This protocol not only helps in bit conversion for message integrity but also provides source authentication, privacy preservation, traceability, and unlinkability. The Grover algorithm is also very effective for handling channel fading in ad hoc networks.

6.5.1 A Trust-Management-Based IoV Forest Fire Scheme

The IoV plays a vital role in enhancing road safety by facilitating important information communication, enabling motorists to make intelligent decisions while on the road. To ensure the integrity of the network and eliminate malicious sensor nodes, trust management is crucial. In this context, various factors are mapped in the forest fire spreading model within VANETs.

The forest fire spreading model considers factors such as the number of sensor node connections, forest density, velocity of sensor nodes (correlated with wind direction), activity of sensor nodes, and the message transmitting ability of neighboring nodes (considered sensor nodes in the network). The presence of malicious nodes that transmit fake messages underscores the importance of credibility checking within the network community. The protocol involves several steps, including analyzing the topology in terms of forest density, fire spreading, wind speed or direction influence, area vegetation size, and topography. It also includes core and complement node selection, trust score estimation, emergency message transmission, important node selection, and trust control of sensor nodes.

The high mobility of the network affects sensor node connectivity, and the G(V,E) representation denotes vehicles (V) and interactions among vehicles with a set of edges connecting to sensor nodes. Using the forest fire model, the probability of data spreading capability for each sensor node in the network or community can be predicted. Short-range dedicated radio and edge devices allow drivers or pedestrians to communicate, reducing road fatalities.

Different communities are developed for message transfer, and the forest fire model aims to identify nodes with higher data spreading capability. The threshold value helps determine the more capable nodes for disseminating messages in the network, termed complementary nodes. In case of emergencies, a node that detects the situation generates a warning message, leading to node selection and trust evaluation. Nodes with trust values below a certain threshold are flagged as malicious and excluded from the community, while those exceeding the trust requirement threshold are retained in the community or added to a blacklist. Core nodes are identified through these steps, and the model is regularly updated for the dynamic vehicular environment. Extensive research indicates that this model is resilient to various network conditions, and carefully selected minimal sensor nodes effectively transmit packets within the network [41].

6.5.2 An FL-Based Privacy-Preserving Protocol for a Vehicular Fog Environment

The smart capabilities of FL in fog-based IoV is particularly helpful in data prediction and control, but IoV suffers from two issues:

- how to preserve privacy protocol with no support of the cloud server
- how to ensure security-preserving FL with low computation and communication overhead and high efficiency using multiparty computation.

The GALAXY framework [42] is useful for low-quality data sets and provides superior properties such as high scalability, confidentiality, high processing efficiency, low error rate, and less resource overhead. To design a threat model, authors proposed an arithmetic circuit (AC) known as a secure circuit evaluation protocol. Here, the circuit is denoted as an acyclic directed graph, and sensor nodes are considered gates connected by interconnected wires. Shamir's sharing is used to execute AC protocol securely and divided into multiple secret shares in a fully connected neural network.

The GALAXY framework provides facilities for fog nodes to maintain privacy in an FL protocol. Here, a lattice is used for secure communication between client and server. A lattice is a discrete additive subgroup of the Euclidean space, and this protocol is known as conditional privacy preserving authentication [43]. Figure 6.6 depicts various components of the security model.

This network framework consists of four entities: trusted authority (TA), application server (AS), vehicles, and RSU nodes. In the figure, TA and AS are upper-layer entities, and the RSUs and vehicles are the bottom layer; a secure socket layer is used for secure communication between entities. The bottom layer deals with dedicated short-range communications (DSRC) for interaction among the multiple nodes through multiple signatures. Zhang et al. proposed a Chinese remainder theorem for secure communication. The sliding window is used in the collection tree protocol, which performs well against bad-mouthing, newcomer, on–off, and Sybil attacks [44].

FL helps to optimize QoS in terms of mobility, computation of resources, efficient bandwidth and communication model. Cluster head selection and cluster matching are used to achieve mobility constraints. Weighted bipartite matching is used to create the clusters. Matching is used to decide which vehicle will move to which cluster, but this protocol has some limitations such as malicious attacks

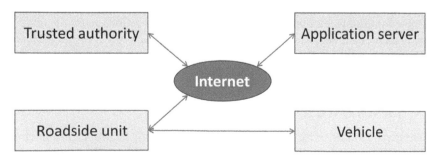

Figure 6.6 Security model.

(false data injection) and outlier detection. Here, we discuss various steps in a cluster-based FL-inspired vehicular network [45].

This protocol follows six steps. The first step focuses on the FL model and its requirements. The second step deals with vehicle velocity and direction and diverse data. Next, the model selects the cluster heads and form clusters. In the fourth step, the broadcast model trains the model, sends updates to the cluster heads, uploads the aggregated model, and aggregates the model. Repeat steps 2–4 until the model converges or stops improving. Step five deals with hierarchical cluster updates and creates new models by aggregating similar updates. Finally, it checks the broadcast model and calculates the preferences. It repeats steps 2–4 until the new models converge or stop improving, adjusting step 3 to take into account of the preferences.

6.5.3 The Role of Blockchain in VANETs

Zhang et al. [46] proposed the AIT protocol, a blockchain and ML-based technique that not only prevents privacy leaks but also requires less communication overhead. This protocol was already tested with SUMO and NS2 software and outperformed existing algorithms in terms of improved scalability, trust score, and rate of malicious sensor node detection. We derive five steps from Figure 6.6.

The first step updates traffic data and predicts malicious behavior of faulty sensor nodes. The second step evaluates linear temporal logic (LTL) using a feed-forward neural network (FFNN), and the output layer provides results in terms of update rate of the trust, upcoming message time prediction, and requirements for information relay. The biases and weights influence to minimize the cost function.

In the third step, some malicious vehicle sends fake message to the RSUs, which creates congestion in the vehicular network. In the fourth step, the unbreakable blockchain prevents malicious RSU message distribution from the sender to the receiver. The Merkle root concept not only helps to handle malicious nodes but also acts as a stub between the RSUs and the vehicle. If the trust level is below 0.5, then it is considered untrustworthy.

If the vehicle ID is valid and αt_i is equal to zero, then $t_i' \leftarrow t_i + \alpha t_i$; otherwise, we stop to update the method. But if $t_i' \geq 0.5$, then trust is validated. Efficient DL is highly accurate and takes less time to train the protocol. The FFNN, RNN, and CNN models take 39, 207, and 61 seconds for training and provide 96%, 95%, and 97% accuracy. The AIT protocol has five stages: traffic data collection and message generation, LTL evaluation by nodes, trust level calculation by local RSU node, trust validation and archiving to the blockchain, and GTL voting and dissemination by all RSUs.

6.5.4 Vehicular Compatibility Routing Scheme in the IoV Using ML

Recent advancements in VANETs aim to enable connected vehicles, emergency warnings, context-aware transportation systems, route compatibility, road safety, and energy and congestion management. VANETs operate locally through DSRC

802.11p and achieves global connectivity via cellular networks (6G, 5G, 4G) and wireless access in vehicular environment. Vehicular communication systems face challenges such as unreliable communication, delay, connectivity issues, minimum hop count, throughput, link quality, and packet delivery ratio in ad hoc multi-hop communications within high-mobility environments. Integrating ML, DL, and AI into VANETs under the umbrella of an intelligent transport system paves the way toward the IoV.

The introduction of cellular vehicle-to-any (C-V2X) systems in 6G will revolutionize mobility in VANETs, facilitating autonomous driving systems, context-aware driving, and cooperative communication systems. Weights can determine the compatibility time between multiple vehicles moving in the same direction or far apart. Supervised classification learning can segregate test cases into predefined classes, enabling the prediction of compatibility values for target vehicles based on previous vehicular data. Integrating 6G networks with ML allows base stations and RSUs to function as sensor nodes in the vehicular area for training purposes.

The proposed classification algorithm can detect compatibility levels among vehicles, ranging from noncompatible (L0) to entertainment communications (L4), support safety (L1), and warning messages (L3). By analyzing previous vehicle information, the algorithm predicts the best path for data delivery and eliminates noncompatible paths. Euclidean distance helps calculate intervehicle distances, while tendencies indicate good connectivity among vehicles moving in the same direction. The feature set considers data on relationships between multiple vehicles, commonly available in vehicular communication technologies.

This information includes the expected vehicular connectivity time among sensor nodes. The source vehicle transmits a route demand communication to detect target routes in a multipath, multi-hop environment. Trust factor calculation ensures safe message transmission if the ratio exceeds a threshold value, promoting reliable routing schemes to maintain longer connectivity among vehicles [29, 76]

6.6 THE ROLE OF ML AND DL TECHNIQUES IN VANETs

New cutting-edge technologies like ML and DL are presently being used in many domains for their robust potential to enhance performance metrics. In the field of VANETs, transportation information is repeatedly collected from numerous sources for multiple applications: data security and routing; malicious sensor node detection; system mobility; and traveler safety, security, and comfort, in short QoS. Here, we discuss a widespread assessment of various ML procedures that are presently being used to address research gaps in the area of vehicle networks [47–65]. We discuss the strong points and flaws of these methodologies for the transportation sector. As a final point, we detect upcoming research opportunities and gaps that can able to leverage capacity of the ML techniques. Table 6.3 presents various ML techniques and their advantages, disadvantages, and applications in VANETs.

Table 6.3 Various ML Techniques Used in VANETs

ML/DL technique	Advantages	Disadvantages	Application area
Support vector machine	Deals with many features and few input instances. Cluster optimization	Choice of optimized kernel	Malicious node detection, various types of attack prevention, spectrum allocation, node clustering
Association rule	Helps to discover correlation	Time-consuming process	Prediction of shortest route and number of road accidents
K-means clustering	No need for labeled data, effective for anonymization of sensitive data	Less efficient, less effective in detecting threats	More stability & security, prediction of road congestion
Reinforcement learning	Helps to extract sensitive information, learns from trial and error, V2X communication using 6G/5G. Effective with large data sets	Takes long time for processing to extract sensitive features	Mobility, driver fault, and shortest route prediction, traffic management, efficient task offloading, dynamic spectrum allocation, resource management in vehicular cloud computing, & efficient network slicing in V2X system
Decision tree algorithm	Easy to use	Consumes large storage space. Becomes complex when multiple DTs are required	Helps to predict malicious vehicle nodes in the network, traffic signal & routing decision management
Convolutional neural network	Scalable, more efficient than artificial neural networks	Computation overheads	Blockchain-inspired security, 6G-based resource management, road accident detection
Deep autoencoders	Extract relevant features if the dataset has high volume, helps to reduce dimension	Takes a lot of time for training, if less relevant data is present in the data set, it gives less accuracy	Network traffic prediction
Restricted Boltzmann machines	Unsupervised learning	High training time, difficult to use on highways	Density of the traffic prediction
Random forest	Select features efficiently with less input value, deals with over-fitting	Inefficient if data set is large	Congestion prediction in the network

(Continued)

Table 6.3 (Continued)

ML/DL technique	Advantages	Disadvantages	Application area
Generative adversarial network	Predefined iterations for construction of various samples in the data set	Training the discrete vehicular data is a challenge	Reduces data transmission delay & communication latency; Helps to improve the rate of message delivery; Able to predict vehicle trajectories
Particle swarm optimization)	No need for hypothesis	Needs cooperation of multiple vehicles, less secure communications	Helps to optimize intra-cluster distance
Deep reinforcement learning	Effective deep learning technique	Hard to achieve	Efficient resource allocation & traffic management on the road, schedules proper communication channels; Selects the relay nodes, which helps in multipoint routing by considering the history under various types of road constraints
Principal component analysis	Dimension reduction	Not applicable in all situation to deal with dimension reduction	Low computational complexity, optimization of data caching in V2X system
Naïve Bayes	Helps to eliminate irrelevant attributes, Robust, mobile	Difficult to extract important information & interrelationships	Helps to predict behavior of the vehicle driver
Recurrent neural network	Provides good results with sequential & discrete information	Issues of bursting gradients	Provides mobility, detection of obstacles, efficient resource reservation using cutting-edge techniques (cloud, fog, & edge computing)
Ant colony optimization	Gradient free	More time complexity	Helps to eliminate malicious sensor nodes
Jelly fish search optimization	Helps in data dissemination	Not more secure	Traffic flow control
Ensemble learning	Handles over-fitting, less variance	More time complexity	Malicious node detection, efficient localization, improved decision

K-nearest neighbor)	Helps in classification	To predict optimum value is difficult; Time-consuming process	Secure, intrusion detection, maintains clusters, efficient localization
Deep belief networks	Iterative demonstration of various attributes	Many initialization stages because of large number of variables	Able to predict automobile driver activities & travel times, secure 5G & 6G vehicular communication
Ensemble of deep learning networks	Mobility model	High computation cost	Needs GPS information for efficient routing; Helps to detect attacks
Long short-term memory network & gated recurrent unit	Ability to adapt long-time dependencies	Complexity increases, consumes high bandwidth, over-fitting problem	Efficient routing decisions & road traffic prediction
Stochastic diffusion search	Helps to handle exploitation	Dynamic topology	Helps to reduce traffic congestion
Artificial swarm intelligence	Easy, less complex	Delays in computation, dynamic topology	Prevents attacks

Veres and Moussa [66] discussed how DL is helpful in intelligent transportation systems. Various DL techniques such as multilayer perceptron, recurrent neural networks, convolutional neural networks, autoencoders, and graph neural networks are used to provide optimized QoS in terms of missing data imputation and noisy data. Supervised learning is used to predict traffic flows and destinations and estimate travel times; unsupervised learning is useful in trajectory clustering; and reinforcement learning is used to find traffic signal and helpful for maximizing revenue.

Long short-term memory techniques are useful in travel time estimation, route based approaches and severity of traffic accident prediction. Pan et al. proposed an efficient resource allocation and task offloading algorithm using federated learning. The rapid development of satellite-founded space systems and VANETs has led to a novel prototype called space-assisted vehicular networks (SAVNs) [10, 67]. Low earth orbit satellites with huge coverage are reconnoitered to support large data exchanges. SAVN protocols permit on-demand and real-time information processing by effectively offloading tasks from the data-guarded vehicles to the data-abundant servers with remaining computation resources.

The SAVN protocol aims to provide information processing facilities and unified coverage for customer vehicles. However, ultra-reliable and low-latency based communication (URLLC) demands posed by developing vehicular applications are challenging to meet with current data computation offloading methods in the SAVN platform. The traditional deep reinforcement is not suitable for SAVNs because they do not utilize background observations.

To tackle this issue and achieve throughput maximization while meeting various URLLC protocol constraints, Pan et al. [67] proposed using the asynchronous federated deep Q learning (AF-DQN) and the URLLC-inspired computation offloading algorithm called ASTEROID protocol. They utilized Lyapunov optimization for resource allocation and task offloading. The AF-DQN protocol addresses task offloading concerns, while a queue backlog-aware procedure is employed for resource allocation on the server side. Pan et al. [69] discuss various constraints of URLLC, including queuing, transmission, result feedback, and computational delays. They used the deep reinforcement algorithm to improve the URLLC-based task offloading.

Alowish et al. [70] described how to not only disseminate message integrating 5G with fog computing but also reduce road casualties. The asynchronous advantage actor critic technique [70–72] is used for driver assistance. Traffic flow can be controlled by using jellyfish search optimization. This protocol performs better than many existing procedures in terms of safety score, prediction error, weather information, latency, data dissemination efficiency, accuracy, energy consumption, and rate of false alarm. Al-Sultan et al. describes driver behavior prediction using a dynamic Bayesian network. Detectable driver behaviors included drowsiness, exceeding the vehicle speed limit, traffic signal violation, and sudden lane changes for emergency control, road safety, and collision avoidance [73].

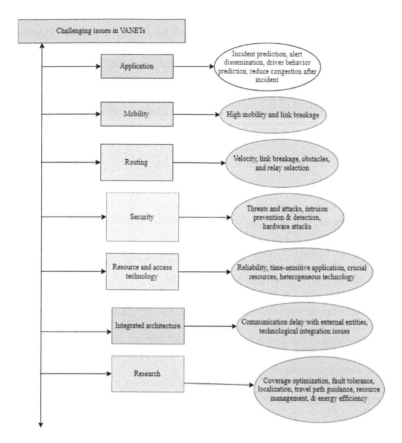

Figure 6.7 Challenges in VANETs.

6.7 FUTURE DIRECTIONS

Figure 6.7 presents challenges related to VANETs that we identified from the literature review. The challenges are collision detection and avoidance, standard integration, lack of multi-hop routing and ad hoc network, architecture, high latency, infrastructure, low PDR, lower data rate, cost, super effective network connectivity, security and data transfer rate.

6.8 CONCLUSION

This chapter offers beginners a complete understanding of ad hoc networks along with simulation tools, technology, recent protocols and architecture designs, current research status, comparisons, and future direction. Challenges with vehicular ad hoc networks include malicious or selfish node detection/outlier detection; channel utilization; link failure; congestion control; optimized age of information and routing; cluster management; task scheduling; energy depletion; load balancing; fault tolerance; power allocation or power optimization; localization of sensor nodes; resource allocation and task offloading (we can use cloud-fog-edge); privacy leakages from distributed, dynamic, open networks; and proneness to various types of attack. In response, it is necessary to design routing protocols with minimal cost and delay and high throughput and reliability.

REFERENCES

[1] Behura, A. (2021). Optimized data transmission scheme based on proper channel coordination used in vehicular ad hoc networks. *International Journal of Information Technology*, 1–10.

[2] Nguyen, V., Kim, O. T. T., Pham, C., Oo, T. Z., Tran, N. H., Hong, C. S., & Huh, E. N. (2018). A survey on adaptive multi-channel MAC protocols in VANETs using Markov models. *IEEE Access*, *6*, 16493–16514.

[3] Wang, Q., Leng, S., Fu, H., & Zhang, Y. (2011). An IEEE 802.11 p-based multichannel MAC scheme with channel coordination for vehicular ad hoc networks. *IEEE Transactions on Intelligent Transportation Systems*, *13*(2), 449–458.

[4] Yao, Y., Zhang, K., & Zhou, X. (2017). A flexible multi-channel coordination MAC protocol for vehicular ad hoc networks. *IEEE Communications Letters*, *21*(6), 1305–1308.

[5] Kumbhar, F. H., & Shin, S. Y. (2021). Novel Vehicular Compatibility based Ad-hoc Message Routing Scheme in the Internet of Vehicles using Machine Learning. *IEEE Internet of Things Journal*, *9*(4), 2817–2828.

[6] Al-Sultan, S., Al-Doori, M. M., Al-Bayatti, A. H., & Zedan, H. (2014). A comprehensive survey on vehicular ad hoc network. *Journal of Network and Computer Applications*, *37*, 380–392.

[7] Zhang, M., Ali, G. G. M. N., Chong, P. H. J., Seet, B.-C., & Kumar, A. (2019). A novel hybrid MAC protocol for basic safety message broadcasting in vehicular networks. *IEEE Transactions on Intelligent Transportation Systems*, *1–14*. doi:10.1109/tits.2019.2939378.

[8] Rajpoot, V., Garg, L., Alam, M. Z., Parashar, V., Tapashetti, P., & Arjariya, T. (2021). Analysis of machine learning based LEACH robust routing in the edge computing systems. *Computers & Electrical Engineering*, 107574.

[9] Goswami, P., Mukherjee, A., Hazra, R., Yang, L., Ghosh, U., Qi, Y., & Wang, H. (2021). AI based energy efficient routing protocol for intelligent transportation system. *IEEE Transactions on Intelligent Transportation Systems*.

[10] Bajracharya, R., Shrestha, R., Hassan, S. A., Konstantin, K., & Jung, H. (2021). Dynamic pricing for intelligent transportation system in the 6G unlicensed band. *IEEE Transactions on Intelligent Transportation Systems*, *23*(7), 9853–9868.

[11] Behura, A., Srinivas, M., & Kabat, M. R. (2022). Giraffe kicking optimization algorithm provides efficient routing mechanism in the field of vehicular ad hoc networks. *Journal of Ambient Intelligence and Humanized Computing*, 1–20.

[12] Rajpoot, V., Garg, L., Alam, M. Z., Parashar, V., Tapashetti, P., & Arjariya, T. (2021). Analysis of machine learning based LEACH robust routing in the Edge Computing systems. *Computers & Electrical Engineering*, 107574.

[13] Goswami, P., Mukherjee, A., Hazra, R., Yang, L., Ghosh, U., Qi, Y., & Wang, H. (2021). AI based energy efficient routing protocol for intelligent transportation system. *IEEE Transactions on Intelligent Transportation Systems*, 23(2), 1670–1679.

[14] Sajedi, S. N., Maadani, M., & Moghadam, M. N. (2021). F-LEACH: a fuzzy-based data aggregation scheme for healthcare IoT systems. *The Journal of Supercomputing*, 1–18.

[15] Gupta, R., Tanwar, S., & Kumar, N. (2021). B-IoMV: Blockchain-based onion routing protocol for D2D communication in an IoMV environment beyond 5G. *Vehicular Communications*, 100401.

[16] Yazici, A., Kirlik, G., Parlaktuna, O., & Sipahioglu, A. (2013). A dynamic path planning approach for multirobot sensor-based coverage considering energy constraints. *IEEE Transactions on Cybernetics*, 44(3), 305–314.

[17] Haghighi, M. S., & Aziminejad, Z. (2019). Highly anonymous mobility-tolerant location-based onion routing for VANETs. *IEEE Internet of Things Journal*, 7(4), 2582–2590.

[18] Sakai, K., Sun, M. T., Ku, W. S., Wu, J., & Alanazi, F. S. (2017). Performance and security analyses of onion-based anonymous routing for delay tolerant networks. *IEEE Transactions on Mobile Computing*, 16(12), 3473–3487.

[19] Liu, W., & Yu, M. (2014). AASR: authenticated anonymous secure routing for MANETs in adversarial environments. *IEEE Transactions on Vehicular Technology*, 63(9), 4585–4593.

[20] Omar, H. A., Zhuang, W., & Li, L. (2015). Gateway placement and packet routing for multihop in-vehicle internet access. *IEEE Transactions on Emerging Topics in Computing*, 3(3), 335–351.

[21] Guo, C., Li, D., Zhang, G., & Zhai, M. (2018). Real-time path planning in urban area via vanet-assisted traffic information sharing. *IEEE Transactions on Vehicular Technology*, 67(7), 5635–5649.

[22] Al-Absi, M. A., Al-Absi, A. A., Sain, M., & Lee, H. (2021). Moving ad hoc networks—A comparative study. *Sustainability*, 13(11), 6187.

[23] Jahanbakht, M., Xiang, W., Hanzo, L., & Azghadi, M. R. (2021). Internet of underwater things and big marine data analytics—A comprehensive survey. *IEEE Communications Surveys & Tutorials*, 23(2), 904–956.

[24] Gayathri, N. B., Thumbur, G., Reddy, P. V., & Rahman, M. Z. U. (2018). Efficient pairing-free certificateless authentication scheme with batch verification for vehicular ad-hoc networks. *IEEE Access*, 6, 31808–31819.

[25] Bello, O., & Zeadally, S. (2022). Internet of underwater things communication: Architecture, technologies, research challenges and future opportunities. *Ad Hoc Networks*, 135, 102933.

[26] Ahmad, F., Kurugollu, F., Kerrache, C. A., Sezer, S., & Liu, L. (2021). NOTRINO: A novel hybrid trust management scheme for internet-of-vehicles. *IEEE Transactions on Vehicular Technology*, 70(9), 9244–9257.

[27] Li, Y., Yang, B., Wu, H., Han, Q., Chen, C., & Guan, X. (2022). Joint offloading decision and resource allocation for vehicular fog-edge computing networks: a contract-stackelberg approach. *IEEE Internet of Things Journal*, 9(17), 15969–15982.

[28] Kumar, N., Chaudhry, R., Kaiwartya, O., Kumar, N., & Ahmed, S. H. (2020). Green computing in software defined social internet of vehicles. *IEEE Transactions on Intelligent Transportation Systems*, 22(6), 3644–3653.

[29] Rahman, M. A., Rahim, M. A., Rahman, M. M., Moustafa, N., Razzak, I., Ahmad, T., & Patwary, M. N. (2022). A secure and intelligent framework for vehicle health monitoring exploiting big-data analytics. *IEEE Transactions on Intelligent Transportation Systems*, *23*(10), 19727–19742.

[30] Tang, F., Mao, B., Kato, N., & Gui, G. (2021). Comprehensive survey on machine learning in vehicular network: technology, applications and challenges. *IEEE Communications Surveys & Tutorials*, *23*(3), 2027–2057.

[31] Nabati, M., Maadani, M., & Pourmina, M. A. (2021). AGEN-AODV: an intelligent energy-aware routing protocol for heterogeneous mobile ad-hoc networks. *Mobile Networks and Applications*, 1–12.

[32] Mozaffari, S., Al-Jarrah, O. Y., Dianati, M., Jennings, P., & Mouzakitis, A. (2020). Deep learning-based vehicle behavior prediction for autonomous driving applications: A review. *IEEE Transactions on Intelligent Transportation Systems*, *23*(1), 33–47.

[33] Muhammad, K., Ullah, A., Lloret, J., Del Ser, J., & de Albuquerque, V. H. C. (2020). Deep learning for safe autonomous driving: Current challenges and future directions. *IEEE Transactions on Intelligent Transportation Systems*, *22*(7), 4316–4336.

[34] Joo, H., Ahmed, S. H., & Lim, Y. (2020). Traffic signal control for smart cities using reinforcement learning. *Computer Communications*, *154*, 324–330.

[35] Hu, H. X., Tang, B., Zhang, Y., & Wang, W. (2019). Vehicular ad hoc network representation learning for recommendations in internet of things. *IEEE Transactions on Industrial Informatics*, *16*(4), 2583–2591.

[36] Ahmad, I., Rahman, T., Zeb, A., Khan, I., Ullah, I., Hamam, H., & Cheikhrouhou, O. (2021). Analysis of security attacks and taxonomy in underwater wireless sensor networks. *Wireless Communications and Mobile Computing*, *2021*.

[37] Lin, D., Kang, J., Squicciarini, A., Wu, Y., Gurung, S., & Tonguz, O. (2016). MoZo: A moving zone based routing protocol using pure V2V communication in VANETs. *IEEE Transactions on Mobile Computing*, *16*(5), 1357–1370.

[38] Eiza, M. H., Owens, T., Ni, Q., & Shi, Q. (2015). Situation-aware QoS routing algorithm for vehicular ad hoc networks. *IEEE Transactions on Vehicular Technology*, *64*(12), 5520–5535.

[39] Kolandaisamy, R., Noor, R. M., Kolandaisamy, I., Ahmedy, I., Kiah, M. L. M., Tamil, M. E. M., & Nandy, T. (2021). A stream position performance analysis model based on DDoS attack detection for cluster-based routing in VANET. *Journal of Ambient Intelligence and Humanized Computing*, *12*(6), 6599–6612.

[40] Hosmani, S., & Mathapati, B. (2021). R2SCDT: robust and reliable secure clustering and data transmission in vehicular ad hoc network using weight evaluation. *Journal of Ambient Intelligence and Humanized Computing*, 1–18.

[41] Fabi, A. K., & Thampi, S. M. (2022). A trust management framework using forest fire model to propagate emergency messages in the Internet of Vehicles (IoV). *Vehicular Communications*, *33*, 100404.

[42] Li, Y., Li, H., Xu, G., Xiang, T., & Lu, R. (n.d.). Practical privacy-preserving federated learning in vehicular fog computing. *IEEE Transactions on Vehicular Technology*. doi: 10.1109/TVT.2022.3150806.

[43] Li, Q., He, D., Yang, Z., Xie, Q., & Choo, K. K. R. (2022). A lattice-based conditional privacy-preserving authentication protocol for the vehicular ad hoc network. *IEEE Transactions on Vehicular Technology*, *71*(4), 4336–4347.

[44] He, D., Chen, C., Chan, S., Bu, J., & Vasilakos, A. V. (2012). ReTrust: Attack-resistant and lightweight trust management for medical sensor networks. *IEEE Transactions on Information Technology in Biomedicine, 16*(4), 623–632.

[45] Taik, A., Mlika, Z., & Cherkaoui, S. (2022). Clustered vehicular federated learning: Process and optimization. arXiv preprint arXiv:2201.11271.

[46] Zhang, C., Li, W., Luo, Y., & Hu, Y. (2020). AIT: An AI-enabled trust management system for vehicular networks using blockchain technology. *IEEE Internet of Things Journal, 8*(5), 3157–3169.

[47] Mchergui, A., Moulahi, T., & Zeadally, S. (2021). Survey on Artificial Intelligence (AI) techniques for vehicular ad-hoc networks (VANETs). *Vehicular Communications*, 100403.

[48] Yu, J. J. Q., & Gu, J. (2019). Real-time traffic speed estimation with graph convolutional generative autoencoder. *IEEE Transactions on Intelligent Transportation Systems, 20*(10), 3940–3951.

[49] Ning, Z., Dong, P., Wang, X., Obaidat, M.S., Hu, X., Guo, L., et al. (2019). When deep reinforcement learning meets 5G-enabled vehicular networks: a distributed offloading framework for traffic big data. *IEEE Transactions on Industrial Informatics, 16*(2), 1352–1361.

[50] Bitam, S., Mellouk, A., & Zeadally, S. (2015). Bio-inspired routing algorithms survey for vehicular ad-hoc networks. *IEEE Communications Surveys & Tutorials, 17*(2).

[51] Soon, F.C., Khaw, H.Y., Chuah, J.H., & Kanesan, J. (2020). Semisupervised PCA convolutional network for vehicle type classification. *IEEE Transactions on Vehicular Technology, 69*(8), 8267–8277.

[52] Guerrero-Ibanez, J.A., Zeadally, S., & Contreras-Castillo, J. (2017). Internet of vehicles: Ar-chitecture, protocols, and security. *IEEE Internet of Things Journal, 5*(5), 3701–3709.

[53] Guerrero-Ibanez, J.A., Zeadally, S., & Contreras-Castillo, J. (2015). Integration challenges of intelligent transportation systems with connected vehicle, cloud comput-ing, and Internet of things technologies. *IEEE Wireless Communication, 22*(6), 122–128.

[54] Reshma, S., & Chetanaprakash, C. (2020). Advancement in infotainment system in auto-motive sector with vehicular cloud network and current state of art. *International Journal of Electrical and Computer Engineering, 10*(2), 2077.

[55] Guo, J., Song, B., Yu, R., Chi, Y., & Yuen, C. (2019). Fast video frame correlation analysis for vehicular networks by using CVS–CNN. *IEEE Transactions on Vehicular Technology, 68*(7), 6286–6292.

[56] Rehman, A., Rehman, S. U., Khan, M., Alazab, M., & Reddy, T. (2021). CANintelliIDS: detect-ing in-vehicle intrusion attacks on a controller area network using CNN and attention-based GRU. *IEEE Transactions on Network Science and Engineering*.

[57] Hasrouny, H., Samhat, A.E., Bassil, C., & Laouiti, A. (2019). Trust model for secure group leader-based communications in VANET. *Wireless Network, 25*(8), 4639–4661.

[58] Hussain, R., Lee, J., & Zeadally, S. (2020). Trust in VANET: a survey of current solu-tions and future research opportunities. *IEEE Transactions on Intelligent Transportation Systems, 22*(5), 2553–2571.

[59] Zhang, D., Yu, F.R., Yang, R., & Zhu, L. (2020). Software-defined vehicular networks with trust management: A deep reinforcement learning approach. *IEEE Transactions on Intelligent Transportation Systems*, *23*(2), 1400–1414.

[60] Noor-A-Rahim, M., Liu, Z., Lee, H., Ali, G.M.N., Pesch, D., & Xiao, P. (2020). A survey on re-source allocation in vehicular networks. *IEEE Transactions on Intelligent Transportation Systems*, *23*(2), 1400–1414.

[61] Liu, W., & Shoji, Y. (2019). DeepVM: RNN-based vehicle mobility prediction to sup-port intelligent vehicle applications. *IEEE Transactions on Industrial Informatics*, *16*(6), 3997–4006.

[62] Yang, H., Xiong, Z., Zhao, J., Niyato, D., Yuen, C., & Deng, R. (2020). Deep reinforcement learning based massive access management for ultra-reliable low-latency communications. *IEEE Transactions on Wireless Communications*, *20*(5), 2977–2990.

[63] Zeadally, S., Javed, M.A., & E.B. Hamida. (2020). Vehicular communications for ITS: stan-dardization and challenges. *IEEE Communications Standards Magazine*, *4*(1), 11–17.

[64] Rihan, M., Elwekeil, M., Yang, Y., Huang, L., Xu, C., & Selim, M.M. (2020). Deep-VFog: When artificial intelligence meets fog computing in V2X. *IEEE System Journal*, *15*(3), 3492–3505.

[65] Lozano Domínguez, J.M., & Mateo Sanguino T.J. (2019). Review on V2X, I2X, and P2X communications and their applications: a comprehensive analysis over time. *Sensors*, *19*(12), 2756.

[66] Veres, M., & Moussa, M. (2019). Deep learning for intelligent transportation systems: A survey of emerging trends. *IEEE Transactions on Intelligent Transportation Systems*, *21*(8), 3152–3168.

[67] Pan, C., Wang, Z., Liao, H., Zhou, Z., Wang, X., Tariq, M., & Al-Otaibi, S. (2022). Asynchronous federated deep reinforcement learning-based URLLC-aware computation offloading in space-assisted vehicular networks. *IEEE Transactions on Intelligent Transportation Systems, 24*(7), 7377–7389.

[68] Liu, J., Ahmed, M., Mirza, M. A., Khan, W. U., Xu, D., Li, J., . . . & Han, Z. (2022). RL/DRL meets vehicular task offloading using edge and vehicular cloudlet: A survey. *IEEE Internet of Things Journal*, *9*(11), 8315–8338.

[69] Pan, C., Wang, Z., Zhou, Z., & Ren, X. (2021). Deep reinforcement learning-based URLLC-aware task offloading in collaborative vehicular networks. *China Communications*, *18*(7), 134–146.

[70] Alowish, M., Shiraishi, Y., Mohri, M., & Morii, M. (2021). Three layered architecture for driver behavior analysis and personalized assistance with alert message dissemination in 5G envisioned Fog-IoCV. *Future Internet*, *14*(1), 12.

[71] Kaur, R., Ramachandran, R. K., Doss, R., & Pan, L. (2021). The importance of selecting clustering parameters in VANETs: A survey. *Computer Science Review*, *40*, 100392.

[72] Al Mallah, R., Quintero, A., & Farooq, B. (2017). Distributed classification of urban congestion using VANET. *IEEE Transactions on Intelligent Transportation Systems*, 18(9), 2435–2442.

[73] Al-Sultan, S., Al-Bayatti, A. H., & Zedan, H. (2013). Context-aware driver behavior detection system in intelligent transportation systems. *IEEE Transactions on Vehicular Technology*, *62*(9), 4264–4275.

[74] Li, Y., Yang, B., Wu, H., Han, Q., Chen, C., & Guan, X. (2022). Joint Offloading decision and resource allocation for vehicular fog-edge computing networks: A contract-stackelberg approach. *IEEE Internet of Things Journal*, *9*(17), 15969–15982.

[75] Prateek, K., Altaf, F., Amin, R., & Maity, S. (2022). A privacy preserving authentication protocol using quantum computing for V2I authentication in vehicular ad hoc networks. *Security and Communication Networks*, *2022*.

[76] Kumbhar, F. H., & Shin, S. Y. (2021). Novel vehicular compatibility based ad-hoc message routing scheme in the internet of vehicles using machine learning. *IEEE Internet of Things Journal, 9*(4), 2817–2828.

Chapter 7

Urban Smart Parking Systems

A Taxonomic Approach

Vipul Singh Negi and Suchismita Chinara

7.1 INTRODUCTION

Parking has become a significant concern for our society as the number of vehicles manufactured in 2022 reached 800 million in India [1]. All these vehicles will require proper parking spots, which are hard to find at peak business hours. According to a survey from 2019, 95% of Indian vehicles are usually parked [2]. This raises the question of how to manage these many vehicles efficiently.

Parking lot size is also an issue, although a larger issue in the USA because so many people drive large pickup trucks and SUVs; in India and the UK, people prefer smaller cars. The size of the standard parking space in the USA is 8.5 ft × 18 ft, which totals 153 sq. ft. and in UK and India, it is 7.84 × 15.75 ft by area, which is 123.50 sq. ft [3]. This means sizeable portions of road must be allocated for on-street parking in the USA. The solution to the problem of mismanaged parking is to develop an automated smart parking system. Smart parking systems (SPS) contain certain modules such as parking space allocation, smart metering for paid parking, a navigation system to the nearest parking lot as well as inside the parking lot, a monitoring system, and the most important of them all: automatic licence plate recognition to authenticate vehicles.

7.1.1 Modules of Smart Parking Systems

Figure 7.1 presents the five modules of a smart parking system: parking space allocation, smart metering for paid parking, automatic license plate recognition, auto navigation, and real-time tracking and monitoring.

Parking space allocation: The first part of any SPS is how you allocate parking spaces. This can be done in two ways: reservation based and park as you come. In reservation-based parking, a mobile or web application is involved that shows first all nearby spaces and then which spaces are available. The user can choose their parking space according to their convenience. In park-as-you-come, spaces are assigned to users as they arrived based on various strategies. The most common is using a genetic algorithm to find the best

DOI: 10.1201/9781003486930-10

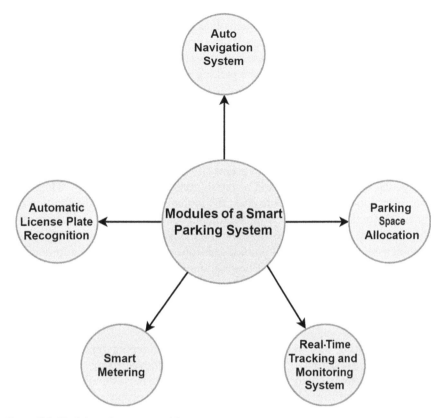

Figure 7.1 Modules of a smart parking system.

position. Thomas et al. [4] proposed one such genetic algorithm to solve this problem and found that the region utilisation and trolley efficiency score increased. The waiting time was also reduced by 5 hours using a genetic algorithm.

Smart metering for paid parking: Smart metering is achieved using mobile applications. The user registers their vehicle at the parking lot and receives a timestamp. When users pull out of their parking spaces, the camera detects the vacant space and generates an e-receipt for the user to pay. When the user reaches the exit parking gate, the payment info is validated by the servers, and the gate opens automatically. There are other methods available for smart payments: self-checkout terminals, vehicle to grid, sensor-integrated point-of-sale terminals, weight-sensing self-checkout kiosks, fastag, and many more [5].

Automatic licence plate recognition: Automatic licence plate recognition uses cameras and computer vision techniques. Luque et al. [6] proposed a smart vehicle presence sensor, the SPIN-V. The SPIN-V contains a Raspberry Pi 3 computer to attach all the components into an HC-SR04 ultrasonic sensor to detect the presence of a vehicle, a Raspberry Pi v2 camera for licence plate detection using computer vision techniques such as optical character recognition (OCR), a LED strip to indicate parking status, a buzzer to guide the user for proper parking inside the allocated parking spot, and a battery source. The main component of this system is licence plate recognition. The pi camera takes the image of the vehicle, loads the image, does background subtraction, and text detection, puts on the ROI filter, and then uses OCR to convert the data into text format.

Auto navigation system: Auto navigation for parking contains two segments: navigating to the parking lot and navigating inside the parking lot. When the user starts looking for a place to park, the system first requires the location of the nearby parking facilities. After making an educated survey of all the available facilities, the user selects one, and the navigation to the facilities begins. A good navigation system will provide real-time traffic congestion information and the quickest way to reach the destination. Google and Apple Maps already provide this feature, which can be integrated into smart parking mobile applications. The second navigation for inside the parking lot requires a 3D map which can be generated by using deep learning to identify and plot the coordinates of the walls and pillars of the parking lots.

Real-time tracking and centralised monitoring: Keeping track of parking vacancies is a must-have feature that can be achieved using a centralised monitoring system which will log all the details, and these details can be used later to make traffic prediction robust. Song et al. [7] proposed parking space detection using self-supervised federated learning and increased accuracy by 3% using the mAP metric. Chippalkatti et al. [8] proposed monitoring the ambient temperature and light available in the parking lot. Centralised monitoring is also helpful for parking lot owners, making it easy to keep tabs on all vehicles. This will increase the security of the vehicles and build trust in the SPS technology.

7.2 LITERATURE SURVEY

Early parking lots and garages featured workers physically present for ticketing and navigation. This methodology was barely productive. It was effective for outdoor parking but became difficult in indoor scenarios because of less manoeuvrability. Then came VANETs (vehicular ad hoc networks) with their multitude of applications, such as adaptive cruise control for situational awareness, traffic light violation detection and prevention, and optimal speed advisor for traffic information systems.

With VANETs, the precise positioning of the vehicle can be tracked by vehicle to vehicle or vehicle to roadside unit communication [9]. Then came the era of parking guidance and information systems (PGIS), which were very reliable and robust due to their use of message boards, but the boards were a weak point, and they have been replaced with dynamic LED displays that show real-time data. Parking lots have seen significant changes and methodologies in recent years, some of which we discuss here.

Shin et al. [10] consider the following objectives regarding the smart parking guidance algorithm: driving distances to and from the parking facility, expected cost of the parking lot, and traffic congestion. Chippalkatti et al. [8] proposed an IoT-based smart parking system that used an MQTT protocol for communication. A website was created to facilitate parking lot booking on which four parking slots were available. This system was designed with Arduino boards, which can be easily scaled as per demand. LDR and LM35 sensors were used for luminosity and temperature monitoring, respectively.

Kotb et al. [11] divided the concept of smart parking into modules. Module one is the parking guidance system, which relies on sensors categorized as on or off roadway. On roadway sensors are placed on roads, and systems use pneumatic tubes; loop detectors; and magnetic, acoustic, piezoelectric, and radio frequency identification (RFID) sensors. For off roadway systems, the sensors are placed above the roadway, specifically ultrasonic, infrared, and CCTV cameras. The second module is parking reservation systems that prevent large numbers of users from attempting to park at the same lot, creating congestion. These systems can be classified as deterministic or stochastic, pricing based, and mobile and web based.

Bagula et al. [12] discuss optimal sensor placement in the parking lot scenario. They classify this problem as a multiobjective optimisation problem. They also provide performance parameters such as the distance between the sensor and the sink, maximum coverage, and covered cells, to name a few.

Jones et al. [13] proposed obtaining two categories of GPS data from mobile phones, cruising and not cruising, and verifying those values with map matching. They used an accelerometer, magnetometer, and gyroscope with GPS to detect the states of cruising and not cruising. They also defined a threshold below which a movement would not register as a state change when the vehicle moved into the smaller parking lot area. Five mobile devices were used with travelling time between 5 min and 25 min. This application is crowdfunded, and if the mobile application doesn't have a certain number of users, it will fail, as the methodology relies on good-quality sensor data.

AlHarbi et al. proposed a solution for the area north of Jeddah in Saudi Arabia using a mobile application. The application was divided into three modules. Module one is for finding and reserving the parking space; the second is for the reservation timer, which is strictly maintained; and the final module is the spot location guide, which provides navigation.

Huang et al. [14] proposed FedParking, an SPS using federated learning. It performed parking space estimation using an LSTM (long short-term memory) model but preserved privacy by using federated learning. The major benefit of this system is that it does not store the user's parking data; only the deep learning model weights are shared with the organisation to improve parking space estimation.

7.3 SPS-ENABLING COMPONENTS

Smart parking requires a large number of electronic components. The number of sensors used in a smart parking scenario directly reflects the final product. Usually, SPS contains ultrasonic and infrared cameras that authenticate vehicles using license plate recognition, which was previously done using computer vision but has now been replaced with convolution neural networks, which are much more effective and robust. Specialised DL models for IoT equipment have also been developed, reducing vehicle authentication's inference times. Table 7.1 presents some of the most commonly used sensors for automated car parking systems.

Table 7.1 Components of SPS

Sensor	Use case
	Raspberry Pi Camera • License plate identification • Monitoring parking spaces
	Ultrasonic Sensor • For indoor parking • Mounted on top of the parking space
	IR Sensor • Mounted in front • Works for both indoors and outdoors

Radar Sensor
- Electromagnetic fields are used to measure
- Does the same thing as IR or ultrasonic

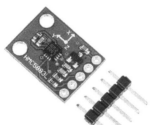

Magnetometer Sensor
- Placed below the car
- Best for outdoor parking

Raspberry Pi Board
- Good wireless connectivity
- Can use computer vision
- Headless mode runs seamlessly.

7.4 TYPES OF PARKING LOTS

Traditionally, parking lots are categorised as indoor or outdoor, but they can be classified further, for instance based on the bounding spaces inside the parking lot, for example, parallel, 30°, 45°, and 60° parking. Each of these methodologies can save valuable space and make navigating inside the parking complex efficient and easier, but here, we will follow the indoor and outdoor parking scenarios represented in Figure 7.2.

7.4.1 Indoor Parking

With limited space, indoor parking is the best methodology in cities, whether single-level parking in the basements of buildings or multiple-level lots and garages. The major problem this method of parking faces is navigation because GPS is not always reliable in indoor conditions. Ata et al. [15] proposed a parking system using Dijkstra's algorithm. In this approach, parking spaces are assigned based on distance. When the vehicle enters the parking lot, the algorithm checks for the

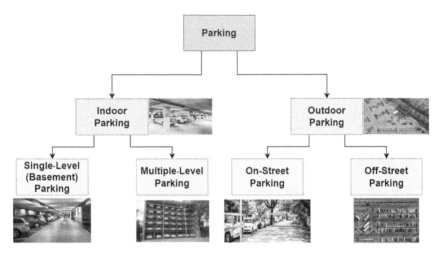

Figure 7.2 Parking lot types.

nearest vacant parking space to the user. The authors' proposed system classified the vehicles into midsize or compact cars and prioritised by size into their own spaces.

Single-level (basement) parking: Single-level parking is usually in basements of apartments or mall complexes. These save much space but also increase the complexity of the parking; the ceilings are usually low, and basements are filled with columns and walls to separate the parking zones. Ultrasonic sensors are the best-suited methodology for indoor basement lots because the sensors are planted on the ceilings. Machine learning (ML)-based methodology to detect and map the walls and columns is the best solution one can imagine. Once the ML method discovers the coordinates of the obstacles, those can be mapped according to the dimensions of the parking lot. Figure 7.3 depicts a pictorial representation of single-level parking.

Multiple-level parking: These parking lots are mainly built near airports and big residential complexes. They are designed by the type of vehicle or the duration of stay. Multiple-level parking lots have the same problems as those with single-level parking with additional challenges. The major one is which vehicle should be assigned to which floor, but the simple solution is for long-term parking to be on higher floors. Most of these parking systems have lifts to stack vehicles to save space, and the lifts prefer lighter vehicles. The authors of [8] used temperature and light sensors to monitor vehicle states. IR sensors are best suited for this type of parking as they are mounted in front (Figure 7.4).

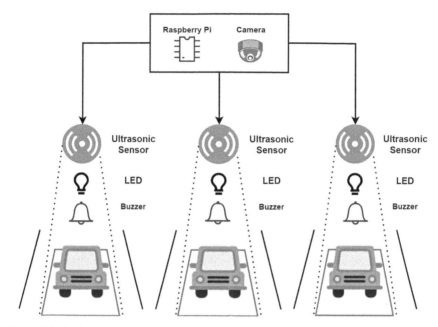

Figure 7.3 Single-level parking lot.

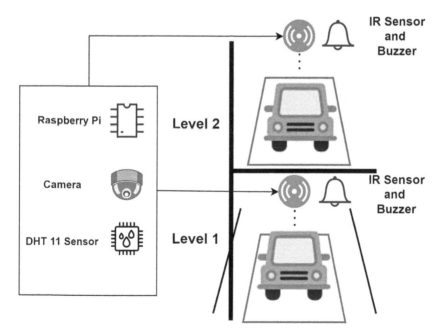

Figure 7.4 Multiple-level parking lot.

7.4.2 Outdoor Parking

Outdoor parking can be associated with specific venues (sporting venue, shopping mall, public offices, etc.), known as off-street parking, or on the streets. They do not provide the security and reliability of indoor enclosures, but with SPS, they can make monitoring reliable.

On-street parking: On-street parking popular in places with less space and usually relies on public roads. On-street parking is the most challenging scenario for smart parking systems, as proper monitoring of a street is already tricky. The sensor is placed on the ground, so pressure sensors are best suited for this type of parking. The sensor is placed at the curb of the footpath in a cylindrical plastic box [11]. The vehicle will be parked and assisted using the IR and pressure sensors. Cameras usually fail in these scenarios as trees around the public roads usually block them. Navigating on-street parking is the easiest, as GPS coordinates are highly effective in outdoor environments. The lack of security is the main drawback of this type of parking because there are no cameras to monitor the vehicles. Another big problem with this parking method is the theft of the sensors as these parking spaces are in open streets. Figure 7.5 shows a pictorial representation of on-street parking.

Off-street parking: These are the most used parking lots because they are readily available nearby restaurants, shops, and public offices. They are further classified into small business-owned off-street parking and big corporation-based gigantic parking lots. The small ones can be managed efficiently without much trouble as they require fewer sensors; one can easily set up such a system with

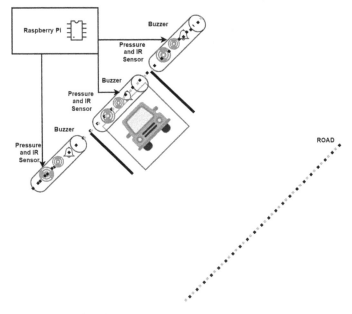

Figure 7.5 On-street parking lot.

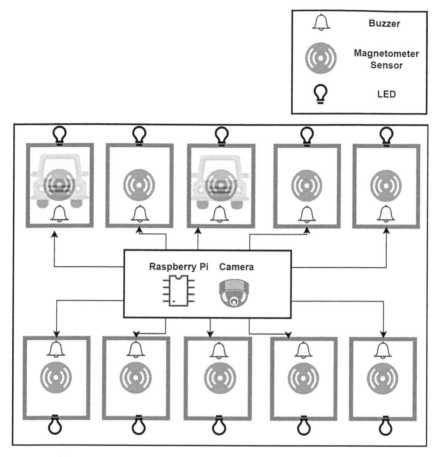

Figure 7.6 Off-street parking lot.

a Raspberry Pi, a Pi camera, and a few ESP32 boards with IR sensors. This can be connected with the small business wifi and managed using Node-Red [16]. For the giant corporations, magnetometer sensors are placed at the centre of each parking lot. Floris et al. [17] proposed a vehicle detection system using magnetometer sensors. Figure 7.6 shows a pictorial representation of off-street parking for giant corporations.

7.5 CHALLENGES IN THE CURRENT SYSTEMS

Route finding and navigation: Applications like Google and Apple Maps have greatly improved this objective, where you can easily spot parking destinations nearby. They also provide navigation to these parking lots, but the main thing they need to provide is the availability of parking spaces. For instance, when a large number of people attend the same event, these maps usually provide the best choice, but everyone receives the same choice, creating congestion. Saleem et al. [18] proposed an IoT-based smart parking recommendation system developed by exploiting the semantic IoT data of traffic and parking sensors. They also developed the real-time provision of expected parking availability (occupancy statistics) based on historical IoT data. The best thing about this proposed approach is its compliance with GDPR.

Internal mapping and navigation of the parking lot: Indoor navigation is challenging because traditional sensors such as GPS lose their effectiveness while performing indoors. A deep learning model could be trained to identify walls and columns and plot the coordinates to create a 3D model of the parking lot. Gerstweiler et al. [19] proposed a mobile AR navigation system for complex indoor environments using computer vision.

Robust payment systems: A robust payment system is required to make the parking experience seamless. The POS machines work for now, providing QR codes, card swipes, and tap-to-pay functionality, but the idea of sps is to automate this as well. The moment a vehicle enters the parking space, the time counter should automatically begin and stop when the vehicle leaves its parking spot. Instead of paying using a POS machine, it would be better if payment were available in a mobile application. The National Payments Corporation of India (NPCI) developed the National Electronic Toll Collection program to meet the electronic tolling requirements of the Indian market. This system is called FASTag and uses RFID tags to pay highway tolls. The FASTag sticker is pasted on the corner of the vehicle's windshield, and when it is close to a toll booth, it automatically detects the tag and deducts the toll from the payment method attached to the account. A similar RFID-based system would solve the problem in smart parking systems [20].

Prediction of available space using time series: The nature of the activity determines which parking lot will be best suited for the user. Huang et al. [14] used federated learning as their learning framework [21] and LSTM for prediction. Federated learning aims to train deep learning models without sharing the data. The process entails transmitting the corresponding weights to a global server, aggregating everything, and passing it down to the local devices. Prediction can be beneficial in predicting the footfall from older data so that the navigation system can be more robust.

7.6 CONCLUSION

Urban smart parking systems have started to grow in many countries, but most focus on the big off-street and indoor parking lots. Indoor parking lots lack navigation, and that can be solved using AR techniques in the future. The biggest challenge is on-street parking and its lack of security measures. Sensor maintenance and power management have the utmost priority because the system will malfunction and be utterly useless without them. Parking lot owners must continuously maintain these two modules because they are the backbone of any smart parking system.

REFERENCES

[1] International Organization of Motor Vehicle Manufacturers. 2022 production statistics. www.oica.net/category/production-statistics/2022statistics/. Accessed on: 2023–07–28.

[2] CSE India. Pampering Parking: How to manage Urban India's Parking Needs. http://cdn.cseindia.org/attachments/0.27615500_1518692167_jasolaparkingreport2018.pdf. Accessed on: 2023–07–28.

[3] Civil Jungle. Parking In India | What Is Parking | Average Parking Space Size. https://civiljungle.com/parking-in-india/. Accessed on: 2023–07–28.

[4] Diya Thomas and Binsu C Kovoor. A genetic algorithm approach to autonomous smart vehicle parking system. *Procedia Computer Science*, 125:68–76, 2018.

[5] Civil Jungle. IoT innovation: Leading companies in smart parking meters for the banking industry. www.electronicpaymentsinternational.com/datainsights/innovators-iot-smart-parking-meters-banking/. Accessed on: 2023–07–28.

[6] Luis F Luque-Vega, David A Michel-Torres, Emmanuel Lopez-Neri, Miriam ACarlos-Mancilla, and Luis E González-Jiménez. Iot smart parking system based on the visual-aided smart vehicle presence sensor: Spin-v. *Sensors*, 20(5):1476, 2020.

[7] Jung Ho Song, Jun Park, Ajit Kumar, Ankit Kumar Singh, Jun Yong Yoon, Jae Won Jang, and Bong Jun Choi. Self-supervised federated learning for parking slot detection. https://journal-home.s3.ap-northeast2.amazonaws.com/site/2023s/abs/0698-LITOD.pdf. Accessed on: 2023–07–28.

[8] Pranav Chippalkatti, Ganesh Kadam, and Vrushali Ichake. I-spark: IoT based smart parking system. In *2018 international conference on advances in communication and computing technology (ICACCT)*, pp. 473–477. IEEE, 2018.

[9] Mujeeb Ur Rehman, Munam Ali Shah, Muhammad Khan, and Shaheed Ahmad. Avanet based smart car parking system to minimise searching time, fuel consumption and co 2 emission. In *2018 24th International Conference on Automation and Computing (ICAC)*, pp. 1–6. IEEE, 2018.

[10] Jong-Ho Shin and Hong-Bae Jun. A study on smart parking guidance algorithm. *Transportation Research Part C: Emerging Technologies*, 44:299–317, 2014.

[11] Amir O Kotb, Yao-chun Shen, and Yi Huang. Smart parking guidance, monitoring and reservations: A review. *IEEE Intelligent Transportation Systems Magazine*, 9(2):6–16, 2017.

[12] Antoine Bagula, Lorenzo Castelli, and Marco Zennaro. On the design of smart parking networks in the smart cities: An optimal sensor placement model. *Sensors*, 15(7):15443–15467, 2015.

[13] Michael Jones, Aftab Khan, Parag Kulkarni, Pietro Carnelli, and Mahesh Sooriyabandara. Parkus 2.0: automated cruise detection for parking availability inference. In *Proceedings of the 14th EAI international conference on mobile and ubiquitous systems: computing, networking and services*, pp. 242–251, 2017.

[14] Xumin Huang, Peichun Li, Rong Yu, Yuan Wu, Kan Xie, and Shengli Xie. Fedparking: A federated learning based parking space estimation with parked vehicle assisted edge computing. *IEEE Transactions on Vehicular Technology*, 70(9):9355–9368, 2021.

[15] KM Ata, A Che Soh, AJ Ishak, H Jaafar, and NA Khairuddin. Smart indoor parking system based on dijkstra's algorithm. *International Journal of Integrated Engineering*, 2(1):13–20, 2019.

[16] Node-RED. Node-RED. https://nodered.org/. Accessed on: 2023–07–28.

[17] Alessandro Floris, Roberto Girau, Simone Porcu, Giovanni Pettorru, and LuigiAtzori. Implementation of a magnetometer based vehicle detection system for smart parking applications. In *2020 IEEE International Smart Cities Conference (ISC2)*, pp. 1–7. IEEE, 2020.

[18] Yasir Saleem, Pablo Sotres, Samuel Fricker, Carmen Lopez de La Torre, Noel Crespi, Gyu Myoung Lee, Roberto Minerva, and Luis Sanchez. Iotrec: The iot recommender for smart parking system. *IEEE Transactions on Emerging Topics in Computing*, 10(1):280–296, 2020.

[19] Georg Gerstweiler, Emanuel Vonach, and Hannes Kaufmann. Hymotrack: A mobile ar navigation system for complex indoor environments. *Sensors*, 16(1):17, 2015.

[20] NPCI. National Electronic Toll Collection. www.npci.org.in/what-wedo/netc-fastag/product-overview. Accessed on 2023–07–28.

[21] Brendan McMahan, Eider Moore, Daniel Ramage, Seth Hampson, and Blaise Agueray Arcas. Communication-efficient learning of deep networks from decentralised data. In *Artificial intelligence and statistics*, pp.1273–1282. PMLR, 2017.

Chapter 8

Machine Learning Approaches in Financial Management of Smart Cities

Susmita Mohapatra, Lopamudra Hota, Sumanta Pyne, and Arun Kumar

8.1 INTRODUCTION

The Oxford English Dictionary [1] defines fraud as "an improper and deliberate act of cheating to gain financial benefit". The Association of Certified Fraud Examiners describes fraud as "a form of deception or misrepresentation by a business or person purposefully which may result in certain unaccounted profits" [2]. Financial fraud, such as credit card fraud, company fraud, and money embezzlement, has gained much awareness and concern recently specifically in smart cities due to digitalisation.

The total damages incurred as a result of financial fraud are immeasurable. Financial fraud detection (FFD) entails differentiating false accounting data from valid data and revealing inappropriate actions, and it allows decision-makers to establish suitable policies to mitigate fraud's impact [3]. Current economic conditions have resulted in a significant rise in accounting fraud cases, making FFD an increasingly important field for regulators, investors, academics, and the media. The demand for identifying, characterising, and reporting accounting fraud has risen as a result of high-profile financial crimes detected and revealed at significant businesses like Lucent, Enron, WorldCom, and Satyam [4].

The authors of [5] define bank fraud as deception perpetrated on a bank or financial institution by a person or entity, and corporate fraud occurs when a company's financial data is knowingly misrepresented in its accounting records to deceive the company's stakeholders and increase company profits or personal financial gain. Ngai et al. [3] described that insurance fraud takes place when an insured attempts to gain financial benefit from an insurer by making fraudulent claims or when the insurer refuses to pay appropriate benefits. Figure 8.1 depicts the basic kinds of financial fraud. This research will focus on financial statement fraud and detection approaches.

According to [4, 6, 7, 8], it is becoming increasingly important to use data mining in FFD to uncover hidden truths from large data sets [3]. To retrieve and identify valuable information from large databases, data mining combines statistics, mathematics, artificial intelligence, and machine learning algorithms [9, 10]. Among the data mining algorithms employed by FFD are naive Bayes (NB), logistic regression (LR), decision trees (DTs), and neural networks (NNs). Review papers

DOI: 10.1201/9781003486930-11

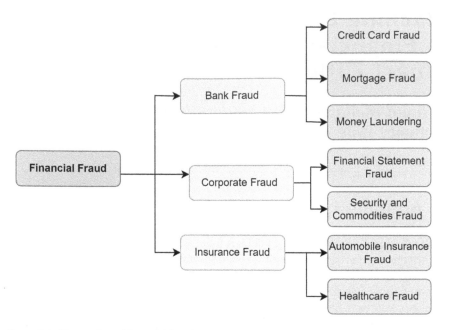

Figure 8.1 Categories of financial fraud.

on this topic have been published in conferences and journals in recent years. Terrorist identification, financial crime detection, intrusion and spam detection, and other statistical techniques related to fraud detection have all been looked into.

There are six parts to this chapter: Section 1 introduces different kinds of accounting fraud. Section 2 provides the general classification of data mining techniques in FFD. Section 3 discusses some broad literature on financial fraud such as what are financial statements, how financial statement fraud occurs in companies of smart cities, and some experimental issues in dealing with FFD. Section 4 presents the classification framework for the deep learning models used for FFD. Section 5 provides the literature review of different researchers who have applied these techniques on multiple data sets, the results obtained, and the challenges with FFD. Section 6 puts an end to our survey and gives some interesting ideas regarding future research.

8.2 CATEGORISATION OF DATA MINING TECHNIQUES

The major six categories of techniques used in data mining are classification, prediction, clustering, regression, outlier detection, and visualisation. In Figure 8.2, we illustrate these techniques. Several algorithms extract relevant relationships from data to support each of the six strategies.

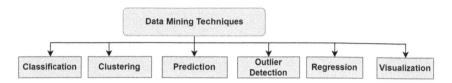

Figure 8.2 Data mining techniques.

8.2.1 Classification

The task of allocating items to one of several specified groups or classes is known as classification. In classification, each attribute set 'x' corresponds to a class label 'y' based on a target function 'f'. A discrete attribute must be used for the class label. It is a widespread issue that affects a wide range of applications. For instance, spam email messages can be identified by the header and content, tumours can be identified by MRI scans, and galaxies can be classified according to their structure.

8.2.2 Clustering

Clustering classifies data items solely based on information about the objects and their relationships. Items within one group should be similar (or related) to each other, while those in another group need to be different (or unrelated) [6]. Clustering amplifies similarity (or homogeneity) within a group, and divergence between groups is greater when the clustering is more distinct. Data segmentation or partitioning, commonly known as clustering, is an unsupervised grouping technique [8]. The most prevalent clustering methods include K-means clustering, DBSCAN, NBC, density peak clustering, and self-organising maps.

8.2.3 Prediction

Using patterns in a data source, predictive analysis calculates numeric and ordered future values [11]. The main fact is that the value of the anticipated attribute is continuous or ordered rather than discontinuous or unordered. The term "predicted attribute" is used to describe this characteristic [8]. Neural networks and logistic models are the algorithms that are mostly employed.

8.2.4 Outlier Detection

Outlier detection is a technique that evaluates the distance between two objects and identifies those that are significantly distinct or nonidentical from the rest of the data [8]. The outliers are the objects in the sample that differ in some way from the rest [12]. Data mining faces many fundamental challenges, including detecting outliers and anomalies. The discounting learning method [7], the local outlier factor algorithm and the local distance-based outlier algorithm are the most often used strategies in outlier detection.

8.2.5 Regression

Regression is a quantitative technique that uses continuous values to suggest an association between predictor variables and response variables [8]. Logit regression has been used as a criterion in numerous empirical research. Fraud detection in the credit card, automobile, crop, and insurance industries, as well as in corporate fraud detection, is often accomplished through regression. There are several frequently used mathematical models, such as logistic regression and linear regression.

8.2.6 Visualisation

Visualisation defines the method of transforming complex input elements into simple structures that helps the users to understand the complicated relationships or patterns revealed by the data mining process [9]. The researchers created a set of tools and apps that use the human visual system's pattern-detecting abilities to dynamically encipher input using size, colour, position, and other optical features. The ideal use of visualisation is to convey complicated patterns through a straightforward display of data or functions [13].

8.3 FINANCIAL FRAUD

Financial fraud refers to the use of unauthorised means or fraudulent schemes to earn profits. Scams can be committed in a variety of financial areas in smart cities, including banks, insurance, taxes, and companies. Cheating such as identity theft, masquerading, tax avoidance, funds misappropriation, and other fiscal fraud, is a burgeoning problem. Despite considerable efforts to tamp down accounting fraud, it is still an issue that has detrimental effects on businesses and the public [14].

8.3.1 Financial Statements

Financial statements describe information related to an enterprise, particularly its accounting results such as revenues, expenditures, gains, losses, possible future issues, and management comments on business operations. All companies are obliged to publish their financial reports annually or quarterly. Accounting statements may be used to show corporate results. Contributors, shareholders, and borrowers use accounting statements to research and compare economic health and business profits [14].

Financial statements contain four categories: balance sheet, cash flow statement, income statement, and explanatory notes. The cash flow statement reflects the success of a firm in financing its operating costs, in its investment fund, and in repaying its borrowings. The balance sheet gives an updated summary of the debts, assets, and shareholders' equity. The profit and loss account or income statement strongly emphasises the cost and profit of the firm during a period. Company profits or revenues are given here, which removes expenditures from incomes. The descriptive notes are extra information that provides clarity regarding certain items posted in the statements [14].

8.3.2 Financial Statement Fraud Detection

Misleading financial statements can contain dishonest investments, fraudulent inputs connected to sales and earnings, abuse of taxes, or decreasing obligations, expenses, or losses [4]. Although it is costly, inaccurate, time-consuming, and ineffective, manual inspection is the most common method of detecting fraud [15], whereas fraud can be most effectively detected using artificial intelligence, particularly machine learning technologies. When fraud is detected using data mining, immediate action is taken to reduce overhead costs [16]. The major data mining methods employed in FFD are logit models, DTs, BBNs, and NNs, as they provide solutions to the problems found in the identification and categorisation of tampered data [17].

8.3.2.1 Manipulations in the Cash Flow Statement Balance Sheet

Financial reports that contain objective, accurate, and trustworthy details represent the foundation of the business. Fraudulent accounting methods can degrade the quality of the statements. It is arduous to identify and reduce fraud in cash flow statements and balance sheets in comparison with profits and losses in the profit and loss account [18].

8.3.2.1.1 Manipulations in the Balance Sheet

The most common types of corporate fraud that are linked to the categories on the balance sheets are excessive receivables, misstatement of inventories, goods, and final products, undermining of liabilities, and lack of borrowings. Balance sheet fraud relates to manipulating incomes and expenditures in the profit and loss statement and the movement of cash in cash flow statements and it is difficult to detect if the cheater has covered their tracks well.

8.3.2.1.2 Manipulations in the Cash Flow Statement

The facts provided in the cash flow statement are more secure since it is easier to tamper with the amounts in incomes, expenditures, debts, and assets than the amounts in cash inflows and outflows [18]. There are four main ways to manipulate in cash flow statement [19]:

- shifting an income from accounting to operations
- shifting expenditures from operations to investments
- moving funds from operations using funds from selling a part of or the whole enterprise
- moving funds from operations using extra unfeasible activities

8.3.2.2 Experimental Issues in Financial Statement Fraud Detection

8.3.2.2.1 Problem Representation

First, we must understand the problem before tackling a difficult subject such as financial statement fraud detection [20], for instance, describing what financial fraud is, why it occurs, and who benefits. Fraud detection models include classification, clustering, prediction, regression, outlier detection, visualisation, etc. [21].

8.3.2.2.2 Feature Selection

In data mining and knowledge-based systems, feature selection is critical. In domains where data sets with many features are accessible, such as machine learning, pattern recognition, and statistics, the subject of choosing attributes is widely studied [22]. If the set of features is not selected properly, it may result in issues such as insufficient information, noisy or irrelevant data, or a poor blend of features. Feature selection approaches include entropy-based feature selection, simple t-statistic methodology, and 10-fold cross-validation, among others [23].

8.3.2.2.3 Performance Metrics

The key determinant of the suitability of data mining algorithms is their success in solving a specific problem. This generally happens in the case of financial statement fraud, when even minor performance improvements can result in significant financial gains [21]. The performance of different algorithms can be measured through precision, recall, area under the curve (AUC), Mathews correlation coefficient (MCC), accuracy, F-measure, and others.

8.4 DEEP LEARNING TECHNIQUES FOR FINANCIAL ACCOUNTING FRAUD DETECTION

Deep learning involves processing complex and bulk data through artificial neural networks (ANNs). It is a type of ML that imitates the design and functions of the human brain. Machines learn through examples using deep learning algorithms. Deep learning is frequently employed in business, advertising, entertainment, and the healthcare industry.

Deep learning models employ several different algorithms. They require a great deal of data and computing power, but almost any kind of data may be used to run them. While no algorithm is flawless, certain algorithms are more effective at carrying out particular tasks. The following paragraphs discuss each algorithm in greater detail.

8.4.1 Convolutional Neural Networks

In addition to object detection and image processing, CNNs, or convolutional neural networks, include several layers. CNNs may be utilised for a variety of tasks, including satellite image identification, medical image analysis, time-series forecasting, and anomaly detection. Convolutional, dropout, max-pooling, and fully linked multilayer perceptron layers are only a few of the several layer types used in CNNs.

8.4.1.1 Convolution Layer

In CNNs, the convolution function is performed by a convolution layer with several filters. The most complicated and expensive layer in a CNN model is the convolution layer. Local connectivity, on the other hand, limits connections between neurons in a layer to those in the layers above and below the neurons, thereby reducing the size of CNN parameters. In addition, the CNN model's parameters are reduced when shared weights are applied. In the previous layer, feature maps are drawn using the convolution kernel, and then activation functions are used to obtain the output features maps [24]. The convolutional layer's formula is as follows:

$$x_j^l = f\left(\sum_{i \in M_j} x_i^{l-1} * k_{ij}^l + b_j^l\right)$$

where the $\times$ denotes the convolution operation, M_j denotes the collection of all the input feature maps, x_j^l represents the j-th feature graph in l-th convolution layer, k_{ij}^l denotes the weight of the convolution kernel j in the layer l, b_j^l denotes the bias, and f denotes the activation function.

8.4.1.2 Rectified Linear Unit

In CNNs, elements are operated on via a ReLU layer. In this case, we get a rectified feature map as an output.

8.4.1.3 Pooling Layer

A pooling layer is then applied to the rectified feature map. Feature maps are down-sampled by pooling to reduce their dimensions. The pooling layer flattens the two-dimensional array of features from the pooled feature map so that it may be represented as a single, extended, continuous, linear vector. The pooling layer's max pooling and average pooling functions are frequently employed to carry out down-sampling operations and lessen complexity. The pooling operation's mathematical equation is the following:

$$S_j = \frac{1}{|R_j|} \cdot \sum_{i \in R_j} a_j$$

where a_j denotes the value in the pooling area output by the activation function of the i-th activation value, and s_j denotes the pooling value of the j-th pooling region, R_j.

8.4.1.4 Fully Connected Layer

The fully connected mechanism considers the flattened matrix from the pooling layer as input to classify and identify the images. Figure 8.3 shows an illustration of a CNN processing flow.

8.4.2 Long Short-Term Memory Networks

LSTM-based recurrent neural networks (RNNs) learn and remember both short- and long-term dependencies. The natural tendency is to retain earlier information for a long time. LSTM networks gradually store information. Due to their potential

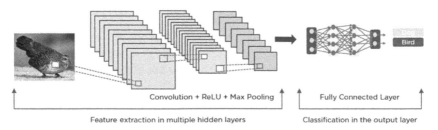

Figure 8.3 Image processed via CNN [25].

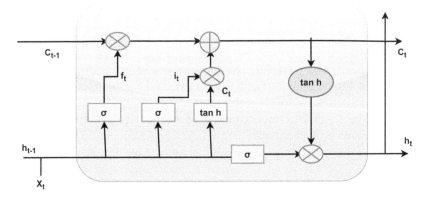

Figure 8.4 Structure of an LSTM cell.

to remember past data, they aid in time-series prediction. Four interconnected layers make up an LSTM that collectively form a structure that resembles a chain. Apart from time-series predictions, they are utilised for music creation, speech recognition, handwritten character recognition, language modelling, sentiment analysis, language translation, financial time series analysis, predictive analysis, and drug discovery. Figure 8.4 depicts an LSTM cell's entire flow.

In the beginning, LSTM cells ignore unimportant details of the prior state. The state values of the cells are then selectively updated. Finally, they provide the output of certain cell state components.

Because each LSTM cell is associated with the network's memory, its structure is similar to that of an RNN. The gates used in LSTM cells are the forget gate f_t, input gate i_t, output gate o_t, and an input modulation gate $\hat{c}_t$. The forget gate f_t determines which attributes are extracted and computed. The input gate determines whether the data is fed into the memory cell, whereas the output gate selects the data that will be the result from the memory cell. The relationships between the gates are shown in equations (3)–(8), where $\otimes$ stands for element-wise multiplication:

$$f_t = \sigma(U_f x_t + W_f h_{t-1} + b_f) \tag{3}$$

$$i_t = \sigma(U_i x_t + W_f h_{t-1} + b_i) \tag{4}$$

$$o_t = \sigma(U_o x_t + W_o h_{t-1} + b_o) \tag{5}$$

$$h_t = \tanh(c_t) \otimes o_t \tag{6}$$

$$\hat{c}_t = \tanh(U_c x_t + W_c h_{t-1} + b_c) \tag{7}$$

$$c_t = f_t \otimes c_{t-1} + i_t \otimes \hat{c}_t \tag{8}$$

8.4.3 Recurrent Neural Networks

An RNN is an extremely popular deep-learning architecture that can process consecutive data. RNN can provide predictions on sequential data with a better degree of accuracy and is effective at capturing the relationships between each data point. The input variable for the modelling process is preserved as significant historical information that will be computed with current data. A detail of the computational architecture is shown in Figure 8.5. The same hidden state that contains the input variable also consists of the calculated result of the data. This input data will be added to the hidden layer along with the t + 1 data for calculation. The activation function used in the hidden layer of the RNN is called a hyperbolic tangent function (tanh):

$$y'_t = \tanh\left(w_{ht}\, y'_{t-1} + w_{xt} x_t + b_t\right) \tag{9}$$

Due to the directed cycles created by connections between RNNs, the outputs from the LSTM may be used as inputs to the current phase. RNNs can memorise previous inputs due to its built-in memory. Applications for RNNs often include handwriting recognition, machine translation, natural language processing, time-series analysis, and image captioning.

Information is fed into the input at time t from the output at time t − 1. The output at time t feeds into the input at time t + 1 in a similar manner. RNN is capable of being processing inputs of any length. The approach takes into account historical information, and the model size is independent of the input size.

8.4.4 Generative Adversarial Networks

The training data is utilised to generate new data instances using deep learning generative algorithms like GANs. The generator, which generates false input, and

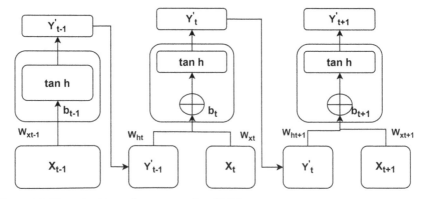

Figure 8.5 The principle and structure of an RNN.

the discriminator, which incorporates that input into its learning process, are the two fundamental parts of GANs. GANs have become more popular over time. For the study of dark matter, they may be employed to enhance astronomical images and replicate gravitational sensing. By utilising picture training, GANs are utilised by video game producers to recreate low-resolution, 2D textures in earlier video games in 4K or greater resolutions. Rendering 3D objects and creating realistic visuals included cartoon characters are all possible using GANs. Figure 8.6 depicts the operation of GANs.

By discriminating between the true sample data and the false data created by the generator, the discriminator gains the ability to differentiate between them. The discriminator quickly recognises false data generated by the generator during initial training. Generators and discriminators receive the results from the GAN to update the model.

8.4.5 Radial Basis Function Networks

The activation job of radial basis function networks (RBFNs), a distinct form of feedforward NN, uses a radial basis function. An input, a hidden, and an output layer are common elements of these models, which are used for time-series prediction, regression, and classification.

By comparing input instances with examples from the training set, data may be categorised using RBFNs. At their input layer, RBFNs are fed by an input vector. RBF neurons are present in a layer. Each data category's associated nodes are included in the output layer, and the function determines the weighted average of the inputs. The outputs of the hidden layer neurons are inversely correlated with the distance from their centres and exhibit Gaussian transfer functions. The network output is created by linearly combining the radial-basis functions and neuron parameters of the input.

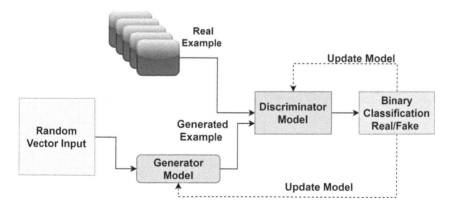

Figure 8.6 Generative adversarial networks.

8.4.6 Multilayer Perceptron

Multiple layers of perceptron with an activation function collectively form an MLP, a specific kind of feedforward NN. An ultimately linked output layer and an input layer make up MLPs. They can be used to create speech recognition, pattern recognition, and machine translation software as the number of input and output layers are same but there are numerous hidden layers.

MLP data is transmitted to the network's input layer. The signal only flows in a single direction because of the graph-like connections between the neurons' layers. MLPs use the weights between the input layer and the hidden layers to compute the input. MLPs choose which nodes to fire by using activation functions. ReLUs, sigmoid functions, and tanh are a few examples of activation functions. Using a training set of data, MLPs instruct the model to recognise correlations and establish relationships between independent and target variables. Figure 8.7 depicts the MLP to computes weights, and bias, and applies the proper activation functions to classify images of cats and dogs.

Layer-by-layer feature transformation is used to create a new feature space from the sample's feature representation in the original space, which facilitates classification or prediction. Deep neural networks, which have more powerful learning capabilities and greater flexibility, are another name for it [9].

8.4.7 Self-Organising Maps

Self-organising maps (SOMs) use self-organising ANNs to reduce the dimensionality of the data, enabling data visualisation. High-dimensional data is challenging for people to see, a problem that data visualisation attempts to solve. To help individuals understand this highly detailed data, SOMs were developed.

SOMs choose a random vector from the training set, then assign starting weights to each node. SOMs look over each node to identify which weights are

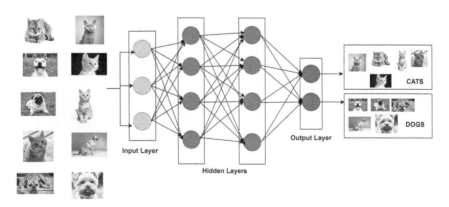

Figure 8.7 Multilayer perceptron.

the most likely input vector. The winning node is known as the best matching unit (BMU). As SOMs learn about the BMU's neighbourhood, the number of neighbours gradually declines. SOMs assign a winning weight to the sample vector. The closer a node is to a BMU, the more its weight varies. The further the neighbour is from the BMU, the less it learns. SOMs repeat step two for N iterations. A SOM receives the data and converts it into 2D RGB values. The colours are then divided and grouped.

8.4.8 Deep Belief Networks

To develop generative models in DBNs, latent, stochastic variables are placed in a hierarchy of layers. Binary values define latent variables, also referred to as hidden units. There are links between the layers of a stack of Boltzmann machines, allowing each RBM layer in a DBN to interact with both the layer above it and the layer below it. DBNs are used for motion-capture data, video recognition, and image identification.

DBNs are trained via greedy algorithms. The greedy learning approach is used to learn the top-down, generative weights layer by layer. DBNs execute the Gibbs sampling phases on the top two hidden layers. In this stage, the instances that the top two hidden layers have specified are extracted from RBM. DBNs collect a sample from the units that are visible using a single iteration of ancestral sampling over the rest of the model. DBNs find that the values of the latent variables in each layer may be inferred in a single bottom-up pass. Figure 8.8 illustrates a DBN architecture.

8.4.9 Restricted Boltzmann Machines

An efficient stochastic ANN called an RBM can learn a probability distribution from an input set. RBMs are used for a variety of applications, such as collaborative filtering, dimensionality reduction, topic modelling, classification, regression, and feature learning. The fundamental units of DBNs are RBMs.

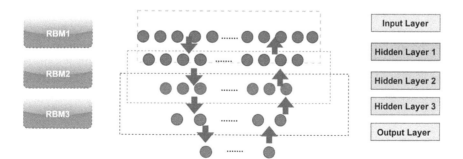

Figure 8.8 Deep belief network architecture.

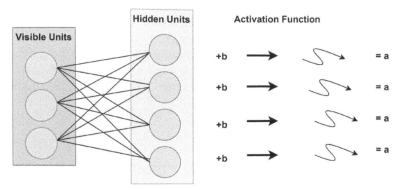

Figure 8.9 Restricted Boltzmann machine.

RBMs are made up of a visible and a hidden unit layer, and all visible units are connected to all hidden ones. RBMs only have a bias unit that is connected to both the visible and hidden units and they lack output nodes. Forward pass and backward pass are the two stages of RBMs. When RBMs receive inputs, they convert them into a collection of integers that are used to encrypt the inputs for the forward pass.

In RBMs, each input is combined with a unique weight and a single overall bias. The hidden layer receives the output from the algorithm. RBMs use the collection of numbers in the backward pass to transform them into the reconstructed inputs. RBMs integrate each activation with its weight and global bias before sending the output to the accessible layer for reconstruction. The RBM then evaluates the quality of the outcome at the visible layer by comparing the reconstruction with the original input. Figure 8.9 depicts the operation of RBMs.

8.4.10 Autoencoders

An AE is a specific type of feedforward NN with identical input and output. These trained NNs reproduce the data from the input layer to the output layer. They are designed to solve unsupervised learning problems. Among the uses of AEs include image processing, popularity prediction, and drug development.

An encoder and a decoder are the two main parts of AEs. The design of AE allows them to take input and change it into a new representation. Then, they make an effort to precisely reproduce the original input. An AE NN receives input when a digit's image is not visible. AEs first encode the picture before condensing the input's size into a more compact form. The AE produces the rebuilt picture after decoding the original image.

8.5 ANALYSIS OF EXISTING TECHNIQUES

This section presents a detailed in-depth analysis of financial fraud detection algorithms used in the literature. Table 8.1 lists the deep learning techniques used by

Table 8.1 Financial Fraud Detection Techniques

Sl. No	Author	Feature selection methods, sampling techniques	Algorithms/methods applied	Sample size	Classification accuracy	Challenges
1	Shengyong et al. [22]	• Chinese word segmentation • Word vector calculation	LR, RF, SVM, XGB, ANN, CNN, LSTM (128), LSTM (256), GRU (128), GRU (256)	5130 firms: 244 fraudulent and 4886 nonfraudulent	**LSTM (256): 94.98%** **GRU (256): 94.62%**	• Limited sampling period • Data source only involves Chinese listed companies
2	Raghavan et al. [26]	K-fold cross-validation	KNN, RF, SVM, AE, RBM, DBN, CNN	**European data set:** 492 frauds and 284,315 nonfraud **Australian data set:** 307 frauds and 383 nonfraud **German data set:** 300 frauds and 700 nonfraud	**European data set:** Ensemble (KNN, SVM, CNN): MCC –0.8226 AUC – 0.8964	Dynamic environments (i.e. the pattern of fraud changes consistently)
3	Craja et al. [27]	HAN for word selection	LR, SVM, RF, XGB, ANN, & HAN	1163 firms: 201 frauds and 962 nonfraud	XGB – 90.83% HAN (AUC) – 92.64%	Model performance shifts in quality among different data types
4	Alghofaili et al. [28]	None	RF, LR, SVM, LSTM, AE	284,807 data points: 492 frauds and 284,315 nonfraud	**LSTM:** Accuracy –99.96% Loss Rate –0.21% Time – 405 s **Autoencoder:** Accuracy – 70.27% Loss Rate –69.08% Time – 318 s	ML models are not capable enough to predict new patterns or deal with big data

(Continued)

Table 8.1 (Continued)

Sl. No	Author	Feature selection methods, sampling techniques	Algorithms/methods applied	Sample size	Classification accuracy	Challenges
5	Wang et al. [29]	None	DNN	3117 firms: 908 fraudulent and 2209 non-fraudulent	**DNN:** Accuracy – ~80% Loss Rate – ~50%	• Existence of missing data and outliers • Sample from one specific country
6	Jan et al. [30]	• 14 financial and 4 non-financial variables • Random sampling	RNN, LSTM	153 firms: 51 fraudulent and 102 non-fraudulent	**RNN:** Accuracy –87.18% Training Time – 0.3 s **LSTM:** Accuracy –94.88% Training Time – 1.5 s	Need to analyse other deep learning models
7	Chen et al. [31]	Queen cohort selection for chromosomes	C4.5 DT, LR, NN, KNN, GA, GA-SVM, PSO-SVM, QGA-SVM	100 firms: 25 fraud and 75 nonfraud	QGA-SVM: 90.50%	Diversity and value of big data
8	Temponeras et al. [32]	• 10-fold cross-validation • Average value of 10-fold cross-validation	C4.5 DT, 3-NN (KNN), LR, SMO, DDMP	164 firms: 41 frauds and 123 nonfraud	DDMP: 93.7%	Robustness of the DDMP model
9	Kirkos et al. [33]	• 10-fold cross-validation • Financial ratios such as leverage, profitability, sales performance, solvency, and financial distress	ID3, NN, BBN	76 firms: 38 frauds and 38 nonfraud	BBN: 90.3%	Data discretisation due to software limitations
10	Yao et al. [2]	PCA, XGBoost	SVM, RF, DT, ANN, LR	240 firms: 120 each frauds and nonfraud	**RF:** 75%	• The data set is not large enough • Variables included can be increased

| 11 | Mohammadi et al. [34] | None | BN, DA, LR, ANN, SVM | 330 firms: 165 frauds and 165 nonfraud | **ANN:** FFS detection accuracy – 69.8% Overall detection accuracy – 75% Type I error rate – 30.2% Overall error rate – 25% | • The whole data sample was used in both preprocessing and classification algorithm evaluation • Near-optimal performance allowed for comparison of the techniques, but it was challenging to determine how generalisable the relative classifier performance was. |
| 12 | Amel-Zadeh et al. [35] | None | DNN, RNN, CART, OLS, LASSO | 27,410 firms | **Random Forest:** Mean squared error (MSE) – 0.055 Mean absolute error (MAE) – 0.153 **Lasso Regression:** MSE – 0.055 MAE – 0.154 **DNN:** MSE – 0.058 MAE – 0.16 | Relatively large average forecasting errors |

SVM – support vector machine, LR – logistic regression, RF – random forest, DT – decision tree, KNN – K-nearest neighbor, ANN – artificial neural network, AE – autoencoders, RBM – restricted Boltzmann machine, DBN – deep belief network, RNN – recurrent neural network, CNN – convolutional neural network, LSTM – long short-term memory, XGB – extreme gradient boosting, GRU – gated recurrent unit, SMO – sequential minimal optimisation, DDMP – deep dense multilayer perceptron, HAN – hierarchical attention network, DNN – deep neural network, PSO – particle swarm optimisation, GA – genetic algorithm, QGA – quantum genetic algorithm, ID3 – iterative dichotomiser 3, OLS – ordinary least squares, BBN – Bayesian belief network, LASSO – least absolute shrinkage and selection operator, CART – classification and regression tree.

different authors on a variety of data sets to detect financial fraud, their classification accuracy, and the challenges faced by them during the experiment.

With the help of deep learning models, the authors of [28] aim to create a better system for spotting financial fraud. Using accounting statement information and textual data from yearly reports of 5130 Chinese companies, this system combined numeric characteristics and textual information. The authors built a financial index system first that included both financial and nonfinancial indices. After that, a word vector was used to retrieve the textual elements from the managerial comments of the yearly reports. Then, effective DL models were used, and their performances were compared.

The empirical findings demonstrate significantly better performance with the suggested deep learning approaches over more conventional machine learning techniques. According to the 94.98% and 94.62% correct classification rates of the LSTM and grated recurrent unit networks, respectively, the recovered textual characteristics show good classification results and significantly support the identification of financial fraud. By splitting the whole data set into 20 balanced subsets and mixing each nonfraudulent group with the fraudulent instances, the authors were able to find a solution for their unbalanced data set.

A comparison of various ML techniques, including RF, KNN, and SVM, and DL methods, including DBN, AE, RBM, and CNN was conducted in [26]. The authors used three data sets, from Europe in general, Australia, and Germany, and three evaluation metrics, area under the ROC curve, MCC, and cost of failure, and they determined that SVM combined with CNN was the most reliable method for large data sets. Several ensemble approaches provided good enhancements for small data sets, including SVMs, random forests, and KNNs. CNN performed better than AEs, RBM, and DBN [36]. Machine learning models need to be retrained, and new datasets must be collected as fraud patterns change over time.

The authors of [29] suggested a method for spotting accounting statement fraud by fusing data from accounting ratios with managerial observations in business annual reports. To retrieve text characteristics from the managerial discussion and analysis (MD&A) part of yearly reports, they used a hierarchical attention network (HAN). In addition to financial ratios, the approach also collected the context and content of managerial remarks that are used to identify false reporting. The methodology offered interpretable indicators, sometimes known as "red-flag" statements, to help stakeholders decide if a special yearly report needs to be looked into further.

Empirical findings showed that the lexical characteristics of MD&A sections collected by the HAN produced positive categorisation outcomes and significantly strengthened accounting ratios; the DL model could correctly detect fraud cases, in contrast to the majority of ML models that are unsuccessful in identifying cases of fraud but do an exceptional job of detecting authentic records. It may be more appropriate to combine these models to support stakeholders in determining fraud rather than selecting a single model due to the variation in performances on diverse data.

Using an actual data set of credit card fraud, the authors of [30] created a framework for the identification of accounting scams built on the LSTM approach. They compared an autoencoder with various machine learning methods already in use, including RF, SVM, and LR. With the use of big data, their model attempted to refine both the efficiency and the accuracy of ongoing identification techniques. Even while certain ML algorithms have shown positive outcomes, they may eventually reach a point where they are unable to improve accuracy, making it impossible for them to forecast new patterns or handle bulk data. On the contrary, DL techniques are capable of grasping even complicated patterns and dynamically adapting to new fraud patterns. The authors discovered that when it comes to solving fraud detection issues, the LSTM approach can attain ideal performance.

Deep learning was initially applied to identifying accounting scams in the research [31]. Using 82 financial indicators and the rate of change of financial indicators along with nonfinancial indicators, an NN model with three layers was employed to discriminate fraud in the accounting statements of Chinese listed companies. As a result, regulatory authorities are now better able to tackle fraud more effectively.

The authors used information from Chinese-listed firms for their investigation; therefore, the prediction outcomes might not be generalisable to the different accounting rules and economic situations in different nations. To fill in the gaps in the input, the average and median were employed. In the end, the model might show different outcomes due to the variation in the samples and the existence of outliers.

Both numerical and nonnumerical data of Taiwan Stock Exchange-listed firms from the Taiwan Economic Journal between 2001 and 2019 were investigated by the authors of [32]. They chose a sample of 153 firms, 51 of which were fraudulent. Using the strong deep learning algorithms RNN and LSTM, they built financial fraud detection models and found that the LSTM model performed better on every performance metric (confusion matrix accuracy, precision, sensitivity, specificity, and F1-score, as well as the Type I and Type II error rates and AUC scores). In comparison with RNN, which has an accuracy of 87.18%, the LSTM model has a high accuracy of 94.88%. Therefore, both models exhibit good performance and are appropriate for identifying financial statement fraud. The study authors conclude that nonfinancial factors, which represent various economic situations, capital markets, financial laws, and business categories, must also be taken into account when analysing accounting frauds along with the typically employed accounting variables.

8.6 CONCLUSION AND FUTURE SCOPE

The successful implementation of machine learning in financial management within smart cities requires quality data; robust model development; and considerations for privacy, security, and regulatory compliance. With this chapter, we examined some of the major challenges confronted by the literature on fraudulent accounting statements. In real time, there are fewer fraud cases than nonfraud cases, and fraud patterns change over time; therefore they are difficult to catch. Therefore, the fraud detection model should be more robust. The principal characteristic of the detection model is its validity or correctness as the data in real time is more diverse and multidimensional. The volumes of information in data may be massive, and the rates of misclassification should be low.

Given these difficulties, there are numerous unanswered questions in the literature that provide excellent opportunities for further research. As unsupervised algorithms were used less than the supervised approaches like classification and regression, future fraud detection studies must concentrate on unsupervised and semi-supervised methods. Combining financial and textual data boosts fraudulent financial statement detection.

The application of machine learning techniques like NB, LR, SVM, and DT was the main focus of the research and development effort in the field of fraud detection in smart city financial sectors. These methods have certain drawbacks, such as poor processing speeds, inefficient memory use, and a lack of parallelism when working with complicated nonlinear data. Deep learning is the ideal method for getting around the problems with traditional machine learning algorithms that were just mentioned. Computational models with several processing layers are now able to learn data representation at various levels of abstraction due to deep learning. Modern object identification, object detection, and speech recognition have all been greatly improved by these methods. Deep learning models also have dynamic designs that can adjust to new patterns and can effectively analyse massive data in terms of accuracy, memory, and speed. Thus, even with enormous amounts of data, their performance is superior to machine learning.

REFERENCES

[1] Stevenson A (2009) Oxford Concise English Dictionary, 11th edition. Oxford University Press, Oxford.
[2] Yao J, Zhang J, Wang L (2018) A financial statement fraud detection model based on hybrid data mining methods. Paper presented at the 2018 International Conference on Artificial Intelligence and Big Data (ICAIBD), Beijing, 26–28 May.
[3] Ngai EW, Hu Y, Wong YH, Chen Y, Sun X (2011) The application of data mining techniques in financial fraud detection: A classification framework and an academic review of the literature. Decision Support Systems 50(3): 559–569. doi: 10.1016/j.dss.2010.08.006.
[4] Yue D, Wu X, Wang Y, Li Y, Chu CH (2007) A review of data mining-based financial fraud detection research. Paper presented at the 2007 International Conference on Wireless Communications, Networking and Mobile Computing, Beijing, 21–25 September.
[5] Phua C, Lee V, Smith K, Gayler R (2010) A comprehensive survey of data mining-based fraud detection research. https://doi.org/10.48550/arXiv.1009.6119.

[6] Zhang D, Zhou L (2004) Discovering golden nuggets: data mining in financial application. IEEE Transactions on Systems, Man, and Cybernetics, Part C (Applications and Reviews) 34(4): 513–522. doi:10.1109/TSMCC.2004.829279.

[7] Yamanishi K, Takeuchi JI, Williams G, Milne P (2004) On-line unsupervised outlier detection using finite mixtures with discounting learning algorithms. Data Mining and Knowledge Discovery 8(3): 275–300. doi:10.1023/B:DAMI.0000023676.72185.7c.

[8] Han J, Kamber M, Pei J (2012) Data mining trends and research frontiers. In: The Morgan Kaufmann Series in Data Management Systems (ed) Data Mining, 3rd edition. Elsevier, Amsterdam, pp. 585–631.

[9] Turban E, Sharda R, Delen, D (2010) Decision Support and Business Intelligence Systems, 9th edition. Prentice Hall Press, New Jersey.

[10] Frawley WJ, Piatetsky-Shapiro G, Matheus CJ (1992) Knowledge discovery in databases: An overview. AI magazine 13(3): 57–57. doi:10.1609/aimag.v13i3.1011.

[11] Ahmed SR (2004) Applications of data mining in retail business. Paper presented at the International Conference on Information Technology: Coding and Computing (ITCC), New York, 5–7 April.

[12] Agyemang M, Barker K, Alhajj R (2006) A comprehensive survey of numeric and symbolic outlier mining techniques. Intelligent Data Analysis 10(6): 521–538. doi:10.3233/IDA-2006-10604.

[13] Eick SG, Fyock DE (1996) Visualizing corporate data. IEEE Potentials 15(5): 6–11. doi:10.1109/45.544032.

[14] Ashtiani M N, Raahemi B (2021) Intelligent fraud detection in financial statements using machine learning and data mining: A systematic literature review. IEEE Access. doi:10.1109/ACCESS.2021.3096799.

[15] West, J, Bhattacharya M (2016) Intelligent financial fraud detection: A comprehensive review. Computers & Security 57: 47–66. doi:10.1016/j.cose.2015.09.005.

[16] Sheshasayee A, Thomas SS (2017) Implementation of data mining techniques in upcoding fraud detection in the monetary domains. Paper presented at the 2017 International Conference on Innovative Mechanisms for Industry Applications (ICIMIA), Delhi, 21–23 February.

[17] Sharma A, Panigrahi P K (2013) A review of financial accounting fraud detection based on data mining techniques. International Journal of Computer Applications 39(1): 37–47. doi:10.5120/4787-7016.

[18] Dimitrijević D (2015) The detection and prevention of manipulations in the balance sheet and the cash flow statement. Ekonomski horizonti 17(2): 137–153. doi:10.5937/ekonhor1502137d.

[19] Schilit H, Perler J (2010) Financial Shenanigans: How to Detect Accounting Gimmicks & Fraud in Financial Reports, 3rd edition. McGraw-Hill Education, New York.

[20] West J Bhattacharya M (2015, June). Mining financial statement fraud: An analysis of some experimental issues. In: Proceedings of the 2015 IEEE 10th Conference on Industrial Electronics and Applications (ICIEA), Wellington, pp. 461–466. https://doi.org/10.1109/ICIEA.2015.7334157

[21] Singh P, Jat SC (2020). A survey to detect financial fraud using deep learning approaches. International Journal of Scientific and Technology Research 9(3): 16–20.

[22] Shengyong D, Xiuguo W (2022, February). An analysis on financial statement fraud detection for chinese listed companies using deep learning. IEEE Access 10: 22516–22532.

[23] Ravisankar P, Ravi V, Rao GR, Bose I (2011). Detection of financial statement fraud and feature selection using data mining techniques. Decision Support Systems 50(2): 491–500. doi: 10.1016/j.dss.2010.11.006

[24] Biswal A (2022). Top 10 deep learning algorithms you should know. In 2022. www.simplilearn.com/tutorials/deep-learningtutorial/deep-learning-algorithm. Accessed 5 September 2022.

[25] Sharma A, Patel M, Tiwari M (2019). A comparative study to detect fraud financial statement using data mining and machine learning algorithms. International Research Journal of Engineering and Technology 6(8): 1492–1495. www.irjet.net/archives/V6/i8/IRJET-V6I8325.pdf

[26] Raghavan P, El Gayar N (2019, December). Fraud detection using machine learning and deep learning. In: Proceedings of the 2019 International Conference on Computational Intelligence and Knowledge Economy (ICCIKE), UAE, pp. 334–339. https://doi.org/10.1109/ICCIKE47802.2019.9004231.

[27] Craja P, Kim A, Lessmann S (2020). Deep learning for detecting financial statement fraud. Decision Support Systems. doi: 10.1016/j.dss.2020.113421.

[28] Alghofaili Y, Albattah A, Rassam MA (2020). A financial fraud detection model based on LSTM deep learning technique. Journal of Applied Security Research 15(4): 1–19.

[29] Wang Y, Li R, Niu Y (2021). A deep neural network based financial statement fraud detection model: Evidence from China. In: Proceedings of 2021 4th Artificial Intelligence and Cloud Computing Conference, Tokyo, pp. 145–149. doi: 10.1145/3508259.3508280.

[30] Jan C-L (2021). Detection of financial statement fraud using deep learning for sustainable development of capital markets under information asymmetry. Sustainability 13(9879): 1–20. doi: 10.3390/su13179879.

[31] Chen YJ, Wu CH (2017, July). On big data-based fraud detection method for financial statements of business groups. In: Proceedings of the 2017 6th IIAI International Congress on Advanced Applied Informatics (IIAI-AAI), Tokyo, pp. 986–987. doi: 10.1109/IIAI-AAI.2017.13.

[32] Temponeras GS, Alexandropoulos SAN, Kotsiantis SB, Vrahatis MN (2019, July). Financial fraudulent statements detection through a deep dense artificial neural network. In: Proceedings of the 2019 10th International Conference on Information, Intelligence, Systems and Applications (IISA), Greece, pp. 1–5.

[33] Kirkos E, Spathis C, Manolopoulos Y (2007). Data mining techniques for the detection of fraudulent financial statements. Expert Systems with Applications 32(4): 995–1003.

[34] Mohammadi M, Yazdani S, Khanmohammadi MH, Maham K (2020). Financial reporting fraud detection: An analysis of data mining algorithms. International Journal of Finance & Managerial Accounting 4(16): 1–12.

[35] Amel-Zadeh A, Calliess JP, Kaiser D, Roberts S (2020). Machine learning-based financial statement analysis. Econometrics: Econometric & Statistical Methods – Special Topics eJournal: 1–69. doi: 10.2139/ssrn.3520684

[36] Perols J (2011). Financial statement fraud detection: An analysis of statistical and machine learning algorithms. Auditing: A Journal of Practice & Theory 30(2): 19–50. doi: 10.2308/ajpt-50009.

Internet of Things for Smart Cities

Chapter 9

Traffic Control Using IoT Technologies and LoRaWAN for Smart Cities

J. Uma Mahesh and Judhistir Mahapatro

9.1 INTRODUCTION

The most recent real-time applications of IoT networks are in smart cities and smart grids. Many sensor devices are utilised in these applications to collect data. These sensors send data to the main network via gateways. In some circumstances, data flows from devices from the main network side to end devices. The primary principle behind LoRaWAN (long-range wide area network) is that end devices broadcast data to a gateway, even if the gateway is far away while using very little energy.

Gateways are overloaded because real-time Internet of Things (IoT) applications consist of a large number of sensor nodes sending via individual links to the gateway. On the other hand, single-hop communication restricts the neighbour nodes from acting as the relay nodes. Thus, single-hop LoRaWAN under-utilises network resources and suffers from packet loss issues as a result of electromagnetic interference and other roadblocks (smart city vehicles and buildings, trees, hills, and so on). In other words, non-line of sight increases packet losses.

Recent research articles explained that multi-hop communication is the alternative to single-hop communication. LoRaWAN is an LPWAN (low-power wide area network). It combines the LoRa physical layer with the LoRaWAN media access layer [1]. LoRaWAN shows good power consumption and coverage, and its MAC layer has become a popular choice for implementation in the IoT era. However, the packet collision rate is high as the ALOHA communication protocol is used as a MAC layer protocol.

In LoRaWAN, the end nodes transmit their data without bothering with the listen before transmit protocol [2, 3]. LoRaWAN performance degrades due to this issue, particularly in terms of transmission delay and energy usage. To overcome this problem, LoRaWAN allows spreading factors, which use the chirp spread spectrum of the physical layer for sending multiple packets at a time. The time on air and transmission power rise for specific spreading factors, which impacts network performance. This is suitable for small-area coverage networks [4–7], but using the LoRaWAN protocol for large-area coverage network applications is still an open research challenge.

DOI: 10.1201/9781003486930-13

In this chapter, we propose a mechanism for dynamically adjusting the configuration parameters of LoRaWAN by using a real-time data set known as the LoRaWAN at the Edge Data Set (LoED). In this LoED, data was gathered from a large LoRaWAN environment with nine gateways and is being utilised for various smart city applications. This data set comprises nine urban gateways with line of sight, limited line of sight, and no line of sight. This data set is ideal for various smart city applications since it allows the analysis of traffic from various angles in order to reduce network traffic. Our numerical results are based on time-series data, and we recommend tuned configurable parameters for two cases: indoor gateway placement with no line of sight and outdoor gateway placement with good line of sight.

This chapter is divided into several sections. Section 2 comprehensively describes LoRaWAN and how this is employed in smart cities using machine learning (ML) and briefly highlights our contributions. Section 3 provides an overview of the IoT and the LoRa/LoRaWAN protocol's capabilities. Section 4 presents the system model and metrics used to compare the two case studies. Section 5 presents numerical results using temporal data analysis. Section 6 concludes the chapter.

9.2 RELATED WORKS

The authors of [7] developed a numerical model that can forecast the success probability of packets in a LoRaWAN network for two-way traffic; however, this methodology cannot be easily scaled up to large LoRa/LoRaWAN networks. The authors of [8] and [10] highlight the significance of efficient traffic management using IoT networks. In [9], the authors suggest ML and reinforcement learning approaches to optimise resource allocation and traffic flow in dense IoT networks. It shows remarkable improvements in network efficiency and energy consumption. The authors of [11] focus on network requirements and capabilities of smart city applications, examine protocols, and provides network design examples. The authors of [12] proposed the prediction of traffic congestion using a bidirectional recurrent neural network. The authors of [13] presented a social IoT-based network architecture for smart cities that improved urban life and considered parameters such as speed, traffic type and pollution to predict real-time congestion and pollution. The authors of [14] studied the impact of important transmission parameters on LoRa networks and underlined the importance of optimisation of these parameters. The authors of [15] discussed a computer-based intelligent traffic control system for smart cities. This system uses image processing and real-time analysis to optimise traffic flow, reduce traffic congestion, and improve control of traffic lights. Using a network of cameras, it records real-time data about vehicles and pedestrians, enabling cities to make informed decisions about traffic management and improve emergency vehicle accessibility and prevent accidents.

The authors of [16] analysed how incorporating green design, IoT, and ecosystems might increase smart city sustainability. The key elements and dimensions are computed using a system model to assist in creating a smart ecosystem that increases the overall sustainability of smart cities. When artificial intelligence (AI) and the IoT come together, they enable the creation of smart cities that improve urban life [17]. ML algorithms [18, 19] allow machines to use data to improve their overall performance on a given subject without being explicitly programmed, but mathematics is used. Using only input data, AI helps systems to identify patterns and forecasting outcomes. As the authors stated in [20], ML algorithms can be used in smart cities to analyse data and perform predictions by considering specific features of relevant applications. These algorithms can improve the efficiency of city growth while also increasing general safety; they can also estimate visitor flows, detect crime tendencies, and analyse usage. Waste management, energy efficiency, and traffic control are just a few smart city tasks that can benefit from machine learning.

9.2.1 Our Contributions

The latest research confirms the effectiveness of LoRaWAN in controlling traffic flow in cities. Decision-making for such applications in smart cities heavily relies on ML. The following list of points summarises this chapter contribution:

- **Comparative performance analysis:** In the context of a smart parking application, we present a comparative performance analysis of gateway 4 and gateway 9. We analyse metrics such as gateway ID, received signal strength, spreading factor, coding rate, and message types to assess each gateway's strengths and weaknesses in managing parking data.
- **Indoor deployment insight (Gateway 4):** Analysis highlights the challenges Gateway 4 faces when deployed indoors without a clear line of sight. Despite potential network performance and signal reception limitations, Gateway 4 still proves valuable in providing parking information to motorists. These findings are important for understanding the feasibility of using indoor gateways in the smart parking application.
- **Outdoor deployment (Gateway 9):** Analysis shows the benefits of Gateway 9 when placed outdoors with a clear line of sight. Gateway 9 has better network performance and a larger coverage area, allowing it to provide real-time updates on parking availability more effectively. This result underscores the importance of placing the gateway outdoors for optimal performance in the smart parking application.
- **Practical recommendations**: The comparative analysis provides practical recommendations for configuring and building LoRaWAN networks in the smart parking context. These recommendations consider the specific characteristics and challenges associated with each gateway type. They aim to optimise network performance and reliability, improving drivers' overall parking experience.

- **Gateway placement indoors with no line of sight:** Using the LoED and applying temporal data analysis, we assess network performance metrics in terms of received signal strength indicator (RSSI), signal-to-noise ratio (SNR), and impact of spreading factor and coding rate with respect to packet transmissions for Gateway 4, which is placed indoors with no line of sight. The analysis provides insights into the challenges faced by indoor no-line-of-sight LoRaWAN networks. It identifies certain parameters that need to be adjusted or tweaked to improve network performance in such scenarios.
- **Gateway placement outdoors with good line of sight:** Shifted focus to Gateway 9, placed on top of a building with a good line of sight. In this chapter, we assess network performance and highlight the strengths and weaknesses of LoRaWAN networks in outdoor environments with a clear line of sight. There are recommendations for optimising performance and taking advantage of outdoor placements.

By conducting these case studies and leveraging the cited contributions, we aim to provide practical insights and recommendations for improving LoRaWAN network performance indoors and outdoors.

9.3 TECHNICAL OVERVIEW OF LORAWAN

9.3.1 Internet of Things

The IoT is pervasive across multiple disciplines. The automation of manual chores into smart processes, spanning industrial controls, automotive environments, healthcare, and more, will continue to increase the need for IoT in the future. Five hundred billion devices are going to interact with each other by 2030 [21]. According to the most recent study in IoT, the LoRa/LoRaWAN protocol has its place as the dominant industry standard for IoT applications requiring real-time capabilities, as shown in Figure 9.1.

9.3.2 Role of IoT Technologies

The use of IoT technologies in smart city traffic management is critical. IoT technologies provide the necessary infrastructure to collect real-time data, enable connectivity between different devices and systems, and enable intelligent decision-making. Here, we discuss some key aspects that highlight the role of IoT technologies [22].

- **Data collection and sensing**: IoT devices such as sensors, cameras, and connected vehicles play a crucial role in collecting real-time data on traffic conditions, vehicle movements, and environmental parameters. These devices collect data on traffic flow, congestion, parking availability, air

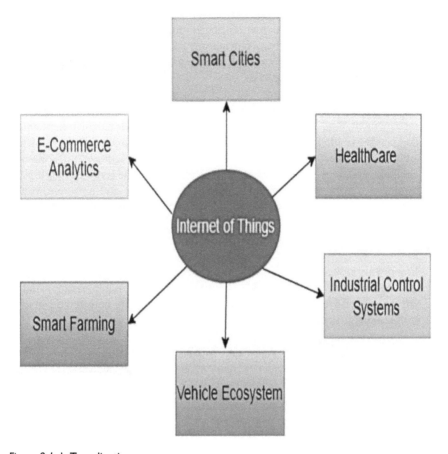

Figure 9.1 IoT applications.

quality, and other relevant factors, providing you with a comprehensive view of the urban transport ecosystem.

- **Data analysis and insights**: IoT technologies make it easier to handle, examine, and comprehend massive amounts of data created by inter-connected devices. Advanced analytics techniques, including machine learning and data mining, can extract valuable insights from the data collected, identifying traffic patterns, congestion hotspots, and potential bottlenecks. These insights help optimise signal control, predict traffic conditions, and proactively implement measures for effective traffic control.
- **Connectivity and communication**: IoT technologies such as wireless communication protocols (e.g. LoRaWAN, cellular networks) enable seamless connectivity between devices and systems in smart cities. This connectivity

enables real-time data exchange between traffic management centres, traffic lights, vehicles, pedestrians, and other transport infrastructure components. IoT enables real-time traffic information to be disseminated to drivers, pedestrians, and other stakeholders, enabling them to make informed decisions and choose efficient routes.

- **Intelligent decision-making**: IoT technologies, combined with advanced AI analytics and algorithms, enable intelligent decision-making in traffic management. Real-time data from IoT devices combined with historical data and predictive models enable authorities to optimise signal control of traffic signals, dynamically reroute vehicles, and implement adaptive traffic management strategies. IoT technologies also enable the integration of multiple modes of transport, such as public transit, ridesharing, and non-motorised options, creating a seamless and connected urban mobility ecosystem.
- **Scalability and Flexibility**: IoT technologies provide scalability and flexibility to meet the growing number of devices and changing traffic demands in smart cities. IoT implementation permits the placement of numerous low-power, linked devices and sensors across the city, enabling in-depth data collection capabilities. IoT technologies also enable integrating different systems and technologies, facilitating interoperability between different traffic management infrastructure components.

IoT technologies are critical in smart city traffic management [10]. They offer real-time data collecting, data analysis, networking, intelligent decision-making, and scalability, allowing traffic management authorities to adopt successful traffic flow, congestion, and urban mobility plans.

9.3.3 LoRa Overview

LoRa (long range) is a wireless and open-source technology invented by a French start-up called Cycleo, developed by the Semtech Corporation in 2012 [10]. LoRa describes a low-powered sensor that transmits minuscule packets of data at a rate of between 0.3 and 5.5 kbps to a receiver across a considerable distance. It is a physical layer that uses radio frequency and chirp spread spectrum (CSS), which can operate with any media access protocol. The major goal of LoRa is to offer battery-powered devices long-range (maximum 15 km), low-data-rate (maximum 50 kbps), wireless network services. Table 9.1 shows how LPWAN differs from other wireless technologies in terms of communication range.

IoT sensors adopt a variety of wireless network protocols based on the typical performance requirements of applications. It is useful to know the advantages and disadvantages of the most widely used wireless protocols compared with LPWAN, especially in terms of main features such as energy efficiency, coverage, cost and data rate. Table 9.2 shows a comparison of various wireless technologies in terms of important features such as power, coverage, data rate, and cost.

Table 9.1 LPWAN versus Other Wireless Protocols

WPAN	WLAN	LPWAN	WMAN	WWAN
Zigbee, Bluetooth (100M)	Wifi (100M)	Sigfox and narrow-band IoT, 10KM and above, resides in WMAN	WIMAX (10KM)	2G, 3G, 4G, 5G

Table 9.2 Comparison of Wireless Protocols

Metric	Bluetooth	Bluetooth low energy	ZigBee	WiFi	Cellular M2M	LPWAN
Area coverage (>10km)	✗	✗	✗	✗	✓	✓
Low data transfer rate (<fewer than 5 kilobits per second, or 20 to 256 bytes each message)	✓	✓	✓	✗	✗	✓
Sufficient power (a single battery should last 5 to 10 years)	✓	✓	✓	✗	✗	✓
Low price	✓	✓	✓	✓	✗	✓

IoT applications are divided into two types: fixed and changeable. Street lighting and farming are examples of fixed type, while livestock and vehicles are examples of changeable type. Because of its unique adaptive data rate feature in the physical layer, LoRaWAN is best suited for fixed-type IoT applications.

ADR policy enhances network performance by improving battery life, coverage, and end-to-end connectivity. This ADR property is not available to Sigfox and narrow-band IoT (NB-IoT) networks. The layered structure of LoRaWAN comprises three levels: the LoRa physical layer, the LoRa MAC layer, and the LoRa application layer. The modulation technique determines the first LoRa physical layer, also known as the modulation layer, such as CSS. The LoRa physical layer is compatible with free ISM bands. The second layer is the LoRaWAN MAC layer, which is discussed more in the LoRaWAN section.

9.3.4 Low-Power Wide Area Network

LPWAN combines several technologies, including LoRaWAN, NB-IoT, Sigfox, random phase multiple access, weightless, and others and uses low power and long-range coverage to communicate with end devices. LoRa is an open-source technology allowing users to establish networks in unlicensed radio frequency

zones. Table 9.3 provides a quick overview of LoRaWAN and other LPWAN protocols. LoRaWAN is better than other LPWAN products in terms of availability,
mobility, and up-link/downlink communication.

9.3.5 LoRaWAN Architecture

The architecture of LoRaWAN supports direct communication between end
devices and gateways, as shown in Figure 9.2.

Table 9.3 Existing LPWAN Protocol Comparison

Metric	Sigfox	LoRaWAN	NB-IoT
Mobility metric	Poor	Good	Poor
Availability metric	Europe	Worldwide	Worldwide
Cost radio modules	<5$	<10$	<12$
Uplink/downlink communication	✓	✓	✓

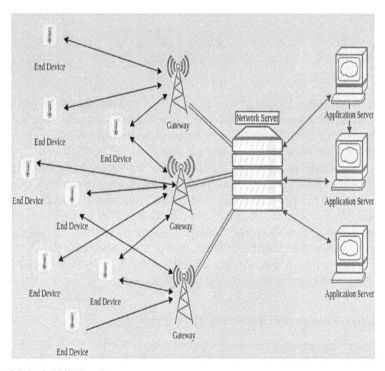

Figure 9.2 LoRaWAN architecture.

Due to the distinctive features of LoRaWAN, it is gaining popularity for use in many real-time applications. In the case of dense LoRaWAN, it is prudent to employ multi-hop communication between end devices and the gateway rather than single-hop communication, and various studies on multi-hop communication confirm that it enhances network performance.

LoRaWAN fails in dense and sparse networks and large-scale IoT applications, such as smart cities, that require many end devices or sensor nodes to communicate with multiple gateways. Gateways communicate with the network server, and the network server communicates with application server and end devices. In LoRa, bidirectional communication occurs between the end device and the gateway, the gateway and the network server (uplink), and the gateway and the end device (downlink).

Here, end devices are sending the same data repeatedly to multiple gateways because the end device transmits its data to any gateways within its radio frequency, and it is tedious for network servers to preprocess duplicate data received from multiple gateways. The LoRaWAN is configured in a star topology, with end nodes and gateways communicating both ways. After being sent via the gateway, the message is sent to the application server by the network server. The end user processes the sensor data before delivering a response message to the network server. The network server selects the appropriate gateway when sending the acknowledgement to the end node. The LoRaWAN protocols are set forth by the LoRa alliance. The range between a LoRa sender and a receiver is determined by the environment in which the device is used. Node devices are divided into three categories.

- **Class A:** When required, the end device sends a packet to the gateway and opens two receive windows to receive queued messages from the gateway.
- **Class B:** The node operates in the same way as a Class A node with more receive windows at predefined intervals. End devices are time-synchronised using gateway beacons.
- **Class C:** Maximum number of receiving slots is unsuitable for battery-powered activities since they are constantly listening.

9.3.5.1 LoRa Physical Layer

This layer employs forward error correction (FEC) and CSS for transmitting the signal. The physical layer trade-offs between the bandwidth and the sensitivity. CSS is robust to non-line of sight, outperforming when interferences exist with the help of the spreading factor provided by the LoRaWAN media access layer. Understanding the essential terms of LoRaWAN parameters such as chip, symbols, chirps, spreading factor, coding rate, and data rate is required for design, development, and deployment.

9.3.5.2 LoRa Gateway

The LoRa gateway is made up of two components: a radio module with an antenna and a microprocessor. The gateway is mains-powered and internet-connected, and it can listen to 100 devices simultaneously at each spreading factor frequency. Many gateways can receive the data packets originating from the source.

9.3.5.3 Chips, Chirps, Spreading Factor, and Symbols

The number of symbols in a LoRa system is determined by the number of chips in the system. Assume that the symbol's value is between 1 and 256. This symbol is made up of 8 bits. Figure 9.3 shows 256 symbols or chips.

Equation (9.1) and equation (9.2) calculate the chip rate and symbol rate, respectively:

$$R_C = ChipRate = \frac{Chips}{Second} \qquad (9.1)$$

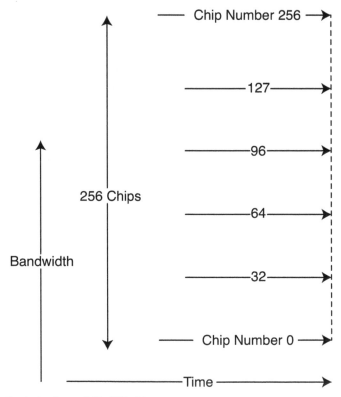

Figure 9.3 Symbol values within 256 chips.

$$R_S = SymbolRate = \frac{Symbols}{Second} \tag{9.2}$$

The bandwidth of one pulse is equal to the chip rate given in equation (3):

$$R_C = \frac{1}{BW} \tag{9.3}$$

We took the spreading factor from [7, 8, 9, 10, 11, 12]. Based on this set of values, we could transmit symbols over bandwidth. R_s from equation (2) can be represented in terms of bandwidth, given in equation (4):

$$R_S = \frac{BW}{2^{SF}}. \tag{9.4}$$

SF can be used to compute the performance of chip rate and symbol rate. We know that symbols are a combination of N chips $\in \{128, 256, 512, 1024, 2048, 4096\}$.

$$SF = log_2(N) \tag{9.5}$$

9.3.5.4 Chirp Spread Spectrum

CSS-generated chirps vary linearly with time to achieve low cost, low power consumption, and noise immunity. The chirp signal either grows or drops over time. If it increases, called up-chirp, then the minimum and maximum frequency can be represented as $f_{min} = 0$ KHz and $f_{max} = 256$ KHz, respectively, as shown in Figure 9.4(a). If it continuously decreases, called down-chirp, it can be described as $f_{max} = 256$ KHz. to $f_{min} = 0$ KHz, as shown in Figure 9.4(b). Consider the symbol 96, which has a decimal value of 96 and whose binary representation is 1100000, which indicates that this symbol has seven bits and the spreading factor is 7; substituting this binary representation generates $2^{SF} = 2^7 = 128$ chips. The symbols begin on chip 96 and continue all the way to chip 128, and the chips are shifted in a cyclical pattern from 0 to 95, as depicted in Figure 9.4(c).

9.3.5.5 Coding Rate and Data Rate

While transmitting simultaneous data packets, it is possible to lose bits due to interference, but FEC is an error-correcting method offered by LoRa that restores

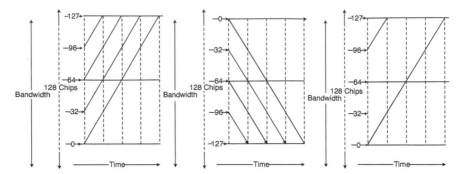

Figure 9.4 Chirp data symbols: (a) up-chirp with spread factor (SF) = 7, (b) down-chirp with SF = 7, and (c) cyclically shifted up-chirp data symbols.

lost bits. It augments the initial data with extra bits. In LoRa, the coding rate is defined as given in equation (6):

$$CodingRate = \frac{4}{4 + Code} \tag{9.6}$$

where Code 1, 2, 3, and 4 redundant bits are used in coding, and then the data rate increases and consequently more power is consumed. Data Rate can be computed as given in equation (7):

$$DR = (\frac{SF \times R_C}{2^{S \times F}}) \times (\frac{4}{4 + Code}) \tag{9.7}$$

LoRaWAN offers significant benefits for traffic management in smart cities. It provides long-distance communication, low power consumption, and high penetration capability, ensuring reliable connectivity across large geographic areas and demanding urban environments. LoRaWAN is highly scalable and cost-effective, and it allows for flexible deployment, making it suitable for managing large numbers of devices to meet traffic management needs.

9.4 ADDRESSING TRAFFIC MANAGEMENT CHALLENGES IN SMART CITIES WITH LORAWAN

In order to conduct a thorough analysis of the problems with traffic management in smart cities, it is necessary to pinpoint the main problems and comprehend how deploying LoRaWAN can assist in solving these problems. Here, we summarise some of the traffic management issues and how LoRaWAN can help find solutions:

(i) **Traffic Congestion**

   Challenge: Urban regions frequently experience traffic congestion, which increases delays, fuel consumption, and pollution [23].

   Solution: Real-time traffic monitoring and data gathering from numerous sensors placed throughout the city are made possible by LoRaWAN. This information can be used to identify crowded locations, evaluate traffic patterns, and adjust the timing of traffic signals to ease congestion [24].

(ii) **Lack of Real-Time Information**

   Challenge: Drivers and traffic management authorities struggle to make educated decisions due to a lack of real-time traffic information [25].

   Solution: Intelligent sensors and cameras that gather real-time traffic data can be used thanks to LoRaWAN. Drivers can access this information via mobile apps, dynamic signage, or connected vehicles to choose alternate routes and make wise decisions [26].

(iii) **Road Safety**

   Challenge: Because traffic accidents and injuries are such a major problem, guaranteeing traffic safety is critical to traffic management [27].

   Solution: The installation of intelligent technologies, such as connected automobiles and pedestrian detection sensors, can be supported by a LoRaWAN-based smart city infrastructure. To improve traffic safety, these systems can connect and send real-time alerts and warnings to drivers and pedestrians [28].

(iv) **Inefficient Parking Management**

   Challenge: Finding parking places in congested urban locations can be difficult, which exacerbates traffic congestion and causes frustration [29].

   Solution: Smart parking systems that employ sensors to determine whether parking spaces are available can be implemented thanks to LoRaWAN. Drivers can easily access this information via smartphone apps or sophisticated parking guidance systems to identify parking spaces [30].

(v) **Multimodal Integration**

   Challenge: To effectively reduce traffic congestion, various transportation options must be integrated, including car-sharing services, trains, bicycles, and buses [31].

   Solution: LoRaWAN can help create integrated transportation systems by facilitating communication between diverse kinds of transportation. This can make seamless ticketing, real-time arrival information, and coordinated planning possible to maximise multimodal transit and reduce reliance on private automobiles [32, 33].

In summary, LoRaWAN can help better control demanding situations in smart cities by enabling real-time statistics collection, green visitor monitoring, and advanced communication between different transportation ecosystem components. By leveraging the benefits of LoRaWAN, including long-distance connectivity, low power consumption, and scalability, cities can implement powerful visitor control solutions that result in increased visitor flow, reduced congestion, increased road safety, and overall greater urban mobility.

9.5 THE CHALLENGES WITH LORAWAN TECHNOLOGY

In order to develop an effective traffic management mechanism using LoRaWAN, optimising the transmission parameters and implementing an intelligent recommender system based on machine learning and temporal data analysis can significantly improve traffic management capabilities. Here are the best solutions for each aspect:

- **Optimising transmission parameters**: Conduct a comprehensive network environment analysis, including local electromagnetic conditions and performance targets. Implement algorithms that dynamically adjust transmission power, coding rate, spreading factor, and bandwidth based on real-time network conditions. To continuously improve network performance and traffic management, use ML algorithms to learn and change the transmission parameters [34].
- **Intelligent Recommendation**: Build a recommendation system that leverages machine learning algorithms to analyse historical and real-time traffic data. Use temporal data analysis to identify patterns, trends, and correlations in traffic flow, congestion, and other relevant factors. Implement predictive models to predict guest scenarios and optimise visitor control strategies in advance. Update information from sensors, cameras, and other IoT devices to provide accurate and timely directions to visitors. It includes smooth optimisation, congestion control, and efficient routing [35].
- **Integration with traffic management systems**: Integrating LoRaWAN-based traffic management into existing city infrastructures requires deploying LoRaWAN-enabled devices across the city. Data exchange protocols and standards are implemented to ensure interoperability between different systems. Real-time statistics collected from sensors and vehicles are used to optimise visitor traffic and reduce congestion. Cooperation with shipping authorities, city planners and era carriers guarantees seamless integration and compliance with regulatory requirements. This integration improves visitor control capabilities and creates a greener, more sustainable shipping ecosystem [36].
- **Continuous monitoring and evaluation**: Continuous monitoring is essential to ensure that the traffic management system works properly. Feedback

from sensors, cameras, and users helps evaluate effectiveness. ML algorithms analyse performance data to find areas that need improvement. Regular updates and refinements are made based on the evaluation results. By implementing these concepts, smart cities improve safety, traffic flow, and congestion while raising the overall quality of life. Traffic authorities can make data-driven judgments to efficiently manage traffic difficulties using improved transmission parameters and a smart suggestion system [37].

9.6 SYSTEM MODEL AND PROPOSED SOLUTION

The LoRaWAN study is built on real-time data from the LoRaWAN Edge Data Set. This data set is perfect for smart city research and applications. We investigate the usefulness of LoRaWAN in real-time scenarios, specifically in urban and indoor areas based on gateway placement. First, let's go over the LoED data set.

9.6.1 LoED

This repository is created from nine gateways in central London's urban areas. It contains all raw payload information and metadata collected from the gateways provided in Table 9.4. The nine gateways collected approximately 11,263,001

Table 9.4 Metrics for the LoRaWAN at the Edge Data Set

Physical layer metric	Description
Physical payload	Payload of the packet received
Gateway	Unique identification of the gateway
CRC	CRC physical layer
Frequency	Channel frequency
Spreading factor	Spreading factor value used by end device
Bandwidth	Packet bandwidth
Coding rate	Coding rate of the packet received
RSSI	Received signal strength of the packet
SNR	Signal to noise ratio of the packet
Device address	Address of the end device
Mtype	Message type request and accept of the packet
Fcnt	Frame counter of the received packet
Fport	Port of the packet

packet transmissions with different configuration parameters. These transmissions come from about 145,023 different device addresses [35].

The packet count includes both unique packets and packets that are from duplicate transmissions. These packets represent traffic generated by various smart city applications. The gateways are placed at multiple locations around the city, with five positioned outdoors on building rooftops, providing a clear line of sight to the end nodes. The final four gateways are positioned inside with a limited line of sight. One of the inner gateways is underground and cannot be seen. The collected packets leverage LoRaWAN's specific header mode and allow the retrieval of metadata data associated with specific metrics [38].

9.6.2 Gateway Details

Five of the nine gateways are located outside on top of buildings, allowing a clear line of sight. The remaining four gateways are positioned inside, where the line of sight is partially clear. One of the four inner gateways is purposefully placed on the ground and out of sight. To simplify the identification of gateways, their unique identifiers, represented in hexadecimal, are reformatted to GTWN, where N represents the gateway number. The mapping of the gateway identification numbers from hexadecimal representation to GTWN is provided in Table 9.5.

9.6.3 Comparative Analysis of Gateway Performance for Case Studies 1 and 2 of a Smart Parking System

Assume a smart city application called Smart Parking [37]. It uses IoT devices and LoRaWAN gateways to keep track of parking spaces and give drivers real-time information about available spots. We want to compare the performance of gateways GTW4 and GTW9 in supporting the smart parking system. GTW4 is placed indoors without a clear view, while GTW9 is placed outdoors with a clear

Table 9.5 Gateway Numbering to Gateway ID

Gateway Hexadecimal ID	GTWN
GTW-00000f0c210281c4	GTW1
GTW-00000f0c22433141	GTW2
GTW-00000f0c210721f2	GTW3
GTW-00000f0c224331c4	GTW4
GTW-00800000a0001914	GTW5
GTW-00800000a0001793	GTW6
GTW-00800000a0001794	GTW7
GTW-7276ff002e062804	GTW8
GTW-0000024b0b031c97	GTW9

view. These different locations can affect the network's overall performance, signal reception, and coverage for each gateway.

By analysing the performance of GTW4 and GTW9, we can understand the challenges and benefits associated with their specific deployment locations. This information can help community managers and city planners optimise the smart parking system's performance and reliability based on each gateway's placement. Comparing GTW4 and GTW9 provides valuable insights into how LoRaWAN networks can effectively enhance the smart parking experience in a smart city. With this knowledge, city governments could make informed decisions about gateway placement and manipulate strategies to ensure correct and timely parking protocols for end users. The following steps are performed to optimise the configuration parameters of the gateway deployment for the smart parking system:

- Initialize configuration parameters of LoRa/LoRaWAN: spreading factor, coding rate, transmission power, message type and so on.
- Collect records with respect to metrics from gateways (indoor and outdoor), including metadata of packets transmitted by end devices for the smart parking system.
- Conduct statistical analysis on the configuration parameters of LoRaWAN.
- Analyse gateway performance.
- Determine the optimal gateway configuration parameters.

9.7 NUMERICAL RESULTS AND DISCUSSION

We used the unique identifiers of GTW4 and GTW9 to track their packet transmission and reception rate performance. This identification helps determine the gateways responsible for receiving and transmitting parking data to the network server.

(i) **Impact of spreading factor on placement of gateway**: The spreading factor in LoRaWAN affects the performance of GTW4 and GTW9, which can be evidently seen from Figures 9.5, 9.6, and 9.7. The spreading factor determines the compromise between communication range and data rate.

GTW4 placed indoors with no clear line of sight may benefit from using a higher spread factor. Higher spreading factors increase the range and improve the gateway's ability to receive signals, even in environments with obstructions or interference. This can help GTW4 meet the indoor challenges and improve its performance in providing accurate parking information. On the other hand, GTW9 placed outdoors with a clear view may not require such a high spreading factor; since it has an unobstructed line of sight, it can pick up signals more easily. In this case, a lower spreading factor can be used to increase data rate and reduce transmission time, resulting in faster communication and improved

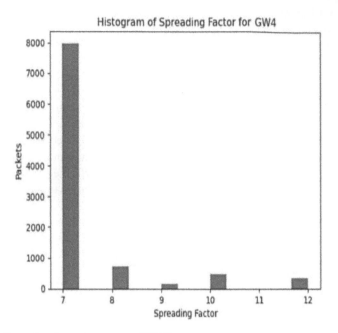

Figure 9.5 Spreading factor impact on GTW4.

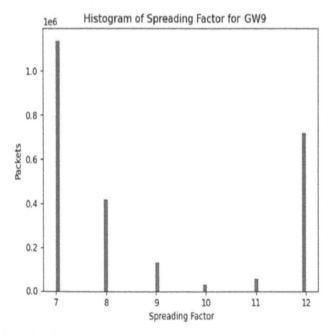

Figure 9.6 Spreading factor impact on GTW9.

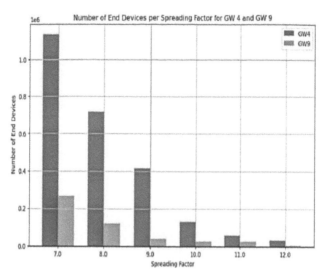

Figure 9.7 Spreading factor versus number of end devices: GTW4 and GTW9.

efficiency. Choosing the appropriate spreading factor for each gateway depends on the specific deployment scenario and the trade-offs between range, data rate, and interference. When choosing the spreading factor for GTW4 and GTW9, it is important to consider the environmental conditions, the signal strength, and the desired performance of the smart parking system.

(ii) **Received Signal Strength Indicator and Signal-to Noise-Ratio**: We compared the RSSIs and SNRs for packets received by GTW4 and GTW9, as shown in Figures 9.8, 9.9, and 9.10. Higher RSSI and better SNR indicate stronger signal reception, thus ensuring reliable transmission of parking data from IoT devices. This is crucial for the accurate detection of parking space occupancy and availability.

(iii) **Spreading factor and bandwidth**: We compared the spreading factor versus bandwidth used by end devices connected to GTW4 and GTW9 for smart parking applications. The results are given in Figure 9.11. The appropriate spreading factor and bandwidth selection ensure efficient parking data transmission and a good balance between data rate and coverage area. Optimal settings contribute to timely updates of park availability.

(iv) **Coding rate and device address**: The coding rate versus device addresses of the smart parking packets received by GTW4 and GTW9 are shown in Figures 9.12 and 9.13. This analysis helps to ensure secure and reliable communication between the IoT devices and the gateways. It enables the proper identification of parking devices and validation of parking data integrity.

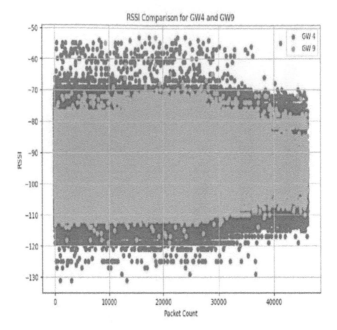

Figure 9.8 Impact of RSSI on GTW4 and GTW9.

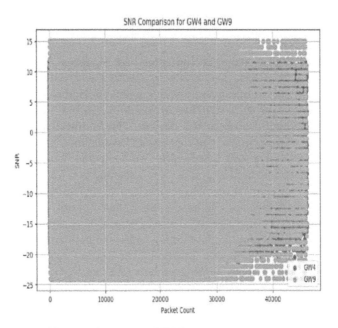

Figure 9.9 Impact of SNR on GTW4 and GTW9.

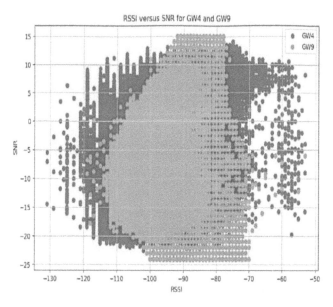

Figure 9.10 RSSI versus SNR for GTW4 and GTW9.

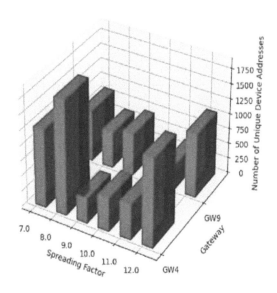

Figure 9.11 Spreading factor versus bandwidth for GTW4 and GTW9.

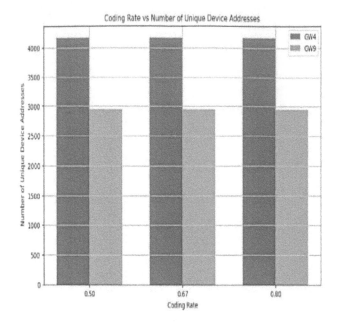

Figure 9.12 Coding factor versus device addresses for GTW4 and GTW9.

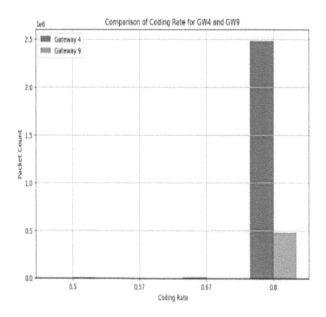

Figure 9.13 Coding rate versus packet count for GTW4 and GTW9.

(v) **Message type, frame counter, and port**: From Figure 9.14, we examine the message types, frame counts, and ports of the packets received by GTW4 and GTW9 in the smart parking application. All end devices participate in the message type (Mtype) mechanism during the LoRaWAN over-the-air-activation (OTAA) process. The Mtype of the LoRaWAN protocol, which indicates the packet type and is represented by a three-bit field in the MAC header, is crucial for this method. In the LoRaWAN data set, Table 9.6 gives each Mtype and its value. These Mtype classifications

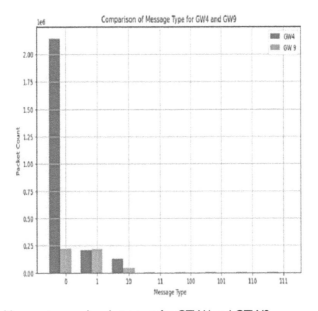

Figure 9.14 Message type and packet count for GTW4 and GTW9.

Table 9.6 Message Types and Their Values

Mtype	Value
Request for join	000
Accepted, request join	001
Request for rejoining	110
Unacknowledged data-up	010
Acknowledged data-up	100
Unacknowledged data-down	011
Acknowledged data-down	101
Proprietary	111

separate and categorise the various sorts of packets transmitted during OTAA operation and data transmission in LoRaWANs.

This data provides insight into the many sorts of parking-related reports, their ordering, and the connected application or service. It aids in the tracking of parking data flow and resource allocation for various sorts of parking-related communications.

When these comparisons are made in the context of the smart parking application, it is possible to evaluate the performance and applicability of Gateway 4 and Gateway 9 for efficiently managing parking data. This analysis can provide insights into each gateway's strengths and weaknesses, assisting in optimising overall network performance and improving the overall parking experience for drivers and city officials.

9.8 CONCLUSIONS AND FUTURE RESEARCH DIRECTIONS

In summary, evaluating Gateway 4 and Gateway 9 in the context of a smart parking system provides valuable insights into their overall performance and suitability for managing parking data. By analysing metrics such as gateway identifier, received signal strength, spreading factor, coding rate, and message types, we can assess the strengths and weaknesses of each gateway. If Gateway 4 is placed indoors without a line of sight, network performance and signal reception challenges occur, but it can still help provide parking information to motorists. Gateway 9 has advantages in terms of faster network speed and a wider coverage area when installed outdoors with a clear line of sight, making it more useful for giving real-time parking updates. This analysis suggests numerous future paths for research and development:

- **Gateway placement optimisation**: Further research can be conducted to optimise gateway placement considering signal coverage, network performance, and cost efficiency. This can result in better coverage and more accurate parking information.
- **Network optimisation**: The analysis clarifies how crucial variables like spreading factor, bandwidth, and coding rate are. Future studies can concentrate on tuning these variables to boost the performance of the smart parking application overall and network efficiency.
- **Integration with advanced technologies**: The accuracy and predictability of a smart parking system can be increased using computational methods such as machine learning and artificial intelligence. This can result in more efficient utilisation of existing parking spaces.
- **Scalability and expansion**: The scalability and growth of smart parking systems are essential as smart cities develop. Future research might solve scalability issues, accommodate more IoT devices and gateways, and

ensure a seamless connection with other smart city applications. Taking into account these potential outcomes will enhance smart parking systems, giving drivers a better experience, maximising the use of parking spaces, and boosting the general effectiveness of smart city operations.

REFERENCES

[1] Z. Qin, G. Denker, C. Giannelli, P. Bellavista and N. Venkatasubramanian, A software defined networking architecture for the Internet-of-Things, in 2014 IEEE Network Operations and Management Symposium (NOMS), Krakow, 2014, pp. 1–9, doi: 10.1109/NOMS.2014.6838365.

[2] A. El-Mougy, M. Ibnkahla and L. Hegazy, Software-defined wireless network architectures for the Internet-of-Things, in 2015 IEEE 40th Local Computer Networks Conference Workshops (LCN Workshops), Clearwater Beach, FL, 2015, pp. 804–811, doi: 10.1109/LCNW.2015.7365931.

[3] K. Sood, S. Yu, and Y. Xiang, Software-defined wireless networking opportunities and challenges for Internet-of-Things: A review, IEEE Internet of Things Journal, vol. 3, no. 4, pp. 453–463, 2016.

[4] D. H. Kim, J. B. Park, J. H. Shin, and J. D. Kim, Design and implementation of object tracking system based on Lora, in 2017 International Conference on Information Networking (ICOIN), January 2017, pp. 463–467.

[5] W. San-Um, P. Lekbunyasin, M. Kodyoo, W. Wongsuwan, J. Makfak, and J. Kerdsri, A long-range low-power wireless sensor network based on u-lora technology for tactical troops tracking systems, in 2017 Third Asian Conference on Defence Technology (ACDT), January 2017, pp. 32–35.

[6] K. Mikhaylov, J. Petajajarvi, and T. Haenninen, Analysis of capacity and scalability of the LoRa low power wide area network technology, in European Wireless 2016; 22th European Wireless Conference, May 2016, pp. 1–6.

[7] T. Petri, M. Goessens, L. Nuaymi, L. Toutain, and A. Pelov, Measurements, performance and analysis of lora fabian, a realworld implementation of LPWAN, in 2016 IEEE 27th Annual International Symposium on Personal, Indoor, and Mobile Radio Communications (PIMRC), September 2016, pp. 1–7.

[8] A. Khaleel, K. Halimjon, L. Amir, U. Nargiza, A. Mona, A. Mai, Internet of Things-aided intelligent transport systems in smart cities: Challenges, opportunities, and future, Wireless Communications and Mobile Computing, vol. 2023, Article ID 7989079, 28 pages, 2023. https://doi.org/10.1155/2023/7989079.

[9] S. U. Minhaj et al., Intelligent resource allocation in LoRaWAN using machine learning techniques, IEEE Access, vol. 11, pp. 10092–10106, 2023, doi: 10.1109/ACCESS.2023.3240308.

[10] B. Hammi, R. Khatoun, S. Zeadally, A. Fayad, and L. Khoukhi, IoT technologies for smart cities, IET Network, vol. 7, pp. 1–13, 2018. doi: 10.1049/iet- net.2017.0163.

[11] D. Kanellopoulos, V.K. Sharma, T. Panagiotakopoulos, and A. Kameas. Networking architectures and protocols for IoT applications in smart cities: Recent developments and perspectives. Electronics, vol. 12, p. 2490, 2023. doi: 10.3390/electronics12112490

[12] S.M. Abdullah, M. Periyasamy, N.A. Kamaludeen, S.K. Towfek, R. Marap-pan, S. Kidambi Raju, A.H. Alharbi, and D.S. Khafaga. Optimising traffic flow in smart cities: Soft GRU-based recurrent neural networks for enhanced congestion prediction using deep learning. Sustainability, vol. 15, p. 5949, 2023. https://doi.org/10.3390/su15075949

[13] M. Fadda, M. Anedda, R. Girau, G. Pau, and D.D. Giusto, A social Internet of Things smart city solution for traffic and pollution monitoring in Cagliari, IEEE Internet of Things Journal, vol. 10, no. 3, pp. 2373–2390, 2023, doi: 10.1109/JIOT.2022.3211093.

[14] A.I. Griva, A.D. Boursianis, S. Wan, P. Sarigiannidis, K.E. Psannis, G. Karagianni-dis, and S.K. Goudos. LoRa-based IoT network assessment in rural and urban scenarios. Sensors, vol. 23, p. 1695, 2023. doi: 10.3390/s23031695

[15] L. Ramachandran, et al., Intelligent based realtime traffic monitoring in smart cities. Irish Interdisciplinary Journal of Science Research (IIJSR), vol. 7, no. 2, pp. 10–15, 2023.

[16] C. Gao, F. Wang, X. Hu, J. Martinez. Research on sustainable design of smart cities based on the Internet of Things and ecosystems. Sustainability, vol. 15, p. 6546, 2023. doi: 10.3390/su15086546

[17] M.E.E. Alahi, A. Sukkuea, F.W. Tina, A. Nag, W. Kurdthongmee, K. Suwannarat, S.C. Mukhopadhyay. Integration of IoT-enabled technologies and artificial intelligence (AI) for Smart City scenario: Recent advancements and future trends. Sensors, vol. 23, p. 5206, 2023. https://doi.org/10.3390/s23115206 [Alpaydin, E. Machine Learning: The New AI.; MIT Press: Cambridge, MA, USA, 2016].

[18] S. Ray. A quick review of machine learning algorithms, in Proceedings of the 2019 International Conference on Machine Learning, Big Data, Cloud and Parallel Computing (COMITCon), Faridabad, 14–16 February 2019, pp. 35–39.

[19] A.K. Tyagi, and P. Chahal. Artificial intelligence and machine learning algorithms, in Research Anthology on Machine Learning Techniques, Methods, and Applications, IGI Global, Hershey, PA, 2022, pp. 421–446.

[20] A.S. Syed, D. Sierra-Sosa, A. Kumar, and A. Elmaghraby. IoT in smart cities: A survey of technologies, practices and challenges. Smart Cities, vol. 4, pp. 429–475, 2021. doi: 10.3390/smartcities4020024

[21] Y.B. Zikria, R. Ali, M.K. Afzal, and S.W. Kim. Next-generation Internet of Things (IoT): Opportunities, challenges, and solutions. Sensors, vol. 21, p. 1174. doi: 10.3390/s21041174

[22] S. Djahel, R. Doolan, and G.-M. Muntean and J. Murphy. A communications-oriented perspective on traffic management systems for smart cities: Challenges and innovative approaches, IEEE Communications Surveys Tutorials, vol. 17, no. 1, pp. 125–151, Firstquarter 2015, doi: 10.1109/COMST.2014.2339817.

[23] D. Asiain, and D. Antol'ın. LoRa-based traffic flow detection for smart-road. Sensors, vol. 21, p. 338, 2021. doi: 10.3390/s21020338

[24] D. Oladimeji, K. Gupta, N.A. Kose, K. Gundogan, L. Ge, and F. Liang. Smart transportation: An overview of technologies and applications. Sensors, vol. 23, p. 3880, 2023. doi: 10.3390/s23083880

[25] E.T. de Camargo, F.A. Spanhol, A.R. Castro e Souza'. Deployment of a LoRaWAN network and evaluation of tracking devices in the context of smart cities. Journal Internet Service Application, vol. 12, no. 8, 2021. doi: 10.1186/s13174-021-00138-7

[26] A. Rao and B. S. Chaudhari. Development of LoRaWAN based traffic clearance system for emergency vehicles, in 2020 Fourth International Conference on I-SMAC (IoT in Social, Mobile, Analytics and Cloud) (I-SMAC), Palladam, 2020, pp. 217–221, doi: 10.1109/I-SMAC49090.2020.9243341.

[27] G. Ali, T. Ali, M. Irfan, U. Draz, M. Sohail, A. Glowacz, M. Sulow- icz, R. Mielnik, Z.B. Faheem, and C. Martis. IoT based smart parking system using deep long short memory network. Electronics, vol. 9, p. 1696, 2020. doi: 10.3390/electronics9101696

[28] T. Boshita, H. Suzuki, and Y. Matsumoto. IoT-based bus location system using LoRaWAN, 2018 21st International Conference on Intelligent Transportation Systems (ITSC), Maui, HI, 2018, pp. 933–938. doi: 10.1109/ITSC.2018.8569920.

[29] S. Hattarge, A. Kekre, and A. Kothari, LoRaWAN based GPS tracking of city-buses for smart public transport system, in 2018 First International Conference on Secure Cyber Computing and Communication (ICSCCC), Jalandhar, 2018, pp. 265–269, doi: 10.1109/ICSCCC.2018.8703356.

[30] S. Muhammad, A. Sagheer, T.M Ghazal, A.K. Muhammad, S. Nizar, and M. Ahmad, Smart cities: Fusion-based intelligent traffic congestion control system for vehicular networks using machine learning techniques, Egyptian Informatics Journal, vol. 23, no. 3, pp. 417–426, 2022.

[31] E. Sallum, N. Pereira, M. Alves, and M. Santos, Performance optimisation on LoRa networks through assigning radio parameters, in 2020 IEEE International Conference on Industrial Technology (ICIT), Buenos Aires, 2020, pp. 304–309, doi: 10.1109/ICIT45562.2020.9067310.

[32] F. Cuomo, D. Garlisi, and A. Martino. Predicting LoRaWAN behavior: How machine learning can help. Computers, vol. 9, p. 60, 2020. doi: 10.3390/computers9030060

[33] S.B. Seo, P. Yadav, and D. Singh. LoRa based architecture for smart town traffic management system. Multimed Tools Applications, vol. 81, pp. 26593–26608, 2022. doi:10.1007/s11042-020-10091-5

[34] J. Sanchez-Gomez, J. Gallego-Madrid, R. Sanchez-Iborra, and A. F. Skarmeta, Performance study of LoRaWAN for smart-city applications, 2019 IEEE 2nd 5G World Forum (5GWF), Dresden, 2019, pp. 58–62, doi: 10.1109/5GWF.2019.8911676

[35] L. Bhatia, M. Breza, R. Marfievici, and J. A. McCann, LoED: The LoRaWAN at the edge dataset: dataset, in Proceedings of the Third Workshop on Data: Acquisition To Analysis (DATA 20). Association for Computing Machinery, New York, USA, 2020, pp. 7–8, doi: 10.1145/3419016.3431491

[36] C. Biyik, Z. Allam, G. Pieri, D. Moroni, M. O'Fraifer, E. O'Connell, S. Olariu, and M. Khalid. Smart parking systems: reviewing the literature, architecture and ways forward. Smart Cities, vol. 4, pp. 623–642, 2021. doi: 10.3390/smartcities4020032

[37] R.K. Kodali, K.Y. Borra, G.N. Sharan Sai, and H.J. Domma, An IoT based smart parking system using LoRa, in 2018 International Conference on Cyber-Enabled Distributed Computing and Knowledge Discovery (CyberC), Zhengzhou, 2018, pp. 151–1513, doi: 10.1109/CyberC.2018.00039.

[38] P. Spadaccino, F.G. Criño, and F. Cuomo. LoRaWAN behaviour analysis through dataset traffic investigation. Sensors, vol. 22, p. 2470, 2022. doi: 10.3390/s22072470.

Chapter 10

Using the Internet of Medical Things to Self-Monitor Vital Parameters

Aishwarya

10.1 INTRODUCTION

The Internet of Medical Things (IoMT) has revolutionised monitoring vital health parameters continuously and unobtrusively. IoMT facilitates seamless connectivity between these monitoring tools and the Internet, facilitating health data collection, sharing, and analysis. This interconnected system empowers individuals to continuously monitor their health metrics, promoting proactive health management and early detection of potential issues. It enables the effortless tracking of essential physiological parameters. By integrating wearable devices, biosensors, and mobile applications, real-time monitoring of these vital signs has become convenient and accessible. Next, we describe the vital parameters and wearable devices for monitoring.

10.1.1 Key Vital Parameters

People can actively monitor their health states using IoMT devices and identify any deviations or changes that might call for medical intervention. Some of the essential physiological measurements include the following:

10.1.1.1 Blood Pressure

The heart is vital in distributing blood throughout tissues and organs. During each heartbeat, blood is propelled into the major arteries of the circulatory system. This circulating blood exerts pressure against the walls of the blood vessels as it traverses the body. Blood pressure (BP) readings comprise two values:

- Systolic blood pressure: During this phase, the heart muscle contracts during its beat, propelling oxygen-rich blood into the blood vessels.
- Diastolic blood pressure: This refers to the pressure within the blood vessels during diastole, the heart's relaxation phase.

DOI: 10.1201/9781003486930-14

BP is measured in millimetres of mercury (mmHg). The values are recorded as a pair, with the higher systolic value preceding the lower diastolic value. For instance, a systolic pressure of 132 mmHg and a diastolic pressure of 88 mmHg is read as 132/88 mmHg.

10.1.1.2 Heart Rate

The rate of heartbeats per minute is a vital measurement [1]. A distinctive medical and health science component is the heart rate measurement and electrical pulse signal analysis, which is accurate, resilient, and less expensive and takes little power [2].

10.1.1.3 Respiratory Rate

An IoMT device to estimate the respiration rate is proposed in [3]. The core objective of this study is to calculate the frequency of breaths taken within a minute. The method analyses the respiration rate (RR) and body temperature using LM35 and MLX90614 sensors. These sensors are connected with the Arduino Mega 2560 microcontroller using the ESP8266 as a Wi-Fi module. This integration allows for efficient data collection and transmission, enabling accurate respiration rate and body temperature assessment.

10.1.1.4 Body Temperature

Monitoring body temperature helps spot fevers or keep track of temperature fluctuations over time. This can be accomplished using digital thermometers, wearable patches, or smart thermometers linked to mobile applications. The authors of [4] utilised a heartbeat sensor and body temperature and consistently logs heart rate data into a designated ".txt" file. Among the commonly employed temperature sensors, prevalent models include LM-35, DS18B20, TMP236, and MAX3020 [5]. Notably, the LM-35 sensor holds prominence in remote patient monitoring in wearable sensor networks [5].

10.1.1.5 Sleep Patterns

Monitoring sleep patterns and spotting probable sleep problems can be made easier by tracking sleep metrics like length, quality, and interruptions. Sleep monitoring features are frequently available on sleep trackers and smartwatches. Chronic stress can adversely affect one's relationships, career, health, and sense of self. The SaYoPillow framework introduces an edge device to enhance the understanding of the correlation between stress and sleep to fully actualise the idea of "smart sleeping" [5, 6]. SaYo-Pillow advocates for the continuous monitoring of physiological signals in real-time, enabling the assessment of sleep quality while considering factors given in Table 10.1.

Table 10.1 Factors Needed for Self-Monitoring in the SaYoPillow [5]

S.no	Factor
1	The number of hours of sleep
2	Snoring range
3	Respiratory rate range
4	Heart rate range
5	Oxygen in the blood range
6	Eye movement rate or amount of REM time
7	Limb movement rate
8	Change in body temperature

10.1.2 Wearable Devices for Vital Parameter Monitoring

Wearable sensors are cutting-edge medical tools that continuously monitor physiological and biological data. Due to their immunity to electromagnetic interference, miniaturisation, ability to detect nano-volumes, integration with fibre, high sensitivity, low cost, adaptability to severe conditions, and corrosion resistance, optical wearable sensors have emerged as a sensing technology.

Biosignals are the bioelectric signals produced by an organ's electrical activity. These are fluctuations in electrical currents attributed to variations in electric potential disparities across specific organs or tissues, encompassing nervous, respiratory, and cardiovascular systems. Based on electrical processes, the human body produces many biosignals. Electrocardiograms (ECGs), photoplethysmograms (PPGs), electroencephalograms (EEGs), electromyograms, electrooculograms, galvanic skin responses, electroretinograms, and electrogastrograms are a few examples of bioelectric signals. The characteristics of ECG, PPG, and EEG signals are shown in this section of the paper, along with their graphical waveforms.

- **(A) Electrocardiogram:** ECG is a technique for diagnosing cardiovascular system issues that use wires, electrodes, and gels. An ECG captures the heart's electrical activity by positioning the electrode above the skin at a specific spot on the body.
- **(B) Photoplethysmogram:** PPG detects blood volume changes.
- **(C) Electroencephalogram:** EEG detects electrical activity in the brain.

10.2 SENSORS AND TECHNIQUES TO MONITOR KEY VITAL PARAMETERS FOR SELF-MONITORING

Here, we discuss the types of IoMT sensors that are used to measure the vital health parameters:

Blood pressure measurement techniques and considerations: In one relevant study [7], the objective was to assess the effectiveness and potential benefits of self-monitoring blood pressure in individuals who had experienced a prior stroke or transient ischemic attack combined with regulated medication adjustments. BP was optimised using quantitative analysis of the data in Statistical Package for the Social Sciences, enabling a comparison of participants' initial characteristics [7]. Descriptive statistics are employed to present continuous data as mean + standard deviation (SD) and categorical variables as count (percentage). The residential areas are grouped as extensive mixed urban and rural areas, small mixed urban and rural areas, and large urban areas. The authors employed thematic analysis to delve into the emerging themes extracted from post-trial interviews with patients and participating general practitioners.

Indications for self-monitoring for BP include living in an urban region, having comorbid conditions, visiting a doctor frequently, receiving guidance on the devices to be used for BP self-monitoring, and having knowledge of self-care for hypertension. Few people actually self-monitor their blood pressure [8].

Temperature sensing and its applications: This research [9] offers a new technique for creating high-stability temperature sensors for bearing spinning parts that has practical applications. The developed CdTe@SiO2/PVA hybrid film demonstrates its applicability as a temperature sensor for swiftly rotating bearing components.

Oxygen saturation monitoring for respiratory health: Continuous respiratory rate and oxygen saturation monitoring remains imperative. On March 11, 2020, the World Health Organization (WHO) officially categorised COVID-19 as a pandemic. According to WHO data, by January 7, 2023, there were 662,757,682 globally confirmed COVID-19 cases, resulting in 6,702,115 fatalities [10]. Respiratory rate is a pivotal physiological indicator for detecting anomalies within the human body, and PPG determines both RR and SpO2 levels. Notably, the Gaussian process regression model outperformed other models in estimating RR and SpO2 readings.

RR, denoting the number of breathing cycles occurring each minute, is often measured in breaths per minute (bpm). For adults, the typical RR ranges from 12 to 22 bpm [11]. Additionally, the frequency of respiration, expressed in hertz (Hz), serves as another common indicator of respiratory rate. RR holds valuable significance in various contexts, including with asthma, sleep apnea, COVID-19, postoperative respiratory instability, and sports science. Wearable sensors that detect RR can be categorised based on the observed stimulus. Notably, differentiating between inhaling through the nose and mouth and exhaling is crucial. Exhalation induces airflow while elevating temperature and humidity levels. This distinction guides the categorisation of wearable sensors for respiratory rate detection.

10.3 DATA COLLECTION, ANALYSIS, AND INTERPRETATION

Data collection is the process of collecting information or data from multiple sources. Data can be collected from multiple sources, such as surveys, interviews, observations, and experiments. In IoMT applications, collected data can include vital signs, activity levels, glucose levels, and other metrics. IoMT sensors on wearable devices capture and transmit real-time patient data; in turn, medical imaging can be digitally captured, stored, and transmitted across networks for analysis and diagnosis, including via remote IoMT access to imaging data. For instance, a system can collect pulse oxygen level and RT-PCR results to easily classify individuals as infected with COVID-19. IoMT devices can also integrate with electronic health record systems, automatically transferring patient data from the devices to the records. This gives healthcare providers up-to-date information for diagnosis and treatment decisions.

In IoMT, mobile applications are increasingly used to collect data. The data is frequently sent to cloud-based services for processing or stored locally on the device. The system incorporates a trio of consortium blockchains to distribute transaction loads and reduce transaction delays effectively. Encrypted health data from medical sensors is transmitted to the doctor through a mobile application, ensuring privacy and security. This information can either be gathered automatically or manually input by the patient or a caregiver [12].

Wearable IoMT sensor devices allow for patients' and providers' real-time monitoring of the patients' health states, but cloud computing is crucial in this process. The stored, processed, and analysed data is safely transported to cloud-based platforms. For managing massive volumes of IoMT data, cloud platforms offer scalability, accessibility, and advanced analytics capabilities.

Leveraging an IoT framework, an essential solution can be developed for secure self-diagnosis of COVID-19 without compromising user data security and with the added benefit of cost-effective cloud-based data analytics. Incorporating advanced technologies such as AI, machine learning, and 5G can potentially diminish the adverse effects of COVID-19 and contribute to its recovery [13]. Implementing this solution can effectively alleviate the impact of COVID-19 utilising readily accessible local resources and expertise.

Real-time feedback and alerts for personal health management: The real-time collection and analysis of health-related data have never been more straightforward, thanks to technological advances and the rising popularity of wearable devices. Real-time feedback and notifications can help with personal health management in various ways, as shown in Figure 10.1.

There should be continuous monitoring of the vital features that give real-time feedback and alerts. Self-monitoring devices can help individuals identify in real

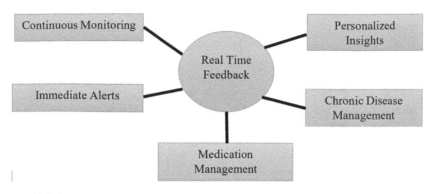

Figure 10.1 Real-time feedback and warnings.

time when vital signs reach problematic levels, which is particularly valuable for sufferers of chronic diseases such as diabetes and heart disease. Devices and systems can also recognise patterns and trends unique to the user to identify possible hazards. Alert notifications can be sent to individuals' mobile devices and even to their medical personnel. Getting immediate notifications can help you handle health issues quickly and possibly avoid serious consequences.

10.4 MACHINE LEARNING AND AI IN SELF-MONITORING

COVID-19 has the potential to be self-diagnosed, self-monitored, and self-managed through the utilisation of individual mobile devices, personal data, cloud services, mobile apps, intelligent IoT systems, AI, machine learning, and 5G technologies. Integrating machine learning algorithms permits continuous real-time monitoring and fine-tuning of sensor capabilities [14]. Figure 10.2 presents a potential framework for an IoMT-based healthcare system.

Data collection is the foundation of any AI IoMT system as it is data that provides insightful results or improves decision-making capability. However, several problems and concerns arise from the vast amounts of sensor-based data that are gathered from such an extensive network. Specialised algorithms are used to deal with data-collecting failures, such as highly concurrent and massive data-gathering algorithms, clustering-based algorithms, and privacy-preserving algorithms [15].

10.5 DATA SECURITY AND PRIVACY CHALLENGES IN IOMT

Security is a crucial concern for data interchange between medical devices in IoMT-based systems. Medical data is extremely sensitive, and IoMT-based systems process and record this data. Because of their diverse design and dependency

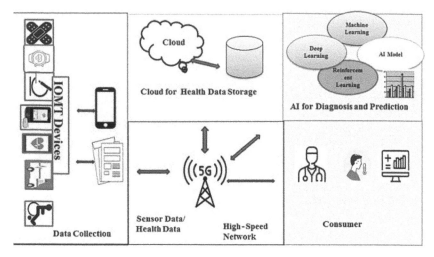

Figure 10.2 AI-based architecture framework for a smart healthcare system [15].

on wireless communication, IoMT-based systems are vulnerable to wireless network-based assaults. Eavesdropping and man-in-the-middle assaults are two of the most severe risks to wireless communication in general, and privacy is a significant concern in the IoMT context as well [16]. Figure 10.3 graphically displays the necessary security concerns to address in IoMT.

10.6 FUTURE DIRECTIONS AND EMERGING TRENDS

Real-time monitoring of patients' healthcare data through the Internet of Medical Things is revolutionising the efficiency and accuracy of patient treatment. However, despite its cutting-edge and recent development, the IoMT faces susceptibility to cyberattacks due to its heterogeneous nature.

Integration of PPG with other biosensors for comprehensive monitoring: Integrating photoplethysmography with other biosensors allows for comprehensive monitoring of various physiological parameters, producing a more holistic and in-depth understanding of a patient's health status. Emerging trends will likely focus on enhancing user-friendly devices and platforms, promoting greater accessibility, and optimising data security and privacy. With an integrated network, the IoMT helps with real-time patient monitoring and enables all relevant healthcare domains to function as a single entity. However, it is strongly advised and necessary to teach IT and medical professionals

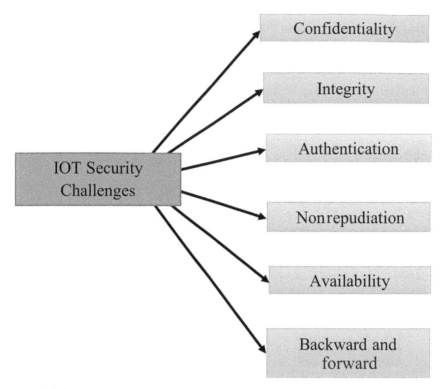

Figure 10.3 Security requirements in IoMT devices.

to protect them against cyberattacks to preserve a high degree of privacy, security, accuracy, and trust [16]. We are exploring the application of block-chain and IoT in demand-side management and supply chain (SC), especially regarding security, privacy, authentication, interoperability, and exchange of medical records.

10.7 CONCLUSION

The Internet of Medical Things represents a groundbreaking application of IoT technology in the integration of medical devices and systems. Through IoMT, individuals can engage in self-monitoring of vital parameters, such as heart rate, blood pressure, and oxygen saturation, using wearable technology and mobile applications. This seamless connectivity between devices and the Internet enables the collection and exchange of health data, which can be analysed using machine learning and AI to identify trends and potential health risks. IoMT empowers individuals to take an active role in their healthcare management, promoting preventive care and early intervention for improved health outcomes. Additionally, smart devices emerge as a key platform for telemedicine applications, offering practical ways to encourage healthy behaviors. Overall, IoMT's potential to enhance real-time monitoring and personalised healthcare makes it a promising and transformative technology in the medical field.

REFERENCES

[1] Chirakanphaisarn, Neramitr, Thadsanee Thongkanluang, and Yuwathida Chiwpreechar. "Heart rate measurement and electrical pulse signal analysis for subjects span of 20–80 years," 2016 Sixth International Conference on Digital Information Processing and Communications (ICDIPC), Beirut, 2016, pp. 70–74, doi: 10.1109/ICDIPC.2016.7470794.

[2] Chirakanphaisarn, Neramitr, Thadsanee Thongkanluang, and Yuwathida Chiwpreechar. "Heart rate measurement and electrical pulse signal analysis for subjects span of 20–80 years." 2016 Sixth International Conference on Digital Information Processing and Communications (ICDIPC). IEEE, 2016.

[3] Hadis, Nor Shahanim Mohamad, et al. "IoT based patient monitoring system using sensors to detect, analyse and monitor two primary vital signs." Journal of Physics: Conference Series 1535.1 (2020).

[4] Ashfaq, Zarlish, et al. "A review of enabling technologies for Internet of Medical Things (IoMT) Ecosystem." Ain Shams Engineering Journal 13.4 (2022): 101660.

[5] Rachakonda, Laavanya, et al. "SaYoPillow: Blockchain-integrated privacy-assured iomt framework for stress management considering sleeping habits." IEEE Transactions on Consumer Electronics 67.1 (2020): 20–29.

[6] Rachakonda, Laavanya, et al. "Sayopillow: Blockchain-integrated privacy-assured iomt framework for stress management considering sleeping habits." IEEE Transactions on Consumer Electronics 67.1 (2020): 20–29.

[7] Doogue, Roisin, et al. "Towards an integrated blood pressure self-monitoring solution for stroke/TIA in Ireland: a mixed methods feasibility study for the TASMIN5S IRL randomised controlled trial." Pilot and Feasibility Studies 9.1 (2023): 9.

[8] Edmealem, Afework, et al. "Blood pressure self-monitoring practice and associated factors among adult hypertensive patients on follow-up at South Wollo Zone Public Hospitals, Northeast Ethiopia." Open Heart 10.1 (2023): e002274.

[9] Pan Zhang, Aizhao Pan, Ke Yan, Yongsheng Zhu, Jun Hong, and Panting Liang. "High-efficient and reversible temperature sensor fabricated from highly luminescent CdTe/ZnS-SiO2 nanocomposites for rolling bearings." Sensors and Actuators A: Physical, 328 (2021): 112758. https://doi.org/10.1016/j.sna.2021.112758.

[10] Vital Signs. Available online: https://my.clevelandclinic.org/health/articles/10881-vital-signs (accessed on August 22 2021)

[11] Mirjalali, S., S. Peng, Z. Fang, C.-H. Wang, S. Wu. "Wearable sensors for remote health monitoring: potential applications for early diagnosis of Covid-19." Advance Materials Technology 7 (2022): 2100545.

[12] Kamal, Randa, Ezz El-Din Hemdan, and Nawal El-Fishway. "Care4U: Integrated healthcare systems based on blockchain." Blockchain: Research and Applications (2023): 100151.

[13] Ahmed, S., J. Yong, and Shrestha, A. "The integral role of intelligent IoT System, cloud computing, artificial intelligence, and 5g in the user-level self-monitoring of COVID-19." Electronics 12 (2023): 1912. https://doi.org/10.3390/electronics12081912

[14] Khan, Aimal, König Tobias, Liebgott Florian, and Greiner Thomas. Self-Monitoring of external magnetic interference in magnetostrictive position sensors using machine learning. In Proceedings of the 2023 8th International Conference on Machine Learning Technologies (ICMLT 23). Association for Computing Machinery, New York, USA, 2023, pp. 8–14. https://doi.org/10.1145/3589883.3589885

[15] Mishra, Divya, Pushpa Singh, and Shivani Agarwal. "AI-and IoT-based architecture in healthcare." Transformation in Healthcare with Emerging Technologies (2022): 1–18.

[16] Bhushan, Bharat, Kumar Avinash, Agarwal Ambuj Kumar, Kumar Amit, Bhattacharya Pronaya, and Kumar Arun. Towards a secure and sustainable Internet of Medical Things (IoMT): Requirements, design challenges, security techniques, and future trends. Sustainability 15 (2023): 6177. https://doi.org/10.3390/su15076177.

Smart Grid Technologies and Renewable Energy

Chapter 11

Renewable Energy Technologies in Smart Cities

Ram Niwash Mahia, Hemant Kaushik,
Raghawendra Mishra and Om Prakash Mahela

11.1 INTRODUCTION

Cities are becoming centers of economic development due to innovations such as utilizing renewable energy (RE). This has created opportunities for sustainable development [1]. Energy demand in smart cities can be met while eradicating carbon footprint and emission of greenhouse gas (GHG) [2]. This can be achieved by increasing the use of RE sources to meet energy demand of smart cities. Various methods are reported to achieve this objective.

In [3], the authors presented a framework for assessing the availability of RE for meeting electricity demand in 45 smart cities in India; the authors established that RE penetration needs to expand from existing levels. In [4], the authors proposed using RE sources to meet 100% of smart city energy demand including for industry and transport requirements in smart cities. In [5], the authors presented a P-Graph technique to design optimal energy systems that link industry with smart cities.

In [6], the authors describe the technologies deployed in a smart city power network: energy storage system (ESS), demand side management, grid security, communication technologies and privacy. A detailed analysis of grid integration of RE resources, ESS, electric vehicles (EVs) and concepts of smart lighting in smart cities is presented in [7]. In [8], the authors presented a study on the use of RE in smart cities, current trends in RE installations and various technologies utilized for storing and distributing RE in smart cities.

We performed a detailed review of the literature, identified 68 relevant studies and established that detailed knowledge of RE sources such as technology, operational methods, key algorithms and energy management system will help to increase the use of RE to meet smart city energy needs. We divide the 68 research papers into the following four major categories:

- The first group [1–8] includes the general ideas of a smart city and RE applications to meet smart city energy demand.
- The second category [9–13] includes the detailed study of factors that comprise a smart city.

DOI: 10.1201/9781003486930-16

- The third category [14–20] includes the detailed study of energy management systems in smart cities.
- The fourth category [21–68] describes RE technology divided into subcategories: [21–22] describe the general concepts of RE sources and categorize them, [22–41] present solar energy technology, [42–57] elaborate wind energy technology, [58–63] illustrate geothermal technology and [64–68] describe miscellaneous concepts of RE sources in smart cities.

11.2 THE CONCEPT OF SMART CITIES

Future smart cities are intended to meet the needs of fast-growing populations. Developments in in information and communication technologies have resulted in the effective management of available resources [9]. Urban migration is increasing rapidly, which is causing new challenges, and creating sustainable and reasonable space in the cities has become challenging task worldwide.

Future models of smart cities ensure citizen well-being through industry development and urban planning. The four core factors of smart city are citizen, life, environment, and governance, and Figure 11.1 presents the subfactors in each category [10]. A detailed study of integrated green energy development of smart cities is reported in [11], including the methods, findings and implications from theoretical and analytical discussion. A detailed study of societal concept of smart city is discussed in [12]. Smart cities differ from smart homes in design components. A brief comparison between smart cities and smart homes is elaborated in Table 11.1 [13].

11.3 ENERGY MANAGEMENT IN SMART CITIES

RE is environmentally friendly and infinite, but efficient and cost-effective methods are needed to harness RE for uninterrupted energy provision. Various categories of energy systems of smart city are elaborated in Figure 11.2 [14]. Major

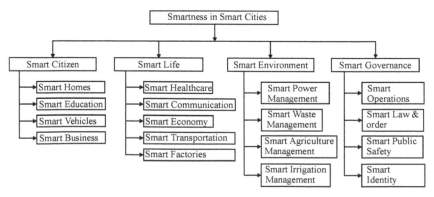

Figure 11.1 Smartness in smart cities.

Table 11.1 Differences between Smart Homes and Smart Cities

S. No.	Categories	Smart home concept	Smart city concept
1	Data storage	On-premise	Cloud computing
2	End-users	Homeowners	Citizens
3	Internet of things devices	50 or more	10 million or more
4	Scale	Small	Large
5	Connectivity	Separated	Integrated
6	Energy saving benefit	Direct	Indirect
7	Feature	Functionality	Compatibility
8	Property	Private property	Public property

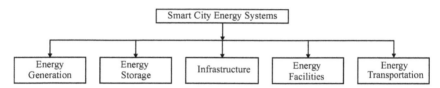

Figure 11.2 Components of smart city energy systems.

Table 11.2 EMS Criteria for Smart Cities

S. No.	Criterion	Description
1	Load/Device	Load is a functional junction
2	Rate	Cost considered proportionate to demand
3	Maximum Limit of Load	Maximum load that can be catered
4	Period	Time of energy utilization
5	Device Priority	The real-time device priority might be high, moderate or low, or it might not be required. Device priority is as follows: Real-time: critical device High: demand is high Moderate: average demand that can be compromised Low: device can be shut down for the nodes Not needed: device is off unless it is required

research focuses in the field of energy management for smart cities include RE integration, power network upgrade, ESS, vehicle to grid, metering infrastructure using emerging technology, demand side management, demand response, artificial intelligence (AI), machine learning (ML), data clouds, security of data, bidirectional energy trade, local trade and distributed grid control [15]. Common EMS criteria for smart cities are elaborated in Table 11.2 [16].

A detailed study of challenges faced in energy management in smart buildings is presented in [17], such as inefficient energy utilization, consumption and drain; the authors discuss in detail the relationships among smart city energy management policies. In [18], the authors presented a detailed study to establish coordination among home energy and EV parking lot management systems in a smart city. The system modeled, simulated and computationally implemented a real-life study. In [19], the authors presented a fuzzy rough set that supported self-sustainable energy management for smart cities; a traditional heating and cooling system is modified to minimize the electricity consumption. In [20], the authors presented a priority-driven seven-layer mechanism for green energy management in a smart city.

11.4 RENEWABLE ENERGY TECHNOLOGIES

Thermal power generation units and RE units are used for meeting smart city energy demand [21]. Coal-fired thermal power plants produce environmental emissions like sulfur dioxides, carbon dioxides and nitrogen oxides that degrade air quality and contribute to climate change effects such as acid rain [22]. Hence, RE is the natural choice for meeting the sustainable energy requirements of smart cities. Figure 11.3 presents some major RE sources that can be used for meeting smart city energy requirements, and we next discuss other RE sources (wind, solar, geothermal).

11.4.1 Solar Energy Technologies

Solar thermal and solar photovoltaic (PV) technology is used to meet smart city energy demand. Solar PV systems are commonly installed on rooftops or as centralized power plants integrated with the power networks of smart cities [23]. A grid-equipped solar PV plant is illustrated in Figure 11.4. The PV array, DC–DC converter, inverter, AC filter and distribution panel are the main components [24].

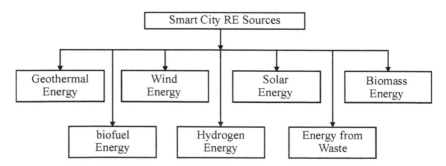

Figure 11.3 Smart city RE sources.

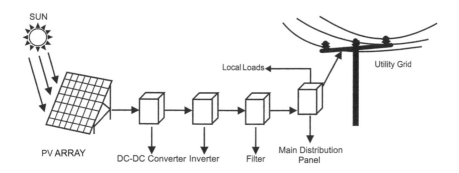

Figure 11.4 Solar PV system.

A detailed study of various components and technology of solar PV units is presented in [25]. Solar thermal technology uses parabolic trough, linear Fresnel, solar tower and solar dish as elaborated in Figure 11.5 [26]. Single-diode equivalent circuit is used to form the solar cells. The output voltage (V) and output current (I) of solar cell are related as described in equation (11.1):

$$I = P_{ph} - I_0 \left\{ exp \left[\frac{q(V + IR_s)}{AkT} \right] - 1 \right\} - \left(\frac{V + IR_s}{R_{sh}} \right) \tag{11.1}$$

where I_{ph}: photo-current of PV cell; I_0: saturation current; A: factor of curve fitting; Rsh: shunt resistance; R_s: series resistance; q: charge on electron and k: Boltzmann constant.

The authors of [27, 28] presented detailed studies of a smart city solar thermal power system. In [29], the authors presented a study of challenges in incorporating PV systems into smart city power grids and introduced a method using digital twin simulations for connecting solar energy units into smart cities. In [30], the authors presented a method using random forest regression and artificial neural network for the accurate prediction of solar power output in smart cities. In [31], the authors presented a naïve Bayes classifier for cooling and heating using a solar energy system in smart cities. Scholars have produced detailed literature related to different solar energy technologies, technical problems encountered and their possible solutions for smart city application [32–41].

11.4.2 Wind Energy Technologies

Wind turbines are used to meet energy demand for smart cities because of their competitive costs and ease of implementation. However, they are limited by their site-specific requirements for optimum wind speed [42]. A wind power plant (WPP)

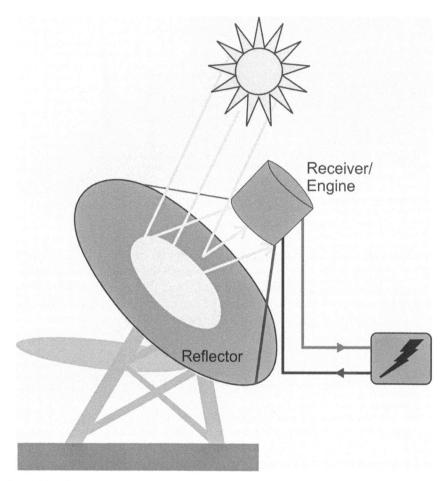

Figure 11.5 Solar thermal power plant.

is elaborated in Figure 11.6, and different energy conversion stages are described in Figure 11.7. Turbines convert wind energy into rotational kinetic energy (KE) and couple with generators that convert the rotational KE to electrical power. Generally, 25–30% of wind energy is converted to useful electrical power [43]. Mechanical output of wind turbine which has been converted into electrical power is given by equation (11.2):

$$P_m = \frac{1}{2}\rho A v^3 C_p(\lambda, \beta) \qquad (11.2)$$

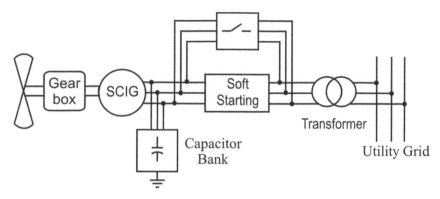

Figure 11.6 Wind-turbine-based WPP.

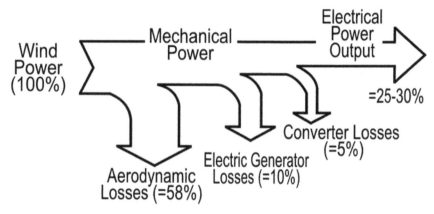

Figure 11.7 Different energy conversion stages in a WPP.

where A: area swept by rotor blades; λ: tip-speed ratio; C_p: power coefficient; and β: blade pitch angle.

Researchers in [44] proposed back-propagation neural network clustering to enhance stability and harmonic reduction in wind turbines for use in smart cities. The authors of [45] conducted a detailed analysis of expanding sustainable wind energy to meet smart city energy demand. Others proposed a method of optimizing the neural network parameters for the short-term forecasting of wind energy to meet smart city energy requirements [46]. Detailed literature findings related to different wind energy technologies, technical problems encountered and their possible solutions for smart city applications are available in [47–57].

11.4.3 Geothermal Energy Technologies

Geothermal energy (GE) is generated and stored inside the core of the earth; it is clean in nature and sustainable, it can be recycled, it is economically viable and it has utilization potential. It has zero carbon emissions as well. The temperature of Earth's core is 6650 °C, but the heat from the core is obtained from different layers. GE is an important source of cooling for passive buildings in smart cities. Hot water is extracted to the earth's surface, pressurized and flash-steamed in a turbine that in turn rotates a generator to produce electricity. Steam is cooled and reinjected into the reservoir to form the closed loop. A geothermal energy generation block scheme is illustrated in Figure 11.8 [58–60].

A detailed study for harvesting the heat energy from geothermal for use in sustainable cities is reported in [61]. Main applications are fuel saving, energy efficient buildings, reduction in temperature and improved outdoor thermal comfort. In [62], the authors introduced a regional energy system optimization approach for investigating techno-economic capabilities of low-carbon lithium extraction directly from deep geothermal plants. A detailed study related to extraction of geothermal energy and utilization for smart city applications is reported in [63].

11.4.4 Miscellaneous Energy Technologies

Utilization of hydrogen energy as fuel for meeting energy storage requirements for future use in smart cities is presented in [64]. Hydrogen is produced through electrolytes using green energy that is further used to produce electricity to stabilize the grid. In [65], the authors presented a detailed study related to sustainable energy ecosystems at an airport that used the hydrogen-supported RE grid storage, RE-powered supply chain, spatiotemporal energy migration solutions and single

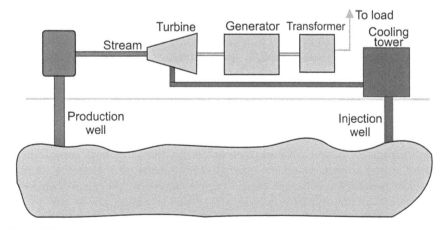

Figure 11.8 Geothermal energy generation.

and multiobjective optimization methods, along with multicriteria decision-making. In [66], the authors presented a method for the design, analysis and optimization of a 100% RE-powered network. In [67], the authors designed a distributed method for balancing the energy supply and demand in smart cities, and the design and use of an integrated smart city model are presented in [68].

11.5 COMPARATIVE STUDY

Following the in-depth literature review for this chapter, we present a comparative study of solar panel and other RE technologies. Table 11.3 presents a comparison of smart city solar panel technologies, and Table 11.4 presents a brief study of various RE technologies used for smart city applications.

Table 11.3 Solar Panel Technologies

S. No.	Parameter	Crystalline silicon	Thin film	Remark
1	Technology	Monocrystalline silicon, polycrystalline silicon, string ribbon	Amorphous silicon, cadmium telluride, copper indium gallium selenide, organic photovoltaic	
2	Voltage rating (Vmp/Voc)	80%–85%	72%–78%	Higher voltage is better
3	Temperature coefficient	High	Small	Low value is effective at high ambient temperature
4	Fill factor of the current–voltage curve	73%–82%	60%–68%	100% is ideal PV cell
5	Panel design	Anodized aluminum	Without frame, sandwiched between glasses, low cost, low weight	
6	Panel efficiency	13%–19%	4%–12%	
7	Inverter compatible with size	Low temperature is better	Factors like temperature, Voc-Vmp difference and isolation resistance are to be considered	
8	DC wiring	As per industry standards	Might require large numbers of circuit combiners and fuses	
9	Type of application	Residential, commercial, utility	Commercial, utility	

Table 11.4 RE Technology Applications in Smart Cities

S. No.	RE source	Generation of electric power	Thermal power generation	Efficiency	General application
1	Solar PV	Yes	No	<30%	House, buildings, heating, electricity, power plant
2	Solar thermal	Yes	Yes	<60%	House, buildings, heating, electricity, power plant
3	Wind	Yes	No	<60%	Power plant
4	GE	Yes	Yes	<60%	House, buildings, heating, electricity, power plant
5	Biomass	Yes	Yes	<60%	House, buildings, heating, electricity, power plant

11.6 CONCLUSION

In this chapter, we critically reviewed the concepts of smart cities and RE technology used to meet smart city energy requirements. Based on the critical review of 68 research papers, we determined that smart cities incorporate IoT in healthcare, communications, the economy, transportation, factories, homes, education, vehicles, business, power management, waste management, agriculture management and smart governance. Smart city energy management includes energy generation, ESS, infrastructure, energy facilities and energy transportation. Common RE technologies for meeting smart city energy demand include solar, wind and geothermal, and the recent development of hydrogen energy will be a major component in the grid stability of smart cities. This review will help engineers, scientist and academicians develop smart cities.

11.7 ACKNOWLEDGMENT

This research work is supported by Innovader Research Labs, Innovader IITian Padhaiwala LearnLab Pvt. Ltd., Jaipur, India.

REFERENCES

[1] Jessica Clement, Benoit Ruysschaert, Nathalie Crutzen, "Smart city strategies—A driver for the localization of the sustainable development goals?," Ecological Economics, Volume 213, 2023, 107941, https://doi.org/10.1016/j.ecolecon.2023.107941.

[2] Raghunathan Krishankumar, Dragan Pamucar, Muhammet Deveci, Manish Aggarwal, Kattur Soundarapandian Ravichandran, "Assessment of renewable energy sources for smart cities' demand satisfaction using multi-hesitant fuzzy linguistic

based choquet integral approach," Renewable Energy, Volume 189, 2022, Pages 1428–1442, https://doi.org/10.1016/j.renene.2022.03.081

[3] Hari Krishnan Govindarajan, Ganesh L.S., "Renewable energy for electricity use in India: Evidence from India's smart cities mission," Renewable Energy Focus, Volume 38, 2021, Pages 36–43, https://doi.org/10.1016/j.ref.2021.05.005.

[4] J.Z. Thellufsen, H. Lund, P. Sorknæs, P.A. Østergaard, M. Chang, D. Drysdale, S. Nielsen, S.R. Djørup, K. Sperling, "Smart energy cities in a 100% renewable energy context," Renewable and Sustainable Energy Reviews, Volume 129, 2020, 109922, https://doi.org/10.1016/j.rser.2020.109922.

[5] Stephan Maier, Michael Narodoslawsky, "Optimal Renewable Energy Systems for Smart Cities," Editor(s): Jiří Jaromír Klemeš, Petar Sabev Varbanov, Peng Yen Liew, Computer Aided Chemical Engineering, Elsevier, Volume 33, 2014, Pages 1849–1854, https://doi.org/10.1016/B978-0-444-63455-9.50143-4.

[6] Tarun Kataray, B. Nitesh, Bharath Yarram, Sanyukta Sinha, Erdem Cuce, Saboor Shaik, Pethurajan Vigneshwaran, Abin Roy, "Integration of smart grid with renewable energy sources: Opportunities and challenges—A comprehensive review, Sustainable Energy Technologies and Assessments," Volume 58, 2023, 103363, https://doi.org/10.1016/j.seta.2023.103363.

[7] T. Atasoy, H. E. Akınç, Ö. Erçin, "An analysis on smart grid applications and grid integration of renewable energy systems in smart cities," 2015 International Conference on Renewable Energy Research and Applications (ICRERA), Palermo, 2015, pp. 547–550, doi: 10.1109/ICRERA.2015.7418473.

[8] K. Sravya, M. Himaja, K. Prapti, K. M. V. V. Prasad, "Renewable energy sources for smart city applications: A review," 3rd Smart Cities Symposium (SCS 2020), Online Conference, 2020, pp. 684–688, doi: 10.1049/icp.2021.0963.

[9] Aysan Bashirpour Bonab, Maria Fedele, Vincenzo Formisano, Ihor Rudko, "Urban quantum leap: A comprehensive review and analysis of quantum technologies for smart cities," Cities, Volume 140, 2023, 104459, https://doi.org/10.1016/j.cities.2023.104459.

[10] Abdul Rehman Javed, Faisal Shahzad, Saif ur Rehman, Yousaf Bin Zikria, Imran Razzak, Zunera Jalil, Guandong Xu, "Future smart cities: requirements, emerging technologies, applications, challenges, and future aspects," Cities, Volume 129, 2022, 103794, https://doi.org/10.1016/j.cities.2022.103794.

[11] Aysan Bashirpour Bonab, Francesco Bellini, Ihor Rudko, "Theoretical and analytical assessment of smart green cities," Journal of Cleaner Production, Volume 410, 2023, 137315, https://doi.org/10.1016/j.jclepro.2023.137315.

[12] Hadi Alizadeh, Ayyoob Sharifi, "Toward a societal smart city: Clarifying the social justice dimension of smart cities," Sustainable Cities and Society, Volume 95, 2023, 104612, https://doi.org/10.1016/j.scs.2023.104612.

[13] Hakpyeong Kim, Heeju Choi, Hyuna Kang, Jongbaek An, Seungkeun Yeom, Taehoon Hong, "A systematic review of the smart energy conservation system: From smart homes to sustainable smart cities," Renewable and Sustainable Energy Reviews, Volume 140, 2021, 110755, https://doi.org/10.1016/j.rser.2021.110755.

[14] Celal Hakan Canbaz, Orhan Ekren, Banu Y. Ekren, Vikas Kumar, "Chapter 32—Evaluation of fuel production technologies by using renewable energy for smart cities," Editor(s): John R.Vacca, Smart Cities Policies and Financing, Elsevier, 2022, Pages 457–470, ISBN 9780128191309, https://doi.org/10.1016/B978-0-12-819130-9.00038-3.

[15] Ubaid ur Rehman, Pedro Faria, Luis Gomes, Zita Vale, "Future of energy management systems in smart cities: A systematic literature review," Sustainable Cities and Society, Volume 96, 2023, 104720, https://doi.org/10.1016/j.scs.2023.104720

[16] Muhammad Babar, Akmal Saeed Khattak, Mian Ahmad Jan, Muhammad Usman Tariq, "Energy aware smart city management system using data analytics and Internet of Things," Sustainable Energy Technologies and Assessments, Volume 44, 2021, 100992, https://doi.org/10.1016/j.seta.2021.100992.

[17] Rajalakshmi Selvaraj, Venu Madhav Kuthadi, S. Baskar, "Smart building energy management and monitoring system based on artificial intelligence in smart city," Sustainable Energy Technologies and Assessments, Volume 56, 2023, 103090, https://doi.org/10.1016/j.seta.2023.103090.

[18] Mohamed Lotfi, Tiago Almeida, Mohammad S. Javadi, Gerardo J. Osório, Cláudio Monteiro, João P.S. Catalão, "Coordinating energy management systems in smart cities with electric vehicles," Applied Energy, Volume 307, 2022, 118241, https://doi.org/10.1016/j.apenergy.2021.118241.

[19] Sumedha Sharma, Amit Dua, Mukesh Singh, Neeraj Kumar, Surya Prakash, "Fuzzy rough set based energy management system for self-sustainable smart city," Renewable and Sustainable Energy Reviews, Volume 82, Part 3, 2018, Pages 3633–3644, https://doi.org/10.1016/j.rser.2017.10.099.

[20] Marwa Ben Arab, Mouna Rekik, Lotfi Krichen, "A priority-based seven-layer strategy for energy management cooperation in a smart city integrated green technology," Applied Energy, Volume 335, 2023, 120767, https://doi.org/10.1016/j.apenergy.2023.120767.

[21] M. Alagumeenaakshi, S. Umamaheswari, A. Annisha Mevis, S. Seetha and G. Hema, "Monitoring and controlling of solar photovoltaic cells using LoRa technology," 2021 International Conference on Advancements in Electrical, Electronics, Communication, Computing and Automation (ICAECA), Coimbatore, 2021, pp. 1–6, doi: 10.1109/ICAECA52838.2021.9675732.

[22] Gajendra Singh Chawda, Om Prakash Mahela, Neeraj Gupta, Mahdi Khosravy, Tomonobu Senjyu, "Incremental conductance based particle swarm optimization algorithm for global maximum power tracking of solar-PV under nonuniform operating conditions," Applied Sciences, Volume 10, Issue 13, 2020, 4575, https://doi.org/10.3390/app10134575

[23] Om Prakash Mahela, and Abdul Gafoor Shaik. "Comprehensive Overview of Grid Interfaced Solar Photovoltaic Systems," Renewable and Sustainable Energy Reviews (Elsevier), Volume 68, Part 1, 2017, Pages 316–332. https://doi.org/10.1016/j.rser.2016.09.096

[24] Lisa Baindu Gobio-Thomas, Muhamed Darwish, Valentina Stojceska, "Environmental impacts of solar thermal power plants used in industrial supply chains," Thermal Science and Engineering Progress, Volume 38, 2023, 101670, https://doi.org/10.1016/j.tsep.2023.101670.

[25] Talal Alqahtani, "Performance evaluation of a solar thermal storage system proposed for concentrated solar power plants," Applied Thermal Engineering, Volume 229, 2023, 120665, https://doi.org/10.1016/j.applthermaleng.2023.120665.

[26] S. Bracco, F. Delfino, P. Laiolo and M. Rossi, "The smart city energy infrastructures at the Savona campus of the University of Genoa," 2016 AEIT International Annual Conference (AEIT), Capri, 2016, pp. 1–6, https://doi.org/10.23919/AEIT.2016.7892774.

[27] K.B. Porate, K.L. Thakre, G.L. Bodhe, "Impact of wind power on generation economy and emission from coal based thermal power plant," International Journal of
Electrical Power & Energy Systems, Volume 44, Issue 1, 2013, Pages 889–896,
https://doi.org/10.1016/j.ijepes.2012.08.029.

[28] O. A. Rosyid, "Comparative performance testing of solar panels for smart city microgrids," 2017 International Conference on Smart Cities, Automation & Intelligent
Computing Systems (ICON-SONICS), Yogyakarta, Indonesia, 2017, pp. 81–86,
doi: 10.1109/ICON-SONICS.2017.8267826.

[29] Bohan Li, Weijun Tan, "A novel framework for integrating solar renewable source
into smart cities through digital twin simulations," Solar Energy, Volume 262, 2023,
111869, https://doi.org/10.1016/j.solener.2023.111869.

[30] P. Tejaswi, O.V. Gnana Swathika, "Chapter Eleven—Machine learning algorithms-
based solar power forecasting in smart cities," Editor(s): Vedik Basetti, Chandan
Kumar Shiva, Mohan Rao Ungarala, Shriram S. Rangarajan, Artificial Intelligence
and Machine Learning in Smart City Planning, Elsevier, 2023, Pages 171–179,
https://doi.org/10.1016/B978-0-323-99503-0.00001-6.

[31] C.R. Mahesha, Mritha Ramalingam, Sujith S., P. Kalyanasundaram, N.B. Soni, G.
Nalinashini, S. Suresh Kumar, Ravishankar Sathyamurthy, V. Mohanavel, "Sustainable cooling and heating in smart cities using solar energy system planning," Energy
Reports, Volume 8, Supplement 8, 2022, Pages 826–835, https://doi.org/10.1016/j.
egyr.2022.09.208.

[32] Om Prakash Mahela, and Abdul Gafoor Shaik, "Power quality recognition in distribution system with solar energy penetration using S-Transform and Fuzzy C-Means
clustering," Renewable Energy (Elsevier), Volume 106, June 2017, Pages 37–51.
https://doi.org/10.1016/j.renene.2016.12.098

[33] Gori Shankar Sharma, Om Prakash Mahela, Baseem Khan, Akhil Ranjan Garg,
"Estimation of Solar Insolation along with worldwide Airport situated on differ-
ent Latitude locations: A case Study of for Rajasthan State, India," Book "Arti-
ficial Intelligence-based Energy Management Systems for Smart Microgrids,"
Editor(s): Baseem Khan, Sanjeevikumar Padmanaban, Hassan Haes Alhelou, Om
Prakash Mahela, S. Rajkumar, CRC Press, Taylor & Francis Group, eBook ISBN
#9781003290346. https://doi.org/10.1201/b22884

[34] Surendra Singh, Avdhesh Sharma, Akhil Ranjan Garg, Om Prakash Mahela, "Spotting the Power Quality Events Associated to Utility Distribution Power Network
with Solar Energy Power Generation," IEEE 2023 8th International Conference for
Convergence in Technology (I2CT), Pune, April 7–9 2023.

[35] Dharmendra Chouhan, M.K. Bhaskar, Om Prakash Mahela, "Protection of Utility
Network with Solar Power GenerationFault Events Recognition to Design a Current Based Transmission Line Protection Scheme Using Signal Processing Techniques," 2022 IEEE Second International Conference on Advances in Electrical,
Computing, Communications and Sustainable Technologies (ICAECT 2022), Bhilai, April 21–22, 2022.

[36] Rajkumar Kaushik, Om Prakash Mahela and Pramod Kumar Bhatt, "Events Recognition and Power Quality Estimation in Distribution Network in the Presence of
Solar PV Generation," 10th IEEE International Conference on Communication Systems and Network Technologies (CSNT2021), IEEE MP Section and Shri GSITS
Indore, April 24–25, 2021.

[37] Atul Kulshrestha, Om Prakash Mahela, Mukesh Kumar Gupta, "Identification and Classification of Faults in Utility Grid with Solar Energy Using Discrete Wavelet Transform and Decision Rules," 12th IEEE International Conference on Computational Intelligence and Communication Networks (CICN 2020), BIAS Bhimtal, Nainital, September 24–25, 2020. https://doi.org/10.1109/CICN49253.2020.9242564

[38] Mohd Zishan Khoker, Om Prakash Mahela, and Gulhasan Ahmad, "A Voltage Algorithm using Discrete Wavelet Transform and Hilbert Transform for Detection and Classification of Power System Faults in the Presence of Solar Energy," 2020 IEEE International Students' Conference on Electrical, Electronics and Computer Science (SCEECS 2020), MANIT Bhopal, India, February 22–23, 2020. https://doi.org/10.1109/SCEECS48394.2020.7

[39] Roshan Kumar Pathak, Sunil Agarwal, Om Prakash Mahela, and Ravi Raj Choudhary, "Recognition of Faults in Grid Connected Solar Photovoltaic Farm Using Current Features Evaluated Using Stockwell Transform Based Algorithm," 2020 IEEE International Students' Conference on Electrical, Electronics and Computer Science (SCEECS 2020), MANIT Bhopal, February 22–23, 2020, https://doi.org/10.1109/SCEECS48394.2020.13

[40] Om Prakash Mahela, Kapil Dev Kansal and Sunil Agarwal, "Detection of Power Quality Disturbances in Utility Grid with Solar Photovoltaic Energy Penetration," 8th IEEE India International Conference on Power Electronics (IICPE-2018), MNIT Jaipur, December 13–14, 2018, https://doi.org/10.1109/IICPE.2018.8709597

[41] Varsha Rani, Om Prakash Mahela and Himanshu Doraya. Power Quality Improvement in the Distribution Network with Solar Energy Penetration Using Distribution Static Compensator. In: IEEE International Conference on Computing, Power and Communication Technologies 2018 (GUCON 2018), Galgotias University, Greater Noida, September 28–29, 2018, https://doi.org/10.1109/GUCON.2018.8674983

[42] Pengfei Duan, Marzieh Askari, Kimia Hemat, Ziad M. Ali, "Optimal operation and simultaneous analysis of the electric transport systems and distributed energy resources in the smart city," Sustainable Cities and Society, Volume 75, 2021, 103306, https://doi.org/10.1016/j.scs.2021.103306.

[43] Om Prakash Mahela, and Abdul Gafoor Shaik. Comprehensive Overview of Grid Interfaced Wind Energy Generation Systems, Renewable and Sustainable Energy Reviews (Elsevier), Volume 57, 2016, Pages 260–281, https://doi.org/10.1016/j.rser.2015.12.048.

[44] Zhi Yuan, Weiqing Wang, Xiaochao Fan, "Back propagation neural network clustering architecture for stability enhancement and harmonic suppression in wind turbines for smart cities," Computers & Electrical Engineering, Volume 74, 2019, Pages 105–116, https://doi.org/10.1016/j.compeleceng.2019.01.006.

[45] H. Sano, "Smart winds?: Green energy and a window of opportunity for Brazilian small cities," 2017 IEEE First Summer School on Smart Cities (S3C), Natal, 2017, pp. 103–107, https://doi.org/10.1109/S3C.2017.8501360.

[46] K. B. Navas R, J. Banu K, R. Katyal, S. B, P. S and J. K. Reddy, "A Novel Short Term Wind Speed Forecasting based on Hybrid Neural Network: A Case Study on Smart City in India," 7th Iran Wind Energy Conference (IWEC2021), Shahrood, 2021, pp. 1–4, https://doi.org/10.1109/IWEC52400.2021.9466972.

[47] Gajendra Singh Chawda, Abdul Gafoor Shaik, Om Prakash Mahela, Sanjeevikumar Padmanaban, "Performance Improvement of Weak Grid-connected Wind Energy System Using FLSRF Controlled DSTATCOM," IEEE Transactions on Industrial

Electronics, Volume 70, Issue 2, 2023, Pages 1565–1575, https://doi.org/10.1109/TIE.2022.3158012

[48] Abhishek Gupta, Ramesh Kumar Pachar, Om Prakash Mahela and Baseem Khan, "Fault Detection and Classification to Design a Protection Scheme for Utility Grid with High Penetration of Wind and Solar Energy," International Journal of Energy Research, Volume 2023, Article ID 4418741, Pages 1–16, https://doi.org/10.1155/2023/4418741

[49] Asmamaw Sewnet, Baseem Khan, Esayas Gidey, Om Prakash Mahela, Adel El-Shahat, Almoataz Y. Abdelaziz, "Mitigating Generation Schedule Deviation of Wind Farm Using Battery Energy Storage System," Energies, Volume 15, Issue 5, 2022, 1768. https://doi.org/10.3390/en15051768

[50] Om Prakash Mahela, Vikram Singh Bhati, Gulhasan Ahmad, Baseem Khan, P. Sanjeevikumar, Akhil Ranjan Garg, and Rajendra Mahla, "A Protection Scheme for Distribution Utility Network in the Presence of Wind Energy Penetration," Computers and Electrical Engineering (Elsevier), Volume 94, 2021, Paper No. 107324, https://doi.org/10.1016/j.compeleceng.2021.107324

[51] Om Prakash Mahela, Baseem Khan, Hassan Haes Alhelou, Pierluigi Siano, "Power Quality Assessment and Event Detection in Distribution Network with Wind Energy Penetration Using Stockwell Transform and Fuzzy Clustering, " IEEE Transactions on Industrial Informatics, Volume 16, Issue 11, 2020, Pages 6922 –6932, https://doi.org/10.1109/TII.2020.2971709

[52] Om Prakash Mahela, Baseem Khan, Hassan Haes Alhelou, Sudeep Tanwar, "Assessment of Power Quality in the Utility Grid Integrated with Wind Energy Generation," IET Power Electronics, Volume 13, Issue 13, 2020, Pages 2917–2925. https://doi.org/10.1049/iet-pel.2019.1351

[53] Om Prakash Mahela, Neeraj Gupta, Mahdi Khosravy, and Nilesh Patel, Comprehensive Overview of Low Voltage Ride through Methods of Grid Integrated Wind Generator, IEEE Access, Volume 7, Issue 1, 2019, Pages 99299–99326. https://doi.org/10.1109/ACCESS.2019.2930413

[54] Rajkumar Kaushik, Om Prakash Mahela and Pramod Kumar Bhatt, "Hybrid Algorithm for Detection of Events and Power Quality Disturbances Associated with Distribution Network in the Presence of Wind Energy," IEEE International Conference on Advance Computing and Innovative Technologies in Engineering (ICACITE 2021), Galgotias College of Engineering College and Technology, Greater Noida, March 4–5, 2021. https://doi.org/10.1109/ICACITE51222.2021.9404665

[55] Atul Kulshrestha, Om Prakash Mahela, Mukesh Kumar Gupta, "A Discrete Wavelet Transform and Rule Based Decision Tree Based Technique for Identification of Fault in Utility Grid Network with Wind Energy," 2021 First IEEE International Conference on Advances in Electrical, Computing, Communications and Sustainable Technologies (ICAECT 2021), Shri Shankarachariya Technical Campus (SSTC), Bhilai, February 19–20, 2021, https://doi.org/10.1109/ICAECT49130.2021.9392428

[56] Surbhi Thukral, Om Prakash Mahela, Bipul Kumar, "Detection of Transmission Line Faults in the Presence of Wind Energy Power Generation Source Using Stockwell's Transform," IEEE International Conference on Issues and Challenges in Intelligent Computing Techniques (ICICT 2019), 27–28th September, 2019, KIET Group of Institutions, Delhi-NCR, Ghaziabad, https://doi.org/10.1109/ICICT46931.2019.8977695

[57] Om Prakash Mahela, Kapil Dev Kansal and Sunil Agarwal, "Detection of Power Quality Disturbances in Utility Grid with Wind Energy Penetration," 8th IEEE India International Conference on Power Electronics (IICPE-2018), MNIT Jaipur, December, 13–14, 2018, Scopus indexed proceeding, https://doi.org/10.1109/IICPE.2018.8709578

[58] Kai Wang, Bin Yuan, Guomin Ji, Xingru Wu, "A comprehensive review of geothermal energy extraction and utilization in oilfields," Journal of Petroleum Science and Engineering, Volume 168, 2018, Pages 465–477, https://doi.org/10.1016/j.petrol.2018.05.012.

[59] Yuqing Wang, Yingxin Liu, Jinyue Dou, Mingzhu Li, Ming Zeng, "Geothermal energy in China: Status, challenges, and policy recommendations," Utilities Policy, Volume 64, 2020, 101020, https://doi.org/10.1016/j.jup.2020.101020.

[60] Diego Moya, Clay Aldás, Prasad Kaparaju, "Geothermal energy: Power plant technology and direct heat applications," Renewable and Sustainable Energy Reviews, Volume 94, 2018, Pages 889–901, https://doi.org/10.1016/j.rser.2018.06.047.

[61] Yuqing Wang, Yingxin Liu, Jinyue Dou, Mingzhu Li, Ming Zeng, "Geothermal energy in China: Status, challenges, and policy recommendations," Utilities Policy, Volume 64, 2020, 101020, https://doi.org/10.1016/j.jup.2020.101020.

[62] Jann Michael Weinand, Ganga Vandenberg, Stanley Risch, Johannes Behrens, Noah Pflugradt, Jochen Linßen, Detlef Stolten, "Low-carbon lithium extraction makes deep geothermal plants cost-competitive in future energy systems," Advances in Applied Energy, Volume 11, 2023, 100148, https://doi.org/10.1016/j.adapen.2023.100148.

[63] Tasnuva Sharmin, Nazia Rodoshi Khan, Md Saleh Akram, M Monjurul Ehsan, "A State-of-the-Art Review on Geothermal Energy Extraction, Utilization, and Improvement Strategies: Conventional, Hybridized, and Enhanced Geothermal Systems," International Journal of Thermo fluids, Volume 18, 2023, 100323, https://doi.org/10.1016/j.ijft.2023.100323.

[64] Qusay Hassan, Aws Zuhair Sameen, Olushola Olapade, Mohammad Alghoul, Hayder M. Salman, Marek Jaszczur, "Hydrogen fuel as an important element of the energy storage needs for future smart cities, International Journal of Hydrogen Energy, 2023, https://doi.org/10.1016/j.ijhydene.2023.03.413.

[65] Yuekuan Zhou, "Low-carbon transition in smart city with sustainable airport energy ecosystems and hydrogen-based renewable-grid-storage-flexibility," Energy Reviews, Volume 1, Issue 1, 2022, 100001, https://doi.org/10.1016/j.enrev.2022.100001.

[66] Chanhee You, Jiyong Kim, "Optimal design and global sensitivity analysis of a 100% renewable energy sources based smart energy network for electrified and hydrogen cities," Energy Conversion and Management, Volume 223, 2020, 113252, https://doi.org/10.1016/j.enconman.2020.113252.

[67] Ammar Oad, Hafiz Gulfam Ahmad, Mir Sajjad Hussain Talpur, Chenglin Zhao, Amjad Pervez, "Green smart grid predictive analysis to integrate sustainable energy of emerging V2G in smart city technologies," Optik, Volume 272, 2023, 170146, https://doi.org/10.1016/j.ijleo.2022.170146.

[68] Azzam Abu-Rayash, Ibrahim Dincer, "Development and application of an integrated smart city model," Heliyon, Volume 9, Issue 4, 2023, e14347, https://doi.org/10.1016/j.heliyon.2023.e14347.

Chapter 12

Optimal Placement of Distributed Energy Generators Using Multiobjective Harmony Search Algorithm for Loss Reduction in Microgrid for Smart Cities

Jitendra Kumar Jangid, Anil Kumar Sharma,
Rajiv Goyal, Avinash Sharma, Om Prakash
Mahela and Baseem Khan

12.1 INTRODUCTION

Microgrid (MG) operations in smart cities are expanding because of the fast increases in energy utilization around the world. Energy supply and deficiency greatly affect the development of a smart city including its economy. Renewable energy sources provide an alternative option to fulfill the increased energy demands of smart cities. Energy is transmitted through distributed generators (DGs) installed throughout smart city power system networks. DG systems are reliable, and their operation is effective.

Wind and solar units are emerging as the most effective DG plants. Placing them at appropriate locations in existing smart city systems is a complex task [1]. DGs can be connected to either the transmission or the distribution network, but maximum benefits can be obtained if DG plants are integrated with MGs. Nonoptimal DG plant size and placement can result in less efficient operations [2].

Recently, intelligent techniques are being applied for the optimal integration of DG units. In [3], the authors designed a method for determining DG plant size and integrating the generators into an electrical grid to enhance voltage stability and decrease active power loss; their proposed method effectively reduced the load fluctuations. They used the voltage stability margin index and curve fitting to recognize the buses for integrating DG plants and validated their study on 33- and 69-bus IEEE networks, and they demonstrated the effectiveness, robustness and good performance of their method.

In [4], the authors introduced an improved technique for estimating the optimal DG size for minimizing power losses and enhancing voltage profiles; this also helps in voltage stability. The authors used multiobjective particle swarm optimization (PSO) to optimize the locations and sizes of DG plants. In [5], the authors introduced a method to minimize line losses and total harmonic distortion (THD) and improve the voltage profile of a distribution network by optimizing DG size and integration along with network structure. Further, the authors examined the impacts of THD on network performance.

In [6], the authors designed an algorithm for identifying the optimal locations for DGs using teaching–learning-based and honeybee-mating optimization. Their method combined the merits of both techniques and was effective for measuring the impacts of current capacity on existing DGs. They also established that adding fuzzy clustering with the multiobjective process improves the DG placement performance.

In [7], the authors formulated a method for placing multiple DGs and optimizing their sizes to minimize active power losses and maintain bus voltages within acceptable limits. To achieve this objective, they implemented a fuzzy logic approach to deploy DGs in an IEEE 33-node system and achieved the stable operation of their considered power network. In [8], the authors used PSO to optimize the sizes and placement of DG systems with a microgrid using nonlinear integer reduction, which effectively reduced total capital cost, operation cost, maintenance cost and the replacement of DG units. Further, the authors maintained the voltage and energy limits of every DG unit, the power supplied to the utility network and the system reliability constraints.

In [9], the authors applied the artificial bee colony (ABC) to optimize DG sizes and locations to minimize network losses and enhance voltage; the authors rated the efficacy of the designed ABC optimization on IEEE 14-node and 57-node systems. In [10], the authors used GA to optimize DG locations and sizes for DG units, specifically to estimate voltage constraints, active and reactive power loss constraints and DG size constraints. The authors studied IEEE 14-node, 30-node and IEEE 57-node networks.

In [11], the authors applied DG units to eliminate power system congestion; they investigated nonlinear impacts of DG units on power system parameters including power transmitted between two network locations. The authors alternated current optimal power flow considering two variables along with mixed-integer programming for the optimized deployment and sizes of DG units to solve the problem of transmission congestion. The study was carried out on IEEE 14-bus systems, and the authors improved a number of variables including reducing generation costs, transmission loss, congestion rent, and locational marginal price and improving voltages. Detailed studies related to DG placement, MGs and renewable energy sources are available in [12–37].

12.1.1 Research Contributions

Here, we present a method using the multiobjective harmony search algorithm (MOHSA) to determine the optimal placement and sizes of DG plants to reduce active and reactive power loss and total MG voltage deviations in a smart city.

The main research contributions of this work are as follows: First, we design a MOHSA for optimal DG size and placement by optimizing three objective functions using MOHSA: total active power loss minimization function (PLMF), total reactive power loss minimization function (QLMF) and total voltage deviation minimization function (VDMF).

Next, we check the efficacy of MOHSA in terms of the active power loss reduction indictor (PLRI), total reactive power loss reduction indictor (QLRI) and total voltage deviation reduction indictor (VDRI). We also measure the overall effectiveness of the proposed MOHSA in terms of payback period to recover investments in the DG unit deployment. To confirm our findings, we tested a network with no DG unit and then networks with one, two, three, four and five DG plants. We performed the study on an IEEE 33-bus MG test network using MATLAB®.

12.1.2 Organization of Chapter

This chapter is designed in eight sections. Research introduction, research gaps, research contributions and paper structure are discussed in Section 1. The study test network is elaborated in Section 2. The proposed MOHSA algorithm and mathematical formulations are elaborated in Section 3. Section 4 describes the performance indicators utilized to rate the different study cases. Simulation results are demonstrated in Section 5. Section 6 describes the cost–benefit analysis of optimal DG placement and computation of payback period; we also compare performances in this section. The paper concludes with Section 7.

12.2 THE PROPOSED IEEE 33-BUS TEST SYSTEM

The IEEE 33-junction feeder was initially designed by Baran and Wu in 1989; this test system has 33 junctions and 32 fixed feeders. Since this system has the utility grid connected at bus-1, which is represented by a generator, this system was the best candidate for the smart city microgrid design. There are reactive power compensating units associated with the test feeder, but there is no power generation unit connected to the test feeder. The first bus of the feeder is integrated to the utility grid. The bus voltage varies from 0.9 p.u. to 1.05 p.u. [38].

The configuration of the MG test network is illustrated in Figure 12.1; the test feeder is a 12.66kV network having a substation and 33 junctions. Table 12.1 details the junction data for the test system we used for this study including active power demand on each bus and total reactive power demand on each bus. The active and reactive test feeder loads were 3.715 (MW) and 2.3 (MV AR), respectively. The detailed test feeder branch data is presented in Table 12.2, which lists the interconnection of various branches between different nodes. The resistance and reactance of each branch are also given in Table 12.2. The reactance-to-resistance (X/R) ratio for all branches is comparatively small (i.e., 0.33 to 3.31), which

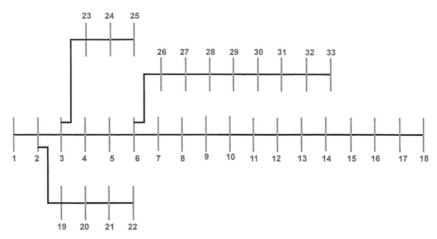

Figure 12.1 The IEEE 33-bus test smart city microgrid used in the study.

Table 12.1 Bus Data for the IEEE 33-Junction Smart City Microgrid System

Bus no.	Bus type	Active demand (MW)	Reactive demand (MW)	Minimum voltage (p.u.)	Maximum voltage (p.u.)
1	PV	0	0	1.0	1.0
2	PQ	0.1	0.06	1.05	0.90
3	PQ	0.09	0.04	1.05	0.90
4	PQ	0.12	0.08	1.05	0.90
5	PQ	0.06	0.03	1.05	0.90
6	PQ	0.06	0.02	1.05	0.90
7	PQ	0.20	0.10	1.05	0.90
8	PQ	0.20	0.10	1.05	0.90
9	PQ	0.06	0.02	1.05	0.90
10	PQ	0.06	0.02	1.05	0.90
11	PQ	0.045	0.03	1.05	0.90
12	PQ	0.06	0.035	1.05	0.90
13	PQ	0.06	0.035	1.05	0.90
14	PQ	0.12	0.08	1.05	0.90
15	PQ	0.06	0.01	1.05	0.90
16	PQ	0.06	0.02	1.05	0.90
17	PQ	0.06	0.02	1.05	0.90
18	PQ	0.09	0.04	1.05	0.90
19	PQ	0.09	0.04	1.05	0.90
20	PQ	0.09	0.04	1.05	0.90

Bus no.	Bus type	Active demand (MW)	Reactive demand (MW)	Minimum voltage (p.u.)	Maximum voltage (p.u.)
21	PQ	0.09	0.04	1.05	0.90
22	PQ	0.09	0.04	1.05	0.90
23	PQ	0.09	0.05	1.05	0.90
24	PQ	0.42	0.20	1.05	0.90
25	PQ	0.42	0.20	1.05	0.90
26	PQ	0.06	0.025	1.05	0.90
27	PQ	0.06	0.025	1.05	0.90
28	PQ	0.06	0.02	1.05	0.90
29	PQ	0.12	0.07	1.05	0.90
30	PQ	0.20	0.60	1.05	0.90
31	PQ	0.15	0.07	1.05	0.90
32	PQ	0.21	0.10	1.05	0.90
33	PQ	0.06	0.04	1.05	0.90

Table 12.2 Branch Data for the IEEE 33-Junction Smart City Microgrid System

Branch Number	From Bus	To Bus	$R(\Omega)$	$X(\Omega)$
1	1	2	0.0922	0.047
2	2	3	0.493	0.2511
3	3	4	0.366	0.1864
4	4	5	0.3811	0.1941
5	5	6	0.819	0.707
6	6	7	0.1872	0.6188
7	7	8	0.7114	0.2351
8	8	9	1.03	0.74
9	9	10	1.044	0.74
10	10	11	0.1966	0.065
11	11	12	0.3744	0.1238
12	12	13	1.468	1.155
13	13	14	0.5416	0.7129
14	14	15	0.591	0.526
15	15	16	0.7463	0.545
16	16	17	1.289	1.721
17	17	18	0.732	0.574
18	2	19	0.164	0.1565
19	19	20	1.5042	1.3554
20	20	21	0.4095	0.4784
21	21	22	0.7089	0.9373

(Continued)

Table 12.2 (Continued)

Branch Number	From Bus	To Bus	R(Ω)	X(Ω)
22	3	23	0.4512	0.3083
23	23	24	0.898	0.7091
24	24	25	0.896	0.7011
25	6	26	0.203	0.1034
26	26	27	0.2842	0.1447
27	27	28	1.059	0.9337
28	28	29	0.8042	0.7006
29	29	30	0.5075	0.2585
30	30	31	0.9744	0.963
31	31	32	0.3105	0.3619
32	32	33	0.341	0.5302

indicates that the test system is a practical distribution system [39]. We used solar and wind DGs to test optimal placement and optimal sizes and discuss their active and reactive power details in Section 12.5 Simulation Results.

12.3 THE PROPOSED MOHSA

This section describes the proposed MOHSA that we implemented to determine optimal sizes and locations of DG plants for minimizing losses of active power, reactive power and voltage deviations in the microgrid.

12.3.1 Design of Objective Functions

As we noted earlier, this study had three objective functions: to minimize total active power loss (TAPL), total reactive power loss (TRPL) and total voltage deviations (TVD) on all junctions of the test MG network. The TAPL minimization function (PLMF) is obtained by equation (12.1):

$$PLMF = \sum_{i=1}^{m} (I_{i.real}^2 \times R_i) \tag{12.1}$$

Here, m is the number of branches in the network, I indicates branch current and R indicates branch resistance. The TRPL minimization function (QLMF) is obtained by equation (12.2):

$$QLMF = \sum_{i=1}^{m} (I_{i.img}^2 \times R_i) \tag{12.2}$$

The TVD minimization function (VDMF) is obtained by equation (12.3):

$$VDMF = \sum_{i=1}^{m} (1 - V_i)^2 \qquad (12.3)$$

Here, V is the voltage of a bus in the test network.

12.3.2 Constraints

We tested for the optimal sizes and deployment of the DG systems considering the constraint limits of junction voltages, DG rating, thermal limits of feeders and active and reactive power loss, which are described in this section. Bus voltage limits are given by equation (12.4):

$$V_i^{min} \leq V_i \leq V_i^{max} \qquad (12.4)$$

Following the Indian electricity grid codes, we set the voltage limits at 97% to 103% of the rated junction voltage. That is, we aimed to maintain the voltage between 0.97 p.u. and 1.03 p.u. with the placement of DG units. The thermal limit feeder constraint is obtained by equation (12.5):

$$I_{i,j} \leq I_{rated} \qquad (12.5)$$

The limit for the DG units is obtained by equation (12.6):

$$S_{DG_i}^{min} \leq S_{DG_i} \leq S_{DG_i}^{max} \qquad (12.6)$$

We set the lower and upper limits of the DG units to 0 and 2 kVA, respectively, for this study.

12.3.3 Multiobjective Harmony Search Algorithm

The harmony search algorithm (HSA) is a population metaheuristic method that gained attention for applications in power systems because of parameters that control investigation by random, elitism degree and exploitation [40]. Further, the HSA takes into account all the available solutions to choose a new solution, in contrast with other optimization techniques that consider only a few solutions, such as the GA [41]. If the HSA uses two or objective functions for optimization purpose, it becomes an MOHSA.

The HSA is based on the concept that musicians improve a harmony. As a musician seeks a good melody by evaluating and optimizing sets of sounds at each practice, the algorithm obtains the optimum of a function by its variables at every iteration [41]. A pseudo code used to implement harmony identification algorithm is elaborated in Algorithm 1. There are three phases for this algorithm: initiate the harmony memory (HM) (line 2), improve the harmony (line 4) and update the memory (line 7) [42]. The initial HMS harmonies are random, and harmonies are improved in new NI generations. When the new solution is superior to the previous one, the solution changes, and if not, the previous solution is retained (memory update).

Algorithm 1: Harmony search

1:   **function** HARMONY SEARCH
2:   $HM = x_i \in \Omega, i \in (1, \dots\dots, HMS)$
3:   **for** t = 0, . . . , NI **do**
4:   $x^{new} = IMPROVE(HM)$
5:   $x^{worst} = \min_{xi} f(x_i), x_i \in (HM)$
6:   **if** $f(x^{new}) > f(x^{worst})$ **then**
7:   $HM = (HM \cup \{x^{new}\}) \setminus \{x^{worst}\}$
8:   **end if**
9:   **end for**
10: **end function**

The HSA improvement mechanism is illustrated by Algorithm 2. Here, r, $r1$, $r2$ and $r3$ are random variables. The parameters are harmony memory consideration rate (HMCR), pitch adjustment rate (PAR) and bandwidth (BW), and improvement takes place in three stages:

(1)   Memory consideration (line 4): existing harmony component is taken from memory.
(2)   Pitch adjustment (line 6): perturbates the considered component.
(3)   Random selection (line 9): generates a new component randomly.

Algorithm 2: Harmony search improvisation function

1:   **function** $IMPROVISE(HM):x^{new}$
2:   **for** $i = 0, \dots, n$ **do**
3:   **if** $r_1 <$ HMCR **then**
4:   $x_i^{new} = x_i^k, k \in (1, \dots, HMS)$
5:   **if** $r_2 <$ PAR **then**
6:   $x_i^{new} = x_i^{new} \pm r_3 \times BW$
7:   **end if**
8:   **else**
9:   $x_i^{new} = x_i^{(L)} + r \times (x_i^{(U)} - x_i^{(L)})$

10:   end if
11:   end for
12:   end function

12.4 PERFORMANCE INDICATORS

We assessed our fulfillment of our objectives based on a set of performance indicators we described here.

12.4.1 TAPL Reduction

We measured total active power loss reduction as the PLRI, calculated as

$$PLRI = \frac{TAPL \; without \; DG - TAPL \; with \; DG}{TAPL \; without \; DG} \times 100\% \qquad (12.7)$$

12.4.2 TRPL Reduction

We measured total reactive power loss reduction as QLRI, calculated as

$$QLRI = \frac{TRPL \; without \; DG - TRPL \; with \; DG}{TRPL \; without \; DG} \times 100\% \qquad (12.8)$$

12.4.3 TVD Reduction

We measured total voltage deviation reduction as VDRI, calculated as

$$PLRI = \frac{TVD \; without \; DG - TVD \; with \; DG}{TVD \; without \; DG} \times 100\% \qquad (12.9)$$

12.5 SIMULATION RESULTS

Here, we present our results from attempting to optimize the sizes and deployment of solar and wind DGs in a smart city microgrid network for loss reduction using a proposed MOHSA. We present the voltage profiles and objective function values for optimal placement of one, two, three, four and five DG plants as well as with no generator.

12.5.1 Microgrid with No Distributed Energy Generators

We simulated the test IEEE 33-bus MG network considering no DG plants and computed the objective functions, the TAPL, TRPL and TVD. Figure 12.2 gives the functions in the pareto optimal solution, reflecting that TAPL, TRPL, and TVD

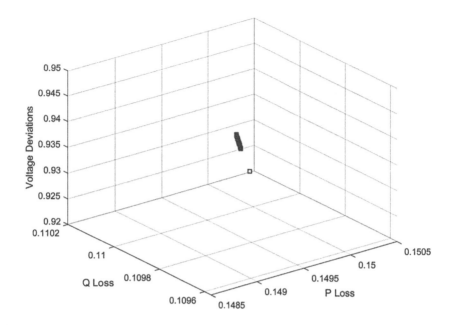

Figure 12.2 Objective functions in the pareto optimal solution with no distributed energy generator.

Table 12.3 Objective Function Values

S. No.	Case Study	TAPL	TRPL	TVD
I	No DG units	148.828 kW	109.573 kVAr	0.947 p.u.
2	One DG unit	140.750 kW	103.643 kVAr	0.871 p.u.
3	Two DG units	114.154 kW	87.261 kVAr	0.427 p.u.
4	Three DG units	93.344 kW	73.322 kVAr	0.433 p.u.
5	Four DG units	99.371 kW	77.150 kVAr	0.342 p.u.
6	Five DG units	97.457 kW	76.799 kVAr	0.342 p.u.

were, respectively, 148.828 kW, 109.573 kVAr and 0.947 p.u. Table 12.3 presents the remaining objective function values.

Figure 12.3 displays the voltage profile measured on all 33 junctions of the IEEE test system during the network simulation considering no DG plants. The figure shows that the voltage at bus-1 is unity and that it reduces as the distance of the bus increases relative to bus-1. The lowest voltage, 0.93 p.u., was observed at bus-32.

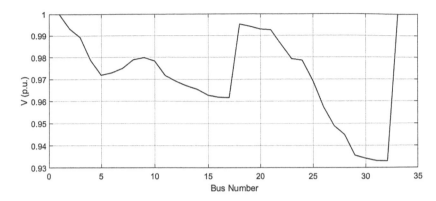

Figure 12.3 Voltages on network junctions in the absence of a distributed energy generator.

Table 12.4 Optimal DG Plant Locations and Sizes

S. No.	Case Study	Bus Number	Size of DG Plant	Total DG Size
1	No DG units	–	–	–
2	One DG unit	7	1.9998 kW	1.9998 kW
3	Two DG units	10	1.5096 kW	2.7192 kW
		29	1.2096 kW	
4	Three DG units	12	1.1153kW	3.5600 kW
		23	1.2337kW	
		28	1.2110 kW	
5	Four DG units	11	1.2182 kW	5.1570 kW
		24	1.4047 kW	
		29	1.2555 kW	
		30	1.2786 kW	
6	Five DG units	13	1.2061 kW	6.6332 kW
		23	1.2215 kW	
		24	1.0929 kW	
		29	1.2205 kW	
		32	1.8922 kW	

12.5.2 One DG Unit

Next we simulated the test MG network considering one DG plant and calculated TAPL, TRPL and TVD to determine the unit's optimal deployment and size using MOHSA. The optimal size of one DG plant is 1.9998 kW, and it should be integrated on bus-7 of the test network (Table 12.4). The TAPL, TRPL, and TVD pareto optimal solutions are presented in Figure 12.4; the figure shows that all three functions decrease, to 140.750 kW, 103.643 kVAr and 0.871 p.u., respectively.

Figure 12.5 displays the voltages measured at all 33 junctions of the IEEE test system during network simulation with one DG unit. Again, the voltage at bus-1 is unity, and it reduces as the distance of the bus increases relative to bus-1. The minimum voltage, 0.938 p.u., is observed at bus-31 and bus-32.

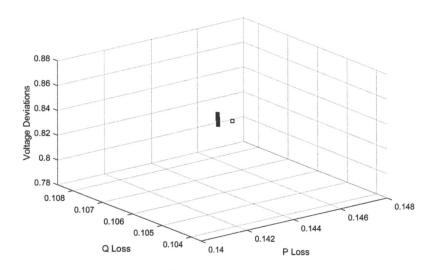

Figure 12.4 Pareto optimal objective functions with one DG unit.

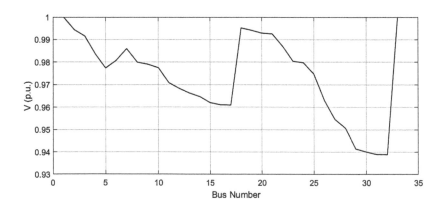

Figure 12.5 Voltages at network junctions with one DG unit.

12.5.3 Two DG Units

Next we simulated the test MG network considering two DG plants and calculated TAPL, TRPL and TVD to determine the units' optimal deployment and sizes using MOHSA. For two DGs, the optimal sizes and locations are 1.5096 kW and 1.2096 kW on bus-10 and bus-29, respectively (Table 12.4). The TAPL, TRPL, and TVD pareto optimal solutions are presented in Figure 12.6; the figure shows that the functions were, respectively, 114.154 kW, 87.261 kVAr and 0.427 p.u. (Table 12.3).

Figure 12.7 displays the voltages measured at all 33 junctions of the IEEE test system during network simulation with two DG units. The voltage at junction-1

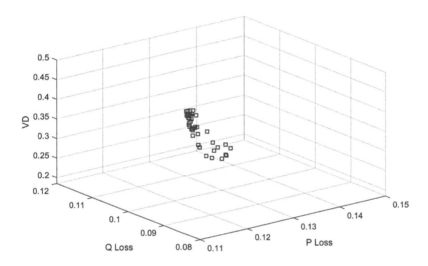

Figure 12.6 Pareto optimal objective functions with two DG units.

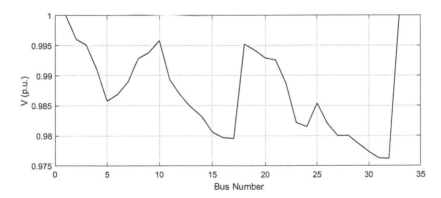

Figure 12.7 Voltages at network junctions with two DG units.

is unity, it reduces as the distance of the bus increases relative to bus-1, and the minimum voltage, 0.976 p.u., is observed at bus-31 and bus-32.

12.5.4 Three DG Units

Next we simulated the test MG network considering three DG plants and calculated TAPL, TRPL and TVD to determine the units' optimal deployment and sizes using MOHSA. For three DGs, the optimal sizes and locations are 1.1153 kW, 1.2337 kW and 1.2110 kW on bus-12, bus-23 and bus-28, respectively (Table 12.4). The TAPL, TRPL, and TVD pareto optimal solutions are presented in Figure 12.8; the figure shows that the functions were, respectively, 93.344 kW, 73.322 kVAr and 0.433 p.u. (Table 12.3).

Figure 12.9 displays the voltages measured at all 33 junctions of the IEEE test system during network simulation with three DG units. The voltage at bus-1 is unity, it reduces as the distance of the bus increases relative to bus-1, and the minimum voltage, 0.966 p.u., is observed at bus-31 and bus-32.

12.5.5 Four DG Units

Next we simulated the test MG network considering four DG plants and calculated TAPL, TRPL and TVD to determine the units' optimal deployment and sizes using MOHSA. For four DGs, the optimal sizes and locations are 1.2182 kW, 1.4047 kW, 1.2555 kW and 1.2786 kW on bus-11, bus-24, bus-29 and bus-30,

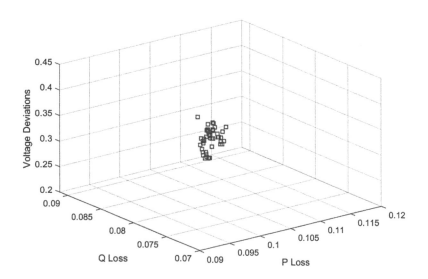

Figure 12.8 Pareto optimal objective functions with three DG units.

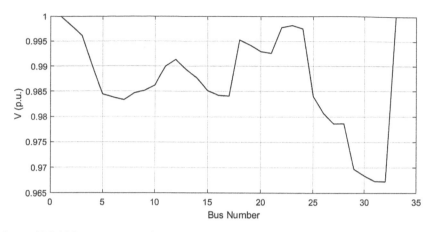

Figure 12.9 Voltages at network junctions with three DG units.

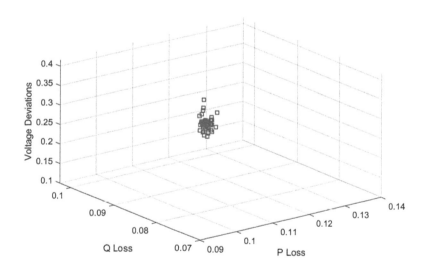

Figure 12.10 Pareto optimal objective functions with four DG units.

respectively (Table 12.4). The TAPL, TRPL, and TVD pareto optimal solutions are presented in Figure 12.10; the figure shows that the functions were, respectively, 99.371kW, 77.150 kVAr and 0.342 p.u. (Table 12.3).

Figure 12.11 displays the voltages measured at all 33 junctions of the IEEE test system during network simulation with four DG units. The voltage at bus-1 is again unity, and it again reduces as the distance of the bus increases relative to the

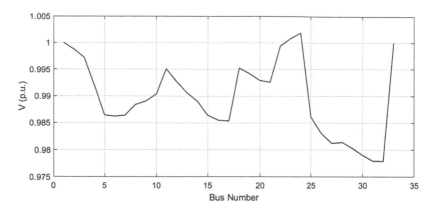

Figure 12.11 Voltages at network junctions with four DG units.

bus-1; the minimum voltage, 0.977 p.u., is again observed at bus-31 and bus-32. However, it is also observed that voltage exceeds unity at bus-24 because of the optimal deployment of the DG units.

12.5.6 Five DG Units

Next we simulated the test MG network considering five DG plants and calculated TAPL, TRPL and TVD to determine the units' optimal deployment and sizes using MOHSA. For five DGs, the optimal sizes and locations are 1.2061 kW, 1.2215 kW, 1.0929 kW, 1.2205kW and 1.8922 kW on bus-13, bus-23, bus-24, bus-29 and bus-32, respectively (Table 12.4). The TAPL, TRPL, and TVD pareto optimal solutions are presented in Figure 12.12; the figure shows that the functions were, respectively, 97.457kW, 76.799 kVAr and 0.342 p.u. sequentially (Table 12.3).

Figure 12.13 displays the voltages measured at all 33 junctions of the IEEE test system during network simulation with five DG units. The voltage at bus-1 is unity, it reduces as the distance of the bus increases relative to bus-1, and the minimum voltage, 0.976 p.u., is observed at bus-31 and bus-32.

12.5.7 Analysis of Performance Indicators

We calculated and analyzed PLRI, QLRI and VDRI for all cases and discuss the findings here. We used the method defined in Section 12.4.1 TAPL Reduction to compute the TAPL reduction indicator (PLRI) using the active power losses in Table 12.3. Table 12.5 presents the PLRI for all cases of study and shows that PLRI is highest with three DG units and the lowest with one unit. Adding DG units did not further improve the PLRI.

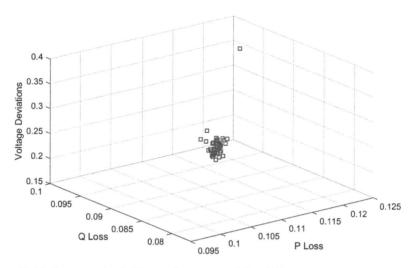

Figure 12.12 Pareto optimal objective functions with five DG units.

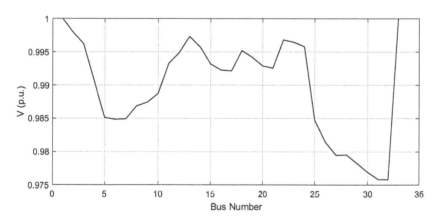

Figure 12.13 Voltages at network junctions with five DG units.

Table 12.5 Performance Indicators

S. No.	Case	PLRI	QLRI	VDRI
1	One DG unit	5.428	5.412	8.025
2	Two DG units	23.298	20.363	54.910
3	Three DG units	37.280	33.084	54.277
4	Four DG units	33.231	29.590	63.886
5	Five DG units	34.517	29.911	63.866

We used the method defined in Section 12.4.2 TRPL Reduction to compute the TRPL reduction indicator (QLRI) using the reactive power losses in Table 12.3. Table 12.5 presents the QLRI for all cases of study and shows that QLRI is highest with three DG units and lowest with one unit. Adding DG units did not further improve the QLRI.

We used the method defined in Section 12.4.3 TVD Reduction to compute the TVD reduction indicator (VDRI) using the total voltage deviations in Table 12.3. Table 12.5 presents the VDRI for all cases of study and shows that VDRI is highest with four and five DG units and lowest with one unit.

12.6 COST–BENEFIT ANALYSIS AND COMPUTATION OF PAYBACK PERIOD

Here, we discuss our cost-benefit analysis of our optimized deployment of optimally sized DG units and how we computed the payback period for the return on the investment in deploying the units. Next we discuss total system losses and loss savings for the optimal unit numbers and sizes at the optimal locations.

12.6.1 Loss Savings and Size of DG Plants

Table 12.6 presents the active power loss saving (PLS) for each optimized DG unit deployment and size and total size of all DG units. We used the parameters in Table 12.6 to calculate the cost–benefit analysis for the DG unit placement.

12.6.2 Cost–Benefit Analysis

We performed this study's cost–benefit analyses based on the current electricity tariffs in the state of Rajasthan in India and the current cost to install a solar PV power system in Rajasthan. The current average electricity tariff (ET) in Rajasthan is INR 7.65/kWh [43]. It costs nearly INR 82,000 to install a 10 kW DG unit (PV system) [44]. The cost of solar PV installation also includes cost of wiring,

Table 12.6 Loss Savings and DG Unit Sizes

S. No.	Case	Total active power loss	Loss saving w.r.t. case of without DG units	Total size of DG units
1	No DG units	148.828 kW	–	–
2	One DG unit	140.750 kW	8.078 kW	1.9998 kW
3	Two DG units	114.154 kW	34.674 kW	2.7192 kW
4	Three DG units	93.344 kW	55.484 kW	3.5600 kW
5	Four DG units	99.371 kW	49.457 kW	5.1570 kW
6	Five DG units	97.457 kW	51.371 kW	6.6332 kW

operation and maintenance. The payback time is the time after which all installation costs have been recovered.

We compute the monthly cost savings (MCS) due to the placement of DG plants using the PLS, the ET and equation (12.10):

$$MCS\,(Rs.) = PLS\,(kW) \times 30 \times 24 \times ET(Rs./kWh) \times \frac{4}{24} \qquad (12.10)$$

Here, we assumed that total power generation is available for a duration of 4 hours in a cycle of 24 hours. Total capital cost occurred on use of DG units (TCCDG) is calculated as follows:

$$TCCDG(Rs.) = \frac{TSDG(kW) \times 82000}{10} \qquad (12.11)$$

The payback period (PP) in years is computed by the ratio of TCCDG and MCS as follows:

$$PP(month) = \frac{TCCDG}{MCS} \qquad (12.12)$$

Next we separately calculate the monthly cost savings, total capital costs for DG unit placement and payback period for each case.

12.6.2.1 One DG Unit

Equation 12.13 calculates the MCS for the optimal placement of one DG unit (MCS1) of 1.9998 kW:

$$MCS1 = 8.078 \times 30 \times 24 \times 7.65 \times \frac{4}{24} = Rs.7415.604 \qquad (12.13)$$

Total capital cost to install one DG unit (TCCDG1) is calculated as

$$TCCDG1(Rs.) = \frac{1.9998 \times 82000}{10} = Rs.16398.36 \qquad (12.14)$$

PP in months is computed by the ratio of TCCDG1 and MCS1 as equation (12.15):

$$PP1 = \frac{16398.36}{7415.604} = 2.211\,months \qquad (12.15)$$

12.6.2.2 Two DG Units

Equation 12.16 calculates MCS2 for the optimal deployment of two DG plants of 2.7192 kW:

$$MCS2 = 34.674 \times 30 \times 24 \times 7.65 \times \frac{4}{24} = Rs.31830.732 \qquad (12.16)$$

Total capital cost to install two DG units (TCCDG2) is calculated as

$$TCCDG2(Rs.) = \frac{2.7192 \times 82000}{10} = Rs.22297.44 \qquad (12.17)$$

PP2 in months is computed by the ratio of TCCDG2 and MCS2 as equation (12.18):

$$PP2 = \frac{22297.44}{31830.732} = 0.701\,month \qquad (12.18)$$

12.6.2.3 Three DG Units

Equation 12.19 calculates MCS3 for the optimal deployment of three DG plants of 3.5600 kW:

$$MCS3 = 55.484 \times 30 \times 24 \times 7.65 \times \frac{4}{24} = Rs.50934.312 \qquad (12.19)$$

Total capital cost to install three DG units (TCCDG2) is calculated as

$$TCCDG3(Rs.) = \frac{3.5600 \times 82000}{10} = Rs.29192.00 \qquad (12.20)$$

PP3 in months is computed by the ratio of TCCDG3 and MCS3 as equation (12.21):

$$PP3 = \frac{29192.00}{50934.312} = 0.573\,month \qquad (12.21)$$

12.6.2.4 Four DG Units

Equation (12.22) calculates MCS4 for the optimal deployment of four DG units of 5.1570 kW:

$$MCS4 = 49.457 \times 30 \times 24 \times 7.65 \times \frac{4}{24} = Rs.45401.526 \qquad (12.22)$$

Total capital cost to install four DG units (TCCDG4) is calculated as

$$TCCDG4(Rs.) = \frac{5.1570 \times 82000}{10} = Rs.42287.40 \qquad (12.23)$$

Payback period (PP4) in months is computed by the ratio of TCCDG4 and MCS4 as equation (12.24):

$$PP4 = \frac{42287.40}{45401.526} = 0.931\,month \qquad (12.24)$$

12.6.2.5 Five DG Units

Equation 12.25 calculations MCS5 for the optimal deployment of five DG plants of 6.6332 kW:

$$MCS5 = 51.371 \times 30 \times 24 \times 7.65 \times \frac{4}{24} = Rs.47158.578 \qquad (12.25)$$

Total capital cost to install five DG plants (TCCDG5) is calculated as

$$TCCDG5(Rs.) = \frac{6.6332 \times 82000}{10} = Rs.54392.24 \qquad (12.26)$$

PP5 in months is computed by the ratio of TCCDG5 and MCS5 as equation (12.27):

$$PP5 = \frac{54392.24}{47158.578} = 1.153 \, month \qquad (12.27)$$

12.6.2.6 Cost–Benefit Analysis Results

The active power loss savings, total sizes of the DG units, monthly cost savings, total capital costs for DG unit placement and payback periods for all cases are provided in Table 12.7.

The results in Table 12.7 indicate that active power loss reduction was greatest and the payback period was shortest with three DG units installed. Installing more decreased the PLS and increased the payback period. We therefore conclude based on the cost–benefit analysis that three DG units is the most cost-effective solution.

12.6.3 Performance Comparative Study

Next, we compared the performance of the proposed MOHSA with that of the GA reported in [45] for determining the optimal placement of optimally sized DG units. Table 12.8 presents the performance comparison findings in terms of different performance indicators and payback period.

Table 12.7 Cost–Benefit Analysis Results

S. No.	Case	PLS (kW)	TSDG (kW)	MCS (Rs.)	TCCDG (Rs.)	PP (months)
1	One DG unit	8.078 kW	1.9998 kW	7415.604	16398.36	2.211
2	Two DG units	34.674 kW	2.7192 kW	31830.732	22297.44	0.701
3	Three DG units	55.484 kW	3.5600 kW	50934.312	29192.00	0.573
4	Four DG units	49.457 kW	5.1570 kW	45401.526	42287.40	0.931
5	Five DG units	51.371 kW	6.6332 kW	47158.578	54392.24	1.153

Table 12.8 Comparative Performances of MOHSA and GA

S. No.	Indicator	Proposed MOHSA	GA
1	PLRI	37.280	31.293
2	QLRI	33.084	27.012
3	VDRI	54.277	45.908
4	DG Capacity	3.560 kW	3.984 kW
5	Active power loss saving	55.484 kW	49.248 KW
6	Payback period	0.573 Month	0.775 Month

Table 12.8 shows that active power loss saving, PLRI, QLRI and VDRI are all higher with our proposed MOHSA than with the GA reported in [45]. Further, the DG units can be smaller with MOHSA, and the payback periods are shorter. In short, MOHSA outperforms GA for determining the optimal placement of DG units.

12.7 CONCLUSION

In this study, we applied a multiobjective I to determine the optimal size and location of distributed energy generators to minimize the losses of active power, reactive power and voltage deviations in a smart city microgrid power network. We achieved this by using the MOHSA to optimize three objective functions: PLMF, QLMF and VDMF, which we measured using the performance indicators PLRI, QLRI and VDRI. We rated overall effectiveness in terms of payback period, the time until the investment in the DG units is recovered.

We performed the study looking at a microgrid network with no DG unit and then with one, two, three, four and five units and concluded that active power loss savings were the greatest and the payback period was the shortest with three DG units. Installing more DG plants increased the PLS and the payback period. Based on the cost–benefit analysis, three DG units is the most cost-effective solution. Further, the PLRI, QLRI and VDRI were the best with three DG units. We compared the performance of the designed MOHSA with the GA reported on in the literature and showed that active power loss saving, PLRI, QLRI, VDRI, size of DG units and payback period were all better with MOHSA than with GA. We conducted this study effectively on a microgrid designed with an IEEE 33-bus test network in MATLAB.

12.8 ACKNOWLEDGMENT

This research work is supported by Innovader Research Labs, Innovader IITian Padhaiwala LearnLab Pvt. Ltd., Jaipur, India.

REFERENCES

[1] S. Ravindran, T. Aruldoss Albert Victoire, "A bio-geography-based algorithm for optimal siting and sizing of distributed generators with an effective power factor model," Computers & Electrical Engineering, Vol. 72, 2018, pp. 482–501, https://doi.org/10.1016/j.compeleceng.2018.10.010.

[2] P.P. Barker, R.W. De Mello, "Determining the impact of distributed generation on power systems. I. Radial distribution systems," Power Engineering Society Summer Meeting, Vol. 3, pp. 1645–1656. doi: 10.1109/PESS.20 0 0.868775.

[3] Sirine Essallah, Adel Khedher, Adel Bouallegue, "Integration of distributed generation in electrical grid: Optimal placement and sizing under different load conditions" Computers and Electrical Engineering, Vol. 79, 2019, p. 106461.

[4] Raida Sellami, Farooq Sher, Rafik Neji, "An improved MOPSO algorithm for optimal sizing & placement of distributed generation: A case study of the Tunisian offshore distribution network (ASHTART)," Energy Reports, Vol. 8, 2022, pp. 6960–6975.

[5] Faheem Ud Din, Ayaz Ahmad, Hameed Ullah, Aimal Khan, Tariq Umer, Shaohua Wan, "Efficient sizing and placement of distributed generators in cyber-physical power systems," Journal of Systems Architecture, Vol. 97, 2019, pp. 197–207, https://doi.org/10.1016/j.sysarc.2018.12.004.

[6] Seyed Iman Taheri, Mauricio B.C. Salles, Alexandre B. Nassif, "Distributed energy resource placement considering hosting capacity by combining teaching–learning-based and honey-bee-mating ilberttion algorithms," Applied Soft Computing, Vol. 113, Part B, 2021, p. 107953, https://doi.org/10.1016/j.asoc.2021.107953.

[7] R. B. Magadum and D. B. Kulkarni, "Optimal placement and sizing of multiple distributed generators using fuzzy logic," 2019 Fifth International Conference on Electrical Energy Systems (ICEES), 2019, pp. 1–6, doi: 10.1109/ICEES.2019.8719240.

[8] F. Tooryan and E. R. Collins, "Optimum size and placement of distributed generators in microgrid based on reliability concept," 2018 IEEE Power and Energy Conference at Illinois (PECI), 2018, pp. 1–6, doi: 10.1109/PECI.2018.8334992.

[9] R. Deshmukh and A. Kalage, "Optimal placement and sizing of distributed generator in distribution system using artificial bee colony algorithm," 2018 IEEE Global Conference on Wireless Computing and Networking (GCWCN), 2018, pp. 178–181, doi: 10.1109/GCWCN.2018.8668633.

[10] M. M. Gidd, S. L. Mhetre and I. M. Korachagaon, "Optimum position and optimum size of the distributed generators for different bus network using genetic algorithm," 2018 Fourth International Conference on Computing Communication Control and Automation (ICCUBEA), 2018, pp. 1–6, doi: 10.1109/ICCUBEA.2018.8697595.

[11] M. Khanabadi, M. Doostizadeh, A. Esmaeilian and M. Mohseninezhad, "Transmission congestion management through optimal distributed generation's sizing and placement," 2011 10th International Conference on Environment and Electrical Engineering, 2011, pp. 1–4, doi: 10.1109/EEEIC.2011.5874788.

[12] Gajendra Singh Chawda, Abdul Gafoor Shaik, Om Prakash Mahela, Sanjeevikumar Padmanaban, "Performance improvement of weak grid-connected wind energy system using FLSRF controlled DSTATCOM," IEEE Transactions on Industrial Electronics, vol. 70, no. 2, 2023, pp. 1565–1575, doi: 10.1109/TIE.2022.3158012

[13] Pramod Kumar, Nagendra Kumar Swarnkar, Om Prakash Mahela, Baseem Khan, Divya Anand, Aman Singh, Juan Luis Vidal Mazon, and Fahd S. Alharithi,

"Optimal sizing and deployment of renewable energy generators in practical transmission network using grid oriented multi-objective harmony search algorithm for loss reduction and voltage profile improvement," International Transactions on Electrical Energy Systems, Vol. 2023, 2023, Article ID 6315918, https://doi.org/10.1155/2023/6315918

[14] Ekata Kaushik, Vivek Prakash, Raymond Ghandour, Zaher Al Barakeh, Ahmed Ali, Om Prakash Mahela, Roberto Marcelo Álvarez, and Baseem Khan. "Hybrid combination of network restructuring and optimal placement of distributed generators to reduce transmission loss and improve flexibility," Sustainability, Vol. 15, no. 6, 2023, p. 5285. https://doi.org/10.3390/su15065285

[15] Takele Ferede Agajie, Armand Fopah-Lele, Ahmed Ali, Isaac Amoussou, Baseem Khan, Mahmoud Elsisi, Om Prakash Mahela, Roberto Marcelo Alvarez, and Emmanuel Tanyi, "Optimal sizing and power system control of hybrid solar pv-biogas generator with energy storage system power plant", Sustainability, Vol. 15, no. 7, p. 5739, 2023, https://doi.org/10.3390/su15075739

[16] Om Prakash Mahela, Mayank Parihar, Akhil Ranjan Garg, Baseem Khan, Salah Kamel, "A hybrid signal processing technique for recognition of complex power quality disturbances," Electric Power Systems Research, Vol. 207, Paper No. 107865, https://doi.org/10.1016/j.epsr.2022.107865

[17] Rajkumar Kaushik, Om Prakash Mahela, Pramod Kumar Bhatt, Baseem Khan, Akhil Ranjan Garg, Hassan Haes Alhelou, and Pierluigi Siano, "Recognition of islanding and operational events in power system with renewable energy penetration using a stockwell transform based method", IEEE Systems Journal, Vol. 16, no. 1, 2022, pp. 166–175. https://doi.org/10.1109/JSYST.2020.3020919

[18] Ravinder Kumar, Hari Om Bansal, Aditya R. Gautam, Om Prakash Mahela, and Baseem Khan, "Experimental investigations on particle swarm optimization based control algorithm for shunt active power filter to enhance electric power quality," IEEE Access, Vol. 10, 2022, pp. 54878–54890. https://doi.org/10.1109/ACCESS.2022.3176732

[19] Ekata Kaushik, Vivek Prakash, Om Prakash Mahela, Baseem Khan, Almoataz Y. Abdelaziz, Junhee Hong and Zong Woo Geem, "Optimal placement of renewable energy generators using grid-oriented genetic algorithm for loss reduction and flexibility improvement," Energies, Vol. 15, Paper No. 1863, https://doi.org/10.3390/en15051863

[20] Ekata Kaushik, Vivek Prakash, Om Prakash Mahela, Baseem Khan, Adel El-Shahat, and A.Y. Abdelaziz, "Comprehensive overview of power system flexibility during the scenario of high penetration of renewable energy in utility grid," Energies, Vol. 15, Paper No. 516, https://doi.org/10.3390/en15020516

[21] Gori Shankar Sharma, Om Prakash Mahela, Mohamed G. Hussien, Baseem Khan, Sanjeevikumar Padmanaban, M. B. Shafik and Z. M. Salem Elbarbary, "Performance evaluation of a MW-size grid-connected solar photovoltaic plant considering the impact of tilt angle" Sustainability, Vol. 14, 2022, Paper No. 1444, https://doi.org/10.3390/su14031444

[22] Nagendra Kumar Swarnkar, Om Prakash Mahela, Baseem Khan, and Mahendra Lalwani, "Multivariable passive method for detection of islanding events in renewable energy based power grids," IET Renewable Power Generation, Vol. 16, 2022, pp. 497–516. https://doi.org/10.1049/rpg2.12355

[23] Om Prakash Mahela, Mahdi Khosravy, Neeraj Gupta, Baseem Khan, Hassan Haes Alhelou, Rajendra Mahla, Nilesh Patel, and Pierluigi Siano, "Comprehensive overview of multi-agent systems for controlling smart grids," CSEE Journal of Power and Energy Systems, Vol. 8, no. 1, 2022, pp. 115–131, https://doi.org/10.17775/CSEEJPES.2020.03390

[24] Pawan Singh, Baseem Khan, Om Prakash Mahela, Hassan Haes Alhelou, G. Hayek, "Managing energy plus performance in data centers and battery-based devices using an online non-clairvoyant speed-bounded multiprocessor scheduling," Applied Sciences, Vol. 10, no. 7, 2020, p. 2459, https://doi.org/10.3390/app10072459

[25] Om Prakash Mahela, Abdul Gafoor Shaik, "Comprehensive overview of grid interfaced solar photovoltaic systems," Renewable and Sustainable Energy Reviews (Elsevier), Vol. 68, Part 1, 2017, pp. 316–332. https://doi.org/10.1016/j.rser.2016.09.096

[26] Om Prakash Mahela, Abdul Gafoor Shaik, "Comprehensive overview of grid interfaced wind energy generation systems," Renewable and Sustainable Energy Reviews (Elsevier), Vol. 57, 2016, pp. 260–281. https://doi.org/10.1016/j.rser.2015.12.048

[27] Om Prakash Mahela, Abdul Gafoor Shaik, "Topological aspects of power quality improvement techniques: A comprehensive overview," Renewable and Sustainable Energy Reviews (Elsevier), Vol. 58, 2016, pp. 1129–1142. https://doi.org/10.1016/j.rser.2015.12.251

[28] Om Prakash Mahela, and Abdul Gafoor Shaik, "A review of distribution static compensator," Renewable and Sustainable Energy Reviews (Elsevier), Vol. 50, 2015, pp. 531–546, https://doi.org/10.1016/j.rser.2015.05.018

[29] Rajkumar Kaushik, Om Prakash Mahela, Pramod Kumar Bhatt, "Hybrid algorithm for detection of events and power quality disturbances associated with distribution network in the presence of wind energy," IEEE International Conference on Advance Computing and Innovative Technologies in Engineering (ICACITE 2021), Galgotias College of Engineering College and Technology, Greater Noida, India, March 4–5, 2021, https://doi.org/10.1109/ICACITE51222.2021.9404665

[30] Rahul Choudhary, Om Prakash Mahela, Surendra Singh, Krishna Gopal Sharma and Akhil Ranjan Garg, "Restructuring of transmission network to cater load demand in northern parts of rajasthan using renewable energy," International Conference on Computational Intelligence and Emerging Power System (ICCIPS 2021), 9–10 March 2021, Government Engineering College, Ajmer, https://doi.org/10.1007/978-981-16-4103-9

[31] Atul Kulshrestha, Om Prakash Mahela, Mukesh Kumar Gupta, "Identification and classification of faults in utility grid with solar energy using discrete wavelet transform and decision rules," 12th IEEE International Conference on Computational Intelligence and Communication Networks (CICN 2020), BIAS Bhimtal, Nainital, September 24–25, 2020, https://doi.org/10.1109/CICN49253.2020.9242564

[32] Ram Narayan Shah, Om Prakash Mahela, Sushma Lohia, "Recognition and mitigation of power quality disturbances in renewable energy interfaced hybrid power grid," 12th IEEE International Conference on Computational Intelligence and Communication Networks (CICN 2020), BIAS Bhimtal, Nainital, September 24–25, 2020, https://doi.org/10.1109/CICN49253.2020.9242623

[33] Aditi Singh, Ahmad Hasan Khan, Ankit Kumar Sharma, Om Prakash Mahela, "Recognition of disturbances in hybrid grid using discrete wavelet transform and

stockwell transform based algorithm," First IEEE International Conference on Measurement, Instrumentation, Control and Automation (ICMICA 2020), NIT Kurukshetra, April 2–4, 2020, https://doi.org/10.1109/ICMICA48462.2020.9242867

[34] Jaya Sharma, Bipul Kumar, Om Prakash Mahela, Akhil Ranjan Garg, "Protection of distribution feeder using stockwell transform supported voltage features," IEEE 9th Power India International Conference (PIICON 2020) from 28 Feb to 01 March, 2020 – Deenbandhu Chhotu Ram University of Science and Technology, Murthal, https://doi.org/10.1109/PIICON49524.2020.9113014

[35] Mohd Zishan Khoker, Om Prakash Mahela, and Gulhasan Ahmad, "A voltage algorithm using discrete wavelet transform and ilbert transform for detection and classification of power system faults in the presence of solar energy," 2020 IEEE International Students' Conference on Electrical, Electronics and Computer Science (SCEECS 2020), MANIT Bhopal, India, February 22–23, 2020, https://doi.org/10.1109/SCEECS48394.2020.7

[36] Om Prakash Mahela, Kapil Dev Kansal and Sunil Agarwal, "Detection of power quality disturbances in utility grid with solar photovoltaic energy penetration," 8th IEEE India International Conference on Power Electronics (IICPE-2018), Electronic, MNIT Jaipur, December 13–14, 2018, DOI: 10.1109/IICPE.2018.8709597

[37] Om Prakash Mahela, Himmani Joshi, Deepak Sharma and Shuvam Sahay, "Detection of open circuiting of secondary winding of current transformer using combined feature of ilbert transform and stockwell transform," 2018 IEEE 8th Power India International Conference (PIICON 2018), NIT Kurukshetra, December 10–12, 2018, DOI: 10.1109/POWERI.2018.8704354

[38] M. E. Baran, F. F. Wu, "Network reconfiguration in distribution systems for loss reduction and load balancing," IEEE Transactions on Power Delivery, Vol. 4, no. 2, 1989, pp. 1401–1407.

[39] S. H. Dolatabadi, M. Ghorbanian, P. Siano, N. D. Hatziargyriou, "An enhanced IEEE 33 bus benchmark test system for distribution system studies," IEEE Transactions on Power Systems, Vol. 36, no. 3, 2021, pp. 2565–2572. Doi: 10.1109/TPWRS.2020.3038030.

[40] X.-S. Yang, "Harmony search as a meta-heuristic algorithm," in *Music-Inspired Harmony Search Algorithm*, ser. Studies in Computational Intelligence, Z. Geem, Ed. Springer Berlin/Heidelberg, 2009, vol. 191, pp. 1–14.

[41] Z. W. Geem, J. H. Kim, G. Loganathan, "A new heuristic optimization algorithm: Harmony search," *Simulation*, Vol. 76, no. 2, 2001, pp. 60–68.

[42] Z. W. Geem, "State-of-the-art in the structure of harmony search algorithm," in *Recent Advances In Harmony Search Algorithm*, ser. Studies in Computational Intelligence, Z. Geem, Ed. Springer Berlin/Heidelberg, 2010, vol. 270, pp. 1–10.

[43] RERC. Tariff for supply of Electricity-2020. Rajasthan Electricity Regulatory Commission, India, 2021. https://energy.rajasthan.gov.in/content/raj/energy-department/en/departments/jvvnl/Tariff_orders.html.

[44] Solar Panel Installation Cost in India. Loom Solar, India 2021. www.loomsolar.com/blogs/collections/solar-panel-installation-cost-in-india.

[45] P. Gopu, S. Naaz, K. Aiman. "Optimal placement of distributed generation using genetic algorithm," Proceedings of the 2021 International Conference on Advances in Electrical, Computing, Communication and Sustainable Technologies (ICAECT), Bhilai, 19–20 February 2021.

Chapter 13

Integrated Vehicle-to-Grid Control of a Smart City Power Network Microgrid

Ram Niwash Mahia, Raghawendra Mishra,
Shalabh Gupta and Om Prakash Mahela

13.1 INTRODUCTION

Microgrids (MGs) are an effective solution for integrating generated renewable energy (RE) with smart city power networks. However, MGs have the limitations of limited RE storage and low improved energy efficiency. Multi-MGs help to solve these problems. Multi-MGs have the advantages of increased RE, improved economy, high energy connectivity with grid operations, and reduced impact on smart city networks [1].

Incorporating electric vehicles (Evs) into smart city MGs can lead to increased fluctuations in voltage, frequency changes, and decreased power availability. The control methods for vehicle-to-grid (V2G) in smart city MGs are coordinated for charging and regulation but have low efficiency, charging control constraints, high complexity, and high computation demand [2]. Recently, researchers have reported on many approaches for the integrated control of MGs including with V2G interfaces.

The authors of [3] report on a detailed study of smart MG control and estimation techniques; they can be DC or AC. In [4], the authors presented a detailed study of the topologies, control schemes, and implementations of a DC-based MG. In [5], the authors introduced a controller for an AC MG that used a false data injection attack. They also designed a distributed adaptive secondary controller for the AC MG that helped to regulate the frequency at the rated value and the voltage in the prescribed limits when controllers were impacted by the attack.

In [6], the authors proposed a model smart city MG with a water heating system incorporated that used the basic principle of an electric spring to coordinate and control the resources in the MG. Water heating system is a load of non-critical nature. In [7], the authors proposed a method for selecting MG control layers that will effectively defend against cyberattacks. The MG contained various distributed generation plants, and the authors adopted hierarchical control. The communication channels for distributed generation make MGs more vulnerable, and cybersecurity issues are pronounced.

In [8], the author proposed a synchronous generator-supported error tracking controller for AC/DC bidirectional converters. It could maintain balance of both AC

DOI: 10.1201/9781003486930-18

and DC power and also effectively minimized frequency and voltage fluctuations without normalization. In [9], the authors proposed back-stepping control for inverters connected in parallel in a smart city MG. In [10], the authors proposed a convex, time-varying, optimization-supported consensus controller that could be used for secondary control of the MG even in the island mode of operations. Detailed studies on smart city technologies such as wind power plants (WPPs), solar PV plants (SPVPs), MGs, Evs, and smart city power network issues are available in [11–41].

We conclude from our in-depth literature review that V2G technology interfaced with MG has the potential to meet smart city energy demand using RE. We consider the main contributions of our research work to be that we designed a smart city MG that incorporated a WPP, diesel generator (DGs), a SPVP, both residential and industrial loads, and V2G technology and that we designed a bidirectional power flow control method for the V2G technology to control the grid parameters during dynamic states.

13.2 BLOCK DIAGRAM OF A PROPOSED SMART CITY MICROGRID

The block scheme of the proposed smart city MG for this study is described in Figure 13.1. It consists of generators and two buses, MG Bus-1 and MG Bus-2, that are integrated with each other through a transformer T-MG. MG

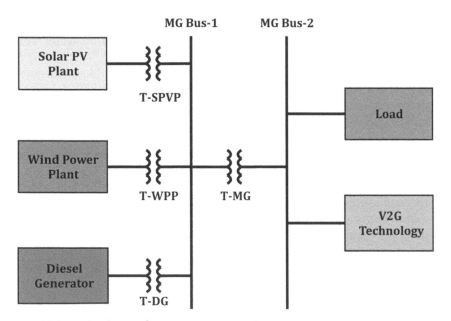

Figure 13.1 Block scheme of a smart city microgrid.

Bus-1 is operated at 25 kV voltage, and MG Bus-2 is operated at 600V. The generators—the SPVP, a WPP, and a DG—are connected to MG Bus-1; load and V2G technology are connected to MG Bus-2. The MG is operated at 60Hz frequency.

The SPVP is integrated to MG Bus-1 using the transformer T-SPVP. The WPP is integrated to MG-Bus-1 using the transformer T-WPP, and DG is integrated to MG-Bus-1 using the transformer T-DG. We give detailed descriptions of the generators, load, V2G technology, transformers, and control methods for each unit in the next section. We developed the MG in MATLAB® software using blocks of different components in phasor mode to ensure the fast simulation of a 24 hour scenario.

13.2.1 Wind Power Plant

The WPP is realized by a wind turbine coupled with a doubly fed induction generator. It is rated at 4.5MW and generates power that is linearly linked with wind speed: When the wind speed achieves a nominal value, the WPP produces nominal power. The WPP is disconnected from the grid from when the maximum wind speed is reached until wind speed gains nominal value. A simulated wind profile is illustrated in Figure 13.2. The nominal wind speed we considered for the study was 13.5 m/s, and the maximum wind speed was 15 m/s.

13.2.2 Solar Power Plant

The SPVP is realized using solar PV plates connected in series and parallel combinations; its rated capacity is 8MW. The SPVP generates power that is proportional to three factors: (1) total area over which the PV panels are installed, (2) the efficiency of the panels, and (3) the solar irradiance. The power generated by the

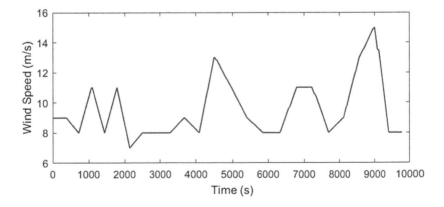

Figure 13.2 Simulated wind profile of the WPP.

PV farm is expressed as a product of efficiency, area covered by the PV farm, and irradiance in W/m². The total area considered for the PV farm is 80,000 m². The panels' efficiency is 10%. A simulated pattern of solar irradiance is illustrated in Figure 13.3; partial shading is projected for a period of 5 minutes at a factor of 0.7 for 12 hours (43,200 s).

13.2.3 Diesel Generator

The DG is realized with a synchronous machine. The details of its technical parameters are provided in Table 13.1. The DG acts as the base power generator and is considered a swing bus in the proposed microgrid; it balances the power generated and consumed in the MG. Frequency deviations in the grid are determined by analysis of rotor speed of the synchronous DG.

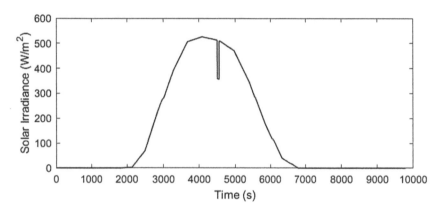

Figure 13.3 Simulated irradiance levels for the solar PV plant.

Table 13.1 Technical Parameters of the Diesel Generator

S. No.	Name of Parameter	Parameter Value
1	Nominal power	15 MW
2	Line-to-line voltage	25 kV
3	Rated frequency	60 Hz
4	Stator resistance (pu)	0.003
5	Inertia constant	3.7
6	Friction factor	0
7	Pole pairs	1
8	Direct-axis synchronous reactance (X_d) in pu	1.305
9	Quadrature-axis synchronous reactance (X_q) in pu	0.474

The governor system is realized using the transfer functions. There are two inputs to the governor: reference speed and measured speed. The mechanical power of the DG is considered the output. Motor inertia and generator inertia are combined. The model consists of a regulator that can be expressed by the following transfer function:

$$Hc = \frac{K.(1+T3\times s)}{1+T1\times s+T1\times T2\times s^2}$$

The actuator is implemented as

$$Ha = \frac{(1+T4.s)}{(s(1+T5.s)(1+T6.s))}$$

The various time constants are given in Table 13.2.

13.2.4 Vehicle-to-Grid Technology

We propose a V2G system to regulate the frequencies of events that happen on a smart city MG in a given 24 hours (full day). V2G controls the charge on the integrated batteries, and available power is used to regulate the system during daytime events. We base our simulations on the following five car user profiles:

- Profile 1: People are traveling to an office and can charge their car batteries at work.
- Profile 2: People are traveling to an office and can charge their car batteries at work, but they have a longer ride.
- Profile 3: People are traveling to an office where they cannot charge their car batteries.
- Profile 4: People stay at home.
- Profile 5: People are traveling to work night shifts.

Table 13.2 Time Constants

S. No.	Symbol of Time Constant/Gain	Parameter Value
1	Regulator gain K	29
2	T1	0.01 s
3	T2	0.02 s
4	T3	0.2 s
5	T4	0.25
6	T5	0.009
7	T6	0.0384
8	Engine time delay Td (s)	0.024

We simulated these five profiles, and they can all be modified; the user can set the vehicle numbers for each profile and also change the rated capacity, power, and power converter efficiency. The cars in the V2G are rated at 40 kW and 85k Wh with system efficiency of 90%. Since there are 100 cars in all the profiles, the total rated capacity of the V2G technology is 4 MW. Table 13.3 presents three use scenarios for the different profiles.

The cars are maintained in two modes, in regulation or in charge. The cars in charge mode continuously take power from the grid and charge their batteries, and cars in regulation mode generally will not exchange power with the MG.

13.2.5 Load

There are two load types: residential and industrial. An asynchronous motor is implemented to simulate the impact of an industrial inductive load on the MG, and we use a load of 0.16MVA. The asynchronous motor is controlled by a square relationship between the rotor speed and mechanical torque. Figure 13.4 graphically displays the residential load consumption pattern.

Table 13.3 Case Study Scenarios

S. No.	Profile	Number of cars		
		Scenario 1	Scenario 2	Scenario 3
1	Profile 1	35	40	30
2	Profile 2	25	20	30
3	Profile 3	10	10	15
4	Profile 4	20	15	15
5	Profile 5	10	15	10

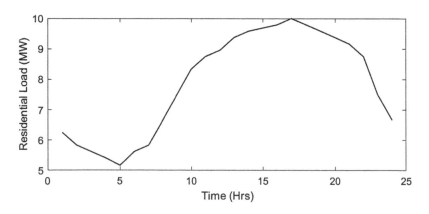

Figure 13.4 Residential load consumption profile.

13.2.6 Details of Transformers

Four transformers are used to design the smart city MG. T-MG connects the two MG buses, which are operated on different voltage levels. T-SPVP connects the solar PV plant to MG Bus-1 to step the voltage generated by the SPVP from 270 V to 25 kV. T-WPP connects the wind power plant to MG Bus-2 to step the voltage generated by WPP from 575 V to 25 kV. T-DG connects the wind power plant to MG Bus-2. This is a one-to-one transformer because the DG generates power at 25 kV, the same as MG Bus-1. Table 13.4 offers details on the transformers.

13.2.7 Proposed EV Charging Philosophy

The EV battery acts as a variable load, and the EV supply system can provide a bidirectional power flow by permitting the EVs to charge and discharge. The voltage and frequency controls of the EV supply system determine the current flow into and out of the EV. A meter measures the EV's electricity consumption. The main onboard vehicle components are the EV inlet, the charger, and the energy storage system. The vehicle inlet and the supply connector interface, and if the EV supply is AC and AC is supplied to the vehicle, the reverse flow will also be AC. The vehicle converts DC battery power to AC output power with an inverter.

13.2.7.1 Bidirectional Charger System

A bidirectional converter is needed to control the current charge and discharge between the AC bus and the EV battery [10]. Figure 13.5 graphically displays the control topology we used for the V2G system design. The bidirectional charger connects the grid and EVs in two stages: (1) grid-connected AC/DC converter and (2) DC/DC converter.

Table 13.4 Description of Transformers

S. No.	Symbol of transformer	Transformer ratio	MVA rating
1	T-SPVP	25 kV/270 V	10 MVA
2	T-WPP	25 kV/575 V	6 MVA
3	T-DG	25 kV/25 kV	20 MVA
4	T-MG	25 kV/600 V	20 MVA

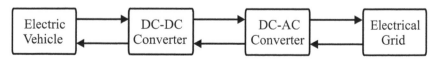

Figure 13.5 Bidirectional charger system.

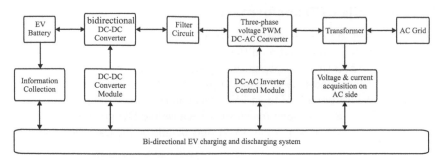

Figure 13.6 Structure of the bidirectional charge and discharge mechanism.

13.2.7.2 V2G Control Mechanism

The EV charging and discharging mechanism uses a three-phase power supply (AC grid) that is connected to batteries and a control loop using a transformer, inverter, filter, and bidirectional DC/DC converter. The structure is elaborated in Figure 13.6. The inverter has a voltage-type PWM converter that is used for energy exchange between the AC grid and the DC bus; this converter works to rectify actions during charging mode and when the battery is taking energy from the grid, and it works in inversion mode when the EV battery is discharging. Figure 13.6 displays the components of the V2G control circuit.

The overall control structure for V2G has double-loop AC/DC inverter mechanism and a single-loop DC/DC converter stage. The battery monitoring system monitors parameters including state of charge (SOC), state of health, voltage, and temperature, and the controller decides how to charge the battery based on conditions such as the SOC. Currents and voltages can be measured with the AC/DC control of the inverter. The inverter takes care of active and reactive power references for bidirectional power flow with the AC grid in both the charging and discharging (V2G) modes. The operator sets the number of EVs and sends the power requirement to the EVs via V2G for action like frequency regulation and load leveling.

13.3 DETAILED DESCRIPTION OF DESIGN AND IMPLEMENTATION OF SMART CITY MG AND V2G TECHNOLOGY CONTROL

Here, we give a detailed description of how we implemented the V2G control in the smart city MG:

- **Step 1:** The MG is designed in MATLAB using Simulink blocks following the block diagram elaborated in Figure 13.1 using the previously described WPP,

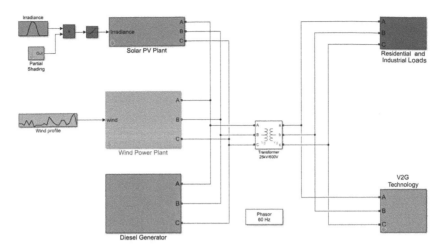

Figure 13.7 Overview of all the component connections in the smart city MG.

SPVP, loads, transformers, DG, and V2G technology. Figure 13.7 gives an overview of the MG component layout in the MATLAB environment. The WPP, SPVP, loads, transformers, and DG are realized using the Simulink models.

- **Step 2:** V2G technology is designed using various components of Simulink library. The major input components that need to change are modeled for input by clicking on the V2G block. The Figure 13.8 contains a snapshot of interactive window where users can input the details.
- **Step 3:** For V2G Technology regulation and charge control are simulated separately. Parameters are measured for both the regulation and charge control.
- **Step 4:** Here we describe the design and control mechanisms for each car user profile and the important steps in the control design:

  o The 1D lookup table block is used to simulate EV battery SOC; following is the string of SOC for a period of 24 hours:

  ▪ [−1 0.9 0.7 0.7 0.7 0.8 0.8 0.8 0.8 0.8 0.9 0.9 0.9 0.9 0.9 0.9 0.8 0.8 0.8 0.9–1 0.9 0.9 0.9].

  o The 1D lookup table block is also used to simulate the plug state for both the SOC and the charge controller. Following is the plug state string for a period of 24 hours:

  ▪ [−1 0.9 0.7 0.7 0.7 0.8 0.8 0.8 0.8 0.8 0.9 0.9 0.9 0.9 0.9 0.9 0.8 0.8 0.8 0.9–1 0.9 0.9 0.9]

  o Charge control is designed using the SR-flip flop and logical operators.
  o SOC is designed using various combinations of the integrator, switches, multipliers, sums, etc.

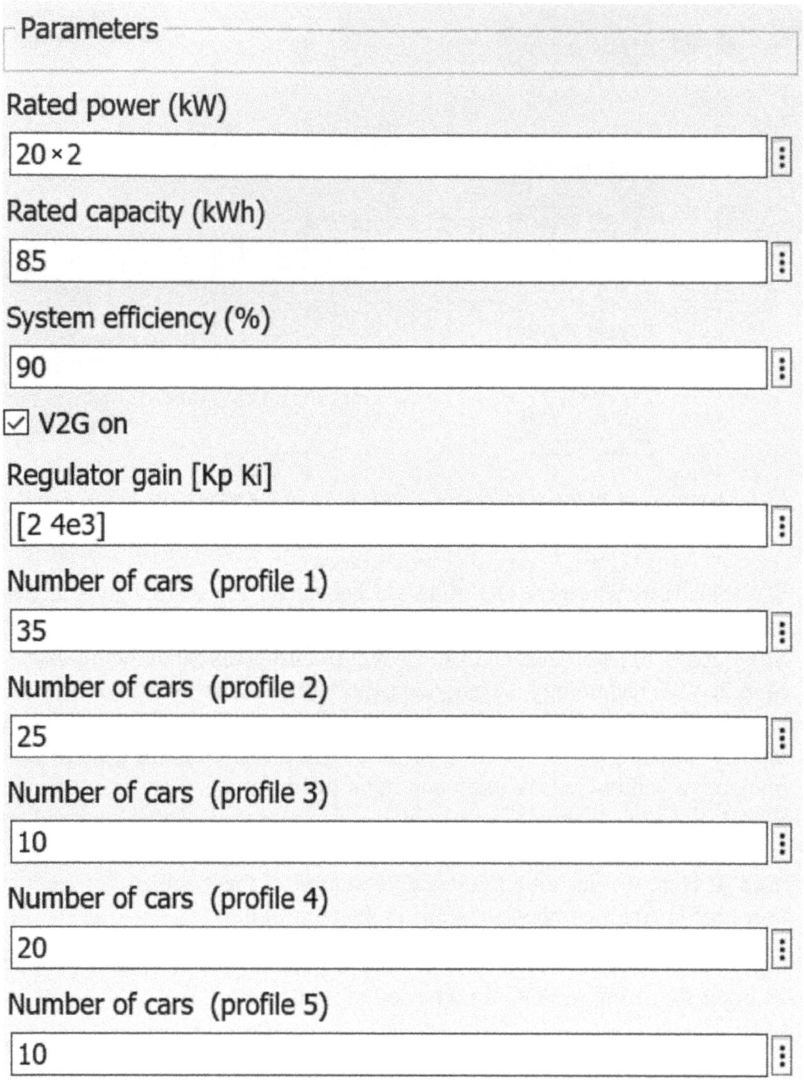

Parameters

Rated power (kW)

| 20×2 | ⠇ |

Rated capacity (kWh)

| 85 | ⠇ |

System efficiency (%)

| 90 | ⠇ |

☑ V2G on

Regulator gain [Kp Ki]

| [2 4e3] | ⠇ |

Number of cars (profile 1)

| 35 | ⠇ |

Number of cars (profile 2)

| 25 | ⠇ |

Number of cars (profile 3)

| 10 | ⠇ |

Number of cars (profile 4)

| 20 | ⠇ |

Number of cars (profile 5)

| 10 | ⠇ |

Figure 13.8 The V2G data input window for V2G.

13.4 SIMULATION

The simulation is performed for a period of 24 hours. Irradiance levels follow a general pattern where maximum intensity is observed at midday. Wind varies with multiple peaks and lows during the day. Normal household consumption patterns are reflected by the residential load; low consumption is seen in day time and high consumption in evening hours, and consumption slowly decreases during night hours. The following events affect the grid frequency during daytime:

- The asynchronous motor kicks in at the third hour.
- Partial shading at noon with the SPVP affects the generation of solar power.
- The wind farm trips at 22 hours because the wind speed exceeds the maximum permitted speed.

A power profile of all the generators and loads is given for the complete day cycle to identify the contributions from every generator and the V2G capacity at peak regulation.

13.5 SIMULATION RESULTS AND DISCUSSION

Here, we discuss the simulation results for study scenario 1, scenario 2, and scenario 3. We give detailed descriptions of the results: power supplied by the generators, MG frequency, residential and industrial load profiles, V2G charging and regulation active and reactive power, and car SOC. At the end of chapter a performance comparative study is included to establish efficacy of MG and V2G technology to control the grid parameters.

13.5.1 Scenario 1

We simulated the proposed MG for the scenario 1 parameters in Table 13.3, specifically 35, 25, 10, 20, and 10 cars in profiles 1–5, respectively. Figure 13.9 displays the power supplied by the DG, WPP, and SPVP and the total power injected into the MG.

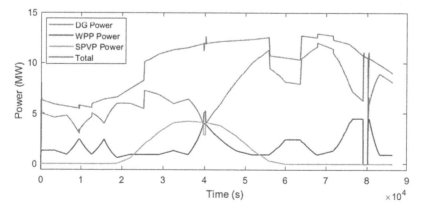

Figure 13.9 Power supplied by generators in scenario 1.

In scenario 1, the total power is the sum of the power supplied by the DG, WPP, and SPVP; partial shading at 43,200 s reduced the solar generation, in turn triggering an increase in generation by the DG. Further, the DG supplies power to mitigate variations in WPP power generation. When wind generation is reduced suddenly at 79,000 s (approximately) due to high wind speed above 15m/s, DG generation increased, and when solar generation was high, DG power supply decreased. In short, in scenario 1, the DG, WPP, and SPVP maintained coordinated control of the DG, WPP, and SPVP including mitigating all load and charging power variations.

The patterns of residential and industrial load variations are illustrated in Figure 13.10. The load patterns were the same for all three scenarios in the study. We observed that industrial load turned on near 3AM and then continued to take load from the MG and that residential load reached a maximum of 10 MW but varied over the entire 24 hours. We also observed small, sudden magnitude changes in the load pattern curve.

Figure 13.11 graphically displays the MG frequencies during scenario 1. The figure shows that the frequency normally held at the nominal frequency of 60Hz but that there were small magnitude changes when either the generation suddenly changed or the V2G charging power changed. However, the frequency did immediately regain the nominal value.

Figure 13.12 displays the V2G charging and regulation power taken from the MG in scenario 1. The figure shows that the V2G charging power changed depending on the car user profile and that the regulation power was only taken or supplied depending on disturbances in the MG. We established that V2G technology can effectively regulate any sudden or dynamic changes in the MG. Figure 13.13 shows the V2G charging and regulation reactive power in scenario 1 and indicates that both charging and regulation reactive power changed when there were sudden load or generation changes. During normal operating conditions, the reactive power exchange was zero. Therefore, we conclude that V2G technology can effectively regulate any sudden or dynamic reactive power changes in the MG.

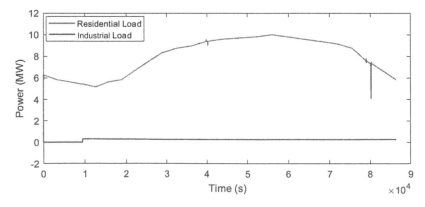

Figure 13.10 Industrial and residential loads in scenario 1.

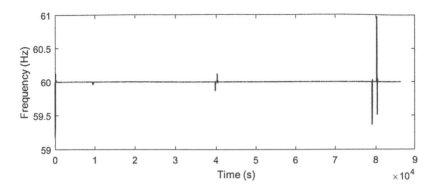

Figure 13.11 Scenario 1 frequencies.

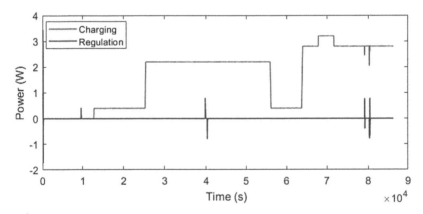

Figure 13.12 V2G charging and regulation power in scenario 1.

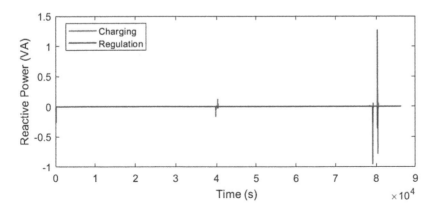

Figure 13.13 V2G charging and regulation reactive power in scenario 1.

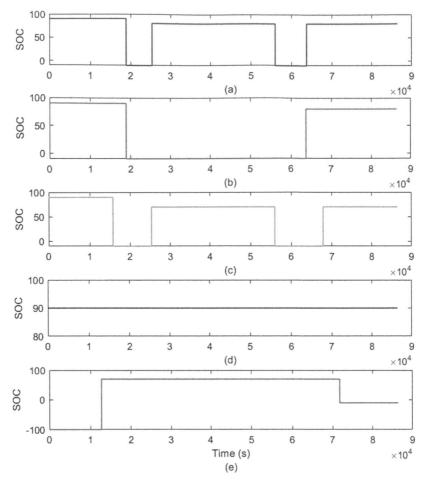

Figure 13.14 Scenario 1 state of charge: (a) profile 1, (b) profile 2, (c) profile 3, (d) profile 4, (e) profile 5.

Figure 13.14(a–e) displays the SOCs for car user profiles 1–5 and indicates that SOC depends on the car status. However, the SOC for cars included in profile 4 was constant at 90%. Negative SOC indicates that the car is on the road and not plugged in, and positive SOC indicates that the car are plugged in.

13.5.2 Scenario 2

Figure 13.15 displays the power supplied by the DG, WPP, and SPVP and the total power injected into the MG for profiles 1–5 in scenario 2. Partial shading at 43,200 s reduced the solar generation, which increased the DG generation; DG

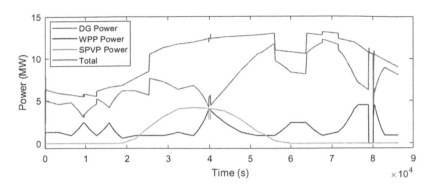

Figure 13.15 Power supplied by generators in scenario 2.

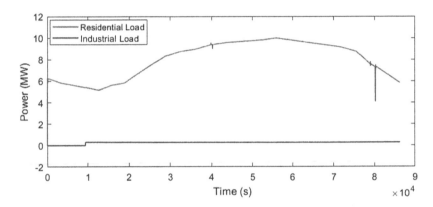

Figure 13.16 Industrial and residential loads in scenario 2.

also supplied power to mitigate the variations in the power generation from the WPP. When wind generation reduced suddenly at approximately 79,000 s due to high wind speed above 15m/s, DG energy generation increased, and when solar generation was high, DG power generation decreased. We established that in scenario 2, the DG, WPP, and SPVP supplied sufficient total load to charge the cars and manage the residential and industrial loads in a coordinated and controlled manner. The generators effectively mitigated all load and charging power variations in scenario 2.

Figure 13.16 displays the residential and industrial load variations in scenario 2. The industrial load activates near 3 AM and then continues to take load from the MG. The residential load peaks at 10 MW but varies over the entire 24 hours. The load pattern curve also reflects sudden small magnitude changes.

Figure 13.17 displays the MG frequencies in scenario 2. The figure shows that the frequency normally remained at the nominal frequency of 60 Hz but that there were small magnitude changes when the generation changed suddenly or the V2G charging power changed; however, the frequency immediately rebounded to the nominal value following these sudden changes.

Figure 13.18 displays the V2G charging and regulation power in scenario 2, and the figure shows that the cars' charging power changed depending on the user profile. Further, regulation power was only taken or supplied depending on the nature of disturbance in the MG. In short, we established that V2G technology can effectively regulate any sudden or dynamic MG changes in scenario 2.

Figure 13.19 shows the V2G charging and regulation reactive power in the MG in scenario 2.

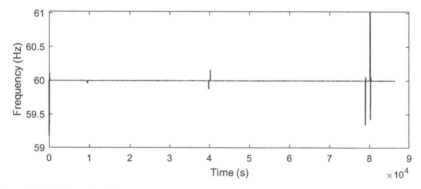

Figure 13.17 Scenario 2 frequencies.

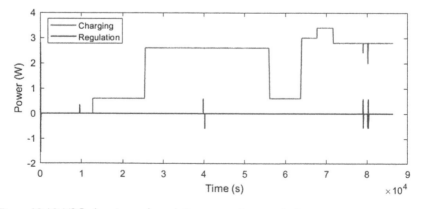

Figure 13.18 V2G charging and regulation power in scenario 2.

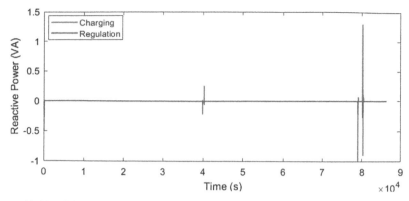

Figure 13.19 V2G charging and regulation reactive power in scenario 2.

Figure 13.20(a–e) displays the scenario 2 SOCs for car user profiles 1–5 and reflects that the SOCs depend on the user car status. Again, however, the SOC for cars included in profile 4 was constant at 90%.

13.5.3 Scenario 3

Figure 13.21 displays the power supplied by the DG, WPP, and SPVP and the total power injected into the MG for profiles 1–5 in scenario 3.

Partial shading at 43,200 s reduced the solar generation, which increased the DG generation; DG power also mitigates variations in WPP power generation. When high wind speed above 15m/s suddenly reduced the wind generation at approximately 79,000 s, the DG generation increased, and at the time of high solar generation, the DG power supply decreased. We established that in scenario 3, the DG, WPP, and SPVP supplied sufficient total load to charge the cars and manage the residential and industrial loads in a coordinated and controlled manner. The generators effectively mitigated all load and charging power variations in scenario 3.

Figure 13.22 displays the pattern of residential and industrial load variations in scenario 3. The industrial load activates near 3 AM and then continues to take load from the MG. The residential load peaks at 10 MW but varies over the entire 24 hours. The load pattern curve also reflects small sudden magnitude changes.

Figure 13.23 displays the MG frequencies in scenario 3. The figure shows that the frequency normally remained at the nominal frequency of 60 Hz but that there were small magnitude changes when the generation changed suddenly or the V2G charging power changed; however, the frequency immediately rebounded to the nominal value following these sudden changes.

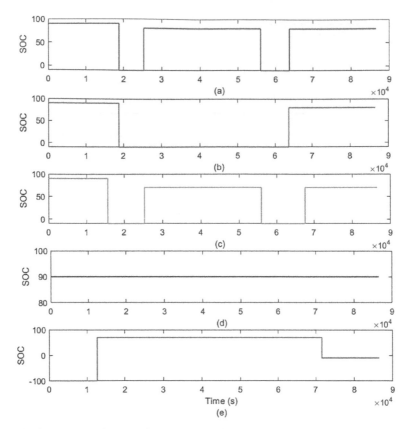

Figure 13.20 Scenario 2 state of charge: (a) profile 1, (b) profile 2, (c) profile 3, (d) profile 4, (e) profile 5.

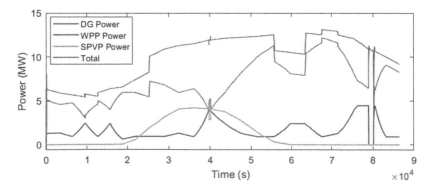

Figure 13.21 Power supplied by generators in scenario 3.

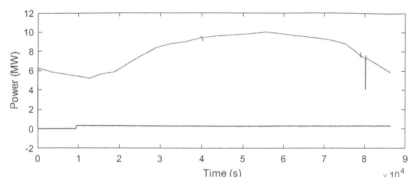

Figure 13.22 Industrial and residential loads in scenario 3.

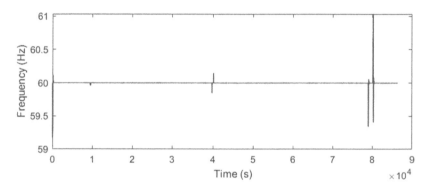

Figure 13.23 Scenario 3 frequencies.

Figure 13.24 displays the V2G charging and regulation power in scenario 2, and the figure shows that the cars' charging power changed depending on the user profile. Further, regulation power was only taken or supplied depending on the nature of disturbance in the MG. In short, we established that V2G technology can effectively regulate any sudden or dynamic MG changes in scenario 3.

Figure 13.25 shows the V2G charging and regulation reactive power in the MG in scenario 3. Specifically, the figure shows that in scenario 3, the V2G charging and regulation reactive power change when there are sudden changes in load or generation; during normal operating conditions, the reactive power exchange is 0. Therefore, we conclude that V2G technology can effectively regulate any sudden or dynamic reactive power changes in the MG in scenario 3.

Figure 13.26(a–e) displays the scenario 3 SOCs for car user profiles 1–5 and reflects that the SOCs depend on the user car status. However, the SOC for cars included in Profile 4 was constant at 90%. Negative values of SOC indicates that car is on road and not plugged in. Positive values of SOC indicates that cars are plugged in.

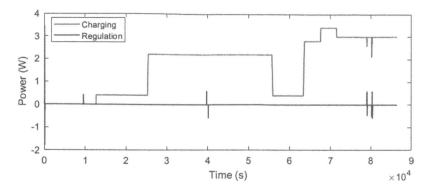

Figure 13.24 V2G charging and regulation power in scenario 3.

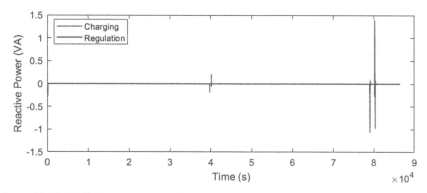

Figure 13.25 V2G charging and regulation reactive power in scenario 3.

13.6 PERFORMANCE COMPARATIVE STUDY

Here, we compared the performance of designed V2G technology integrated with MG with the conceptual framework reported in [42], and we observed frequency deviations of 2%. However, our proposed methodology was effective for regulating frequencies with less than 1% variation.

13.7 CONCLUSION

In this chapter, we designed a smart city MG that incorporated the following components: WPP, DG, SPVP, both residential and industrial loads, and V2G technology and included a bidirectional power flow method for controlling grid parameters during dynamic states. The following are the main conclusions of this study:

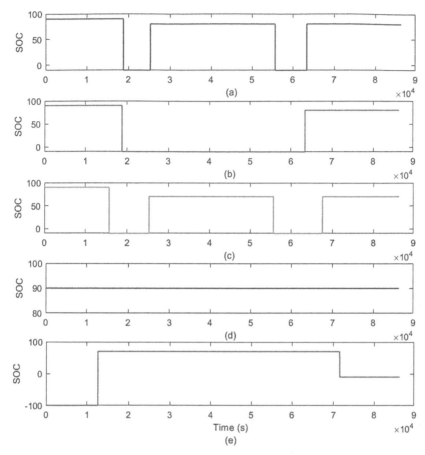

Figure 13.26 Scenario 3 state of charge: (a) profile 1, (b) profile 2, (c) profile 3, (d) profile 4, (e) profile 5.

- We tested five different V2G car user profiles in three separate operating scenarios.
- The proposed smart city MG can effectively maintain the load-generation balance. Variations in generation by one generator are mitigated by the other generators.
- The proposed smart city MG with V2G technology effectively absorbed load variations.
- The proposed control of V2G technology effectively maintained the smart city MG frequency at the rated value of 60% with deviation less than 1%.
- The proposed control of V2G technology effectively provided bidirectional power flow depending on the cars in a profile.

13.8 ACKNOWLEDGMENT

This research work is supported by Innovader Research Labs, Innovader IITian Padhaiwala LearnLab Pvt. Ltd., Jaipur, India.

REFERENCES

[1] Zhengji Meng, Xuekai Hu, Lei Wang, Shaobo Yang, Liang Meng, Hao Zhou, Ziwei Cheng, Tongfei Cui, "Research on internal external collaborative optimization strategy for multi microgrids interconnection system," Energy Reports, Vol. 9, Supplement 7, 2023, 1616–1626, https://doi.org/10.1016/j.egyr.2023.04.212.

[2] Hussein Abubakr, Abderezak Lashab, Juan C. Vasquez, Tarek Hassan Mohamed, Josep M. Guerrero, "Novel V2G regulation scheme using Dual-PSS for PV islanded microgrid," Applied Energy, Vol. 340, 2023, 121012, https://doi.org/10.1016/j.apenergy.2023.121012

[3] Nsilulu T. Mbungu, Ali A. Ismail, Mohammad AlShabi, Ramesh C. Bansal, A. Elnady, Abdul Kadir Hamid, "Control and estimation techniques applied to smart microgrids: A review," Renewable and Sustainable Energy Reviews, Vol. 179, 2023, 113251, https://doi.org/10.1016/j.rser.2023.113251.

[4] Babangida Modu, Md Pauzi Abdullah, Mufutau Adewolu Sanusi, Mukhtar Fatihu Hamza, "DC-based microgrid: Topologies, control schemes, and implementations," Alexandria Engineering Journal, Vol. 70, 2023, 61–92, https://doi.org/10.1016/j.aej.2023.02.021.

[5] Qingyu Su, Haoyu Fan, Jian Li, "Distributed adaptive secondary control of AC microgrid under false data injection attack," Electric Power Systems Research, Vol. 223, 2023, 109521, https://doi.org/10.1016/j.epsr.2023.109521.

[6] Fei Li, Chang Liu, Jianhua Zhang, Guangsen Guo, Yongdi Chen, Xiaocheng Wei, Resilience optimal control strategy of microgrid based on electric spring, Energy Reports, Vol. 9, Supplement 2, 2023, 236–245, https://doi.org/10.1016/j.egyr.2023.02.074.

[7] Mahdi Sadegh Zarei, Hajar Atrianfar, "A hierarchical framework for distributed resilient control of islanded AC microgrids under false data injection attacks," ISA Transactions, 2023, https://doi.org/10.1016/j.isatra.2023.03.044.

[8] Zhilin Lyu, Jiaqi Yi, Jian Song, Bin Liu, "Coordinated optimal control and dispatching operation of grid-connected AC/DC hybrid microgrid group," Electric Power Systems Research, Vol. 221, 2023, 109430, https://doi.org/10.1016/j.epsr.2023.109430.

[9] F. Iraji, V. Azarm, E. Farjah and T. Ghanbari, "A suitable power sharing control of parallel-connected inverters in microgrids," 2017 5th International Conference on Control, Instrumentation, and Automation (ICCIA), Shiraz, 2017, pp. 313–318, doi: 10.1109/ICCIAutom.2017.8258699.

[10] F. Alshammari and A. El-Refaie, "Time-varying optimization-based consensus control for microgrid's secondary control," 2021 IEEE Power & Energy Society Innovative Smart Grid Technologies Conference (ISGT), Washington, DC, 2021, pp. 1–5, doi: 10.1109/ISGT49243.2021.9372276.

[11] Gajendra Singh Chawda, Abdul Gafoor Shaik, Om Prakash Mahela, Sanjeevikumar Padmanaban, "Performance improvement of weak grid-connected wind energy system using FLSRF controlled DSTATCOM," IEEE Transactions on Industrial Electronics, Vol. 70, no. 2, 2023, pp. 1565–1575, doi: 10.1109/TIE.2022.3158012

[12] Nagendra Kumar Swarnkar, Om Prakash Mahela and Mahendra Lalwani, "Multivariable Signal Processing Algorithm for Identification of Power Quality Disturbances" Electric Power Systems Research, (Elsevier), Vol. 221, 2023, 109480, DOI: https://doi.org/10.1016/j.epsr.2023.109480

[13] Ekata Kaushik, Vivek Prakash, Raymond Ghandour, Zaher Al Barakeh, Ahmed Ali, Om Prakash Mahela, Roberto Marcelo Álvarez, and Baseem Khan, "Hybrid combination of network restructuring and optimal placement of distributed generators to reduce transmission loss and improve flexibility," Sustainability, Vol. 15, no. 6, 2023, 5285, https://doi.org/10.3390/su15065285

[14] Surendra Singh, Avdhesh Sharma, Akhil Ranjan Garg, Om Prakash Mahela, Baseem Khan, Ilyes Boulkaibet, Bilel Neji, Ahmed Ali, and Julien Brito Ballester, "Power quality detection and categorisation algorithm actuated by multiple signal processing techniques and rule based decision tree," Sustainability, Vol. 15, no. 5, 4317, https://doi.org/10.3390/su15054317

[15] Takele Ferede Agajie, Armand Fopah-Lele, Ahmed Ali, Isaac Amoussou, Baseem Khan, Mahmoud Elsisi, Om Prakash Mahela, Roberto Marcelo Alvarez, and Emmanuel Tanyi, "Optimal sizing and power system control of hybrid solar PV-biogas generator with energy storage system power plant", Sustainability, Vol. 15, no. 7, 2023, 5739, https://doi.org/10.3390/su15075739

[16] Om Prakash Mahela, Mayank Parihar, Akhil Ranjan Garg, Baseem Khan, Salah Kamel, "A hybrid signal processing technique for recognition of complex power quality disturbances," Electric Power Systems Research (Elsevier), Vol. 207, Paper No. 107865, https://doi.org/10.1016/j.epsr.2022.107865

[17] Rajkumar Kaushik, Om Prakash Mahela, Pramod Kumar Bhatt, Baseem Khan, Akhil Ranjan Garg, Hassan Haes Alhelou, and Pierluigi Siano, "Recognition of islanding and operational events in power system with renewable energy penetration using a stockwell transform based method", IEEE Systems Journal, Vol. 16, no. 1, 2022, 166–175. DOI: 10.1109/JSYST.2020.3020919

[18] Amit Kumar Sharma, Rupendra Kumar Pachauri, Sushabhan Choudhury, Om Prakash Mahela, Baseem Khan, and Ankur Kumar Gupta, "Improved power maxima point of photovoltaic system using umbrella optimizing technique under PSCs: An experimental study," IET Renewable Power Generation, 2022, DOI: 10.1049/rpg2.12486

[19] Ravinder Kumar, Hari Om Bansal, Aditya R. Gautam, Om Prakash Mahela, and Baseem Khan, "Experimental investigations on particle swarm optimization based control algorithm for shunt active power filter to enhance electric power quality," IEEE Access, Vol. 2022, 54878–54890, DOI: 10.1109/ACCESS.2022.3176732

[20] Ekata Kaushik, Vivek Prakash, Om Prakash Mahela, Baseem Khan, Almoataz Y. Abdelaziz, Junhee Hong and Zong Woo Geem, "Optimal placement of renewable energy generators using grid-oriented genetic algorithm for loss reduction and flexibility improvement," Energies, Vol. 15, Paper No. 1863, https://doi.org/10.3390/en15051863

[21] Gori Shankar Sharma, Om Prakash Mahela, Mohamed G. Hussien, Baseem Khan, Sanjeevikumar Padmanaban, M. B. Shafik and Z. M. Salem Elbarbary, "Performance evaluation of a MW-size grid-connected solar photovoltaic plant considering the impact of tilt angle," Sustainability (MDPI), Vol. 14, 2022, Paper No. 1444. https://doi.org/10.3390/su14031444

[22] Asmamaw Sewnet, Baseem Khan, Esayas Gidey, Om Prakash Mahela, Adel El-Shahat, Almoataz Y. Abdelaziz, "Mitigating generation schedule deviation of wind farm using battery energy storage system," Energies, Vol. 15, no. 5, 2022, 1768, https://doi.org/10.3390/en15051768

[23] Om Prakash Mahela, Yagya Sharma, Shoyab Ali, Baseem Khan and Sanjeevikumar Padmanaban, "Estimation of islanding events in utility distribution grid with renewable energy using current variations and stockwell transform," IEEE Access, Vol. 9, 2021, 69798–69813, https://doi.org/10.1109/ACCESS.2021.3078315

[24] Nagendra Kumar Swarnkar, Om Prakash Mahela, Baseem Khan, and Mahendra Lalwani, "Multivariable passive method for detection of islanding events in renewable energy based power grids," IET Renewable Power Generation, Vol. 16, 2022, 497–516. https://doi.org/10.1049/rpg2.12355

[25] Rupendra Kumar Pachauri, Om Prakash Mahela, Baseem Khan, Ashok Kumar, Sunil Agarwal, Hassan Haes Alhelou, Jianbo Bai, "Development of arduino assisted data acquisition system for solar photovoltaic array characterization under partial shading conditions," Computers and Electrical Engineering (Elsevier), Vol. 92, 2021, Paper No. 107175, https://doi.org/10.1016/j.compeleceng.2021.107175

[26] Rupendra Kumar Pachauri, Jianbo Bai, Isha Kansal, Om Prakash Mahela, Baseem Khan, "Shade dispersion methodologies for performance improvement of classical total-cross-tied photovoltaic array configuration under partial shading conditions," IET Renewable Power Generation, Vol. 15, 2021, 1796–1811, https://doi.org/10.1049/rpg2.12147, March 2021

[27] Nagendra Kumar Swarnkar, Om Prakash Mahela, Baseem Khan, and Mahendra Lalwani, "Identification of islanding events in utility grid with renewable energy penetration using current based passive method," IEEE Access, Vol. 9, 2021, 93781–93794, https://doi.org/10.1109/ACCESS.2021.3092971

[28] Aditya Kachhwaha, G. I. Rashed, Akhil Ranjan Garg, Om Prakash Mahela, Baseem Khan, M. B. Shafik, and Mohamed Hussien, "Design and performance analysis of hybrid battery & ultracapacitor energy storage system for electrical vehicle active power management," Sustainability (MDPI), Vol. 14, no. 2, 2022, Paper No. 776. https://doi.org/10.3390/su14020776

[29] Om Prakash Mahela, Baseem Khan, Hassan Haes Alhelou, Sudeep Tanwar, Sanjeevi kumar Padmanaban, "Harmonic mitigation and power quality improvement in utility grid with solar energy penetration using distribution static compensator", IET Power Electronics, Vol. 14, 2021, 912–922, https://doi.org/10.1049/pel2.12074

[30] Rajkumar Kaushik, Om Prakash Mahela, Pramod Kumar Bhatt, Baseem Khan, Sanjeevikumar Padmanabhan, and Frede Blaabjerg, "A hybrid algorithm for recognition of power quality disturbances," IEEE Access, Vol. 2, 2020, 229184–229200. https://doi.org/10.1109/ACCESS.2020.3046425

[31] Om Prakash Mahela, Abdul Gafoor Shaik, Baseem Khan, Rajendra Mahla, Hassan Haes Alhelou, "Recognition of complex power quality disturbances using S-transform based ruled decision tree," IEEE Access, Vol. 8, 2020, 173530– 73547, https://doi.org/10.1109/ACCESS.2020.3025190

[32] Om Prakash Mahela, Mahdi Khosravy, Neeraj Gupta, Baseem Khan, Hassan Haes Alhelou, Rajendra Mahla, Nilesh Patel, and Pierluigi Siano, "Comprehensive overview of multi-agent systems for controlling smart grids," CSEE Journal of Power and Energy Systems, Vol. 8, no. 1, 2022, 115–131. https://doi.org/10.17775/CSEEJPES.2020.03390

[33] Om Prakash Mahela, Neeraj Gupta, Mahdi Khosravy, and Nilesh Patel, "Comprehensive overview of low voltage ride through methods of grid integrated wind generator," IEEE Access, Vol. 7, 'no. 1, 2019, 99299–99326. https://doi.org/10.1109/ACCESS.2019.2930413

[34] Abdul Gafoor Shaik and Om Prakash Mahela, "Power quality assessment and event detection in hybrid power system," Electric Power Systems Research (Elsevier), Vol. 161, 2018, 26–44, https://doi.org/10.1016/j.epsr.2018.03.026

[35] Om Prakash Mahela and Abdul Gafoor Shaik, "Recognition of power quality disturbances using S-transform based ruled decision tree and fuzzy C-means clustering classifiers," Applied Soft Computing (Elsevier), Vol. 59, 2017, 243–257. https://doi.org/10.1016/j.asoc.2017.05.061

[36] Om Prakash Mahela, and Abdul Gafoor Shaik, "Power quality recognition in distribution system with solar energy penetration using S-transform and fuzzy C-means clustering," Renewable Energy (Elsevier), Vol. 106, 2017, 37–51, https://doi.org/10.1016/j.renene.2016.12.098

[37] Om Prakash Mahela, and Abdul Gafoor Shaik, "Comprehensive overview of grid interfaced solar photovoltaic systems," Renewable and Sustainable Energy Reviews, Vol. 68, Part 1, 2017, 316–332, https://doi.org/10.1016/j.rser.2016.09.096

[38] Om Prakash Mahela, and Abdul Gafoor Shaik, "Power quality improvement in distribution network using DSTATCOM with battery energy storage system," International Journal of Electrical Power and Energy Systems, Vol. 83, 2016, pp. 229–240. https://doi.org/10.1016/j.ijepes.2016.04.011

[39] Om Prakash Mahela, and Abdul Gafoor Shaik, "Comprehensive overview of grid interfaced wind energy generation systems," Renewable and Sustainable Energy Reviews, Vol. 57, 2016, pp. 260–281. https://doi.org/10.1016/j.rser.2015.12.048

[40] Om Prakash Mahela, and Abdul Gafoor Shaik, "Topological aspects of power quality improvement techniques: A comprehensive overview," Renewable and Sustainable Energy Reviews, Vol. 58, 2016, 1129–1142. https://doi.org/10.1016/j.rser.2015.12.251

[41] Om Prakash Mahela, Abdul Gafoor Shaik, and Neeraj Gupta, "A critical review of detection and classification of power quality events," Renewable and Sustainable Energy Reviews, Vol. 41, 2015, 495–505. https://doi.org/10.1016/j.rser.2014.08.070

[42] Christophe Guille, and George Gross, "A conceptual framework for the vehicle-to-grid (V2G) implementation," Energy Policy, Vol. 37, no. 11, 2009, 4379–4390, https://doi.org/10.1016/j.enpol.2009.05.053.

Section 6

Transmission and Distribution of Electrical Power in Smart Cities

Chapter 14

Comprehensive Overview of Utility Network Technologies for Smart Cities

Pramod Kumar, Atul Kulshrestha,
Sanjana Chugh and Om Prakash Mahela

14.1 INTRODUCTION

Smart cities ensure better living for citizens by digitizing every aspect of city life. Electrical power is critical for smart city technology and power networks; each smart application has its own power and connectivity requirements. Key technologies that are being continuously upgraded to meet smart city energy demands include those for power networks and power generation, power quality detection and improvement, network protection, vehicle-to-grid (V2G) communication, and the smart grid [1].

In [2], the authors presented a method for sharing smart grid communication infrastructures that has accelerated less-developed cities' conversions into smart cities. In [3], the authors introduced a solar photovoltaic (PV) power forecasting technique that used small samples and compared and analyzed the prediction effects of different recurrent neural network models. In [4], the authors proposed a daisy chain network and a tree network that used cost-effective wireless communication-actuated microcontrollers for smart city applications that worked to reduce the transmission load on the server using relay commands and network paths. In the study, the authors implemented a smart city street light system that used minimal energy.

In [5], the authors presented detailed aspects of a smart city that ensured power for smart health, smart buildings, and smart transportation. In [6], the authors designed a wireless communication network for electrical energy data acquisition with advantages that included security, reliability, network scalability, and low operation expenses. In [7], the authors proposed a solution for integrated utilities for smart cities that addressed the challenges large gas, water, telecommunication, and electricity systems face in integrating with smart cities. The study solution will help with providing reliable, sustainable services at reduced prices.

In [8], the authors proposed a model of multi-energy flow regulation and operation optimization for the energy Internet. In practical cases, they demonstrated dynamically simulated, complementary, and multi-energy strategies for the power side and consumer side. In [9], the authors presented a solar remote monitoring arrangement using a solar PV-supported power conditioning unit (PCU) that solved issues related to maintenance, management, and mean time to repair the system. The authors deployed an intelligent remote-monitoring system supported by Internet of Things (IoT) to track the solar PV PCU parameters. In brief, we conducted a detailed review of the literature related to smart city technologies and ultimately identified 82 articles for critical analysis. We divide those articles into seven categories:

- Articles in category 1 [1–9] describe general aspects of smart city and technologies deployed for the smart city applications.
- Category 2 articles [10–27] detail the concepts of microgrids and microgrid control.
- Category 3 articles [28–43] detail wind, solar, and diesel generator applications in smart cities.
- Category 4 articles [44–47] describe the concepts of vehicle-to-grid (V2G) technology.
- Category 5 articles [48–66] discuss smart city power quality detection and mitigation technology.
- Category 6 articles [67–78] describe the protection technology for smart city networks.
- Category 7 articles [79–82] describe smart city metering technology.

14.2 SMART CITY MICROGRID

A microgrid (MG) is an energy system that operates in isolated mode or in integration with a main electrical grid and that provides power to a specific area, such as a neighborhood, university campus, military base, or industrial facility [10, 11]. MGs incorporate distributed energy resources (DERs), including renewable energy (RE) sources, energy storage systems (ESS), and loads, which control uses. Figure 14.1 graphically displays a typical MG block scheme, and next we describe some key MG features and components.

- **Generation sources:** A microgrid incorporates diverse generation sources including solar PV panels, wind turbines, diesel or natural gas generators, combined heat and power plants, and ESS. These sources can be renewable or conventional, offering flexibility and resilience to the MG [12, 13].
- **Energy storage systems:** Energy storage is a crucial component of a MG as it permits the capture and utilization of excessive energy produced during periods of high generation or low demand. ESS technologies like batteries, pumped hydro, and flywheels store energy for later use, which ensures stable, reliable power during fluctuations or outages [14].
- **Control systems:** Advanced control systems manage the operation of the MG, optimizing the use of available resources, balancing supply and

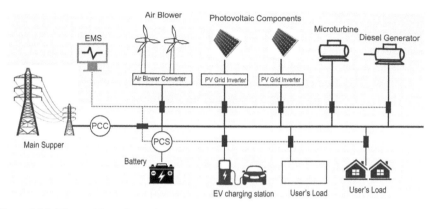

Figure 14.1 Microgrid configuration.

demand, and ensuring system stability. These control systems incorporate sophisticated algorithms that monitor and manage generation, storage, and load balancing to achieve efficient and reliable energy management [15].

- **Islanding capability:** One of the distinguishing features of a MG is its ability to operate in island mode. During a grid outage or emergency, the MG can disconnect from the main grid and continue to supply power to its integrated loads autonomously. This capability enhances the resilience and reliability of the MG, ensuring that critical loads can be powered even in the absence of grid power [16].

- **Grid interconnection:** MGs can be designed to operate in parallel with the main grid, allowing for two-way power flow. They can import electricity from the grid during times of high demand or when local generation is insufficient. Conversely, MGs can export excess power back to the grid when they have surplus power. Grid interconnection provides flexibility and economic benefits by leveraging the main grid as a backup or supplementary power source [17, 18].

- **Demand management:** MGs often incorporate demand-management strategies to optimize the use of energy and minimize peak demand. Load management techniques like demand response and energy-efficient systems allow for better coordination and control of electricity consumption. This helps to minimize costs, enhance energy efficiency, and ensure a more balanced supply–demand profile within the MG [19].

- **Resilience and energy independence:** By integrating various generation sources, energy storage, and intelligent control systems, MGs enhance energy resilience and reduce dependence on the main grid. They offer the potential for energy independence, increased reliability, and the ability to integrate many RE sources [20].

14.2.1 Microgrid Control Algorithms

MGs are local energy arrangements that can operate in isolated mode or in conjunction with a grid. They consist of DERs like solar panels, wind turbines, ESS, and backup generators that generate, store, and distribute electricity within a defined area. To ensure efficient and reliable operation, MGs employ various control methods [21–25]; following are some of the commonly used methods:

- **Centralized control:** In a centralized control approach, a central controller monitors and manages the operation of all DERs in an MG. It optimizes the power generation, storage, and distribution based on factors such as demand, availability of resources, and grid conditions. Centralized control allows for the coordinated management of the entire MG, ensuring the efficient utilization of resources and stable operation.
- **Distributed control:** Distributed control involves decentralizing the control functions across multiple devices within the MG. Each DER or group of DERs has its own local controller that makes decisions based on local measurements and control algorithms. These local controllers communicate with each other to coordinate their actions and maintain system stability. Distributed control provides flexibility and robustness by allowing individual components to respond quickly to local conditions.
- **Hierarchical control:** Hierarchical control uses features of centralized and distributed control methods. It divides the control functions into multiple levels or tiers. At the top tier, a central controller oversees the global operation of the MG, optimizing the overall performance; lower tiers consist of local controllers responsible for managing specific DERs or subsystems. The hierarchical structure enables efficient coordination between different control levels and improves system reliability.
- **Droop control:** Droop control is a method of decentralized control that is commonly used in MGs with multiple DGs like solar panels and wind turbines. Each generator is assigned a set-point or reference voltage/frequency, and the generators adjust their output based on the difference between their actual measurements and the reference values. This allows for power sharing among the generators and helps to maintain system stability. Droop control is generally used in combination with other control methods to achieve effective load sharing and frequency regulation.
- **Energy management system:** An EMS is a software-based control system that monitors, analyses, and controls the operation of a MG. It gathers data from various sensors and meters, performs real-time analysis, and makes control decisions to optimize the MG performance. An EMS can incorporate different control methods, such as centralized, distributed, or hierarchical control, depending on the specific needs and characteristics of the MG.
- **Demand response:** Demand response involves adjusting electricity use in response to price signals or grid conditions. In a MG, demand response can

be used as a control method to balance supply with demand. By actively managing and controlling the energy consumption of connected loads, the MG can optimize its overall operation and reduce reliance on external sources. Demand response can be implemented through automated control systems or by providing incentives for consumers to adjust their consumption patterns.

These control methods are combined and tailored for meeting the specific needs of a microgrid. The choice of control method depends on factors like MG size, DER type, the level of automation desired, and the reliability requirements. Effective control methods ensure the efficient utilization of resources, stable operation, and the ability to operate in isolation mode or in coordination with a grid [26, 27].

14.3 GENERATION TECHNOLOGY FOR SMART CITY NETWORKS

Smart city networks are powered by energy generation from SPP, WPP, and DG, which we describe in more detail in the following sections.

14.3.1 Wind Power Plant

WPPs are used to generate electrical power from kinetic energy (KE) associated with blowing wind. They use a wind turbine, generator, rotor-side converter (RSC), and grid-side converter (GSC). By combining a doubly fed induction generator (DFIG) with RSC and GSC, WPPs can efficiently harness wind energy and seamlessly integrate it into the electrical grid. This configuration allows for variable speed operation, grid synchronization, and grid support functionalities, making wind energy a reliable and viable source of renewable power.

Generally, DFIG is utilized for WPPs. A wind turbine converts the wind energy into electrical power using aerodynamic force generated at the rotor blades. When wind flows across the rotor blades, air pressure on one side of a rotor blade decreases, and the difference in air pressure between the two sides of the blade generates lift and drag forces. The lift force is stronger than the drag, which causes the rotor to spin. Hence, translational KE of wind is transformed into rotational KE. Turbine rotor is connected to generator directly or using a gearbox. Transformation of aerodynamic force to rotation of a generator generates electricity. Therefore, rotational KE is converted to the electrical energy using the generator. All components of the WPP are illustrated in Figure 14.2. Transformer is utilized for stepping up power to grid voltage [28, 29].

DFIGs equipped with a back-to-back converter (RSC and GSC) are widely used in wind turbines. They enable wind turbines to operate with various ranges of speed. The DFIG is a type of electrical generator used in wind turbines; it has

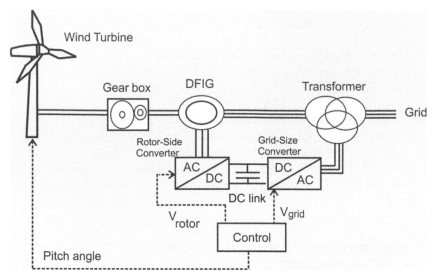

Figure 14.2 DFIG-based wind power plant.

a three-phase wound rotor and a three-phase stator. The rotor is connected to the wind turbine's rotor blades, which converts the wind KE into mechanical energy. DFIG is called "doubly fed" because the stator and rotor windings are both integrated to power grid [30].

The RSC is an electronic power converter integrated to the rotor windings of a DFIG. Its purpose is to control and adjust the rotor current and voltage. Controlling rotor current supports the RSC to allow the wind turbine to operate at variable speeds, thereby optimizing power generation based on wind conditions. It also enables the decoupling of active and reactive power control among rotor and grid [31].

The GSC is another electronic power converter, but it is integrated to stator windings of a DFIG. It is primarily used for converting electrical power generated by generator to a form suitable for grid connection. GSCs are used to control the voltage and frequency of the power that is injected into a utility grid and synchronizes with it. Additionally, the GSC provides grid support functions like reactive power compensation and power control. The overall operation of the wind power plant with DFIG, RSC, and GSC can be summarized as follows [32, 33]:

- **Wind energy conversion:** Wind turbine rotor blades takes KE from wind, which rotates the rotor. The rotational motion is transferred to the DFIG, where it induces an electromotive force.
- **Rotor-side power control:** RSC regulates rotor current and voltage to optimize power taken from wind. By adjusting rotor current independently of

the grid, the RSC permits the wind turbine to operate at variable speeds, matching the wind speed for maximum energy capture.

- **Stator power conversion:** Stator windings of DFIG generate three-phase alternating current (AC) power. This power is then converted by the GSC to the desired voltage and frequency levels for grid connection. The GSC ensures synchronization with the utility grid and regulates active and reactive power supplied to the grid.
- **Grid support functions:** GSC also provides ancillary services to support grid stability and power quality. It can dynamically control reactive power flow, compensating for fluctuations and voltage variations.
- **Transformer:** The primary function of a step-up transformer is to increase the voltage of electrical power supplied by wind turbines. Wind turbine generators typically produce power at a relatively low voltage. By stepping up the voltage, the transformer facilitates the efficient transmission of power over long distances, reducing resistive losses. The higher voltage also aligns with the grid's voltage for connection.

14.3.2 Solar PV Power Plant

A solar PV plant converts solar energy into electrical power via the photovoltaic effect through PV modules, a boost converter, an inverter, a filter, and a transformer [34]. Figure 14.3 displays a block scheme of a solar PV plant. Other descriptions of solar PV components can be found in [35–39].

- **Solar PV modules**: These are the fundamental building blocks of SPP. The PV modules are also known as solar panels which consist of multiple integrated PV cells which convert sunlight directly into electricity. The modules are typically mounted on support structures like rooftops or ground-mounted racks for maximizing the exposure to sunlight.

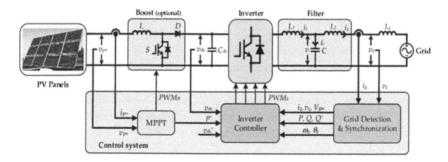

Figure 14.3 Solar PV plant.

- **Inverter**: Inverter has a critical role for grid-connected SPP. It converts direct current (DC) generated by solar panels into AC, which is compatible with the grid. Inverters also ensure that the SPP synchronizes with the grid's voltage, frequency, and phase parameters. They monitor and control the power output, allowing the system to operate at its maximum efficiency.
- **DC–DC boost converter**: Solar PV panels typically generate electricity at relatively low voltage. However, for efficient power transmission and compatibility with the system's requirements, it is often necessary to increase the voltage. A DC–DC boost converter is employed for stepping up the voltage of DC power generated by solar panels. This enables efficient power transfer and optimal utilization of the generated energy.
- **Filters**: Filters used in grid-connected solar PV systems play a crucial role in mitigating power quality issues and ensuring compliance with grid regulations. Harmonic filters are designed to mitigate the availability of harmonics in electrical current generated by solar PV systems. Harmonics are unwanted distortions in the waveform that can cause interference and degrade power quality. Harmonic filters use passive or active components to suppress specific harmonic frequencies, ensuring that the current injected into the grid meets the harmonic standards defined by grid codes.
- **Electrical metering and monitoring**: Bidirectional energy meters measure quanta of power generated by the system and the electricity consumed from the grid. Monitoring systems provide real-time data on system performance, including energy production, efficiency, and any potential faults or issues.
- **Control and regulation**: A control circuit is typically employed to monitor and regulate boost converter output voltage. It adjusts the duty cycles of switching components to maintain a stable output voltage despite variations in input voltage and load. This control mechanism ensures the reliable operation of the SPP.

14.3.3 Diesel Generator

Diesel generators (DGs) use diesel fuel to produce electrical energy; they are generally utilized as backup power source in situations where a reliable and continuous power supply is essential, such as during conditions of power outages or in remote areas without access to a stable electrical grid. Their durability, fuel efficiency, and wide range of power output make them suitable for a variety of applications. However, it is important to ensure regular maintenance and adhere to environmental regulations when operating DGs [40]. A block diagram of a DG indicating different components and control algorithm is shown in Figure 14.4. Here are some key points about diesel generators [41–43]:

- **Operation**: A DG has components like an engine and an alternator. The diesel engine is responsible for converting chemical energy stored in the

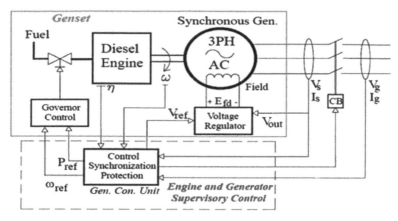

Figure 14.4 Block diagram of a diesel generator.

form of diesel fuel into mechanical energy (ME) that the alternator uses to generate electricity.

- **Fuel efficiency**: DGs have higher fuel efficiency than other types of generators. Diesel fuel has a higher energy density than gasoline, meaning it can produce more power per unit of fuel. This makes DGs a cost-effective solution for long-term or continuous power requirements.
- **Power output**: DGs are designed in different sizes and power ratings and range from small portable units that can provide a few kilowatts of power to large industrial generators that can produce several megawatts. The power output of a DG depends on its engine size and the capacity of the alternator.
- **Durability and reliability**: Diesel engines are known for their durability and reliability. They are designed to withstand heavy loads and operate continuously for extended periods. This makes DGs suitable for demanding applications and critical power needs.
- **Maintenance**: Proper maintenance is crucial to ensure the optimal performance and longevity of a DG. Regular maintenance includes oil and filter changes, fuel system checks, cooling system inspection, and periodic load testing. It is important to follow the manufacturer's guidelines and recommendations for maintenance schedules.
- **Noise and emissions**: Although DGs are generally noisier than other types of generators, advancements in technology have resulted in the development of quieter models. Additionally, diesel engines produce exhaust emissions like nitrogen oxides and particulate matter. Modern DGs are equipped with emission control systems to meet stringent environmental regulations.
- **Applications**: DGs are commonly found in residential buildings, hospitals, data centers, construction sites, mining operations, telecommunications infrastructure, and as backup power for commercial establishments.

- **Automatic start systems**: Many DGs are equipped with automatic start systems that can sense power outages and start the generator automatically. This feature ensures a seamless transition to backup power and eliminates the need for manual intervention.

14.4 VEHICLE-TO-GRID TECHNOLOGY IN SMART CITY NETWORKS

V2G technology uses electric vehicles (EVs) as a means of energy storage and supply, integrating them into the power grid infrastructure. V2G enables bidirectional power flow, allowing EVs to consume electricity from grid and also to deliver excess electricity back to the grid. This concept transforms EVs from simple energy consumers to active participants in the electrical system [44]. Following is the breakdown of how V2G technology works [45, 46]:

- **Charging**: EVs can be charged using conventional charging stations or through a dedicated V2G charger. These chargers allow for two-way power flow between vehicle and grid.
- **Energy storage**: Once EV is fully charged, excess electricity is stored in the vehicle's battery for later use. Stored energy can be used during peak demand periods or power outages when the grid requires additional support.
- **V2G**: When the grid requires additional electricity, the V2G system communicates with the EVs that are connected to the grid. If the vehicle owner has consented, the V2G system can access stored energy in the EV's battery and discharge it to the grid when required.
- **Grid support**: The electricity discharged from EVs can be used to stabilize the grid, meet peak demand, or provide backup power during emergencies. This flexibility can help balance intermittent RE sources and improve the overall reliability of grid.
- **Compensation**: EV owners who participate in V2G programs can be financially compensated for the energy they provide back to the grid. This compensation can take the form of reduced electricity bills, monetary incentives, or other rewards.

Major benefits of V2G technology include improved grid stability, facilitated RE integration, cost savings, emergency power backup, and environmental backup [47].

- **Grid stability**: V2G systems can help stabilize the grid by supplying power in periods of peak demand. This minimizes the requirement of plants for additional power and grid infrastructure.
- **Renewable energy integration**: V2G facilitates the integration of RE sources by allowing excess energy generated from wind or solar power to be stored in EVs that can be released back to grid when required.

- **Cost savings**: EV owners can benefit from reduced electricity costs by charging their vehicles during off-peak hours when electricity rates are lower. Additionally, financial incentives for participating in V2G programs can further offset the cost of owning an EV.
- **Emergency power backup**: During power outages or emergencies, EVs with V2G capabilities can serve as temporary backup power sources for homes, businesses, or critical infrastructure.
- **Environmental impact**: By utilizing stored energy in EV batteries, V2G reduces the reliance on fossil fuel-based power plants, resulting in lower greenhouse gas emissions and a cleaner energy mix.

Although V2G technology holds immense potential, widespread implementation still faces certain challenges, including standardization of communication protocols, addressing concerns related to battery degradation, and establishing regulatory frameworks to govern the interaction between EV owners, utilities, and grid operators. However, as the technology continues to evolve, V2G has the potential to revolutionize the way we utilize and distribute electrical energy.

14.4.1 PQ Detection Technology

Interruptions in power quality are major concerns for both consumers and utilities; the competitive market for power forces utilities to maintain PQ because consumers expect higher-quality service. Now, all utilities as well as power supplier licensees are required to certify that they provide good-quality service. This helps to attract customers and stay competitive.

Signal analysis plays a major role in the detection or recognition and classification of PQ issues. Signal processing methods are utilized for the extraction of features from power signals to identify types of disturbances to analyze PQ. Commonly implemented techniques are fast Fourier transform, short-time Fourier transform. Wavelet transform (WT) and discrete wavelet transform (DWT) are also important techniques utilized in PQ analysis [48].

Low PQ reduces the life of loads and equipment and can harm the performance of load [49]. In [50], a WT-supported energy function is designed for identification of PQ events which includes the voltage sag, swell and flicker. In [51], a broad scenario is discussed for analyzing PQ in a power system using WT, Stockwell transform (ST), Gabor transform (GT) and Wigner distribution function (WDF).

In [52], the authors designed a technique that used energy function using WT to detect PQ events including sag, flicker, and swell. In [53], the authors described various methods supported by signal analysis and artificial intelligence to identify PQ events in an automatic manner; they also investigated the impact of noise on performance. In [54], the authors described that poor quality of power is generally due to disturbances in voltage and current waveforms like transients, spikes, sag, swell, momentary interruption, wave faults, impulses, notches, over-voltage, under-voltage, and distortion harmonics. Different combinations of PQ events known as complex PQ disturbances also impact quality of power.

In [55], the authors described different methods based on signal processing to extract features related to disturbances in power signals to analyze power quality. In [56], the authors described identifying PQ disturbances using artificial neural network and WT. In [57], the authors introduced a method supported by WT that used the energy function to identify PQ events like voltage swell, flicker, and voltage sag on a DFIG wind farm. In [58], the authors broadly described some of the important methods for PQ analysis in power networks such as ST, GT, WT, and WDF. In [59], the authors described common power quality disturbances include voltage sag, impulsive transients, voltage swell, oscillatory transients, etc. Common PQ disturbances are described in Table 14.1.

14.4.2 PQ Mitigation Technology

Common PQ improvement methods used in smart cities include active filter, passive filter, and distribution static compensator (DSTATCOM) [60]. A study of PQ improvement in a three-phase grid integrated PV system with a battery storage system (BESS) is described in [61]. ESS technology to maximize the penetration of solar energy in the grid and improve PQ is described in [62]. Custom power devices like DSTATCOM, dynamic voltage restorer, and unified power quality conditioner are utilized to improve PQ in energy from RE sources [63].

DSTATCOM ensures flexible control of voltage and PQ improvement at the point of connection to the utility grid. If a BESS is integrated on a DC bus, DSTATCOM

Table 14.1 Characteristics and Categories of Power Quality Disturbances

S. No.	Categories	Duration	Typical content	Voltage magnitude
1	Impulsive transient	<1 ms	5 ns to 0.1 ms rise	
2	Oscillatory transient	5 μs–0.3 ms	< 5 MHz	0–8pu
3	Momentary interruption	0.3 cycles–1 min		<0.1 pu
4	Voltage sag	0.3 cycles–1 min		0.1–0.9 pu
5	Voltage swell	0.3 cycles–1 min		1.1–1.8 pu
6	Under voltage	>1 min		0.8–0.9 pu
7	Over voltage	>1 min		1.1–1.2 pu
8	DC offset	Steady state		0–0.1%
9	Notch	Steady state		
10	Harmonic	Steady state	0–100th harmonic	0–20%
11	Power frequency variations	<10 s		
12	Voltage unbalance	Steady state		0.5–2%

becomes effective for exchanging active as well as reactive power with the grid by changing the amplitude and phase angle of converter voltage relative to terminal line voltage [64]. This improves dynamic system performance with respect to the voltage regulation and frequency. It also increases the capacity of DSTATCOM to compensate reactive power, balance the load, and eliminate harmonic current.

A few other researchers have studied DSTATCOM for improving power grid performance. The authors in [65] implemented DSTATCOM considering adaptive neural network control for harmonic reduction, balancing of load, and voltage regulation in an isolated RE system. Shahnia et al. [66] described the detailed use of DSTATCOM for additional power flow in distribution networks of medium and low voltage with single-phase RE resources.

14.5 PROTECTION TECHNOLOGY IN SMART CITY NETWORKS

Smart city power networks have become complex due to the increased penetration of large generators and RE sources. Faults in such complex networks may affect power supplies including causing blackouts. Statistics related to fault types and frequency in power systems can be useful in designing protection schemes. Table 14.2 gives percentages of causes of faults. Distribution faults in various sections of power systems are shown in Table 14.3. Relative probabilities of different kinds of short-circuits on overhead line cables circuits are given in Table 14.4.

Table 14.2 Approximate Percentages of Various Causes of Faults

Cause	Percentage
Lighting	12
Sleet, wind, mechanical (jumper conductors)	20
Equipment failure	20
Switching to a fault	20
Miscellaneous (bird age, tree falling on line, sabotage, accidents etc.)	28

Table 14.3 Frequency of Fault Occurrences in Different Links of a Power System

Equipment	Percentage of Total
Overhead lines	50
Cables	10
Transformers	10
Switchgear	15
Control equipment	3
Instrument transformers (CTs and PTs)	2
Miscellaneous	10

Table 14.4 Relative Probabilities of Incidence of Short Faults on Overhead and Cables

S. No.	Type of faults	Fault occurrence percentage
1.	LG fault	70
2.	Phase to phase	15
3.	Two phases to ground	10
4.	Phase to phase and third phase to ground	2 or 3
5.	All phases to ground	2 or 3
6.	All the three phases shorted	2 or 3

Relay systems for transmission line protection are extremely important devices used for safety-related issues during power system operations; relay systems switch off faulted sections of line in order to avoid harmful fault effects on power system. Recently, numerical relays provide flexibility in protection as these relays can be programmed according to need; signal analysis methods play an important role in determining thresholds for faults in numerical relays. Values higher than the threshold actuate the relay to generate a command to isolate the faulty section. Intelligent methods are utilized for classifying the fault type taken place on network [67].

Approaches like Fourier transform, WT, STFT, Hilbert Huang transform (HHT), WDF, and ST are used for detecting and classifying faults on power system network [68]. In [69], the authors presented an algorithm for diagnosing faults in nonlinear systems with decentralized event-recording measurements. Every sensor used locally available information for transmitting the measurement received from remote filters; the number of filters aimed to collectively estimate state of system and possible faults.

In [70], the authors described a scheme based on WT and linear discriminate analysis to detect and categorize faults. In [71], the authors described how the transmission lines are important elements in a power delivery system. During faults, protection relay is expected to respond fast to isolate faulty sections of line to help maintain stability in the healthy sections of the network. Accurately determining fault location helps with inspecting and repairing faulty lines, demonstrating the importance of relays for protection. Investigators have elaborated on numerous protection schemes for smart city applications and the respective challenges even with high RE penetration [72–78].

14.6 SMART METERING TECHNOLOGY IN SMART CITY NETWORKS

Increased use of digital technology in smart city infrastructures has resulted in policies to use smart meters in the utility sector, which includes electricity, water, and natural gas. This improves service delivery and addresses broader challenges like demand side management [79]. In [80], the authors presented an IoT-supported environmentally friendly green score meter for smart sustainable city applications. In [81], the authors presented fifth-generation networks with the aim of using smart meters, with two objectives. The first was to increase narrow-band-IoT spectral efficacy, and the second was to enhance signal burden for every transmission request. In [82], the authors proposed an IoT-supported wireless energy effective smart meter system. A network of smart meters was designed using star and mesh techniques to deliver energy utilization data to a utility provider.

14.7 CONCLUSION

This chapter presented a detailed review of smart technologies in smart city power networks; we discussed power generation, power quality detection and improvement, network protection, vehicle-to-grid communication, smart grids, and smart metering, key technologies for meeting the energy requirements of smart cities. Smart city energy sources include wind and solar power plants, diesel generators, biomass, and geothermal energy. V2G technology is being used to make transportation smart as well as to improve the stability of smart city power grids. Techniques such as wavelet transform, discrete wavelet transform, Stockwell transform, Wigner distribution function, artificial neural network, and FT are utilized to design devices to monitor power quality in smart city utility networks, and smart metering technology is being used to accurately measure electricity, water, and natural gas. We hope that this review will be helpful for engineers, scientists, and academicians in developing smart city power systems.

14.8 ACKNOWLEDGMENT

This research work is supported by Innovader Research Labs, Innovader IITian Padhaiwala LearnLab Pvt. Ltd., Jaipur, India.

REFERENCES

[1] R. Pandya, K. Velani and D. Karvat, Design of smart power distribution network for smart city-Dholera, 2018 International Conference on Current Trends towards Converging Technologies (ICCTCT), Coimbatore, 2018, pp. 1–5, doi: 10.1109/ ICCTCT.2018.8550980.

[2] G. C. Heck, R. Hexsel, V. B. Gomes, L. Iantorno, L. L. Junior and T. Santana, GRID-CITY: A framework to share smart grids communication with smart city applications, 2021 IEEE International Smart Cities Conference (ISC2), Manchester, 2021, pp. 1–4, doi: 10.1109/ISC253183.2021.9562794.

[3] Q. Lv et al., Photovoltaic power forecasting in dunhuang based on recurrent neural network, 2021 IEEE 23rd Int Conf on High Performance Computing & Communications; 7th Int Conf on Data Science & Systems; 19th Int Conf on Smart City; 7th Int Conf on Dependability in Sensor, Cloud & Big Data Systems & Application (HPCC/DSS/SmartCity/DependSys), Haikou, 2021, pp. 1346–1352, doi: 10.1109/HPCC-DSS-SmartCity-DependSys53884.2021.00203.

[4] M. Azman, J. G. Panicker and R. Kashyap, Wireless daisy chain and tree topology networks for smart cities, 2019 IEEE International Conference on Electrical, Computer and Communication Technologies (ICECCT), Coimbatore, 2019, pp. 1–6, doi: 10.1109/ICECCT.2019.8869252.

[5] U. T. Khan and M. F. Zia, Smart city technologies, key components, and its aspects, 2021 International Conference on Innovative Computing (ICIC), Lahore, 2021, pp. 1–10, doi: 10.1109/ICIC53490.2021.9692989.

[6] Li Yan et al., Study on the remote communication technology in the construction of power user electric energy data acquire system, 2014 China International Conference on Electricity Distribution (CICED), Shenzhen, 2014, pp. 43–46, doi: 10.1109/CICED.2014.6991660.

[7] M. Bran, M. Frigura-Iliasa, H. E. Filipescu, L. Dolga, V. Vatau and M. Iorga, Case study about smart integrated utilities for smart cities, 2020 IEEE 18th World Symposium on Applied Machine Intelligence and Informatics (SAMI), Herlany, 2020, pp. 23–26, doi: 10.1109/SAMI48414.2020.9108772.

[8] C. Kuang, Q. Wang, J. Wan, G. Li and B. Lv, Multi-energy flow regulation and operation method of distribution network based on smart city energy internet, 2020 International Conference on Communications, Information System and Computer Engineering (CISCE), Kuala Lumpur, 2020, pp. 203–206, doi: 10.1109/CISCE50729.2020.00046.

[9] M. P. Kantipudi, S. Rani and S. Kumar, IoT based solar monitoring system for smart city: an investigational study, 4th Smart Cities Symposium (SCS 2021), Online Conference, Bahrain, 2021, pp. 25–30, doi: 10.1049/icp.2022.0307.

[10] I. El-Dessouki and N. Saeed, Smart grid integration into smart cities, 2021 IEEE International Smart Cities Conference (ISC2), Manchester, 2021, pp. 1–4, doi: 10.1109/ISC253183.2021.9562769.

[11] M. U. Mutarraf et al., A communication-less multimode control approach for adaptive power sharing in ship-based seaport microgrid, IEEE Transactions on Transportation Electrification, vol. 7, no. 4, pp. 3070–3082, 2021, doi: 10.1109/TTE.2021.3087722.

[12] C. Li, F. de Bosio, S. K. Chaudhary, M. Graells, J. C. Vasquez and J. M. Guerrero, Operation cost minimization of droop-controlled DC microgrids based on real-time pricing and optimal power flow, IECON 2015–41st Annual Conference of the IEEE Industrial Electronics Society, Yokohama, 2015, pp. 003905–003909, doi: 10.1109/IECON.2015.7392709.

[13] J. Mírez, A modeling and simulation of optimized interconnection between DC microgrids with novel strategies of voltage, power and control, 2017 IEEE Second International Conference on DC Microgrids (ICDCM), Nuremburg, 2017, pp. 536–541, doi: 10.1109/ICDCM.2017.8001098.

[14] F. Zhang et al., Advantages and challenges of DC microgrid for commercial building a case study from Xiamen university DC microgrid, 2015 IEEE First

International Conference on DC Microgrids (ICDCM), Atlanta, GA, 2015, pp. 355–358, doi: 10.1109/ICDCM.2015.7152068.

[15] E. Rodriguez-Diaz, E. J. Palacios-Garcia, A. Anvari-Moghaddam, J. C. Vasquez and J. M. Guerrero, Real-time energy management system for a hybrid AC/DC residential microgrid, 2017 IEEE Second International Conference on DC Microgrids (ICDCM), Nuremburg, 2017, pp. 256–261, doi: 10.1109/ICDCM.2017.8001053.

[16] N. Gurung, A. Vukojevic and H. Zheng, Demonstration of islanding and grid reconnection capability of a microgrid within distribution system, 2022 IEEE PES Innovative Smart Grid Technologies – Asia (ISGT Asia), Singapore, 2022, pp. 655–659, doi: 10.1109/ISGTAsia54193.2022.10003608.

[17] Y. Guan, B. Wei, J. M. Guerrero, J. C. Vasquez and Y. Gui, An overview of the operation architectures and energy management system for multiple microgrid clusters, In iEnergy, vol. 1, no. 3, pp. 306–314, 2022, doi: 10.23919/IEN.2022.0035.

[18] N. Chen, H. Wang, H. Li and D. Xu, Generic Derivation of Optimal Architecture for A Resilient Microgrid with Graph Theory, 2019 IEEE 10th International Symposium on Power Electronics for Distributed Generation Systems (PEDG), Xi'an, 2019, pp. 359–364, doi: 10.1109/PEDG.2019.8807521.

[19] S. Kampezidou, O. Vasios and S. Meliopoulos, Multi-Microgrid Architecture: Optimal Operation and Control, 2018 North American Power Symposium (NAPS), Fargo, ND, 2018, pp. 1–5, doi: 10.1109/NAPS.2018.8600550.

[20] E.D. Escobar, D. Betancur, T. Manrique, I.A. Isaac, Model predictive real-time architecture for secondary voltage control of microgrids, Applied Energy, vol. 345, 2023, 121328, doi: 10.1016/j.apenergy.2023.121328.

[21] A. Nawaz, J. Wu, C. Long, Distributed optimal energy scheduling for grid connected multi-microgrids with architecturized load characteristics, Energy Reports, vol. 8, 2022, pp. 11259–11270, doi: 10.1016/j.egyr.2022.08.256.

[22] P. Mohana Kishore, B. Ravikumar, Refined hybrid microgrid architecture for the improvement of voltage profile, Energy Procedia, vol. 90, 2016, pp. 645–654, doi: 10.1016/j.egypro.2016.11.233.

[23] I. Patrao, E. Figueres, G. Garcerá, R. González-Medina, Microgrid architectures for low voltage distributed generation, Renewable and Sustainable Energy Reviews, vol. 43, 2015, pp. 415–424, doi: 10.1016/j.rser.2014.11.054.

[24] F. Delfino, G. Ferro, M. Robba, M. Rossi, An architecture for the optimal control of tertiary and secondary levels in small-size islanded microgrids, International Journal of Electrical Power & Energy Systems, vol. 103, 2018, pp. 75–88, doi: 10.1016/j.ijepes.2018.05.026.

[25] P. Pant, F. Ibanez, P. Vorobev, T. Hamacher and V. Peric, A simplified microgrid architecture with reduced number of measurement units, 2022 IEEE PES Innovative Smart Grid Technologies Conference Europe (ISGT-Europe), Novi Sad, Serbia, 2022, pp. 1–6, doi: 10.1109/ISGT-Europe54678.2022.9960677.

[26] M. Shakir and Y. Biletskiy, Smart microgrid architecture for home energy management system, 2021 IEEE Energy Conversion Congress and Exposition (ECCE), Vancouver, BC, 2021, pp. 808–813, doi: 10.1109/ECCE47101.2021.9595165.

[27] S. Marzal, R. Salas, R. González-Medina, G. Garcerá, E. Figueres, Current challenges and future trends in the field of communication architectures for microgrids, Renewable and Sustainable Energy Reviews, vol. 82, Part 3, 2018, pp. 3610–3622, doi: 10.1016/j.rser.2017.10.101.

[28] Om Prakash Mahela, and Abdul Gafoor Shaik, Comprehensive overview of grid interfaced wind energy generation systems, Renewable and Sustainable Energy Reviews (Elsevier), vol. 57, pp. 260–281, 2016, doi: 10.1016/j.rser.2015.12.048

[29] Rajkumar Kaushik, Om Prakash Mahela and Pramod Kumar Bhatt, Hybrid algorithm for detection of events and power quality disturbances associated with distribution network in the presence of wind energy, IEEE International Conference on Advance Computing and Innovative Technologies in Engineering (ICACITE 2021), Galgotias College of Engineering College and Technology, Greater Noida, March 4–5, 2021, doi: 10.1109/ICACITE51222.2021.9404665.

[30] Atul Kulshrestha, Om Prakash Mahela, Mukesh Kumar Gupta, A discrete wavelet transform and rule based decision tree based technique for identification of fault in utility grid network with wind energy, 2021 First IEEE International Conference on Advances in Electrical, Computing, Communications and Sustainable Technologies (ICAECT 2021), Shri Shankaracharia Technical Campus (SSTC), Bhilai, February 19–20, 2021, doi: 10.1109/ICAECT49130.2021.9392428

[31] Surbhi Thukral, Om Prakash Mahela, Bipul Kumar, Detection of transmission line faults in the presence of wind energy power generation source using Stockwell's transform, IEEE International Conference on Issues and Challenges in Intelligent Computing Techniques (ICICT 2019), KIET Group of Institutions, Delhi-NCR, Ghaziabad, 27–28th September, 2019. doi: 10.1109/ICICT46931.2019.8977695

[32] Om Prakash Mahela, Kapil Dev Kansal and Sunil Agarwal. Detection of power quality disturbances in utility grid with wind energy penetration, 8th IEEE India International Conference on Power Electronics (IICPE-2018), MNIT Jaipur, December, 13–14, 2018. doi: 10.1109/IICPE.2018.8709578

[33] Om Prakash Mahela, Pragati Prajapati and Soyab Ali. Investigation of power quality events in distribution network with wind energy penetration. 2018 IEEE Students' Conference on Electrical, Electronics and Computer Science (SCEECS 2018), MANIT, Bhopal, February 24–25, 2018, doi: 10.1109/SCEECS.2018.8546945

[34] Om Prakash Mahela, and Abdul Gafoor Shaik. Comprehensive overview of grid interfaced solar photovoltaic systems, Renewable and Sustainable Energy Reviews (Elsevier), vol. 68, Part 1, pp. 316–332, 2017, doi: 10.1016/j.rser.2016.09.096

[35] Om Prakash Mahela, and Abdul Gafoor Shaik. Detection of power quality disturbances associated with grid integration of 100 kW solar PV plant, 1st IEEE Uttar Pradesh Conference-International Conference on Energy Economics and Environment (ICEEE 2015), Galgotia Institute of Engineering and Technology, Noida, March 27–28, 2015, doi: 10.1109/EnergyEconomics.2015.7235070

[36] Pragati Prajapati, Om Prakash Mahela and Soyab Ali. Investigation of power quality events in distribution network with solar energy penetration, 2018 IEEE Students' Conference on Electrical, Electronics and Computer Science (SCEECS 2018), MANIT, Bhopal, February 24–25, 2018, doi: 10.1109/SCEECS.2018.8546930,

[37] Surbhi Thukral, Om Prakash Mahela, and Bipul Kumar. Detection of transmission line faults in the presence of solar PV system using Stockwell's transform. IEEE 7th Power India International Conference on advances in signal processing (PIICON 2016), Government Engineering College, Bikaner, November 25–27, 2016, doi: 10.1109/POWERI.2016.8077304,

[38] Toshiba Suman, Om Prakash Mahela, and Sheesh Ram Ola. Detection of transmission line faults in the presence of solar PV generation using discrete wavelet

transform, IEEE 7th Power India International Conference on advances in signal processing (PIICON 2016), Government Engineering College, Bikaner, Bikaner, November 25–27, 2016, doi: 10.1109/POWERI.2016.8077203,

[39] Kavita Kumari, Atul Kumar Dadhich, and Om Prakash Mahela. Detection of power quality disturbances in the utility grid with solar energy using S-transform, IEEE 7th Power India International Conference on advances in Signal Processing (PII-CON 2016), Government Engineering College, Bikaner, November 25–27, 2016, doi: 10.1109/POWERI.2016.8077351,

[40] A. Gasparjan, A. Terebkov and A. Zhiravetska, Monitoring of electro-mechanical system diesel-synchronous generator, 2015 IEEE 5th International Conference on Power Engineering, Energy and Electrical Drives (POWERENG), Riga, 2015, pp. 103–108, doi: 10.1109/PowerEng.2015.7266303.

[41] D. H. Wang, C. V. Nayar and C. Wang, Modeling of stand-alone variable speed diesel generator using doubly-fed induction generator, The 2nd International Symposium on Power Electronics for Distributed Generation Systems, Hefei, 2010, pp. 1–6, doi: 10.1109/PEDG.2010.5545769.

[42] M. Greig and J. Wang, Fuel consumption minimization of variable-speed wound rotor diesel generators, IECON 2017–43rd Annual Conference of the IEEE Industrial Electronics Society, Beijing, 2017, pp. 8572–8577, doi: 10.1109/IECON. 2017.8217506.

[43] M. Moroz, K. Korol, S. O. Korol, O. Moroz, I. Kuzev and O. Vasylkovskyi, The method for stabilizing the electrical power of a vehicle diesel generator plant, 2021 IEEE International Conference on Modern Electrical and Energy Systems (MEES), Kremenchuk, 2021, pp. 1–4, doi: 10.1109/MEES52427.2021.9598609.

[44] K. P. Inala and K. Thirugnanam, Role of communication networks on vehicle-to-grid (V2G) system in a smart grid environment, 2022 4th International Conference on Energy, Power and Environment (ICEPE), Shillong, 2022, pp. 1–5, doi: 10.1109/ ICEPE55035.2022.9798110.

[45] Z. Xu, W. Shi, J. Wu, H. Qi, X. Zhang and J. Wang, Smart grid dispatching strategy considering the difference of electric vehicle demand, 2020 IEEE 4th Conference on Energy Internet and Energy System Integration (EI2), Wuhan, 2020, pp. 1285–1290, doi: 10.1109/EI250167.2020.9347357.

[46] Vishwajeet Kumar Sinha, Ram Niwash Mahia, and Om Prakash Mahela, Power management in electric vehicles using a hybrid energy storage system, in Book Active Electrical Distribution Network: Issues, Solution Techniques and Applications, Editors: Baseem khan, Om Prakash Mahela, Hassan Haes Alhelou, S. Rajkumar, Sanjeevikumar Padmanaban, doi: 10.1016/B978-0-323-85169-5.00014-9 (In production, Academic Press, Elsevier, 2022, ISBN: 9780323851695)

[47] Ashish Kumar, Ram Niwash Mahia, and Om Prakash Mahela, Modified space vector pulse width modulation technique for speed control of permanent magnet synchronous motor in electric vehicles, in Book Active Electrical Distribution Network: Issues, Solution Techniques and Applications, Editors: Baseem khan, Om Prakash Mahela, Hassan Haes Alhelou, S. Rajkumar, Sanjeevikumar Padmanaban, doi: 10.1016/B978-0-323-85169-5.00002-2

[48] Om Prakash Mahela, Umesh Sharma and Tanuj Manglani, Recognition of power quality disturbances using discrete wavelet transform and fuzzy c-means clustering,

2018 IEEE 8th Power India International Conference (PIICON 2018), NIT Kuruk-shetra, India, December 10–12, 2018, doi: 10.1109/POWERI.2018.8704404.

[49] Rahul Saini, Om Prakash Mahela and Deepak Sharma, Detection and classification of complex power quality disturbances using hilbert transform and rule based decision tree, 2018 IEEE 8th Power India International Conference (PIICON 2018), NIT Kurukshetra, India, December 10–12, 2018, doi: 10.1109/POWERI.2018.8704427.

[50] Ankit Kumar Sharma, Om Prakash Mahela and Sheesh Ram Ola, Detection of power quality disturbances using discrete wavelet transform, IEEE International Conference on Electrical Power and Energy Systems (ICEPES 2016), MANIT, Bhopal, India, December 14–16, 2016, doi: 10.1109/ICEPES.2016.7915973.

[51] S. -H. Cho, G. Jang and S. -H. Kwon, Time-frequency analysis of power-quality disturbances via the gabor–wigner transform, IEEE Transactions on Power Delivery, vol. 25, no. 1, January 2010, pp. 494–499, doi: 10.1109/TPWRD.2009.2034832.

[52] S. A. Deokar and L. M. Waghmare, Integrated DWT–FFT approach for detection and classification of power quality disturbances, International Journal of Electrical Power & Energy Systems, vol. 61, 2014, pp. 594–605, doi: 10.1016/j.ijepes.2014.04.015.

[53] Mishra M, Power quality disturbance detection and classification using signal processing and soft computing techniques: A comprehensive review, International Transactions on Electrical Energy Systems, vol. 29, 2019, e12008, doi: 10.1002/2050-7038.12008.

[54] Vishakha Pandya, Sunil Agarwal, Om Prakash Mahela and Sunita Choudhary, Recognition of power quality disturbances using hybrid algorithm based on combined features of stockwell transform and hilbert transform, 2020 IEEE International Students' Conference on Electrical, Electronics and Computer Science (SCEECS 2020), MANIT Bhopal, India, February 22–23, 2020, doi: 10.1109/SCEECS48394.2020.4.

[55] Om Prakash Mahela, Abdul Gafoor Shaik and Neeraj Gupta, A critical review of detection and classification of power quality events, Renewable and Sustainable Energy Reviews (Elsevier), vol. 41, January 2015, pp. 495–505, doi: 10.1016/j.rser.2014.08.070.

[56] M. S. Sakib, M. R. Islam, S. M. S. H. Tanim, M. S. Alam, M. Shafiullah and A. Ali, Signal processing-based artificial intelligence approach for power quality disturbance identification, 2022 International Conference on Advancement in Electrical and Electronic Engineering (ICAEEE), Gazipur, Bangladesh, 2022, pp. 1–6, doi: 10.1109/ICAEEE54957.2022.9836389.

[57] Om Prakash Mahela, Kapil Dev Kansal and Sunil Agarwal, Detection of power quality disturbances in utility grid with wind energy penetration, 8th IEEE India International Conference on Power Electronics (IICPE-2018), MNIT Jaipur, India, 2018, December 13–14, doi: 10.1109/IICPE.2018.8709578.

[58] G. S. Chawda et al., Comprehensive review on detection and classification of power quality disturbances in utility grid with renewable energy penetration, IEEE Access, vol. 8, 2020, pp. 146807–146830, doi: 10.1109/ACCESS.2020.3014732.

[59] Z. Wang, T. Deng, H. Wang, J. Tao, H. Zhang and Q. Wang, Power quality disturbance recognition method in park distribution network based on one-dimensional vggnet and multi-label classification, 2023 5th Asia Energy and Electrical Engineering Symposium (AEEES), Chengdu, China, 2023, pp. 764–770, doi: 10.1109/AEEES56888.2023.10114115.

[60] O. P. Mahela and A. G. Shaik, Topological aspects of power quality improvement techniques: A comprehensive overview, Renewable and Sustainable Energy

Reviews, vol. 58, pp. 1129–1142, 2016. [Online]. www.sciencedirect.com/science/article/pii/S1364032115016342

[61] R. Kumar, A. Mohanty, S. R. Mohanty, and N. Kishor, Power quality improvement in 3-phase grid connected photovoltaic system with battery storage, Power Electronics, Drives and Energy Systems (PEDES), 2012 IEEE International Conference, December 2012, pp. 1–6.

[62] A. Zahedi, Maximizing solar pv energy penetration using energy storage technology, Renewable and Sustainable Energy Reviews, vol. 15, no. 1, pp. 866–870, 2011. [Online]. Available: www.sciencedirect.com/science/article/pii/S1364032110002984

[63] W. Frangieh and M. B. Najjar, Active control for power quality improvement in hybrid power systems, in Technological Advances in Electrical, Electronics and Computer Engineering (TAEECE), 2015 Third International Conference, April 2015, pp. 218–223.

[64] M. G. Molina and P. E. Mercado, Control design and simulation of dstatcom with energy storage for power quality improvements, in Transmission Distribution Conference and Exposition: Latin America, 2006. TDC '06. IEEE/PES, Aug 2006, pp. 1–7.

[65] S. R. Arya, K. Kant, R. Niwas, B. Singh, A. Chandra, and K. Al-Haddad, Power quality improvement in isolated distributed generating system using dstatcom, in Industry Applications Society Annual Meeting, 2014 IEEE, October 2014, pp. 1–8.

[66] F. Shahnia, R. P. S. Chandrasena, A. Ghosh, and S. Rajakaruna, Application of dstatcom for surplus power circulation in mv and lv distribution networks with single-phase distributed energy resources, Electric Power Systems Research, vol. 117, no. 0, pp. 104–114, 2014. [Online]. www.sciencedirect.com/science/article/pii/S0378779614003071.

[67] Shoaib Hussain, A.H. Osman, Fault location scheme for multi-terminal transmission lines using unsynchronized measurements, International Journal of Electrical Power and Energy Systems, vol. 78, 2016, pp. 277–284.

[68] K. M. Silva, B. A. Souza and N. S. D. Brito, Fault detection and classification in transmission lines based on wavelet transform and ANN, IEEE Transactions on Power Delivery, vol. 21, no. 4, pp. 2058–2062, 2006.

[69] Liu Yang, He Xiao, Wang Zidong and Zhou Dong-Hua, Fault detection and diagnosis for a class of nonlinear systems with decentralized event-triggered transmissions, IFAC-Papers Online, vol. 48, no. 21, 2015, pp. 1134–1139.

[70] Anamika Yadav and Aleena Swetapadma, A novel transmission line relaying scheme for fault detection and classification using wavelet transform and linear discriminant analysis, Ain Shams Engineering Journal, vol. 6, 2015, pp. 199–209.

[71] Joe-Air Jiang, Ching-Shan Chen, and Chih-Wen Liu, A new protection scheme for fault detection, direction discrimination, classification, and location in transmission lines, IEEE Transactions on the Power Delivery, vol. 18, no. 1, 2003.

[72] M. Eissa. Protection techniques with renewable resources and smart grids—A survey, Renewable Sustainable Energy Review, vol. 52, 2015, pp. 1645–1667.

[73] P. Barra, D. Coury, R. Fernandes. A survey on adaptive protection of microgrids and distribution systems with distributed generators, Renewable Sustainable Energy Review, vol. 118, 2020, 109524.

[74] V. Telukunta, J. Pradhan, J.; Agrawal, A.; Singh, M.; Srivani, S.G. Protection challenges under bulk penetration of renewable energy resources in power systems: A review, CSEE Journal Power Energy System, vol. 3, 2017, pp. 365–379.

[75] S.R. Ola, A. Saraswat, S.K. Goyal, S. Jhajharia, B. Rathore, O.P. Mahela. Wigner distribution function and alienation coefficient-based transmission line protection scheme, IET General Transmission Distribution, vol. 14, 2020, pp. 1842–1853.

[76] M. Dehghani, M.H. Khooban, T. Niknam, Fast fault detection and classification based on a combination of wavelet singular entropy theory and fuzzy logic in distribution lines in the presence of distributed generations, International Journal Electronics Power Energy System, vol. 78, 2016, pp. 455–462.

[77] A. Malhotra, O.P. Mahela, H. Doraya, Detection and classification of power system faults using discrete wavelet transform and rule based decision tree, Proceedings of the 2018 International Conference on Computing, Power and Communication Technologies (GUCON), Greater Noida, 28–29 September 2018, pp. 142–147.

[78] T. Suman, O.P. Mahela, S.R. Ola. Detection of transmission line faults in the presence of wind power generation using discrete wavelet transform. Proceedings of the 2016 IEEE 7th Power India International Conference (PIICON), Bikaner, 25–27 November 2016, pp. 1–6.

[79] Godfred Amankwaa, Richard Heeks, Alison L. Browne, Smartening up: User experience with smart water metering infrastructure in an African city, Utilities Policy, Vol. 80, 2023, p. 101478, doi: 10.1016/j.jup.2022.101478.

[80] Manikanda Kumaran K, Manivannan R, Kalaiselvi S, Anitha Elavarasi S, An IoT based environment conscious green score meter towards smart sustainable cities, Sustainable Computing: Informatics and Systems, Vol. 37, 2023, p. 100839, doi: 10.1016/j.suscom.2022.100839.

[81] A.M. Abbas, K.Y. Youssef, I.I. Mahmoud, A.Zekry, NB-IoT optimization for smart meters networks of smart cities: Case study, Alexandria Engineering Journal, vol. 59, no. 6, 2020, pp. 4267–4281, doi: 10.1016/j.aej.2020.07.030.

[82] S.S. Chowdary, M.A. Abd El Ghany, K. Hofmann, IoT based wireless energy efficient smart metering system using zigbee in smart cities, 2020 7th International Conference on Internet of Things: Systems, Management and Security (IOTSMS), Paris, 2020, pp. 1–4, doi: 10.1109/IOTSMS52051.2020.9340230.

Chapter 15

Smart Power Quality Monitoring System for Smart Cities

Ekata Sharma and Om Prakash Mahela

15.1 INTRODUCTION

Recent integrations of electric vehicles (EVs) and distributed generators (DG) into smart city power networks and applications of solid-state controllers in smart cities have resulted in load demand variations, the injection of harmonics into network power, and other power quality (PQ) issues [1]. PQ events generated in smart city power networks include sag with voltage signal, swell with voltage signal, momentary interruption with voltage signal, harmonics with voltage signal, flicker with voltage signal, oscillatory transient with voltage signal, impulsive transient with voltage signal, notch with voltage signal, and spikes with voltage signal [2]. These PQ disturbances impact the security, reliability, and stability of power networks as well as the sensitive equipment equipped in data centers, hospitals, banking establishments, and other sectors of smart cities [3]. Therefore, PQ disturbances need to be detected and remedied as soon as possible after they occur.

Signal analysis and mathematical tools have been developed to detect PQ disturbances. A detailed analysis of various PQ improvement techniques that can be used for smart cities is reported in [4]. In [5], the authors presented a PQ monitoring and detection scheme that considered the time difference and had high efficiency. They improved the detection accuracy by adding time synchronization. In [6], the authors designed a smart city PQ monitoring method using artificial neural network. In [7], the authors designed a hybrid model using machine learning and deep learning to detect and categorize PQ events with high precision and accuracy. Investigators have developed and reported on multiple techniques for detecting PQ disturbances in smart city power networks [8–39].

Based on our critical review of existing methods, we determined that there remains a need for smart PQ monitoring methods with high accuracy for detecting and classifying PQ disturbances in smart city power networks. In response, we conducted this investigation, and here we introduce the study. We designed a smart PQ monitoring system (SPQMS) to detect and categorize PQ disturbances observed with a power network of smart cities using wavelet singular entropy (WSE).

DOI: 10.1201/9781003486930-21

We computed WSE using Shannon entropy by analyzing voltage signals with a PQ disturbance and applying stationary wavelet transform (SWT). We computed a disturbed index to indicate the presence of PQ disturbances with a voltage signal. WSE and disturbed index higher than unity indicated the presence of a PQ disturbance. We computed a feature considering the maximum WSE, which we used to classify the PQ disturbances using decision rules. We detected nine PQ disturbances that we classified with accuracy higher than 98%. We tested the efficacy of the proposed SPQMS by comparing its performance with discrete wavelet transform (DWT) and fuzzy C-means clustering (FCM).

15.2 GENERATION OF PQ DISTURBANCES

In the power network of smart cities, PQ disturbances such as sag in voltage, swell, interruption, flicker, oscillatory transient (OT), impulsive transient (IT), notch, spike, and harmonics are frequently observed. These PQ disturbances are simulated by mathematical modeling available in [40] and described in this chapter where A indicates amplitude, f indicates frequency, V indicates voltage, T indicates time period, τ indicates time constant, ω indicates angular frequency, and u(t) indicates unit step function. Simulated parameters of the investigated PQ disturbances are included in Table 15.1.

15.2.1 Voltage Signal without PQ Event

We used the following mathematical model to simulate a voltage signal without a PQ disturbance:

Table 15.1 Simulated Parameters of Smart City PQ Disturbances

Smart City PQ Disturbance	Simulated
Voltage signal without a PQ disturbance	A = 1 pu, f = 50Hz
SGVS	$\alpha = 0.3, t_1 = 0.06, t_2 = 0.14$
SWVS	$\alpha = 0.3, t_1 = 0.06, t_2 = 0.14$
MIVS	$\alpha = 0.95, t_1 = 0.06, t_2 = 0.14$
HVS	$\alpha_3 = 0.05, \alpha_5 = 0.10, \alpha_7 = 0.15$
FVS	$\alpha_f = 0.15, \beta = 15$
OTVS	$\alpha = 0.8, t_1 = 0.08, \tau = 0.02, t_2 = 0.10$
ITVS	$\alpha = 10, t_1 = 0.085, \tau = 0.02, t_2 = 0.088$
NOVS	K = 0.4, $t_1 = 0.006$, t2 = 0.0065
SPVS	K = 0.4, $t_1 = 0.002, t_2 = 0.0023$

Notes. SGVS: sag with voltage signal, SWVS: swell with voltage signal, MIVS: momentary interruption with voltage signal, HVS: harmonics with voltage signal, FVS: flicker with voltage signal, OTVS: oscillatory transient with voltage signal, ITVS: impulsive transient with voltage signal, NOVS: notch with voltage signal, SPVS: spikes with voltage signal.

$$V(t) = Asin(\omega t) \tag{15.1}$$

15.2.2 Sag

We used the following mathematical model to simulate a PQ event of sag with voltage signal:

$$V(t) = (1 - \alpha(u(t - t_1) - u(t - t_2)))sin(\omega t) \tag{15.2}$$

15.2.3 Swell with Voltage Signal

We used the following mathematical model to simulate a PQ disturbance of swell with a voltage signal:

$$V(t) = (1 + \alpha(u(t - t_1) - u(t - t_2)))sin(\omega t) \tag{15.3}$$

15.2.4 Momentary Interruption with Voltage Signal

We used the following mathematical model to simulate a PQ disturbance of momentary interruption (MI) with a voltage signal:

$$V(t) = (1 - \alpha(u(t - t_1) - u(t - t_2)))sin(\omega t) \tag{15.4}$$

15.2.5 Harmonics with Voltage Signal

We used the following mathematical model to simulate a PQ event of harmonics with a voltage signal:

$$V(t) = \alpha_1 sin(\omega t) + \alpha_3 sin(3\omega t) + \alpha_5 sin(5\omega t) + \alpha_7 sin(7\omega t) \tag{15.5}$$

15.2.6 Flicker with Voltage Signal

We used the following mathematical model to simulate a PQ event of flicker with a voltage signal:

$$V(t) = (1 + \alpha_f sin(\beta \omega t))sin(\omega t) \tag{15.6}$$

15.2.7 OT with Voltage Signal

We used the following mathematical model to simulate a PQ disturbance of OT with a voltage signal:

$$V(t) = sin(\omega t) + \alpha e^{\frac{(t - t1)}{\tau}} sin \omega n(t - t_1)\{u(t_2 - u(t_1))\} \tag{15.7}$$

15.2.8 IT with Voltage Signal

We used the following mathematical model to simulate a PQ disturbance of IT with a voltage signal:

$$V(t) = sin(\omega t) + \alpha e^{\frac{(t-t1)}{\tau}} - \alpha e^{\frac{(t-t1)}{\tau}} \{u(t_2 - u(t_1))\} \qquad (15.8)$$

15.2.9 Notches with Voltage Signal

We used the following mathematical model to simulate a PQ disturbance of notches with a voltage signal:

$$V(t) = sin(\omega t) - sign(sin(\omega t)) \times \left[\sum_{n=0}^{9} K \times \{u(t - (t1 + 0.02n)) - u(t - (t2 + 0.02n))\} \right] \qquad (15.9)$$

15.2.10 Spikes with Voltage Signal

We used the following mathematical model to simulate a PQ disturbance of spikes with a voltage signal:

$$V(t) = sin(\omega t) + sign(sin(\omega t)) \times \left[\sum_{n=0}^{9} K \times \{u(t - (t1 + 0.02n)) - u(t - (t2 + 0.02n))\} \right] \qquad (15.10)$$

15.3 WAVELET SINGULAR ENTROPY AND STATIONARY WAVELET TRANSFORM

WSE is a useful technique for analyzing the complexity or irregularity of signals. However, its effectiveness in detecting PQ disturbances varies. It is recommended to explore and experiment with different threshold values and wavelet functions to achieve optimal detection results. WSE indicates the complexity or irregularity of a signal based on the Shannon entropy of the singular values obtained from the singular value decomposition (SVD) of the wavelet coefficients; the WSE quantifies the amount of information or randomness present in the signal. The primary purpose of WSE is to analyze signals for their complexity, irregularity, or information content. When applying WSE to power quality analysis, it is typically used to detect disturbances that introduce complexity or irregularity to the signal, such as transients, harmonics, or other non-sinusoidal components [41–42].

15.3.1 Stationary Wavelet Transform

Stationary wavelet transform (SWT) is a form of wavelet transform that eradicates the deficiency of translation invariance with DWT. SWT achieves translation invariance by removing down-samplers and up-samplers in the process of DWT. Up-sampling of the coefficients is performed by considering a factor of $2^{(j-1)}$ at j^{th} level of decomposition. A digital form of SWT is illustrated in Figure 15.1, and SWT filters

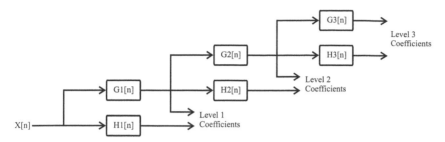

Figure 15.1 Digital implementation of SWT.

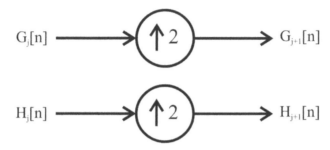

Figure 15.2 SWT filters.

are demonstrated in Figure 15.2. Filters at every level are up-sampled forms of their prior versions. A detailed mathematical SWT formulation is available in [43].

15.3.2 Shannon Entropy

Shannon entropy indicates the uncertainty of random variables. Computation of Shannon entropy is based on Shannon's metric, which is calculated as

$$H = -\sum_{i=1}^{s} (P_i \times ln(P_i))$$

(15.11)

Here, H: Shannon entropy, P_i: probability of given symbol, S: symbols encountered.

15.3.3 Singular Value Decomposition

The SVD of a matrix is performed by factorization of that matrix into three subsequent matrices. SVD indicates the linear transformations in terms of geometrical and theoretical aspects. The SVD of *mxn* matrix A is calculated by equation 15.12:

$$A = U \sum A^T$$

(15.12)

Here, U: *mxm* matrix with orthonormal eigenvectors of AA^T and V^T: transpose of a *nxn* matrix that contains orthonormal eigenvectors of A^TA, and summation symbol indicates matrix of orthogonal nature with r elements equal to root of positive eigenvalues of AA^T or $A^T A$. Both these matrices have positive eigenvalues of the same nature.

15.4 SMART POWER QUALITY MONITORING SYSTEM FOR SMART CITIES

We designed the SPQMS for this chapter's study by computing the WSE of voltage signals that had PQ disturbances following these detailed steps:

- Simulate a PQ disturbance using mathematical models described in Section 12.2 Generation of PQ Disturbances.
- Set the parameters for the WSE, including the wavelet function name (Daubechies wavelet [db4]), the decomposition level (Level 5), and the length of each segment (64 samples).
- Iterate over the signal and calculate the WSE using the sliding window approach.
- For each segment, perform the SWT and compute the singular values of the SWT coefficients, normalize the singular values, and calculate the WSE based on Shannon entropy.
- Set a threshold (1.0) to detect disturbances based on the WSE exceeding the threshold. The indices where the WSE exceeds the threshold are considered disturbed regions.
- A disturbed index is computed that indicates the WSE greater than unity.
- Plot the original signal and the WSE. The disturbed regions are highlighted by overlaying red dots on the corresponding samples in the WSE plot.
- Feature F1 is computed by taking the maximum WSE following this detailed mathematical formulation:

$$F1 = max(abs(WSE)) \tag{15.13}$$

- PQ disturbances are classified using decision rules driven by feature F1.

15.5 DETECTING PQ DISTURBANCES IN A SMART CITY POWER NETWORK: SIMULATION RESULTS

This section details the results of our simulations to detect PQ events in a smart city power distribution network using the proposed SPQMS. Results for voltage signals that do not have a PQ event are also elaborated in this section.

15.5.1 Voltage Signal without PQ Disturbance

The voltage signal without a PQ event is simulated using equation (15.1) and is depicted in Figure 15.3(a). The voltage is analyzed by applying the proposed SPQMS to obtain the WSE and disturbed plot in Figure 15.3(b). F1 is calculated from the WSE and given in Table 15.2.

Figure 15.3(a) illustrates that not every event is related to voltage and that the nature of voltage waveform is purely sinusoidal. Figure 15.3(b) indicates that WSE reaches unity after 64 samples. Further, the disturbed index is also unity after 64 samples. The unit magnitude of the disturbed index indicates that PQ disturbance is not associated with voltage. Table 15.2 indicates that F1 is unity. In short, the proposed SPQMS established that there was no disturbance in the voltage waveform.

15.5.2 Voltage Sag

The sag with a voltage signal is calculated with equation (15.2) and depicted in Figure 15.4(a). This event is processed using the proposed SPQMS to obtain the WSE plot and disturbed index in Figure 15.4(b). F1 is calculated from the WSE and given in Table 15.2.

Figure 15.4(a) illustrates that a sag disturbance is seen with voltage between samples 192 and 448. Figure 15.4(b) indicates that WSE reaches unity after 64 samples, and high WSE is seen twice, starting at samples 192 and 448, which

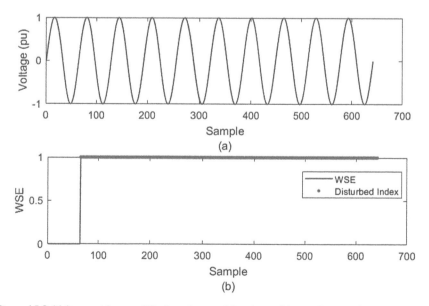

Figure 15.3 Voltage without a PQ disturbance: (a) voltage; (b) wavelet singular entropy.

Table 15.2 FI for Each Tested PQ Disturbance

S. No.	PQ disturbance	Symbol of PQ disturbance	Magnitude of FI
I	Voltage signal without a PQ disturbance	P0	1.000
2	SGVS	PI	1.4010
3	SWVS	P2	1.3187
4	MIVS	P3	2.3430
5	HVS	P4	1.4859
6	FVS	P5	1.2001
7	OTVS	P6	2.2114
8	ITVS	P7	2.0518
9	NOVS	P8	1.3302
10	SPVS	P9	1.2479

Notes. SGVS: sag with voltage signal, SWVS: swell with voltage signal, MIVS: momentary interruption with voltage signal, HVS: harmonics with voltage signal, FVS: flicker with voltage signal, OTVS: oscillatory transient with voltage signal, ITVS: impulsive transient with voltage signal, NOVS: notch with voltage signal, SPVS: spikes with voltage signal.

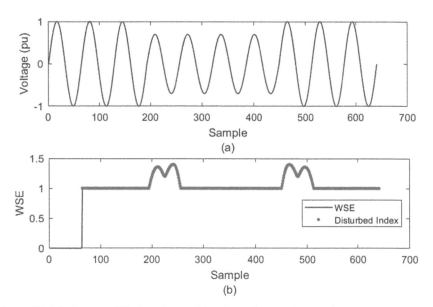

Figure 15.4 Voltage sag PQ disturbance: (a) voltage; (b) wavelet singular entropy.

indicates the start and end of sag disturbance. Further, the disturbed index also reaches unity after 64 samples, and high values indicated the sag disturbances, at 192 and 448. Table 15.2 indicates that F1 is 1.4010. Therefore, the proposed SPQMS established that there was a sag event with voltage.

15.5.3 Voltage Swell

Swell with a voltage signal is calculated with equation (15.3) and depicted in Figure 15.5(a). This event is analyzed by applying the proposed SPQMS to obtain the WSE and disturbed index plot in Figure 15.5(b). F1 is calculated from the WSE and given in Table 15.2.

Figure 15.5(a) illustrates that a swell disturbance is associated with voltage waveform between samples 192 and 448. Figure 15.5(b) indicates that WSE reaches unity after 64 samples and that WSE is high twice, starting at 192 and 448, which indicate start and end of swell event. Further, the disturbed index also reaches unity after 64 samples and is high at 192 and 448 indicating the swell disturbance. Table 15.2 shows that F1 is 1.3187. Hence, the proposed SPQMS established that there was a swell disturbance with voltage. Additionally, the peak WSE and disturbed index for this swell disturbance were lower than they were for the sag disturbance.

15.5.4 Momentary Interruption

The momentary interruption with a voltage signal is calculated with equation (15.4) and depicted in Figure 15.6(a). This disturbance is analyzed using the SPQMS to obtain the WSE and disturbed index plot in Figure 15.6(b). F1 is calculated from the WSE and given in Table 15.2.

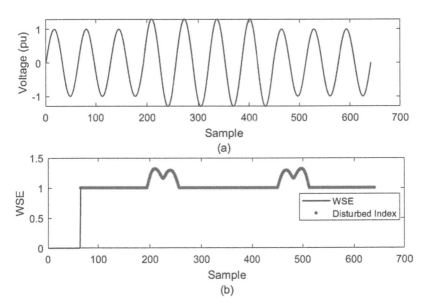

Figure 15.5 Voltage swell PQ disturbance: (a) voltage waveform; (b) wavelet singular entropy.

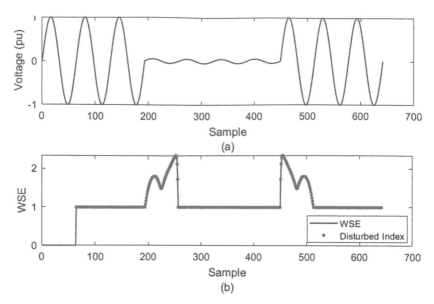

Figure 15.6 Momentary interruption PQ disturbance: (a) voltage waveform; (b) wavelet singular entropy.

Figure 15.6(a) illustrates that a MI disturbance is associated with voltage waveform between samples 192 to 448. Figure 15.6(b) indicates that WSE reaches unity after 64 samples and is high at samples 192 and 448, indicating the start and end of the MI event. A form of ditch is seen in the WSE plot that indicates the MI disturbance. Further, the disturbed index reaches unity after 64 samples and is high at 192 and 448, indicating the MI disturbance associated with the voltage waveform. A form of ditch is observed in the disturbed index plot indicates the MI disturbance. Table 15.2, indicates that F1 is 2.3430. Therefore, the proposed SPQMS established that there was a MI disturbance with voltage. Additionally, the peak WSE and disturbed index for the MI disturbance were higher than the respective values for sag and swell disturbances.

15.5.5 Voltage Harmonics

The harmonics with a voltage signal disturbance is calculated with equation (15.5) and depicted in Figure 15.7(a). This event is analyzed by applying the proposed SPQMS to obtain the WSE and disturbed index plot in Figure 15.7(b). F1 is calculated from the WSE and given in Table 15.2.

Figure 15.7(a) illustrates that the harmonics event is seen with voltage waveform over the complete signal period. Figure 15.7(b) indicates that WSE reaches 1.5 after 64 samples and remains constant over the entire signal period. Further,

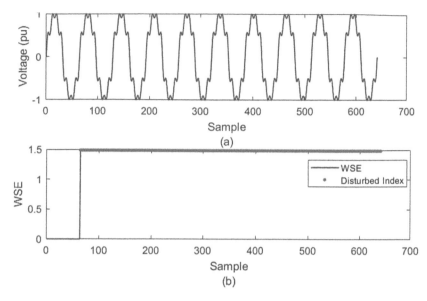

Figure 15.7 Voltage harmonics PQ disturbance: (a) voltage; (b) wavelet singular entropy.

disturbed index reaches 1.5 after 64 samples and also remains constant, indicating the harmonics disturbance with voltage. Table 15.2 indicates that F1 is 1.4859. Therefore, the proposed SPQMS established that there was a harmonics disturbance with voltage. Additionally, the peak WSE and disturbed index for the harmonics disturbance were higher than the respective values of the pure sine wave, which is unity.

15.5.6 Flicker

The flicker with a voltage signal is calculated with equation (15.6) and depicted in Figure 15.8(a). This event is analyzed by applying the proposed SPQMS to obtain the WSE and disturbed index plot in Figure 15.8(b). F1 is computed from the WSE and given in Table 15.2.

Figure 15.8(a) illustrates that the flicker event is associated with voltage over the complete signal interval. Figure 15.8(b) demonstrates that WSE reaches 1.2 after 64 samples and remains constant over the entire signal period. Further, the disturbed index reaches 1.2 after 64 samples and also remains constant, indicating the flicker disturbance with voltage. Table 15.2 indicates that F1 is 1.2001. Therefore, the proposed SPQMS established that there was a flicker disturbance with voltage. Additionally, the WSE and disturbed index for the flicker disturbance exceeded the respective values for pure sine wave and were lower than those for the harmonics disturbance.

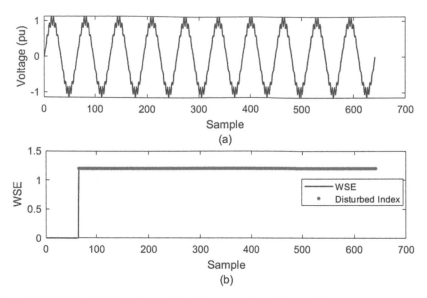

Figure 15.8 Flicker PQ disturbance: (a) voltage waveform; (b) wavelet singular entropy.

15.5.7 Oscillatory Transient

The with a voltage signal is calculated with equation (15.7) and depicted in Figure 15.9(a). This disturbance is calculated using the proposed SPQMS to obtain the WSE and disturbed index plot in Figure 15.9(b). F1 is calculated from the WSE and given in Table 15.2.

Figure 15.9(a) illustrates that an OT event with voltage is seen between samples 256 and 320. Figure 15.9(b) indicates that WSE reaches unity after 64 samples and is high at sample 256, indicating the start of the OT disturbance. A form of bridge is seen in WSE plot that confirms the OT event. Further, the disturbed index reaches unity after 64 samples and is also high at 256, indicating the OT event with voltage. A form of bridge in the disturbed index plot confirms OT event. Table 15.2 indicates that F1 is 2.2114. Therefore, the proposed SPQMS established that there was an OT event with voltage.

15.5.8 Impulsive Transient

The IT with voltage signal is calculated with equation (15.8) and depicted in Figure 15.10(a). This event is calculated using the proposed SPQMS to obtain the WSE and disturbed index plot in Figure 15.10(b). F1 is calculated from the WSE and included in Table 15.2.

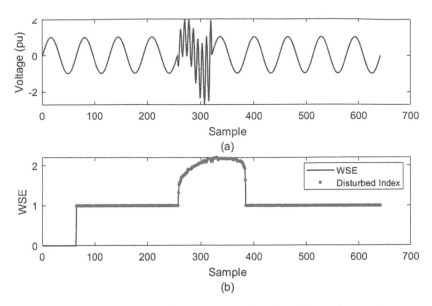

Figure 15.9 Oscillatory transient PQ disturbance: (a) voltage; (b) wavelet singular entropy.

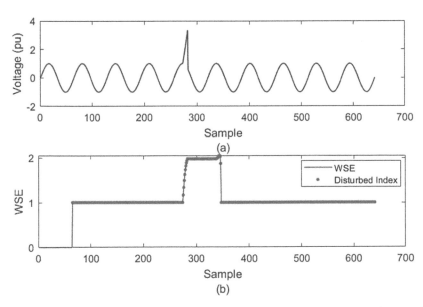

Figure 15.10 Impulsive transient PQ disturbance: (a) voltage waveform; (b) wavelet singular entropy.

Figure 15.10(a) illustrates that an IT disturbance is associated with voltage waveform between samples 272 and 282. Figure 15.10(b) indicates that WSE reaches unity after 64 samples and is high at sample 272, indicating the start of the IT disturbance. A form of step is seen in the WSE plot that indicates the IT event with voltage. Further, the disturbed index reaches unity after 64 samples and is also high at 272, indicating the event. A form of bridge is observed in the disturbed index plot that also indicates the event. Table 15.2 indicates that F1 is 2.0518. Therefore, the proposed SPQMS established that there was an IT event with voltage.

15.5.9 Notch

The notch with a voltage signal is calculated with equation (15.9) and depicted in Figure 15.11(a). This event is analyzed using the proposed SPQMS to obtain the WSE plot and disturbed index in Figure 15.11(b). F1 is calculated from the WSE and included in Table 15.2.

Figure 15.11(a) illustrates that a notch disturbance with voltage is seen over the full signal interval. Figure 15.11(b) indicates that WSE reaches 1.33 after 64 samples and remains constant over the entire signal period. Further, the disturbed index reaches 1.33 after 64 samples and also remains constant, indicating the notch disturbance. Table 15.2 indicates that F1 is 1.3302. Therefore, the proposed SPQMS established that there was a notch disturbance with voltage. Additionally,

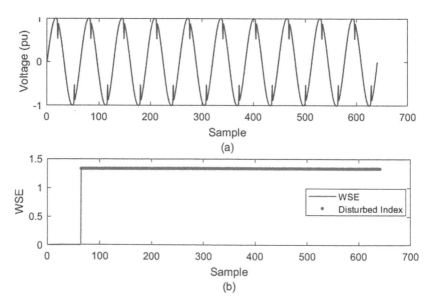

Figure 15.11 Notch PQ disturbance: (a) voltage waveform; (b) wavelet singular entropy.

the peak WSE and disturbed index for the notch disturbance were higher than the respective values for the pure sine wave.

15.5.10 Spike

The spike with a voltage signal is calculated with equation (15.10) and depicted in Figure 15.12(a). This voltage signal with a spike PQ event is processed applying the proposed SPQMS to obtain the WSE plot and disturbed index which are detailed in Figure 15.12(b). F1 is calculated from the WSE and included in Table 15.2.

Figure 15.12(a) illustrates that the spike disturbance is associated with voltage over the complete signal interval. Figure 15.12(b) indicates that WSE reaches 1.25 after 64 samples and remains constant over the entire signal period. Further, the disturbed index reaches 1.25 after 64 samples and also remains constant, indicating the spike disturbance. Table 15.2 indicates that F1 is 1.2479. Therefore, the proposed SPQMS established that there was a spike event with voltage. The peak WSE and disturbed index for the spike disturbance were also higher than they were for the sine wave.

15.6 CLASSIFICATION OF PQ DISTURBANCES

We categorized the PQ disturbances following the decision rules in Figure 15.13 based on F1. We used the SPQMS to calculate WSE by measuring voltages with a PQ disturbance, and F1 is computed as the maximum absolute WSE. Initially, we

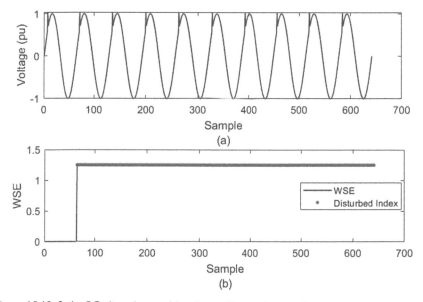

Figure 15.12 Spike PQ disturbance: (a) voltage; (b) wavelet singular entropy.

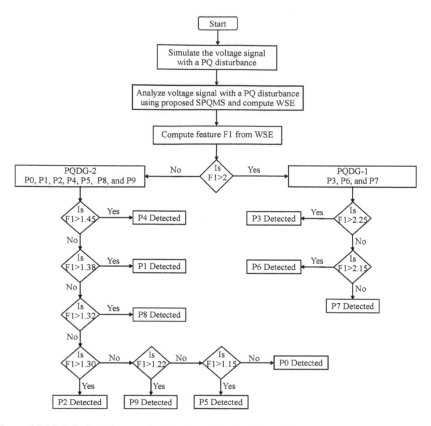

Figure 15.13 PQ disturbance classification using decision rules.

categorized the disturbances into two groups: events with F1 > 2 (PQ disturbance group 1, PQDG-1) and events with F1 < 2 (PQDG-2).

We estimated the accuracy of classification by testing the algorithm to classify a data set of 60 of the investigated PQ disturbances, which we simulated by varying the parameters: time of PQ event, signal frequency, frequency of PQ event, magnitude of PQ disturbance, etc. Categorization accuracy in terms of perfectly classified and inaccurately classified PQ events is given in Table 15.3. The table indicates that average classification accuracy is higher than 98%.

15.7 PERFORMANCE COMPARATIVE STUDY

We compared the performance of the proposed SPQMS with discrete wavelet transform and fuzzy C-means clustering algorithms for detecting PQ events that were reported in [44]. The accuracy with DWT and FCM was less than 96% [44],

Table 15.3 Accurate SPQMS Categorizations of PQ Disturbances Based on FI

S. No.	PQ disturbance	Number of perfectly categorized PQ disturbances	Number of inaccurately categorized PQ disturbances	Accuracy (%)
I	Voltage signal without a PQ disturbance	60	0	100%
2	SGVS	59	I	98.33%
3	SWVS	58	2	96.67%
4	MIVS	60	0	100%
5	HVS	59	I	98.33%
6	FVS	59	I	98.33%
7	OTVS	60	0	100%
8	ITVS	60	0	100%
9	NOVS	59	I	98.33%
10	SPVS	59	I	98.33%
Average classification accuracy				98.832%

Notes. SGVS: sag with voltage signal, SWVS: swell with voltage signal, MIVS: momentary interruption with voltage signal, HVS: harmonics with voltage signal, FVS: flicker with voltage signal, OTVS: oscillatory transient with voltage signal, ITVS: impulsive transient with voltage signal, NOVS: notch with voltage signal, SPVS: spikes with voltage signal.

in contrast with our high accuracy of >98%. The proposed SPQMS outperforms DWT and FCM.

15.8 CONCLUSION

For this chapter, we designed a smart power quality monitoring system to detect and categorize PQ events associated with smart city power networks using wavelet singular entropy. We concluded that the designed SPQMS effectively detected PQ disturbances (voltage sag, swell, harmonics; momentary interruption; oscillatory and impulsive transient, etc.) using the WSE and the disturbed index. We classified the PQ events by applying decision rules based on maximum absolute WSE. The accuracy of the proposed SPQMS at classifying PQ disturbances exceeded 98%, which was superior to the accuracy using DWT and FCM. We performed this study using MATLAB® software.

15.9 ACKNOWLEDGMENT

This research work is supported by Innovader Research Labs, Innovader IITian Padhaiwala LearnLab Pvt. Ltd., Jaipur, India.

REFERENCES

[1] G.K. John, M.R. Sindhu, T.N.P. Nambiar, "Renewable Energy Based Hybrid Power Quality Compensator based on Deep Learning Network for Smart Cities," Artificial Intelligence and Machine Learning in Smart City Planning, 2023, pp. 137–157, doi: 10.1016/B978-0-323-99503-0.00017-X.

[2] M. Longo, D. Zaninelli, M. Roscia and M. Costoiu, "Smart City to Improve Power Quality," 2014 16th International Conference on Harmonics and Quality of Power (ICHQP), Bucharest, Romania, 2014, pp. 458–462, doi: 10.1109/ICHQP.2014.6842861.

[3] S. Makasheva, P. Pinchukov and J. Szołtysek, "The Power Quality as a Pretext for Developing Smart City Concepts," 2020 International Multi-Conference on Industrial Engineering and Modern Technologies (FarEastCon), Vladivostok, Russia, 2020, pp. 1–7, doi: 10.1109/FarEastCon50210.2020.9271462.

[4] D. C. Sekhar, P. V. V. R. Rao and R. Kiranmayi, "Conceptual Review on Demand Side Management, Optimization Techniques for the Improvement of Power Quality in Smart Grids," 2022 Second International Conference on Artificial Intelligence and Smart Energy (ICAIS), Coimbatore, India, 2022, pp. 1640–1647, doi: 10.1109/ICAIS53314.2022.9742779.

[5] F. Yalin et al., "An On-site Detection Scheme of Power Quality Monitoring Device Considering Time Synchronization," 2022 6th International Conference on Smart Grid and Smart Cities (ICSGSC), Chengdu, China, 2022, pp. 93–97, doi: 10.1109/ICSGSC56353.2022.9962995.

[6] K. N. Akpinar and O. Ozgonenel, "Optimization of Artificial Neural Network for Power Quality Disturbances Detection," 2019 7th International Istanbul Smart Grids and Cities Congress and Fair (ICSG), Istanbul, Turkey, 2019, pp. 95–98, doi: 10.1109/SGCF.2019.8782429.

[7] R. Rahul and B. Choudhary, "Machine Learning and Deep Learning Based Hybrid Approach for Power Quality Disturbances Analysis," 2023 International Conference on Computational Intelligence and Knowledge Economy (ICCIKE), Dubai, United Arab Emirates, 2023, pp. 63–68, doi: 10.1109/ICCIKE58312.2023.10131708.

[8] Om Prakash Mahela, Abdul Gafoor Shaik, and Neeraj Gupta. A Critical Review of Detection and Classification of Power Quality Events, Renewable and Sustainable Energy Reviews (Elsevier), Vol. 41, 2015, pp. 495–505, doi: 10.1016/j.rser.2014.08.070

[9] Om Prakash Mahela and Abdul Gafoor Shaik. Power Quality Recognition in Distribution System with Solar Energy Penetration Using S-Transform and Fuzzy C-Means Clustering, Renewable Energy, Vol. 106, 2017, pp. 37–51, doi: 10.1016/j.renene.2016.12.098

[10] Om Prakash Mahela and Abdul Gafoor Shaik. Recognition of Power Quality Disturbances Using S-Transform Based Ruled Decision Tree and Fuzzy C-Means Clustering Classifiers, Applied Soft Computing, Vol. 59, 2017, pp. 243–257, doi: 10.1016/j.asoc.2017.05.061

[11] Abdul Gafoor Shaik and Om Prakash Mahela, Power Quality Assessment and Event Detection in Hybrid Power System, Electric Power Systems Research (Elsevier), Vol. 161, 2018, pp. 26–44, doi: 10.1016/j.epsr.2018.03.026

[12] Om Prakash Mahela, Abdul Gafoor Shaik, Baseem Khan, Rajendra Mahla, Hassan Haes Alhelou, "Recognition of Complex Power Quality Disturbances Using S-Transform Based Ruled Decision Tree," IEEE Access, Vol. 8, 2020, pp. 173530–173547, doi: 10.1109/ACCESS.2020.3025190

[13] Rajkumar Kaushik, Om Prakash Mahela, Pramod Kumar Bhatt, Baseem Khan, Sanjeevikumar Padmanabhan, and Frede Blaabjerg, "A Hybrid Algorithm for Recognition of Power Quality Disturbances," IEEE Access, Vol. 2, 2020, pp. 229184–229200, doi: 10.1109/ACCESS.2020.3046425

[14] Om Prakash Mahela, Baseem Khan, Hassan Haes Alhelou, Sudeep Tanwar, Assessment of Power Quality in the Utility Grid Integrated with Wind Energy Generation, IET Power Electronics, Vol. 13, Issue 13, 2020, pp. 2917–2925, doi: 10.1049/iet-pel.2019.1351

[15] Om Prakash Mahela, Abdul Gafoor Shaik, Neeraj Gupta, Mahdi Khosravy, Baseem Khan, Hassan Haes Alhelou, and Sanjeevikumar Padmanaban, Recognition of the Power Quality Issues Associated with Grid Integrated solar Photovoltaic Plant in Experimental Frame Work, IEEE Systems Journal, Vol. 15, Issue 3, 2021, pp. 3740–3748, doi: 10.1109/JSYST.2020.3027203

[16] Om Prakash Mahela, Mayank Parihar, Akhil Ranjan Garg, Baseem Khan, Salah Kamel, "A Hybrid Signal Processing Technique for Recognition of Complex Power Quality Disturbances," Electric Power Systems Research (Elsevier), Vol. 207, Paper No. 107865, doi: 10.1016/j.epsr.2022.107865

[17] Nagendra Kumar Swarnkar, Om Prakash Mahela and Mahendra Lalwani, "Multivariable Signal Processing Algorithm for Identification of Power Quality Disturbances" Electric Power Systems Research, Vol. 221, 2023, 109480, doi: 10.1016/j.epsr.2023.109480.

[18] Om Prakash Mahela, and Abdul Gafoor Shaik. Recognition of Power Quality Disturbances Using S-Transform and Fuzzy C-Means Clustering. In: IEEE International Conference and Utility Exhibition on Co-generation, Small Power Plants and District Energy (ICUE 2016), BITEC, Bang Na, Bangkok, Thailand, September 14–16, 2016, doi: 10.1109/COGEN.2016.7728955

[19] Rajkumar Kaushik, Om Prakash Mahela and Pramod Kumar Bhatt, "Hybrid Algorithm for Detection of Events and Power Quality Disturbances Associated with Distribution Network in the Presence of Wind Energy," IEEE International Conference on Advance Computing and Innovative Technologies in Engineering (ICACITE 2021), Galgotias College of Engineering College and Technology, Greater Noida, India, March 4–5, 2021, doi: 10.1109/ICACITE51222.2021.9404665

[20] Ram Narayan Shah, Om Prakash Mahela, Sushma Lohia, "Recognition and Mitigation of Power Quality Disturbances in Renewable Energy Interfaced Hybrid Power Grid," 12th IEEE International Conference on Computational Intelligence and Communication Networks (CICN 2020), September 24–25, 2020, BIAS Bhimtal, Nainital, India, doi: 10.1109/CICN49253.2020.9242623

[21] Vishakha Pandya, Ravi Raj Choudhary, Om Prakash Mahela, and Sunita Choudhary, Detection and Classification of Complex Power Quality Disturbances Using Hybrid Algorithm Based on Combined Features of Stockwell Transform and Hilbert Transform, 2020 IEEE International Students' Conference on Electrical, Electronics and Computer Science (SCEECS 2020), MANIT Bhopal, India, February 22–23, 2020, doi: 10.1109/SCEECS48394.2020.5

[22] Vishakha Pandya, Sunil Agarwal, Om Prakash Mahela, and Sunita Choudhary, Recognition of Power Quality Disturbances Using Hybrid Algorithm Based on Combined Features of Stockwell Transform and Hilbert Transform, 2020 IEEE International Students' Conference on Electrical, Electronics and Computer Science (SCEECS 2020), MANIT Bhopal, India, February 22–23, 2020, doi: 10.1109/SCEECS48394.2020.4

[23] Om Prakash Mahela, Kapil Dev Kansal and Sunil Agarwal. Detection of Power Quality Disturbances in Utility Grid with Wind Energy Penetration. In: 8th IEEE India International Conference on Power Electronics (IICPE-2018), MNIT Jaipur, India, December, 13–14, 2018, doi: 10.1109/IICPE.2018.8709578

[24] Om Prakash Mahela, Kapil Dev Kansal and Sunil Agarwal. Detection of Power Quality Disturbances in Utility Grid with Solar Photovoltaic Energy Penetration. In: 8th IEEE India International Conference on Power Electronics (IICPE-2018), MNIT Jaipur, India, December 13–14, 2018, doi: 10.1109/IICPE.2018.8709597

[25] Om Prakash Mahela, Umesh Sharma and Tanuj Manglani. Recognition of Power Quality Disturbances Using Discrete Wavelet Transform and Fuzzy C-means Clustering. In: 2018 IEEE 8th Power India International Conference (PIICON 2018), NIT Kurukshetra, India, December 10–12, 2018, doi: 10.1109/POWERI.2018.8704404

[26] Rahul Saini, Om Prakash Mahela and Deepak Sharma. Detection and Classification of Complex Power Quality Disturbances Using Hilbert Transform and Rule Based Decision Tree. In: 2018 IEEE 8th Power India International Conference (PIICON 2018), NIT Kurukshetra, India, December 10–12, 2018, doi: 10.1109/POWERI.2018.8704427

[27] Rahul Saini, Om Prakash Mahela and Deepak Sharma. An Algorithm Based on Hilbert Transform and Rule Based Decision Tree Classification of Power Quality Disturbances. In: 2018 IEEE 8th Power India International Conference (PIICON 2018), NIT Kurukshetra, India, December 10–12, 2018, doi: 10.1109/POWERI.2018.8704465

[28] Mahaveer Meena, Om Prakash Mahela, Mahendra Kumar and Neeraj Kumar. Detection and Classification of Complex Power Quality Disturbances Using Stockwell Transform and Rule Based Decision Tree. In: IEEE PES International Conference on Smart Electric Drives and Power System (ICSEDPS-2018), G H Raisoni College of Engineering, Nagpur, India, June 12–13, 2018, doi: 10.1109/ICSEDPS.2018.8536028

[29] Mahaveer Meena, Om Prakash Mahela, Mahendra Kumar and Neeraj Kumar. Detection and Classification of Power Quality Disturbances Using Stockwell Transform and Rule Based Decision Tree. In: IEEE PES International Conference on Smart Electric Drives and Power System (ICSEDPS-2018), G H Raisoni College of Engineering, Nagpur, India, June 12–13, 2018, doi: 10.1109/ICSEDPS.2018.8536064

[30] Om Prakash Mahela, Pragati Prajapati and Soyab Ali. Investigation of Power Quality Events in Distribution Network with Wind Energy Penetration. In: 2018 IEEE Students' Conference on Electrical, Electronics and Computer Science (SCEECS 2018), MANIT, Bhopal, India, February 24–25, 2018, doi: 10.1109/SCEECS.2018.8546945

[31] Pragati Prajapati, Om Prakash Mahela and Soyab Ali. Investigation of Power Quality Events in Distribution Network with Solar Energy Penetration. In: 2018 IEEE Students' Conference on Electrical, Electronics and Computer Science

(SCEECS 2018), MANIT, Bhopal, India, February 24–25, 2018, doi: 10.1109/SCEECS.2018.8546930

[32] Ashwin Venkatraman, Kandarpa Sai Paduru, Om Prakash Mahela, and Abdul Gafoor Shaik. Experimental investigation of power quality disturbances associated with grid integrated wind energy system. In: 4th IEEE International Conference on Advanced Computing and Communication Systems (ICACCS 2017), Coimbatore, India, pp. 1–6, January 6–7, 2017, doi: 10.1109/ICACCS.2017.8014686

[33] Ankit Kumar Sharma, Om Prakash Mahela, and Sheesh Ram Ola. Detection of Power Quality Disturbances Using Discrete Wavelet Transform. In: IEEE International Conference on Electrical Power and Energy Systems (ICEPES 2016), MANIT, Bhopal, India, December 14–16, 2016, doi: 10.1109/ICEPES.2016.7915973

[34] Ankit Kumar Sharma, Om Prakash Mahela, and Sheesh Ram Ola. Detection of Power Quality Disturbances in The Utility grid Using Stockwell Transform. In: IEEE 7th Power India International Conference on advances in signal processing (PIICON 2016), Government Engineering College, Bikaner, India, November 25–27, 2016, doi: 10.1109/POWERI.2016.8077376

[35] Kavita Kumari, Atul Kumar Dadhich, and Om Prakash Mahela. Detection of Power Quality Disturbances in the Utility Grid with Wind Energy Penetration Using Stockwell Transform. In: IEEE 7th Power India International Conference on advances in signal processing (PIICON 2016), Government Engineering College, Bikaner, India, November 25–27, 2016, doi: 10.1109/POWERI.2016.8077223

[36] Kavita Kumari, Atul Kumar Dadhich, and Om Prakash Mahela. Detection of Power Quality Disturbances in the Utility Grid with Solar Energy Using S-Transform. In: IEEE 7th Power India International Conference on advances in signal processing (PIICON 2016), Government Engineering College, Bikaner, India, November 25–27, 2016, doi: 10.1109/POWERI.2016.8077351

[37] Om Prakash Mahela, and Abdul Gafoor Shaik. Recognition of Power Quality Disturbances Using S-transform and Rule-Based Decision Tree. In: 2016 IEEE First International Conference on Power Electronics, Intelligent Control and Energy Systems (ICPEICES 2016), DTU, New Delhi, India, July 4–6, 2016, doi: 10.1109/ICPEICES.2016.7853093

[38] Om Prakash Mahela, and Abdul Gafoor Shaik. Detection of Power Quality Disturbances Associated with Grid Integration of 100 kW Solar PV Plant. In: 1st IEEE Uttar Pradesh Conference-International Conference on Energy Economics and Environment (ICEEE 2015), Galgotia Institute of Engineering and Technology, Noida, India, March 27–28, 2015, doi: 10.1109/EnergyEconomics.2015.7235070

[39] Om Prakash Mahela, and Abdul Gafoor Shaik. Power Quality Detection in Distribution System with Wind Energy Penetration using Discrete Wavelet Transform. In: 2nd IEEE International Conference on Advances in Computing and Communication Engineering (ICACCE-2015), Tula's Institute, Dehradun, India, May 1–2, 2015, doi: 10.1109/ICACCE.2015.52

[40] R.H. Tan and V.K. Ramachandaramurthy, "Numerical Model Framework of Power Quality Events," European Journal of Scientific Research, 2010, 43, pp. 30–47.

[41] L. Qing and W. Zengzing, "Study on Non-unit Transient Protection Principle for EHV Transmission Lines Based on Wavelet Singular Entropy," 2009 IEEE Power & Energy Society General Meeting, Calgary, AB, Canada, 2009, pp. 1–6, doi: 10.1109/PES.2009.5275613.

[42] Moslem Dehghani, Mohammad Hassan Khooban, Taher Niknam, "Fast Fault Detection and Classification Based on a Combination of Wavelet Singular Entropy Theory and Fuzzy Logic in Distribution Lines in the Presence of Distributed Generations," International Journal of Electrical Power & Energy Systems, Vol. 78, 2016, pp. 455–462, doi: 10.1016/j.ijepes.2015.11.048.

[43] Rodriguez, Nibaldo, Guillermo Cabrera, Carolina Lagos, and Enrique Cabrera. 2017. "Stationary Wavelet Singular Entropy and Kernel Extreme Learning for Bearing Multi-Fault Diagnosis" Entropy, Vol. 19, no. 10, pp. 541. doi: 10.3390/e19100541

[44] O. P. Mahela, U. K. Sharma and T. Manglani, "Recognition of Power Quality Disturbances Using Discrete Wavelet Transform and Fuzzy C-means Clustering," 2018 IEEE 8th Power India International Conference (PIICON), Kurukshetra, India, 2018, pp. 1–6, doi: 10.1109/POWERI.2018.8704404

Chapter 16

A Smart Protection Scheme for Smart City Transmission Feeders Using K-Means Clustering

Ekata Sharma and Rajendra Mahla

16.1 INTRODUCTION

Smart grids have become essential for meeting the energy demands of smart cities. They help to manage power generation, transmission, and distribution to ensure uninterrupted supply. Transmission lines are critical elements for bulk power supply to smart cities; a fault on the transmission line can lead to an extensive power outage. Hence, smart protection schemes are required so that fault events may be detected and faulty line sections can be disconnected and repaired immediately [1].

The commonly observed faults on smart city power networks are phase-A to ground (PAGF), phase-A and phase-B with ground (PABGF), phase-A and phase-B (PABF), all phases (APF), and all phases with ground (APGF) [2]. Recently, different methods have been designed to detect faults on smart city transmission lines and protect these lines. In [3], the authors used the artificial neural network to detect and localize faults occurring on a 330 kV, 500 km three-phase transmission line. The current and voltage data captured at both ends of line with high accuracy, precision, and speed of execution helps to achieve this objective.

In [4], the authors introduced a robust fault classification method which used the shuffle attention-MobileNetV3 for transmission lines. This method used image recognition to acquire high-resolution fault features and categorize the faults. A fault recognition approach for a transmission network using support vector machine is mentioned in [5]. This approach used time- and frequency-series data recorded at both terminals of the line and had a noise detection accuracy of 99.89% with a signal-to-noise ratio (SNR) 30 dB.

In [6], the authors used discriminant and multivariate statistical analysis to design a fault detection method for a power system network. A hierarchical methodology to detect and classify fault events is introduced in [7]. This method found the exact locations of faults using phasor measurement units and used deep learning, recurrent neural network, and long short-term memory to differentiate the faults with high accuracy. Fault detection, classification, and location algorithms have been reported in the literature [8–35].

DOI: 10.1201/9781003486930-22

A critical review of methods reported in literature established that fault iden-tification performance deteriorates in noisy environments. Smart city infrastruc-tures use many dynamic loads and communication approaches which are the main sources of noise for power signals. Hence, fault recognition algorithms are required which are not affected by noise for smart city power networks. We pur-sued the following as the research objectives for this chapter:

- We designed a smart protection scheme (SPS) for the power transmission and distribution feeders of a smart city by processing the current waveform using K-means clustering.
- We designed a cluster index to cluster the data into healthy or faulty and colour-coded the data as blue for healthy and cyan for faulty.
- The proposed SPS effectively detected PAGF, PABGF, PABF, APF, and APGF.
- The SPS could also detect faults under conditions of variations in fault impedance and fault location, reverse power flow on the smart transmission feeder, and noise.
- The proposed SPS performs better than a DWT-based fault recognition algorithm even in noisy conditions.

16.2 SMART CITY TEST FEEDER

We used a smart two terminal smart transmission feeder (STF) rated at 220 kV to test the efficacy of the designed SPS, specifically, a two-terminal STF equipped between Bus-1 and Bus-2. Loads, transformers, generators, and other transmission feeders are connected on both Bus-1 and Bus-2. These are represented using smart city generators connected on both the buses: SCG-1 and SCG-2 are integrated on Bus-1 and Bus-2, respectively. The STF we utilized to study the protection is elaborated in Figure 16.1. We used Zebra aluminium conductor steel reinforced (ACSR) for the STF. Table 16.1 shows the current-carrying capacity of the Zebra conductor and the Moose and Panther conductors rated at 400 kV and 132 kV, respectively [36].

Figure 16.1 Test smart transmission feeder.

Table 16.1 Current-Carrying Capacity of the Conductors Used for the STFs

S. No.	Code name of conductor	STF voltage	Current-carrying capacity in amperes	
			Design temperature of 650 °C	Design temperature of 750 °C
1	ACSR Panther	132 kV	179.89	340.83
2	ACSR Zebra	220 kV	201.26	496.46
3	ACSR Moose	400 kV	133.60	530.51

Table 16.2 Simulated Parameters of the Test Feeder

S. No.	Smart city test system parameter	Simulated parameter value
1	Length of STF	20 km
2	Voltage of SCG-1	220∠20° kV
3	Voltage of SCG-2	220∠0° kV
4	Equivalent impedance of SCG-1	$17.177 + j45.529\ \Omega$
5	Equivalent impedance of SCG-2	$15.31 + j45.925\ \Omega$
6	Thermal rating of STF	176MVA
7	Positive sequence resistance of STF	0.0749Ω/km/circuit
8	Positive sequence reactance of STF	0.3992Ω/km/circuit
9	Zero sequence resistance of STF	0.2200Ω/km/circuit
10	Zero sequence reactance of STF	1.3392Ω/km/circuit
11	System frequency	60 Hz

Table 16.2 gives the simulated parameters of the generators and STFs [37]. The SPS processes the current signals recorded by the current transformer (CT-1) equipped on the STF close to Bus-1 to detect fault events.

16.3 K-MEANS CLUSTERING

K-means clustering (KMC) uses unsupervised learning to solve clustering problems. KMC groups the unlabelled data set into many clusters and discovers the categories of groups in the data set. K indicates the number of pre-defined clusters which are created in the process. KMC is applied using following activities [38]:

1. Evaluate best value of K centroids using iterative process.
2. Compute the distance of a data point from the centroids using Euclidian distance (ED) formula.

$$ED = \sqrt{(x-x_0)^2 - (y-y_0)^2}\tag{16.1}$$

where (x,y) indicates the data point coordinates and (x_0,y_0) indicates the centroid coordinates.

3. Each data point is assigned to the closest k-center to form data clusters.
4. Compute variance and identify a new centroid for every cluster. Variance indicates the summation of squared distance among the data points and centroid of a cluster:

$$Variance = \sum_{i \in Cluster - 1} d_i^2 \tag{16.2}$$

5. Repeat step 3 to assign each data set to the closest new centroid.
6. Repeat steps 2 to 4 iteratively till the best result is obtained.

In the KMC method, selecting the optimal number of centroids (k) is critical. Generally, the elbow approach is utilized for selecting the optimal k [39].

16.4 SMART PROTECTION SCHEME

We designed the SPS for the power transmission and distribution feeder of a smart city by processing the current waveform using K-means clustering. Table 16.3 describes all the steps of the proposed SPS to detect fault. We tested the SPS on a STF rated at 220 kV, but it could be applied to STFs rated at 132 kV and 400 kV as well. The proposed SPS is equally applicable for smart distribution feeders.

Table 16.3 Steps of SPS Implementation

1. Realize a fault at centre of STF and capture current on Bus-1 terminal using CT-1
2. Assign symbol *signalData* to phase current
3. Perform K-means clustering using MATLAB® function *kmeans*
   [idx, centroids] = kmeans(signalData, k);
4. Calculate distances to cluster centroids using MATLAB *pdist2*
   distances = pdist2(signalData, centroids);
5. Assign each point to the closest cluster using MATLAB *min*
   [~, clusterIndices] = min(distances, [], 2);
6. Identify the fault cluster by MATLAB *mode*
   faultCluster = mode(clusterIndices);
7. Plot the results
8. Repeat steps 2 to 7 for current of other phases

16.5 DETECTION OF FAULT INCIDENTS IN SMART CITY TEST FEEDERS: SIMULATION RESULTS

This section details simulation results to detect PAGF, PABGF, PABF, APF, and APGF using the proposed SPS.

16.5.1 Healthy Condition

Proposed smart two-terminal STF is simulated without any fault event, and current is recorded on Bus-1 terminal of STF using CT-1. Phase-A current waveform is elaborated in Figure 16.2(a). Current is analysed using KMC-supported SPS and cluster index is computed which is described in Figure 16.2(b). A colour bar is also shown to the right of the cluster plot in Figure 16.2(b).

Figure 16.2(a) displays that the current has a pure sinusoidal waveform with no deviations. Figure 16.2(b) depicts that there is only of type of cluster, shown as red pellets on the blue bar at cluster index of unity. The colour of the bar represents the nature of the clusters: The blue central bar indicates healthy data, and indicates faulty data. The figure shows no cyan bar, which indicates healthy data. KMC effectively identified healthy data.

16.5.2 Phase-A to Ground Fault

Proposed smart two-terminal STF is applied to a PAGF in the middle of STF, and phase-A current is recorded on Bus-1 using CT-1. Phase-A current waveform is

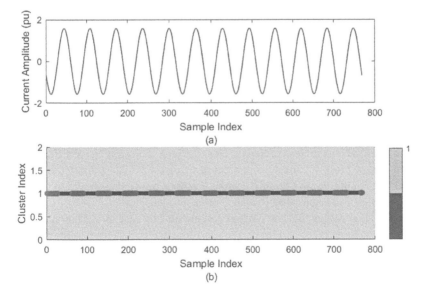

Figure 16.2 Healthy STF: (a) current phase-A waveform; (b) cluster index.

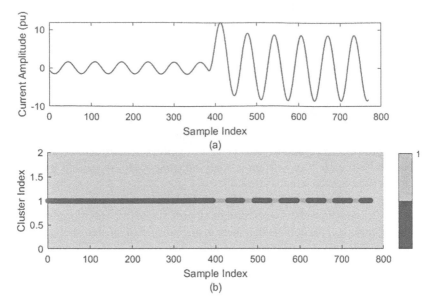

Figure 16.3 PAGF on STF: (a) phase-A current waveform; (b) cluster index.

elaborated in Figure 16.3(a). Current is processed using the KMC-supported SPS and cluster index (Figure 16.3(b)). A colour bar is also shown to the right of cluster plot in Figure 16.3(b).

Figure 16.3(a) indicates that the PAGF increased the magnitude of the current waveform at the 384th sample. Figure 16.3(b) indicates that there are two types of clusters: The red solid line indicates healthy data, and red pellets on the coloured bar at cluster index unity indicate the faulty data. The solid blue central bar indicates healthy data but is not visible because of the solid red bar. In Figure 16.3(b), the cyan bar for samples 385 to 768 indicates faulty data. The proposed KMC algorithm effectively detected PAGF and discriminated it from the healthy data.

Proposed smart two-terminal STF is simulated with a PAGF in the middle of STF, and phase-B current is captured on Bus-1. Phase-B current waveform is elaborated in Figure 16.4(a). Current is processed using the KMC-supported SPS, and cluster index is computed (Figure 16.4(b)). A colour bar is also shown to the right of the cluster plot in Figure 16.4(b).

Figure 16.4(a) shows that the current waveform of phase-B is pure sinusoidal in nature with no deviations. Figure 16.4(b) indicates that there is only one type of cluster, shown as red pellets on the blue bar at cluster index unity. The blue central bar indicates healthy data, as does the absence of cyan. The proposed KMC algorithm established that the phase-B current waveform was healthy during the PAGF event.

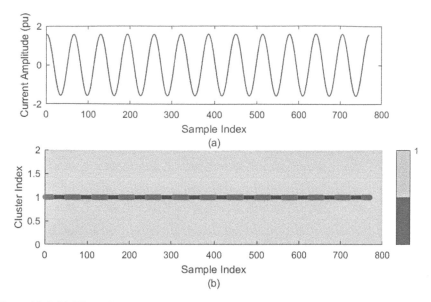

Figure 16.4 PAGF on the smart city transmission feeder: (a) phase-B current waveform; (b) cluster index.

16.5.3 Phase-A and Phase-B with Ground Fault

Proposed smart two-terminal STF is realized on phase-A and phase-B with ground fault at centre of STF, and phase-A current of is recorded on Bus-1 using CT-1. Phase-A current waveform is depicted in Figure 16.5(a). Current is analysed using the KMC-supported SPS, and cluster index is computed (Figure 16.5(b)). A colour bar is also shown to the right of the cluster plot in Figure 16.5(b).

Figure 16.5(a) shows that the magnitude of the phase-A current waveform increased at the 384th sample because of the PABGF. Figure 16.5(b) indicates that there are two clusters, shown as the red solid line and pellets on the coloured bar at cluster index unity; the solid line indicates the healthy data, and the red pellets indicate the faulty data. The blue central bar indicates healthy data but is most obscured by the solid red bar. Figure 16.5(b) also shows a cyan bar for samples 385 to 768, indicating faulty data. The proposed KMC algorithm effectively detected PABGF and discriminated it from the healthy data.

Proposed smart two-terminal STF is simulated with a PABGF in the middle of STF and phase-B current is captured on Bus-1 using CT-1. Phase-B current waveform is depicted in Figure 16.6(a). Current is analysed using the KMC-supported SPS, and cluster index is computed (Figure 16.6(b)). A colour bar is also shown to the right of the cluster plot in Figure 16.6(b).

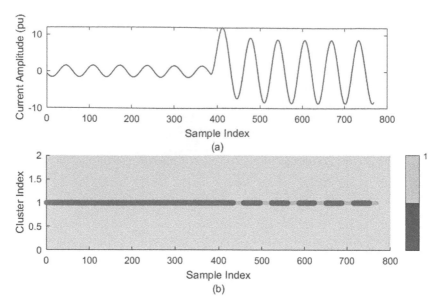

Figure 16.5 PABGF on the smart city transmission feeder: (a) phase-A current waveform; (b) cluster index.

Figure 16.6(a) shows that the magnitude of the phase-B current waveform increases at the 384th sample because of the PABGF. Figure 16.6(b) indicates that there are two clusters, shown as the red solid line and red pellets on the coloured bar at cluster index unity. The solid line indicates the healthy data, and the red pellets indicate the faulty data. The blue central bar indicates a healthy data set but is obscured by the solid red bar. Figure 16.6(b) shows a cyan bar for samples 385 to 768, indicating faulty phase-B data. The proposed KMC algorithm effectively detected PABGF and discriminated it on phase-B from the healthy data set.

Proposed smart two-terminal STF is simulated with a PABGF in the middle of STF and phase-C current is captured on Bus-1 using CT-1. Phase-C current waveform is illustrated in Figure 16.7(a). Current is analysed using the KMC-supported SPS, and cluster index is calculated (Figure 16.7(b)). A colour bar is also shown to the right of the cluster plot in Figure 16.7 (b).

Figure 16.7(a) shows that the phase-C current is purely sinusoidal with no deviations during the PABGF event. Figure 16.7(b) shows only one cluster, shows as the red pellets on the blue bar at cluster index unity. The blue central bar indicates healthy phase-C data. Figure 16.7(b) shows no cyan, which also indicates the healthiness of the data set. The proposed KMC algorithm established that the phase-C current waveform is healthy during a PABGF event.

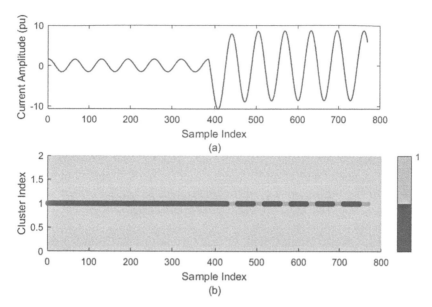

Figure 16.6 PABGF on the smart city transmission feeder: (a) phase-B current waveform; (b) cluster index.

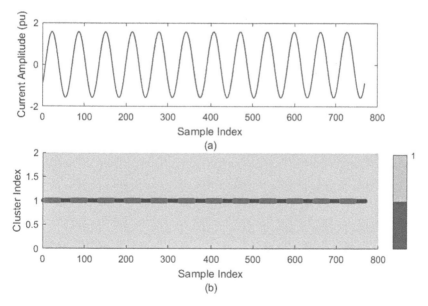

Figure 16.7 PABGF on the smart city transmission feeder: (a) phase-C current waveform; (b) cluster index.

16.5.4 Phase-A and Phase-B Fault

Proposed smart two-terminal STF is realized with a phase-A and phase-B fault at the centre of the STF, and phase-A current is recorded on Bus-1 using CT-1. Phase-A current waveform is illustrated in Figure 16.8(a). Current is analysed using the KMC-supported SPS, and cluster index is calculated (Figure 16.8(b)). A colour bar is also shown to the right of the cluster plot in Figure 16.8(b).

Figure 16.8(a) shows that the magnitude of the phase-A current waveform increased at the 384th sample because of the PABF. Figure 16.8(b) indicates two clusters, shown by the red solid line and pellets on the coloured bar at cluster index unity; the solid line indicates healthy data, and the red pellets indicate faulty data. The blue central bar reflects a healthy data set but is obscured by the solid red bar. Figure 16.8(b) shows a cyan bar for samples 385 to 768, which indicates faulty phase-A data. The KMC algorithm effectively detected PABF in the healthy phase-A data set.

Proposed smart two-terminal STF is simulated with a PABF in the middle of STF, and phase-B current is captured on Bus-1 using CT-1. Phase-B current waveform is illustrated in Figure 16.9(a). Current is analysed using the KMC-supported SPS, and cluster index is calculated (Figure 16.9(b)). A colour bar is also shown to the right of the cluster plot in Figure 16.9(b).

Figure 16.9(a) shows that the phase-C current waveform is purely sinusoidal with no deviations during the PABF. Figure 16.9(b) indicates that there is only

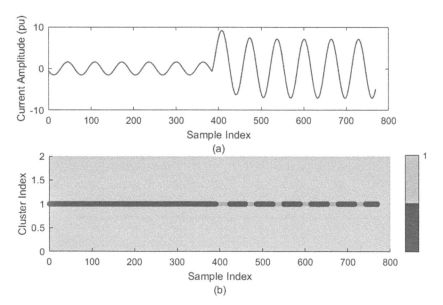

Figure 16.8 PABF on the smart city transmission feeder: (a) phase-A current waveform; (b) cluster index.

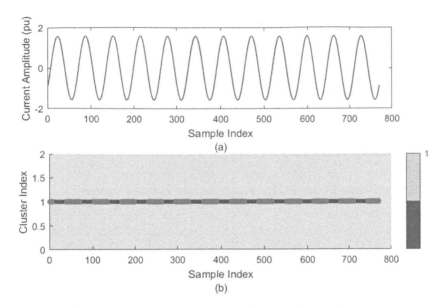

Figure 16.9 PABF on the smart city transmission feeder: (a) phase-C current waveform; (b) cluster index.

cluster, shown as the red pellets on the blue bar at cluster index unity. The blue central bar indicates healthy phase-C data. Figure 16.9(b) shows no cyan on the central bar, also indicating healthy data. The proposed KMC algorithm established that the phase-C current waveform was healthy during the PABF event.

16.5.5 All-Phases Fault

Proposed smart two-terminal STF is simulated with an all-phases fault at middle of STF and current of phase-A is captured on Bus-1 terminal of STF using CT-1. Phase-A current waveform is illustrated in Figure 16.10(a). Current is analysed using the KMC-supported SPS, and cluster index is calculated (Figure 16.10(b)). A colour bar is also shown to the right of the cluster plot in Figure 16.10(b).

Figure 16.10(a) shows that the magnitude of the phase-A current waveform increased at the 384th sample because of the APF. Figure 16.10(b) indicates two clusters, shown as the red solid line and pellets on the coloured bar at cluster index unity; the solid line indicates healthy data, and the red pellets indicate faulty data. The blue central bar indicates healthy data but is obscured by the solid red bar.

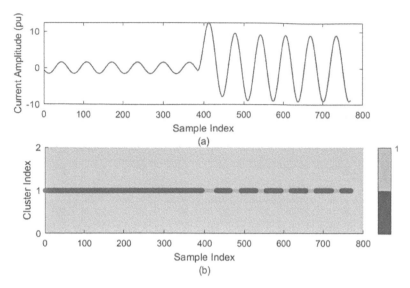

Figure 16.10 APF on the smart city transmission feeder: (a) phase-A current waveform; (b) cluster index.

Figure 16.10(b) shows a cyan bar for samples 385 to 768, which indicates faulty phase-A data. The proposed KMC algorithm effectively detected APF and discriminated it from the healthy phase-A data.

16.5.6 All-Phases and Ground Fault

Proposed smart two-terminal STF is simulated with an all-phases and ground fault at the centre of the STF, and phase-A current is recorded on Bus-1 CT-1. Phase-A current waveform is illustrated in Figure 16.11(a). Current is analysed using the K-means clustering supported SPS and cluster index is evaluated which is illustrated in Figure 16.11(b). A colour bar is also shown to the right of cluster plot of Figure 16.11(b).

Figure 16.11(a) shows that the magnitude of the phase-A current waveform increased at the 384th sample because of the APGF. Figure 16.11(b) indicates two clusters, shown as a red solid line and red pellets on the coloured bar at cluster index unity; the solid line indicates healthy data, and the red pellets indicate faulty data. The blue central bar indicates healthy data but is obscured by the solid red bar. Figure 16.11(b) shows a cyan bar for samples 385 to 768, which indicates faulty phase-A data. The proposed KMC algorithm effectively detected APGF and discriminated it from healthy phase-A data.

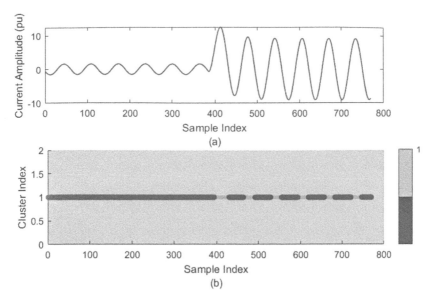

Figure 16.11 APG on the smart city transmission feeder: (a) phase-A current waveform; (b) cluster index.

16.6 CASE STUDIES OF FAULT INCIDENTS IN SMART CITY TEST FEEDERS

This section details the simulation results for testing the proposed SPS in cases of fault impedance and fault location variations, power flow on the STF in the opposite direction, and noise.

16.6.1 Fault Impedance Variation

Proposed smart two-terminal STF is simulated with a phase-A to ground fault in the middle of the STF at fault impedance of 100 Ω, and phase-A current is captured on Bus-1 terminal of STF using CT-1. Phase-A current waveform is illustrated in Figure 16.12(a). Current is analysed using the KMC-supported SPS, and cluster index is calculated (Figure 16.12 (b)). A colour bar is also shown to the right of the cluster plot in Figure 16.12(b).

Figure 16.12(a) illustrates that the magnitude of the phase-A current waveform increased at the 384th sample because of the PAGF with the fault impedance. Figure 16.12(b) indicates that there are two clusters, shown as the red solid line and red pellets on the coloured bar at cluster index unity; the solid line indicates healthy data, and the red pellets indicate faulty data. The blue central

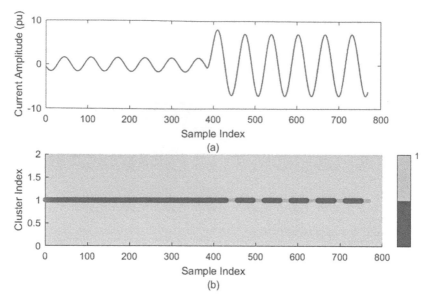

Figure 16.12 PAGF on the smart city transmission feeder with fault impedance of 100 Ω: (a) phase-A current waveform; (b) cluster index.

bar indicates healthy data but is obscured by the solid red bar. Figure 16.12(b) shows a cyan bar for samples 385 to 768, which indicates faulty phase-A data. The proposed KMC algorithm effectively detected the PAGF with 100 Ω fault impedance and discriminated it from the healthy phase-A data. This establishes that the proposed SPS is effective for detecting faults on STFs for fault imped-ances in the range of 0 Ω to 100 Ω.

16.6.2 Fault Location Variation

Proposed smart two-terminal STF is simulated with a PAGF near Bus-2 on the STF, and phase-A current of is captured on Bus-1 using CT-1. Phase-A current waveform is illustrated in Figure 16.13(a). Current is analysed using the KMC-supported SPS, and cluster index is calculated (Figure 16.13(b)). A colour bar is also shown to the right of the cluster plot in Figure 16.13(b).

Figure 16.13(a) illustrates that the magnitude of the phase-A current waveform increased at the 384th sample because of the PAGF on the STF near Bus-2. Fig-ure 16.13(b) indicates two clusters, shown as the red solid line and red pellets on the coloured bar at cluster index unity; the solid line indicates healthy data, and the red pellets indicate faulty data. The blue central bar indicates healthy data but is obscured by the solid red bar. Figure 16.13(b) shows a cyan bar for samples 385 to 768, which indicates faulty phase-A data. The proposed KMC algorithm effectively detected the PAGF on the STF near Bus-2 and discriminated it from

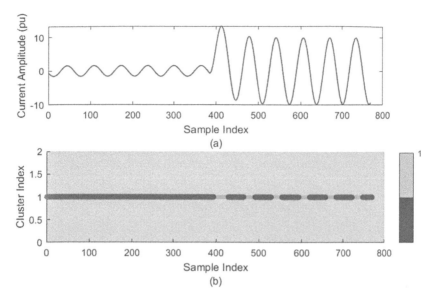

Figure 16.13 PAGF on the smart city transmission feeder near Bus-2: (a) phase-A current waveform; (b) cluster index.

the healthy phase-A data. This establishes that the designed SPS is effective for detecting faults on the STF over the entire line length.

16.6.3 Reverse Power Flow

Proposed smart two-terminal STF is simulated with a PAGF at the centre of the STF considering power flow on the STF from Bus-2 to Bus-1, and phase-A current is captured on Bus-1 using CT-1. Phase-A current waveform is illustrated in Figure 16.14(a). Current is analysed using the KMC-supported SPS, and cluster index is calculated (Figure 16.14(b)). A colour bar is also shown to the right of the cluster plot in Figure 16.14(b).

Figure 16.14(a) illustrates that the magnitude of the phase-A current waveform increased at the 384th sample because of the PAGF with power flow. Figure 16.14(b) indicates two clusters, shown as the red solid line and pellets on the coloured bar at cluster index unity; the solid line indicates healthy data, and the red pellets indicate faulty data. The blue central bar indicates healthy data but is obscured by the solid red bar. Figure 16.14(b) shows a cyan bar for samples 385 to 768, which indicates faulty phase-A data. The proposed KMC algorithm effectively detected the PAGF with power flow on the STF and discriminated it from the healthy phase-A data. This establishes that the proposed SPS is effective for detecting faults on STFs for power flow in both directions.

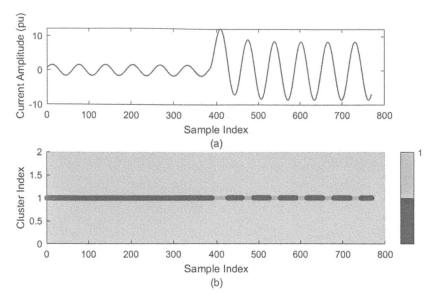

Figure 16.14 PAGF on the smart city transmission feeder with flow in the reverse direction: (a) phase-A current waveform; (b) cluster index.

16.6.4 Noisy Environment

Proposed smart two-terminal STF is realised with a PAGF at the centre of the STF, and phase-A current is recorded on Bus-1 using CT-1. Noise at 20 dB SNR is superimposed on the Phase-A current waveform, shown in Figure 16.15(a). Current is analysed using the KMC-supported SPS, and cluster index is calculated (Figure 16.15(b)). A colour bar is also shown to the right of the cluster plot in Figure 16.15(b).

Figure 16.15(a) illustrates that the magnitude of the phase-A current waveform increased at the 384th sample because of the PAGF. Noise is observed with the signal over the entire signal time. Figure 16.15(b) indicates that two clusters, shown as the red solid line and pellets on the coloured bar at cluster index unity; the solid line indicates healthy data, and the red pellets indicate faulty data. The blue central bar indicates healthy data but is obscured by the solid red bar. Figure 16.15(b) shows a cyan bar for samples 385 to 768, which indicates faulty phase-A data with noise. The proposed KMC algorithm effectively detected the PAGF on the STF with noise of 20 dB SNR is effectively detected and discriminated from the healthy data set on phase-A using the proposed K-means clustering algorithm. This establishes that the proposed SPS is effective for detecting faults on STFs in noisy conditions.

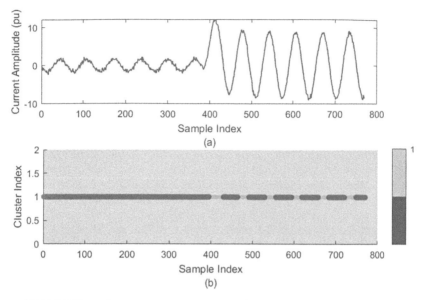

Figure 16.15 PAGF on the smart city transmission feeder with noise of 20 dB SNR: (a) phase-A current waveform; (b) cluster index.

16.7 PERFORMANCE COMPARATIVE STUDY

We compared the performance of the designed K-means clustering-based smart protection scheme with a DWT scheme reported in [40]. The DWT performance deteriorated in the presence of noise, and we observed false tripping commands, whereas the proposed KMC-based SPS is effective for detecting faults at noise levels as high as 20 dB SNR.

16.8 CONCLUSION

For this chapter, we designed a smart protection scheme for smart city power transmission and distribution feeders by processing the current waveforms using K-means clustering. We concluded that the proposed SPS is efficient for detecting faults on STF: phase-A to ground, phase-A and phase-B with ground, phase-A and phase-B, all-phases, and all-phases with ground. The SPS is also efficient for detecting faults in fault impedance variation, fault location variation, reverse power flow on STF, and noise at 20 dB SNR. We conclude that the proposed SPS performs better than a DWT-based algorithm even in noisy conditions. The proposed SPS is effective for protecting both transmission and distribution feeders including the underground and overhead lines in smart city power networks.

16.9 ACKNOWLEDGEMENT

This research work is supported by Innovader Research Labs, Innovader IITian Padhaiwala LearnLab Pvt. Ltd., Jaipur, India.

REFERENCES

[1] Ramesh Guguloth, T.K. Sunil Kumar, Congestion Management in Restructured Power Systems for Smart Cities in India, Computers & Electrical Engineering, Volume 65, 2018, Pages 79–89, *https://doi.org/10.1016/j.compeleceng.2017.04.016.*

[2] Om Prakash Mahela, Vishnu Dutt Sharma, Baseem Khan, Sunil Agarwal, Hassan Haes Alhelou, Identification and Classification of Faults Using Stockwell Transform and Decision Rule, Smart Cities Policies and Financing, 2022, Pages 439–455, *https://doi.org/10.1016/B978-0-12-819130-9.00026-7*

[3] Vincent Nsed Ogar, Sajjad Hussain, Kelum A.A. Gamage, The Use of Artificial Neural Network for Low Latency of Fault Detection and Localisation in Transmission Line, Heliyon, Volume 9, Issue 2, 2023, e13376, *https://doi.org/10.1016/j.heliyon.2023.e13376.*

[4] Yanhui Xi, Weijie Zhang, Feng Zhou, Xin Tang, Zewen Li, Xiangjun Zeng, Pinghua Zhang, Transmission Line Fault Detection and Classification Based on SA-Mobile-NetV3, Energy Reports, Volume 9, 2023, Pages 955–968, *https://doi.org/10.1016/j.egyr.2022.12.043.*

[5] Pavan Venkata, Vivek Pandya, Kushal Vala, Amit V. Sant, Support Vector Machine for Fast Fault Detection and Classification in Modern Power Systems Using Quarter Cycle Data, Energy Reports, Volume 8, Supplement 16, 2022, Pages 92–98, *https://doi.org/10.1016/j.egyr.2022.10.279*

[6] Y. Zhang, J. Zhang, J. Ma and Z. Wang, Fault Detection Based on Discriminant Analysis Theory in Electric Power System, 2009 International Conference on Sustainable Power Generation and Supply, Nanjing, China, 2009, pp. 1–5, *https://doi.org/10.1109/SUPERGEN.2009.5347972.*

[7] Mohammad Reza Shadi, Mohammad-Taghi Ameli, Sasan Azad, A Real-Time Hierarchical Framework for Fault Detection, Classification, and Location in Power Systems Using PMUs Data and Deep Learning, International Journal of Electrical Power & Energy Systems, Volume 134, 2022, 107399, *https://doi.org/10.1016/j.ijepes.2021.107399.*

[8] Atul Kulshrestha, Om Prakash Mahela, Mukesh Kumar Gupta, Baseem Khan, Hassan Haes Alhelou, Pierluigi Siano, Hybridization of Stockwell Transform and Wigner Distribution Function to Design a Transmission Line Protection Scheme, *Applied Sciences, 2020,* Volume 10, Issue 22, 7985, October 2020, *https://doi.org/10.3390/app10227985*

[9] Mohd Zishan Khoker, Om Prakash Mahela, and Gulhasan Ahmad, A Voltage Algorithm using Discrete Wavelet Transform and Hilbert Transform for Detection and Classification of Power System Faults in the Presence of Solar Energy, 2020 IEEE International Students' Conference on Electrical, Electronics and Computer Science (SCEECS 2020), MANIT Bhopal, India, February 22–23, 2020, *https://doi.org/10.1109/SCEECS48394.2020.7*

[10] Shubhmay Karmakar, Gulhasan Ahmad, Om Prakash Mahela, and Ravi Raj Choudhary, Algorithm Based on Combined Features of Stockwell Transform and

Hilbert Transform for Detection of Transmission Line Faults with Dynamic Load, First IEEE International Conference on Power, Control and Computing Technologies (ICPC2T), NIT Raipur, India, January 3–5, 2020, *https://doi.org/10.1109/ICPC2T48082.2020.9071516*

[11] Abhishek Gupta, Ramesh Kumar Pachar, Baseem Khan, Om Prakash Mahela, and Sanjeevikumar Padmanaban, A Multivariable Transmission Line Protection Scheme Using Signal Processing Techniques, *IET Generation, Transmission and Distribution*, Volume 15, pp. 3115–3137, *https://doi.org/10.1049/gtd2.12244*

[12] Jaya Sharma, Bipul Kumar, Om Prakash Mahela, and Akhil Ranjan Garg, Protection of Distribution Feeder Using Stockwell Transform Supported Voltage Features, IEEE 9th Power India International Conference (PIICON 2020) from 28 Feb to 01 March, 2020 – Deenbandhu Chhotu Ram University of Science and Technology, Murthal, India, *https://doi.org/10.1109/PIICON49524.2020.9113014*

[13] Surbhi Thukral, Om Prakash Mahela, and Bipul Kumar. Detection of Transmission Line Faults in the Presence of Solar PV System Using Stockwell's Transform. In: *IEEE 7th Power India International Conference on advances in signal processing (PIICON 2016)*, Government Engineering College, Bikaner, India, November 25–27, 2016, *https://doi.org/10.1109/POWERI.2016.8077304*

[14] Nikita Tailor, Satyanarayan Joshi, Om Prakash Mahela, Transmission Line Protection Schemes Based on Wigner Distribution Function and Discrete Wavelet Transform, IEEE 9th Power India International Conference (PIICON 2020) from 28 Feb to 01 March, 2020 – Deenbandhu Chhotu Ram University of Science and Technology, Murthal, India, *https://doi.org/10.1109/PIICON49524.2020.9113011*

[15] Rajesh Kumar, Om Prakash Mahela, Mahendra Kumar, Nitin Kumar Suyan, Neeraj Kumar, A Current Based Algorithm Using Harmonic Wavelet Transform and Rule Based Decision Tree for Transmission Line Protection, *4th IEEE International Conference On Internet of Things: Smart Innovation and Usages (IoT-SIU 2019)*, 18–19 April, 2019, Krishna Engineering College, Ghaziabad, Uttar Pradesh, India, *https://doi.org/10.1109/IoT-SIU.2019.8777667*

[16] Sunita Choudhary, Om Prakash Mahela, and Sheesh Ram Ola. Detection of Transmission Line Faults in the Presence of Thyristor Controlled Reactor Using Discrete Wavelet Transform. In: IEEE 7th Power India International Conference on advances in signal processing (PIICON 2016), Government Engineering College, Bikaner, India, November 25–27, 2016, *https://doi.org/10.1109/POWERI.2016.8077268*

[17] Bhuvnesh Rathore, Om Prakash Mahela, Baseem Khan, Sanjeevikumar Padmanaban, Protection Scheme using Wavelet-Alienation-Neural Technique for UPFC Compensated Transmission Line, IEEE Access, 2021, Volume 9, pp. 13737–13753, 2021, *https://doi.org/10.1109/ACCESS.2021.3052315*

[18] Amit Kumar Gangwar, Om Prakash Mahela, Bhuvnesh Rathore, Baseem Khan, Hassan Haes Alhelou, and Pierluigi Siano, A Novel K-Means Clustering and Weighted K-NN Regression Based Fast Transmission Line Protection, IEEE Transactions on Industrial Informatics, Volume: 17, Issue: 9, pp. 6034 – 6043, Sept. 2021, *https://doi.org/10.1109/TII.2020.3037869*

[19] Atul Kulshrestha, Om Prakash Mahela, Mukesh Kumar Gupta, Neeraj Gupta, Nilesh Patel, Tomonobu Senjyu, Mir Sayed Shah Danish, Mahdi Khosravy, A Hybrid Fault Recognition Algorithm Using Stockwell Transform and Wigner Distribution Function for Power System Network with Solar Energy Penetration, *Energies, May 2020*, 13(14), 3519, *https://doi.org/10.3390/en13143519*

[20] Akanksha Malhotra, Om Prakash Mahela and Himanshu Doraya. Detection and Classification of Power System Faults Using Discrete Wavelet Transform and Rule Based Decision Tree. In: *IEEE International Conference on Computing, Power and Communication Technologies 2018 (GUCON 2018)*, Galgotias University, Greater Noida, India, September 28–29, 2018, *https://doi.org/10.1109/GUCON.2018.8674922*

[21] Toshiba Suman, Om Prakash Mahela, and Sheesh Ram Ola. Detection of Transmission Line Faults in the Presence of Solar PV Generation Using Discrete Wavelet Transform. In: *IEEE 7th Power India International Conference on advances in signal processing (PIICON 2016)*, Government Engineering College, Bikaner, Bikaner, India, November 25–27, 2016, *https://doi.org/10.1109/POWERI.2016.8077203*

[22] Sheesh Ram Ola, Amit Saraswat, Sunil Kumar Goyal, S. K. Jhajharia, and Om Prakash Mahela. A Technique Using Stockwell Transform Based Median for Detection of Power System Faults. In: *2018 IEEE 8th Power India International Conference (PIICON-2018)*, NIT Kurukshetra, India, December 10–12, 2018, *https://doi.org/10.1109/POWERI.2018.8704459*

[23] Gulhasan Ahmad, Om Prakash Mahela and Sheesh Ram Ola. A Stockwell Transform Based Approach for Detection of Transmission Line Faults in the Presence of Thyristor Controlled Reactor. In: *IEEE International Conference SPIN 2018*, Galgotia University, Greater Noida, India, February 22–23, 2018, *https://doi.org/10.1109/SPIN.2018.8474098*

[24] Ligang Tang, Om Prakash Mahela, Baseem Khan, and Yini Miró, Current and Voltage Actuated Transmission Line Protection Scheme Using Hybrid Combination of Signal Processing Techniques, *Sustainability, March 24*, 2023, *15*(7), 5715; *https://doi.org/10.3390/su15075715*

[25] Abhishek Gupta, Ramesh Kumar Pachar, Om Prakash Mahela and Baseem Khan, Fault Detection and Classification to Design a Protection Scheme for Utility Grid with High Penetration of Wind and Solar Energy, International Journal of Energy Research, Volume 2023, Article ID 4418741, pp. 1–16, *https://doi.org/10.1155/2023/4418741*

[26] Abhishek Gupta, Ramesh Kumar Pachar, Om Prakash Mahela, and Baseem Khan, Fusion of Signal Processing Techniques to Design Current and Voltage Features Based Protection Scheme for Utility Grid with Renewable Energy Penetration *IEEE Access*, 2022, Volume 10, pp. 118222 – 118235, *https://doi.org/10.1109/ACCESS.2022.3219201*

[27] Anup Kumar, Himanshu Sharma, Ram Niwash Mahia, Om Prakash Mahela, Baseem Khan, Design and Implementation of Hybrid Transmission Line Protection Scheme Using Signal Processing Techniques, *International Transactions on Electrical Energy Systems*, Volume 2022, Article ID 7209553, 20 pages, 2022, *https://doi.org/10.1155/2022/7209553*

[28] Om Prakash Mahela, Vikram Singh Bhati, Gulhasan Ahmad, Baseem Khan, P. Sanjeevikumar, Akhil Ranjan Garg, and Rajendra Mahla, A Protection Scheme for Distribution Utility Network in the Presence of Wind Energy Penetration, *Computers and Electrical Engineering*, Volume 94, Paper No. 107324, 2021, *https://doi.org/10.1016/j.compeleceng.2021.107324*

[29] Sheesh Ram Ola, Amit Saraswat, Sunil Kumar Goyal, S. K. Jhajharia, Bhuvnesh Rathore, Om Prakash Mahela, Wigner Distribution Function and Alienation Coefficient Based Transmission Line Protection Scheme, *IET Generation, Transmission and Distribution, Volume 14, Issue 10*, 22 May 2020, pp. 1842–1853, *https://doi.org/10.1049/iet-gtd.2019.1414*

[30] Om Prakash Mahela, Jaya Sharma, Bipul Kumar, Baseem Khan, Hasan Haes Alhelou, An Algorithm for the Protection of Distribution Feeder Using Stockwell and Hilbert Transforms Supported Features, *CSEE Journal of Power and Energy Systems*, ISSN 2096–0042 CN 10–1328/TM, Volume: 7, *Issue: 6*, Nov. 2021, pp. 1278–1288, *https://doi.org/10.17775/CSEEJPES.2020.00170*

[31] Govind Sahay Yogee, Om Prakash Mahela, Kapil Dev Kansal, Baseem Khan, Rajendra Mahla, Hassan Haes Alhelou, Pierluigi Siano, An Algorithm for Recognition of Fault Conditions in the Utility Grid with Renewable Energy Penetration, *Energies*, 13(9), 2383, April 2020, *https://doi.org/10.3390/en13092383*

[32] Sheesh Ram Ola, Amit Saraswat, Sunil Kumar Goyal, S. K. Jhajharia, Baseem Khan, Om Prakash Mahela, Hassan Haes Alhelou, and Pierluigi Siano, A Protection Scheme for a Power System with Solar Energy Penetration, *Applied Sciences 2020*, Volume 10, Issue 4, Paper No. 1516, pp. 1–22, Feb. 2020, *https://doi.org/10.3390/app10041516*

[33] Sheesh Ram Ola, Amit Saraswat, Sunil Kumar Goyal, Virendra Sharma, Baseem Khan, Om Prakash Mahela, Hassan Haes Alhelou, Pierluigi Siano, Alienation Coefficient and Wigner Distribution Function Based Protection Scheme for Hybrid Power System Network with Renewable Energy Penetration, *Energies*, Volume 13, Issue 5, 2020, Paper No. 1120, *https://doi.org/10.3390/en13051120*

[34] Om Prakash Mahela, Mukesh Kumar Gupta, Atul Kulshrestha, Baseem Khan, Rajendra Mahla, Akhil Ranjan Garg, Aditya R. Gautam, Sanjeevikumar Padmanaban, Hybrid protection algorithm for power system with renewable energy generation using Stockwell transform and Wigner distribution function, *IET The Journal of Engineering*, 2022, pp. 1–15, *https://doi.org/10.1049/tje2.12164*

[35] Aditi Singh, Ahmad Hasan Khan, Ankit Kumar Sharma and Om Prakash Mahela, Recognition of Disturbances in Hybrid Grid Using Discrete Wavelet Transform and Stockwell Transform Based Algorithm, First IEEE International Conference on Measurement, Instrumentation, Control and Automation (ICMICA 2020), NIT Kurukshetra, India, April 2, 2020 to April 4, 2020, *https://doi.org/10.1109/ICMICA48462.2020.9242867*

[36] Uttar Pradesh Power Transmission Corporation Limited, India, *https://upptcl.org/upptcl/en/article/current-carrying*, Accessed on July 13, 2023

[37] Kulshrestha, Atul, Om Prakash Mahela, Mukesh Kumar Gupta, Baseem Khan, Hassan Haes Alhelou, and Pierluigi Siano. 2020. Hybridization of the Stockwell Transform and Wigner Distribution Function to Design a Transmission Line Protection Scheme *Applied Sciences* 10, no. 22: 7985. *https://doi.org/10.3390/app10227985*

[38] Guodong Liu, Feng Ji, Wen Sun, Lin Sun, Optimization design of short-circuit test platform for the distribution network of integrated power system based on improved K-means clustering, Energy Reports, Volume 9, Supplement 8, 2023, Pages 716–726, *https://doi.org/10.1016/j.egyr.2023.04.319.*

[39] D. Marutho, S. Hendra Handaka, E. Wijaya and Muljono, The Determination of Cluster Number at k-Mean Using Elbow Method and Purity Evaluation on Headline News, 2018 International Seminar on Application for Technology of Information and Communication, Semarang, Indonesia, 2018, pp. 533–538, *https://doi.org/10.1109/ISEMANTIC.2018.8549751.*

[40] N. Tailor, S. Joshi and O. P. Mahela, Transmission Line Protection Schemes Based on Wigner Distribution Function and Discrete Wavelet Transform, 2020 IEEE 9th Power India International Conference (PIICON), Sonepat, India, 2020, pp. 1–6, *https://doi.org/10.1109/PIICON49524.2020.9113011.*

Section 7

Recent Advancements in Healthcare Systems

Chapter 17

Time–Frequency Features for the Cardiovascular System

Ravi Raj Choudhary, Mamta Rani
and Puneet Kumar Jain

17.1 INTRODUCTION

The heart generates different sounds that contain vibrations and information about the atria, ventricles, blood vessels, and valves. The process where a microphone transducer records and plots these vibrations is called phonocardiography (PCG) [1]. PCG is a standard way to record heart signals and overcome human hearing limitations. Some inappropriate signals may be introduced when recording these signals due to the subject's movement or stethoscope and other ambient sources. Therefore, denoising techniques are crucial for removing or suppressing the noise recorded in PCG signals. From the denoised signal, features are extracted and applied to the machine learning model to classify the signal.

17.1.1 Motivation

According to World Health Organization (WHO) reports, cardiovascular diseases (CVDs) are the leading cause of death worldwide and account for 17.5 million deaths (31% of the total) around the world [2]. Since the COVID-19 pandemic, millions of people are affected by post-COVID cardiovascular heart disease [3], which has also increased the CVD death rate worldwide. To reduce the mortality rate, it is necessary to detect CVD at an early stage and generate an alarm for patients to get clinical help.

17.1.2 Contribution of the Chapter

This research focuses on the automatic analysis of heart sound signals to identify various CVDs early and promptly initiate the appropriate treatment. We conducted an empirical study of time–frequency analysis techniques using a lightweight convolutional neural network (CNN) model for PCG signal classification. PCG signals are acoustic vibrations produced by the heart during its functioning and can provide useful information regarding cardiac health.

DOI: 10.1201/9781003486930-24

17.1.3 The Organisation of the Chapter

This chapter is organised as follows. Section 2 discusses the existing methods proposed for PCG signal feature extraction and classification. The detail of each step used in the study and other materials are described in Section 3, including the preprocessing, decomposition of the signal, and classification using CNN. Section 4 describes and discusses the obtained results. Section 5 concludes the work done in this chapter.

17.2 LITERATURE SURVEY

17.2.1 Feature Extraction in the Time Domain

The majority of classification methods for heart sound signals follow a three-step process: segmentation, feature extraction, and classification. However, there have been a few attempts to directly extract features from the time signal without segmentation [4, 5]. In the available literature, many researchers have focused on using the time–frequency domain for feature extraction.

For instance, Gosh et al. [6] employed the Stockwell transform (ST) to obtain the time–frequency representation of PCG signals. Karhade et al. [7] utilised polynomial chirplet transform to represent PCG signals in time and frequency. Researchers have segmented PCG signals using time–envelope analysis [8], time–frequency analysis [9,10], and machine learning [11], utilising ECG or photoplethysmography signals as reference signals [12, 13]. In [14], singular value decomposition was incorporated with ST, and Gamero and Watrous [15] employed a hidden Markov model with time-cepstral characteristics. In other attempts, self-organising map and holomorphic envelogram [16], time-delay neural network [13] were used. However, these methods showed lower accuracy in automatically identifying foetal heart sounds (FHS), particularly in PCG signals with low signal-to-noise ratios (SNR).

As a consequence, there is a need to devise an improved methodology for FHS identification. For this, short-time Fourier transform (STFT) [17], wavelet transform (WT) [18], and various other techniques have been proposed [19, 20]. Marzorati et al. [21] suggested a convolutional network to identify the FHS. Another noteworthy contribution comes from Bhardwaj et al. [22], who proposed a specific kind of deep learning model known as an explainable CNN for PCG signal classification. This model aimed to identify and categorise heart valve-related diseases.

In conclusion, various time–frequency and automated identification techniques have been explored in the literature for PCG signal analysis, with ongoing efforts to improve accuracy and automate the detection of FHS components, especially in PCG signals with low SNR. Additionally, deep learning models have emerged as promising tools for the classification of heart-related abnormalities using PCG signals.

17.2.2 Classification Methods

Recently, deep learning (DL) approaches applied to the time–frequency (TF) domain of physiological signals have shown promising results in the automated identification of heart abnormalities [23–27]. These methods transform the signal representation using TF analysis and then use DL techniques for classification [24]. For instance, Ren et al. [23] utilised scalogram for binary classification, distinguishing between normal and abnormal categories and employing a combination of VGGNet and SVM-based learning models. Koike et al. [25] used STFT based classifications and employed a transfer learning model.

Despite the successes of DL models, there are still challenges in detecting heart valve diseases (HVDs) with high accuracy. Consequently, there is a need to develop new techniques such as time–frequency DL to accurately detect HVDs using PCG signals. In the field of multiclass classification, Puneet et al. [26, 27] proposed a two-stage classification approach that uses tuned Q-Factor wavelet transform (TQWT) features and a lightweight 1D–CNN model, which has shown promise for accurate classification of multiple heart-related abnormalities.

In summary, deep learning methods with the TF domain transformation have demonstrated significant performance. However, further advancements and novel techniques like time–frequency DL are required to improve accuracy and expand the capabilities of automated disease detection using PCG signals. Additionally, multiclass classification approaches such as two-stage classification with TQWT and lightweight CNN, hold promise for addressing more complex heart-related classification tasks.

17.3 METHODS AND MATERIALS

The steps followed in this study are shown in Figure 17.1. First, the signal is preprocessed and then decomposed; we decompose the signal using DWT and TQWT and use the obtained coefficients using the decomposition to train a 1D–CNN model. The model classifies the PCG signal into five categories. The following subsections describe our steps.

17.3.1 Preprocessing

The data set employed for the experiments is a public data set consists of 1000 signals divided into five classes. Each sample has an 8 kHz sampling frequency. The signal is downsampled to 1 kHz, and the z-score normalisation is applied.

17.3.2 Decomposition of the Signal

Decomposition is performed using DWT and TQWT. These techniques provide the multiresolution analysis of the signal since they decompose the signal into

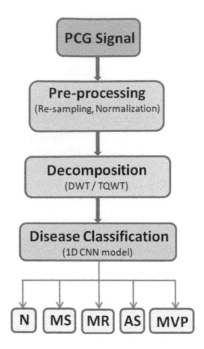

Figure 17.1 Flowchart of the study.

various frequency bands. It helps in the localisation of pathological categories because the signatures of different pathologies lie in different frequency bands. Next, we provide a brief description of the decomposition using DWT and TQWT.

17.3.2.1 Decomposition Using DWT

Mallat proposed a subband tree approach to decompose the signal, as shown in Figure 17.2(a). In this approach, two analysis filters, low-pass and high-pass, are applied to the signal to decompose into two separate frequency bands. Then the filtered signal is downsampled by a factor of two to make the total number of coefficients of both filters close to the original signal. The same process is applied to the approximation coefficients to obtain the next level of detail and approximation coefficients.

In this study, we decomposed the signal to five levels using 'coif-5' as the mother wavelet. Figure 17.2(b) describes the obtained signals using the decomposition of the original signal to five levels. We obtained five detailed level coefficients: 250–500 Hz, 125–250 Hz, 64–125 Hz, 32–64 Hz, and 16–32 Hz for levels 1 through 5, respectively. The approximation level covered the frequency range from 0–16 Hz.

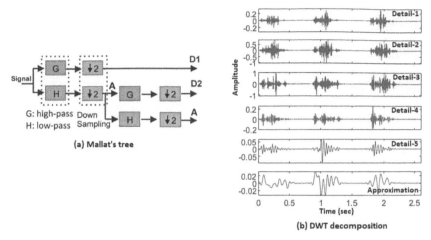

Figure 17.2 DWT: (a) Mallat's tree for DWT decomposition; (b) signal reconstructed using approximation and detailed coefficients at five levels.

17.3.2.2 Decomposition Using TQWT

DWT is a widely used technique for decomposing PCG signals due to its capacity to provide a multiresolution analysis of the signal, which helps differentiate the various categories of pathological and normal signals. However, DWT has a constant quality factor, and due to this, the frequency range of each band remains constant and cannot be adapted to the signal characteristics [17]. In contrast, TQWT is tunable.

As shown in Figure 17.3(a), the decomposition of the signal using TQWT is similar to the DWT decomposition steps. The signal is filtered using two filters, low-pass and high-pass. Then the outputs of these filters are downsampled. However, in contrast to DWT, the bandwidth and the downsampling factor depend on α and β. These two parameters are calculated using redundancy (r) and quality (Q); by tuning Q and r, the bandwidth of each frequency band can be tuned as required.

In this study, we decomposed the signal to 16 levels. We set Q to 1 and r to 8. Figure 17.3 shows the original signal and the 16 decomposed signals. Although the decomposition using TQWT had some redundancy, it could be controlled using r.

17.3.3 Classification Using 1D-CNN

We flatten the obtained coefficients using DWT or TQWT to obtain a 1D array. These 1D arrays are used to train the 1D-CNN model, as described in Figure 17.4. There are eight layers, with three layers having learnable parameters. The size of the input layer equals the number of coefficients in the 1D array obtained using the

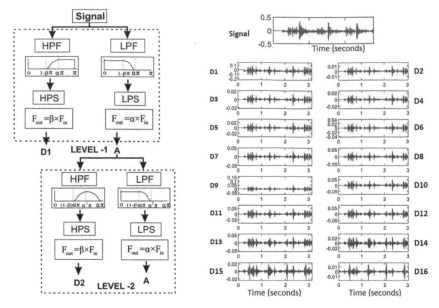

Figure 17.3 TQWT: (a) TQWT decomposition tree; (b) obtained decomposition of the signal using TQWT to 16 levels.

respective decomposition technique. The length of the DWT array is 2942, while for TQWT, it is 13606. There are two pairs of convolution and max-pooling layers, as shown in the figure. The sixth layer is a fully connected layer consisting of five neurons representing the number of classes present in the data set. The softmax layer calculates the probability of a sample being labelled.

17.4 EXPERIMENTAL RESULTS

We conduct the experiments using the proposed setup on a publicly available data set. The description of the data set and the results obtained using 1D-CNN with DWT and TQWT are presented in the following subsections. The experiments are conducted using the Matlab® software.

17.4.1 Data Set Description

The data set contains 200 samples from five different heart sound signal categories, including aortic stenosis (AS), mitral stenosis (MS), mitral valve prolapse (MVP), mitral regurgitation (MR), and normal (N). The original signals were sampled at 8 kHz and downsampled to 1 kHz in the preprocessing step. The typical length of the sample is 3 s and consists of three cardiac cycles.

CNN model summary

♦	Name	Type	Activations	Parameters
1	imageinput 1×2942×1 images with 'rescale-zero-one' normalization	Image Input	1(S) × 2942(S) × 1(C) × 1(B)	0
2	conv_1 8 1×7×1 convolutions with stride [1 1] and padding 'same'	2-D Convolution	1(S) × 2942(S) × 8(C) × 1(B)	64
3	maxpool_1 2×2 max pooling with stride [1 1] and padding 'same'	2-D Max Pooling	1(S) × 2942(S) × 8(C) × 1(B)	0
4	conv_2 4 1×3×8 convolutions with stride [1 1] and padding 'same'	2-D Convolution	1(S) × 2942(S) × 4(C) × 1(B)	100
5	maxpool_2 2×2 max pooling with stride [1 1] and padding 'same'	2-D Max Pooling	1(S) × 2942(S) × 4(C) × 1(B)	0
6	fc 5 fully connected layer	Fully Connected	1(S) × 1(S) × 5(C) × 1(B)	58845
7	softmax softmax	Softmax	1(S) × 1(S) × 5(C) × 1(B)	0
8	classoutput crossentropyex with '1' and 4 other classes	Classification Output	1(S) × 1(S) × 5(C) × 1(B)	0

Figure 17.4 Architecture summary of the CNN model.

17.4.2 Results Obtained Using DWT and 1D-CNN

The 1D-CNN model discussed in the previous section is trained on the data set using the fol- lowing parameters.

- MaxEpochs: 100
- Initial Learn Rate: 0.01
- Shuffling of samples: every epoch
- Mini Batch Size: 128
- Optimiser: stochastic gradient descent with momentum
- GPU: 1

The obtained accuracy and loss curve with respect to each iteration is depicted in Figure 17.5. From the figure, it can be observed that the training and validation accuracy and loss are close to each other, indicating that the model is not overfitted. An initial perturbation is observed while training the model that settles in most of the experiments. The model training consumed 27 seconds on a signal GPU system with 8 GB RAM.

The obtained confusion matrix using the DWT and 1D-CNN is described in Figure 17.6. The overall accuracy for all five class classifications is 97.8%. The obtained results are promising for all the classes. The proposed model classifies the normal vs abnormal signals with 100% accuracy. This feature promotes the use of such a model in remote monitoring applications where the primary focus is to detect the abnormality as soon as possible.

Table 17.1 shows the quantitative results obtained for the DWT with 1D-CNN in terms of sensitivity, specificity, precision, recall, and F1. The sensitivity for MR, MS, and N is 100% while for AS, it is 96.3%, and for MVP, it is 92.8%. Except

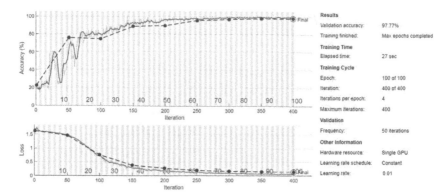

Results	
Validation accuracy:	97.77%
Training finished:	Max epochs completed
Training Time	
Elapsed time:	27 sec
Training Cycle	
Epoch:	100 of 100
Iteration:	400 of 400
Iterations per epoch:	4
Maximum iterations:	400
Validation	
Frequency:	50 iterations
Other Information	
Hardware resource:	Single GPU
Learning rate schedule:	Constant
Learning rate:	0.01

Figure 17.5 Accuracy and loss curve for the CNN model trained on DWT.

Confusion Matrix

1 **52** 19.3%	**0** 0.0%	**0** 0.0%	**2** 0.7%	**0** 0.0%	96.3% 3.7%
2 **0** 0.0%	**49** 18.2%	**0** 0.0%	**0** 0.0%	**0** 0.0%	100% 0.0%
3 **0** 0.0%	**0** 0.0%	**50** 18.6%	**0** 0.0%	**0** 0.0%	100% 0.0%
4 **0** 0.0%	**2** 0.7%	**2** 0.7%	**52** 19.3%	**0** 0.0%	92.9% 7.1%
5 **0** 0.0%	**0** 0.0%	**0** 0.0%	**0** 0.0%	**60** 22.3%	100% 0.0%
100% 0.0%	96.1% 3.9%	96.2% 3.8%	96.3% 3.7%	100% 0.0%	**97.8%** **2.2%**

Output Class

Target Class

Figure 17.6 Confusion matrix obtained for the CNN model trained on DWT.

Table 17.1 Obtained Results for DWT + CNN

Class	Sensitivity	Specificity	Precision	Recall	F1
AS	0.9630	1.0000	1.0000	0.9630	0.9811
MR	1.0000	0.9909	0.9608	1.0000	0.9800
MS	1.0000	0.9909	0.9615	1.0000	0.9804
MVP	0.9286	0.9906	0.9630	0.9286	0.9455
N	1.0000	1.0000	1.0000	1.0000	1.0000

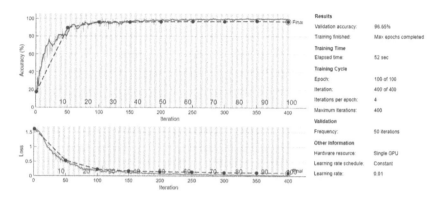

Figure 17.7 Accuracy and loss curve for the CNN model trained on DWT.

for the MVP class, F1 is also more than 98% because the MR and MS frequency ranges overlap. For the normal class, all the parameters are 100%. These results show that the DWT sufficiently exploits the discriminative features for various classes of heart sound signals.

17.4.3   Results Obtained Using TQWT and 1D-CNN

Like the DWT coefficients experiment, the model was trained and tested with TQWT coefficients. The learning progress of the model and the results are provided as follows. Figure 17.7 describes the training iterations and respective accuracy and loss curve. The curves depict that the training and validation accuracy are close to each other, which means the model is not overfitted. Since the length of the coefficient array obtained using the TQWT is larger than that obtained using DWT, the elapsed time for the training is 52 seconds, higher than that for the DWT coefficients.

Figure 17.8 shows the obtained confusion matrix using TQWT coefficients with 1D CNN. Overall accuracy of 96.7% is obtained for the five class

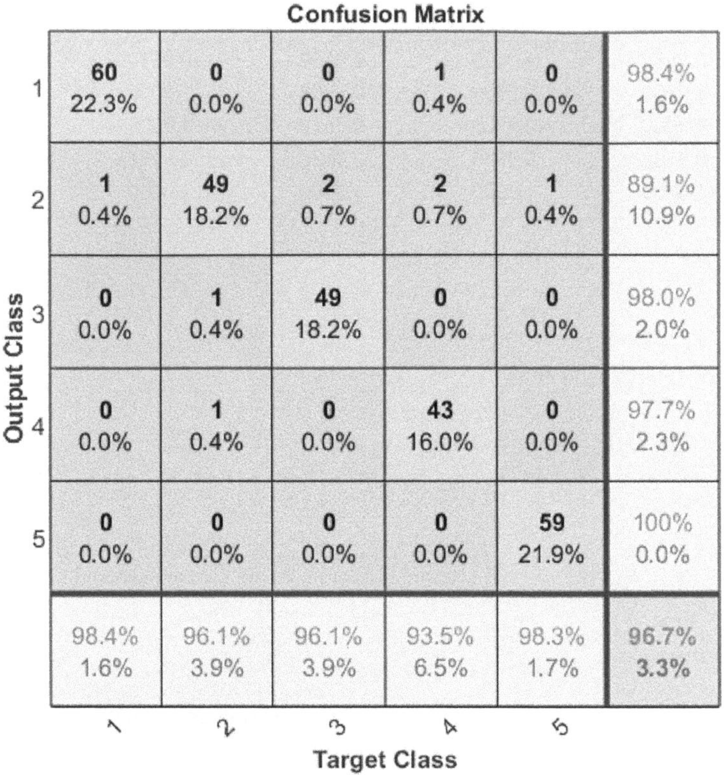

Confusion Matrix

60	**0**	**0**	**1**	**0**	98.4%
22.3%	0.0%	0.0%	0.4%	0.0%	1.6%
1	**49**	**2**	**2**	**1**	89.1%
0.4%	18.2%	0.7%	0.7%	0.4%	10.9%
0	**1**	**49**	**0**	**0**	98.0%
0.0%	0.4%	18.2%	0.0%	0.0%	2.0%
0	**1**	**0**	**43**	**0**	97.7%
0.0%	0.4%	0.0%	16.0%	0.0%	2.3%
0	**0**	**0**	**0**	**59**	100%
0.0%	0.0%	0.0%	0.0%	21.9%	0.0%
98.4%	96.1%	96.1%	93.5%	98.3%	**96.7%**
1.6%	3.9%	3.9%	6.5%	1.7%	**3.3%**

Output Class (rows 1–5) / Target Class (columns 1–5)

Figure 17.8 Confusion matrix obtained for CNN model trained on TQWT.

classifications. Similar to the DWT coefficients, the TQWT coefficients also produced 100% accuracy for distinguishing the normal from the abnormal classes. The results are promising using TQWT coefficients, but they are lower than the results obtained using the DWT coefficients. This indicated that the redundancy in the TQWT coefficients does not improve accuracy at extra computational costs.

Table 17.2 shows the quantitative results for the TQWT with the 1D-CNN method. The obtained F1s for AS, MR, MS, MVP, and N classes are 98.36%, 92.45%, 97.03%, 95.56%, and 99.16%, respectively, showing that the 1D-CNN model is efficient in classifying all five classes. However, these numbers are lower than the numbers produced by the model using the DWT coefficients. High sensitivity (greater than 97%, except MR class) and high specificity (greater than 98.6%) are promising results for a medical application.

Table 17.2 Obtained Results for TQWT + CNN

Class	Sensitivity	Specificity	Precision	Recall	F1-score
AS	0.9836	0.9952	0.9836	0.9836	0.9836
MR	0.8909	0.9907	0.9608	0.8909	0.9245
MS	0.9800	0.9909	0.9608	0.9800	0.9703
MVP	0.9773	0.9867	0.9348	0.9773	0.9556
N	1.0000	0.9952	0.9833	1.0000	0.9916

17.5 CONCLUSION

The work presented in this chapter explored the role of two time–frequency analysis techniques, DWT and TQWT, for classifying heart sound signals. A lightweight 1D-CNN model is proposed for the classification. The results indicate that both the time–frequency analysis techniques can differentiate the prominent features of normal from various abnormal heart sound signals. The performance of the 1D-CNN model is superior with the DWT coefficients to that with the TQWT coefficients. The computational complexity to decompose the signal using DWT is also lower than the TQWT. Moreover, the computational cost of the model with DWT coefficients is also lower since the length of the coefficients array is lower. These results suggest that DWT is preferable for decomposing heart sound signals. We also observed that the model with DWT coefficient classifies the normal vs abnormal heart sound signal with 100% accuracy. Such systems enable monitoring the heart's health in remote locations where the primary goal is to detect the abnormality at an early stage. Future work will focus on classifying PCG signals in the presence of ambient noise incorporating other time–frequency representation techniques.

17.6 ACKNOWLEDGEMENT

This work was funded by Science and Education Research Board (SERB), DST-India project vide SRG/2022/001681.

REFERENCES

[1] B. Bozkurt, I. Germanakis, and Y. Stylianou, "A study of time–frequency features for cnn-based automatic heart sound classification for pathology detection," *Computers in Biology and Medicine*, vol. 100, pp. 132–143, 2018. [Online]. Available: https://www.sciencedirect.com/science/article/pii/S0010482518301744

[2] "Cardiovascular diseases (cvds)." [Online]. Available: www.who.int/en/news-room/fact-sheets/detail/cardiovascular-diseases-(cvds)

[3] M. K. Chung, D. A. Zidar, M. R. Bristow, S. J. Cameron, T. Chan, C. V. Harding, D. H. Kwon, T. Singh, J. C. Tilton, E. J. Tsai, N. R. Tucker, J. Barnard, and J. Loscalzo, "Covid-19 and cardiovascular disease," *Circulation Research*, vol. 128, no. 8, pp. 1214–1236, 2021. [Online]. Available: www.ahajournals.org/doi/abs/10.1161/CIRCRESAHA.121.317997

[4] S.-W. Deng and J.-Q. Han, "Towards heart sound classification without segmentation via autocorrelation feature and diffusion maps," *Future Generation Computer Systems*, vol. 60, pp. 13–21, 2016. [Online]. Available: www.sciencedirect.com/science/article/pii/S0167739X16000121

[5] M. Zabihi, A. B. Rad, S. Kiranyaz, M. Gabbouj, and A. K. Katsaggelos, "Heart sound anomaly and quality detection using ensemble of neural networks without segmentation," in *2016 Com- puting in Cardiology Conference (CinC)*, 2016, pp. 613–616.

[6] S. K. Ghosh, R. N. Ponnalagu, R. K. Tripathy, G. Panda, and R. B. Pachori, "Automated heart sound activity detection from pcg signal using time–frequency-domain deep neural network," *IEEE Transactions on Instrumentation and Measurement*, vol. 71, pp. 1–10, 2022.

[7] J. Karhade, S. Dash, S. K. Ghosh, D. K. Dash, and R. K. Tripathy, "Time–frequency-domain deep learning framework for the automated detection of heart valve disorders using pcg sig- nals," *IEEE Transactions on Instrumentation and Measurement*, vol. 71, pp. 1–11, 2022.

[8] T. Li, T. S. Qiu, and H. Tang, "A heart sound segmentation method based on cyclosta- tionary envelope," in *Instruments, Measurement, Electronics and Information Engineering*, ser. Applied Mechanics and Materials, vol. 347. Trans Tech Publications Ltd, 10 2013, pp. 2280–2283.

[9] S. K. Ghosh and R. N. Ponnalagu, "A novel algorithm based on stockwell transform for boundary detection and segmentation of heart sound components from pcg signal," in *2019 IEEE 16th India Council International Conference (INDICON)*, 2019, pp. 1–4.

[10] Y. Zhang, Z. Ma, X. Zhou, X. Li, Y. Liu, M. Chen, X. Sun, X. Wang, J. Wang, L. Cai, and K. Sun, *Heart Sound Segmentation Based on a Joint HSMM Method*. Cham: Springer International Publishing, 2021, pp. 145–156. [Online]. Available: https://doi.org/10.1007/978-3-030-79474-3_10

[11] Y. He, W. Li, W. Zhang, S. Zhang, X. Pi, and H. Liu, "Research on segmentation and classification of heart sound signals based on deep learning," *Applied Sciences*, vol. 11, no. 2, 2021. [Online]. Available: www.mdpi.com/2076-3417/11/2/651

[12] N. Giordano and M. Knaflitz, "A novel method for measuring the timing of heart sound components through digital phonocardiography," *Sensors*, vol. 19, no. 8, 2019. [Online]. Available: www.mdpi.com/1424-8220/19/8/1868

[13] T. Oskiper and R. Watrous, "Detection of the first heart sound using a time-delay neural network," in *Computers in Cardiology*, 2002, pp. 537–540.

[14] A. Moukadem, A. Dieterlen, N. Hueber, and C. Brandt, "A robust heart sounds segmentation module based on s-transform," *Biomedical Signal Processing and Control*, vol. 8, no. 3, pp. 273–281, 2013.

[15] L. Gamero and R. Watrous, "Detection of the first and second heart sound using probabilistic models," in *Proceedings of the 25th Annual International Conference of the IEEE Engineering in Medicine and Biology Society (IEEE Cat. No.03CH37439)*, vol. 3, 2003, pp. 2877–2880.

[16] D. Gill, N. Gavrieli, and N. Intrator, "Detection and identification of heart sounds using ho- momorphic envelogram and self-organising probabilistic model," in *Computers in Cardiology, 2005*, 2005, pp. 957–960.

[17] D.-H. Pham, S. Meignen, N. Dia, J. Fontecave-Jallon, and B. Rivet, "Phonocardiogram sig- nal denoising based on nonnegative matrix factorisation and adaptive contour representation computation," *IEEE Signal Processing Letters*, vol. 25, no. 10, pp. 1475–1479, 2018.

[18] Y. Chen, S. Wei, and Y. Zhang, "Classification of heart sounds based on the combination of the modified frequency wavelet transform and convolutional neural network," *Medical Biological Engineering Computing*, vol. 58, 07 2020.

[19] S. K. Ghosh, R. Ponnalagu, R. Tripathy, and U. R. Acharya, "Automated detection of heart valve diseases using chirplet transform and multiclass composite classifier with pcg signals," *Computers in biology and medicine*, vol. 118, p. 103632, 2020.

[20] M. Morshed, S. A. Fattah, and M. Saquib, "Automated heart valve disorder detection based on pdf modeling of formant variation pattern in pcg signal," *IEEE Access*, vol. 10, pp. 27 330–27 342, 2022.

[21] D. Marzorati, A. Dorizza, D. Bovio, C. Salito, L. Mainardi, and P. Cerveri, "Hybrid convo- lutional networks for end-to-end event detection in concurrent ppg and pcg signals affected by motion artifacts," *IEEE Transactions on Biomedical Engineering*, vol. 69, no. 8, pp. 2512–2523, 2022.

[22] A. Bhardwaj, S. Singh, and D. Joshi, "Explainable deep convolutional neural network for valvular heart diseases classification using pcg signals," *IEEE Transactions on Instrumentation and Measurement*, vol. 72, pp. 1–15, 2023.

[23] Z. Ren, N. Cummins, V. Pandit, J. Han, K. Qian, and B. Schuller, "Learning image-based representations for heart sound classification," in *Proceedings of the 2018 International Conference on Digital Health*, ser. DH '18. New York, NY, USA: Association for Computing Machinery, 2018, pp. 143–147. [Online]. Available: https://doi.org/10.1145/3194658.3194671

[24] G. S. K. Tang, Chang, "Deep layer kernel sparse representation network for the detection of heart valve ailments from the time–frequency representation of pcg recordings," *BioMed Research International*, 2020. 2020, Article ID 8843963, 16 pages, https://doi.org/10.1155/2020/8843963

[25] T. Koike, K. Qian, Q. Kong, M. D. Plumbley, B. W. Schuller, and Y. Yamamoto, "Audio for audio is better? an investigation on transfer learning models for heart sound classification," in *2020 42nd Annual International Conference of the IEEE Engineering in Medicine Biology Society (EMBC)*, 2020, pp. 74–77.

[26] R. R. Choudhary, P. Kumar Jain, and M. R. Singh, "A two-stage classification of heart sounds using tunable quality wavelet transform features," in *2022 International Conference on Emerg- ing Techniques in Computational Intelligence (ICETCI)*, 2022, pp. 110–114.

[27] P. K. Jain, R. Raj Choudhary, and M. R. Singh, "A light-weight 1-d convolution neural network model for multi-class classification of heart sounds," in *2022 International Conference on Emerging Techniques in Computational Intelligence (ICETCI)*, 2022, pp. 40–44.

Chapter 18

Multidomain Features for Emotion Recognition Using EEG Signals

Shreyan Saha and Puneet Kumar Jain

18.1 INTRODUCTION

Affective computing is the research and development of systems and devices that can recognise, understand, process, and reproduce human sentiments. Computer science, psychology, and cognition are all included in this multidisciplinary field. While the field's origins may be traced back to early philosophical investigations into emotion, Rosalind Picard wrote a paper on affective computing [1] that paved the way for the more modern discipline of computer science.

The primary motivation of the research work in this field is to find the possibility of replicating empathy. The computer should be able to detect and respond to people's emotions and adjust its behaviour accordingly. For instance, affective computing systems can monitor a user's emotional state (through sensors [2], microphone [3], cameras [4], and software logic) and respond with an action, such as recommending a series of videos that fit the person's mood [5].

Affective computing involves extracting significant patterns from the collected signals and then classifying them using machine learning algorithms. Researchers discovered that using physiological signals instead of auditory or visual data can help machine intelligence better, as the latter method has a significant shortcoming in that the classification result is empirical; the correctness of the results obtained cannot be quantified. Auditory and visual data also tend to be less effective than physiological signals because facial expressions can be manipulated to an extent, and audio signals are susceptible to environmental noise. As a result, the suggested standard is now a more exact and reliable classification method based on physiological data.

Human emotions are anatomically produced in the limbic system in the brain's frontal lobe [6]. Analysing signals from the limbic system is preferred for appropriately classifying emotions. To achieve this, we utilise EEG signals representing the brain's electrical activities to recognise and classify emotions. EEG signals are recorded by placing several electrodes on the scalp following the International 10–20 System [7], ensuring consistent and reproducible readings. This standardisation allows for comparisons of readings across different subjects and studies over time, making EEG a valuable tool for emotion analysis and research.

DOI: 10.1201/9781003486930-25

18.1.1 Introduction to Electroencephalography

EEG is an electrophysiological monitoring technology used to record the brain's electrical activity using electrodes placed on the scalp. EEG monitors voltage changes within the neurons caused by ionic currents [8]. Diagnostic applications of EEG are often focused on either the different types of brain waves as observed in the frequency domain (gamma, beta, alpha, theta and delta are the five primary frequency bands in EEG signals) or event-related potentials which looks into potential time bound fluctuations, such as the onset of a stimulus. EEG has been used to diagnose epilepsy [9], tumours, strokes, and other localised brain disorders [10]. EEG has advantages compared to imaging-based techniques in terms of low cost and the ability to assess brain activity in the order of milliseconds. However, due to poor spatial precision, the capacity to evaluate brain activity using EEG deeper than the cortex is limited.

18.1.2 10–20 System of Electrode Placement

The 10–20 system is an international standard for EEG electrode placement, as shown in Figure 18.1. This system relies on measurements of external cranial

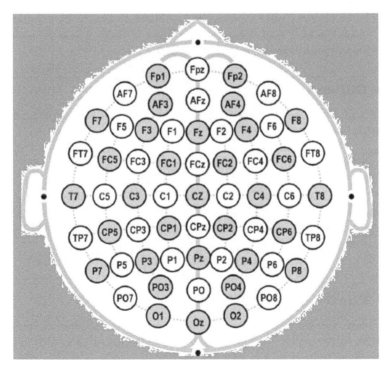

Figure 18.1 The position of electrodes used in the DEAP data set based on the 10–20 system for 32 electrodes (gray circles) [11].

landmarks to determine electrode placement. The assumption is that the positions of these scalp sites and the underlying brain structures maintain a stable relationship. "10–20" refers to the distances between adjacent electrodes. The letters represent the lobes of the brain: frontal (F), temporal (T), central (C), parietal (P), and occipital (O). Even-numbered electrodes belong to the right hemisphere, and odd-numbered to the left; "z" is for midline electrodes.

18.1.3 Problem Definition

Numerous techniques for EEG-based emotion categorisation have been published, but they all have flaws, such as a restricted number of emotion states examined and a lack of significant accuracy in cross-subject training and testing. A general drop in accuracy is noted for algorithms that classify based on a higher number of emotional states. SMOTE [12] (synthetic minority oversampling technique), as an oversampling technique, has not been used to mitigate class imbalance in any of the papers that have been perused.

To that end, DEAP considered a standard data set for emotion recognition, is used to classify and obtain significant accuracy for two and four classes and determine experimentally if SMOTE can bring about a difference in accuracy scores by mitigating class imbalance. The results obtained show that using SMOTE to oversample the minority class increases the resultant accuracies by a significant amount, which can be a vital component in future research where the accuracy may get compromised because of class imbalance.

18.1.4 Objective

With this work, we aimed to classify emotional states using EEG signals. In this direction, the following are the objectives:

- to develop a feature set that can be used for emotion recognition to accurately classify and recognise the various emotions
- to classify emotions based on two and four discrete states of emotions mapped from the valence-arousal (VA) space
- to find a subset of channels which gives comparable accuracy to the entire array of 32 channels
- to address the issue of class imbalance present in the DEAP data set

18.1.5 Contributions of the Work

For this study, we analysed features from multiple domains based on previous observations by Ali et al. [11], Nakisa et al. [13], and Khateeb et al. [14] to select a suitable set of features for the emotion classification task. To address the class imbalance in the dataset, we employed SMOTE. Then, we used the extracted feature set to use support vector machine (SVM), k-nearest neighbour (KNN), decision tree, and random forest algorithms. The experiments involved mapping emotions into two and four discrete states based on VA space as classification labels. The work contributed significantly to emotional state classification in several ways, as follows:

- found a multidomain feature set which can classify emotions in two and four-class models with higher accuracy than the compared methods
- found a subset of 16 channels that produce accuracy values comparable to those obtained using 32 channels, reducing the potential hardware cost for recording EEG signals
- applied SMOTE to remove class imbalance and increase the overall performance and, consequently, the resistance of the model against skewed classification

18.1.6 Chapter Outline

The chapter is structured as follows: Section 2 provides a comprehensive literature survey, offering an overview of relevant works consulted during the preparation of this chapter. In Section 3, the implementation methodology of the proposed model is outlined. Section 4 presents the results of various experiments conducted, including discussions on selecting an optimal subset of channels, investigating the impacts of class imbalance and oversampling, and comparing the proposed model with similar works in the field. Section 5 concludes the chapter by highlighting the key findings and discussing potential future research directions.

18.2 LITERATURE SURVEY

Affective computing is a relatively new field in which studies on emotion classification have been conducted. DEAP is one of the most well-known publicly available data sets, created by Koelstra et al. [5], who used music videos to elicit emotional responses. The authors classified the DEAP data set subject-wise using leave-one trial-out cross-validation to achieve average accuracies of 62.0%, 57.6%, and 55.4%, respectively, on the arousal, valence, and liking scales. The rating distribution for the various scales showed some correlations between the scales. For example, a positive correlation between valence and liking indicated that the subjects preferred music videos which made them happy. Separately, the lower valence and arousal correlation indicates that the subjects can discern these two emotional states.

Previous researchers on the DEAP data set explored various features and methods to identify emotions. For example, Ali et al. [11] developed a feature set comprising time and time–frequency (wavelet) domain features and achieved a maximum accuracy of 83.8% using SVM for a four-class categorisation based on VA space. Similarly, Khateeb et al. [14] used features from time, frequency, and time–frequency and obtained an accuracy of 65.72% for a nine-class categorisation.

A common focus in these studies is to identify a smaller set of channels that can deliver comparable accuracy with that of using the entire array of 32 channels, reducing processing costs.

To achieve this goal, researchers have explored subsets of channels, such as Fp1, Fp2, F3, and F4. To that end, Alarcao et al. [15] surveyed a large number of papers by researchers in the field, the data sets they used, the preprocessing they performed, the number of electrode channels they selected, and finally, the classifiers they used and their accuracy. We pursued this approach in this thesis. Moreover, researchers have investigated EEG frequency bands (gamma, beta, alpha, theta, and delta) to determine which contains the most relevant data for emotion recognition. Studies consistently show that gamma and beta frequency bands are closely linked to emotion recognition, supporting that emotional and cognitive processes are associated with higher-frequency brain activities [14].

Several scholars have made several key observations about EEG signals. Separating valence and arousal into two classes based on the scale's midpoint, according to Koelstra et al., leads to an imbalance in class samples. In light of this problem, F1 should also be reported as a metric as it considers the balance of classes in its calculation. Furthermore, several studies have demonstrated that cross-subject accuracy is substantially less accurate than within-subject accuracy.

Even though different emotions share some brain patterns in common, Zheng et al. [16] show in their research that individual variances exist for other individuals that could lead to differences in the underlying probability distribution from subject to subject. Consequently, it leads to lower average accuracy when the classifier is trained and tested on different subjects. Similarly, Nath et al. [17] state in their paper that because each individual has their own characteristic brain signal pattern, emotion prediction based on features from another individual will significantly degrade the model's performance for predicting an unknown subject. The researchers also discovered that the signals for an individual's various trials are similar; therefore, the pattern for a given emotion can be identified by analysing the signals obtained for that individual. They also argue that by increasing the data size, the differences in strengths of the EEG signals of different individuals can be accounted for. However, since the DEAP data set only contains 32 individuals' EEG signals, it cannot account for this variance in EEG signals. Lan et al. [18] found that the baseline method's mean classification accuracy without domain adaptation is 39.05% for three-class classification using leave-one-subject-out cross-validation, correlating with the findings of the two papers previously mentioned, suggesting that there exists a significant difference between the EEG signal of different subjects.

18.3 PROPOSED METHODOLOGY

The block diagram of the proposed method is shown in Figure 18.2. From the DEAP data set, we extracted the feature matrix to be used for classification with each sample consisting of features from all 32 EEG channels from both time and

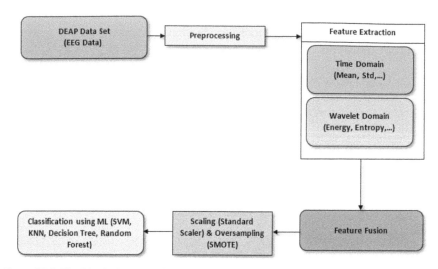

Figure 18.2 The block diagram of the proposed methodology.

wavelet domains. The time features were calculated on all the data points of each channel, whereas the wavelet features were calculated on the first three frequency bands (gamma, beta and alpha) of each channel, bringing the total feature vector size to 768 features.

As there was class sample imbalance, we used SMOTE oversampling to make the number of samples of minority classes equal to that of the majority class. After that, we trained SVM, KNN, decision tree, and random forest on the feature set along with hyperparameter tuning using Bayesian optimisation. The accuracies obtained are based on a fivefold cross-validation of the entire dataset after scaling the dataset to zero mean and unit variance and then using principal component analysis (PCA) to reduce the feature vector to 20% of the number of samples to prevent overfitting.

18.3.1 Feature Extraction

Emotions represent complex mental states triggered by neuronal activity in many areas of the brain. Analysing EEG signals requires extracting important features that can be used for machine learning. Since EEG signals vary with time and are nonstationary, they have characteristic time and frequency information, implying that complementary data can be found in separate signal domains. The features we used in the data set are extracted from time and wavelet domains based on the findings of Ali et al. [11], Nakisa et al. [13], and Khateeb et al. [14] as follows:

18.3.1.1 Time Domain Features

The time features are extracted from the preprocessed signal directly without applying any transform.

- The mean, standard deviation, mean absolute values of the first differences of the signal and the standardised signal, and mean absolute values of the second differences of the signal and the standardised signal
- Hjorth Parameters:
- Activity:

$$A_h = var\ (s_j) \tag{18.1}$$

- Mobility:

$$M_h = \sqrt{\frac{var(s'_j)}{var(s_j)}} \tag{18.2}$$

- Complexity:

$$C_h = \frac{M'_h}{M_h} \tag{18.3}$$

where $\bar{X}\ (n) = (X(n) - \mu x)/\sigma x$ is the standardized signal.

18.3.1.2 Wavelet Domain Features

The EEG signal is a nonstationary signal in which the frequency components are localised in time. Wavelet transform is used to study such signals since it can gather frequency (scales) and time information [19]. The mother wavelet used during wavelet transform is of a finite time span, giving a time-based localisation of the signal's frequency components.

A discrete wavelet transform decomposes a signal into several frequency bands, each band including a time series of signal coefficients with respect to that frequency band [20]. The time resolution of the signal increases, and the frequency resolution decreases with higher frequencies in the signal. This means that a higher frequency component can be more accurately located in time, but there will be more ambiguity to their exact value than with a lower-frequency component [21]. In DWT, there are numerous mother wavelets to choose from, each having some specific characteristic. The db4 mother wavelet, for example, is similar to the spike wave of EEG [19], and hence, it is employed as the mother wavelet in our thesis. The DWT is obtained as below, assuming the parameters as discrete values:

$$DWT(j,k) = \frac{1}{\sqrt{2^j}} \int x(t) \psi \left(\frac{t - 2^j k}{2^j} \right) dt \tag{18.4}$$

The signal $x(t)$ is decomposed by the high-pass filter giving the detail coefficients of that level D_i, where i is the level of decomposition and the low-pass filter h gives the approximation coefficients (A_i). The approximation coefficients are further broken down to get subsequent details and approximation coefficients. The EEG signals are divided into five bands using the db4 mother wavelet function: gamma, beta, alpha, theta, and delta. Each sample now comprises the features extracted from the first three of the five bands for all the channels' data. The features extracted from the frequency bands are

- Wavelet Energy:

$$E_j = \sum_{k=1}^{N} D_j(k)^2)k = 1, 2, \ldots, N \tag{18.5}$$

where j represents the frequency band or decomposition level using DWT and k is the number of wavelet coefficients within the j frequency band.

- Wavelet entropy:

$$En_j = -\sum_{k=1}^{N} \left(D_j(k)^2 \right) log \left(D_j(k)^2 \right) \tag{18.6}$$

- Recursing energy efficiency (REE):

$$REE_{gamma} = \frac{E_{gamma}}{E_{total}} \tag{18.7}$$

- Logarithmic REE (LREE):

$$LREE_{gamma} = log_{10} [\frac{E_{gamma}}{E_{total}}] \tag{18.8}$$

- Absolute logarithmic REE (ALREE):

$$ALREE_{gamma} = | log_{10} \left[\frac{E_{gamma}}{E_{total}} \right] \tag{18.9}$$

18.3.2 SMOTE

One of the main difficulties with imbalanced class classification is that the number of minority class samples is insufficient for a model to identify the class or decision boundary correctly. Oversampling the minority class samples is a possible solution. It can be performed simply by replicating instances from the data set's minority class. Synthesising new minority class instances is an improvement over replicating existing minority class examples. This method of data augmentation can be quite effective.

In 2002, Chawla et al. [12] adopted the SMOTE strategy. SMOTE involves selecting samples close to each other based on a distance metric, connecting the samples with a line, and selecting a new sample at a position along that line. Specifically, a minority class sample is randomly chosen and then the k nearest neighbours for the sample are found (usually, a k of 5 is used). A new sample is synthesised between the two instances at a randomly selected point in the feature space.

18.3.3 Classification Using Machine Learning

For the classification, the following four classifiers are used:

- **K-nearest neighbour:** KNN [22] classifies unlabelled samples of testing data based on their resemblance to training data. Given an unlabelled sample X, the classifier selects K nearest neighbours of the sample based on a distance metric like Euclidean distance. After that, sample X is assigned a class or category which is associated with the maximum number of neighbours.
- **Support vector machine:** Cortes and Vapnik proposed SVM [23], which creates a hyperplane that linearly divides samples into classes while maintaining the maximum possible distance between the class borders. SVM works by trying to find an N-1 dimensional hyperplane that best separates all the data points. Suppose a linear hyperplane cannot separate the data points. The data points are transformed to a higher-dimensional plane using the kernel functions, including linear, polynomial, and radial basis function kernels.
- **Decision trees:** A decision tree [24] is a hierarchical classification algorithm that classifies data via a tree-like graph. The algorithm splits the tree at each level based on decision rules generated from data features to create a model that predicts the value of a target variable. Each branch represents a decision path based on feature values, and each leaf node represents a category label (the decision is made based on a threshold denoting a node's purity or majority class).
- **Random forest:** A random forest [25] is used for solving regression and classification problems. It uses the concept of ensemble classifiers, which combines multiple classifiers to get the final result. Decision trees are the basic unit of a random forest algorithm. Two kinds of ensemble meta-algorithms, bagging and bootstrap aggregation, are used to train the random forest algorithm's generated forest. One of the main benefits of random forest over decision tree is that it avoids the problem of overfitting that the

latter suffers by aggregating the results of all its constituent decision trees' predictions to determine the final outcome, making them much more robust than a single decision tree and consequently increasing the precision of the results.

18.3.4 Hyperparameter Tuning

Hyperparameter tuning enhances a model's efficiency. Our machine learning algorithm deals with three types of data during training:

- Training data comprises samples containing features on which the model is fitted, which is used to predict results for new data.
- The model's parameters are the variables the chosen classifier adjusts based on the training data. For instance, in a neural network, the model's parameters are represented by the weight values assigned to each processing node (neuron), influencing its contribution to the final prediction.
- Hyperparameters are additional parameters that impact the training process but have no direct association with the training data. They influence how the model is trained, such as determining the number of hidden layers in a deep neural network or selecting a distance metric for KNN. Unlike model parameters, hyperparameters usually remain stable during training. Algorithms like grid search, random search, and Bayesian optimisation are used to optimise hyperparameters.

In summary, hyperparameter tuning involves adjusting configuration variables that influence the model's training process, while model parameters are learned from the training data to make accurate predictions.

Bayesian optimisation: In the case of grid search and random search, the hyperparameters were tuned by running multiple experiments with models trained on different hyperparameter settings independent of each other, and because of this, the system is unable to apply what it learned from one model to the next iteration of tuning. Bayesian optimisation [26], a sequential model-based optimisation algorithm, fixes this by selecting the next hyperparameter settings based on the results of the previous iteration.

Instead of a brute force approach to selecting hyperparameters, as is the case with grid and random search, this method uses the results of the previous runs to determine the hyperparameter settings to be used to increase the model performance. This approach is continued until an optimal solution is reached. Bayesian optimisation generates a probabilistic model by mapping hyperparameters to an objective function score probability. Due to the way the hyperparameters are chosen, Bayesian approaches are efficient. Because they prioritise hyperparameters that appear more promising based on previous discoveries, Bayesian techniques can optimise the hyperparameters in fewer iterations than the other two techniques. This is why we utilised this algorithm as the optimiser in the proposed methodology.

18.4 EXPERIMENTAL RESULTS

This section describes the DEAP data set and emotional classes formed, the optimum number of channels experimentally obtained, the performance improvement due to SMOTE, and finally, a comparison study of the performance achieved by the proposed model with that of other models in the same field of study.

18.4.1 Data Set and Class Formation

This section describes the structure of the DEAP data set, the method of creating the emotion labels for the videos, and the classes (two classes and four classes) formed from these labels.

18.4.1.1 DEAP Data Set

DEAP is a publicly available benchmark data set compiled by Koelstra et al. [5]. It contains 40 channels, 32 EEG signals recorded as the 10–20 international system, and eight peripheral physiological signals recorded from 32 participants. The database offers the possibility of classifying emotions experienced by different people while watching music videos. Sixteen females and sixteen males ranging in age from 19 to 37 (mean age is 26.9) years took part in the research for this chapter.

There were 40 videos, one minute in length, each with its own ID and reflecting different genres. The data extracted from the EEG electrodes are divided into two arrays: 1) the array with a dimension of 40 × 40 × 8064 for each user, where these dimensions represent the number of videos shown to each user (40), the number of channels recorded for each video (40), and the number of samples (8064) collected for each channel. 2) Each video's valence, arousal, dominance, and liking rating is stored in another array with dimensions 40 × 4.

We used the Self-Assessment Manikin (SAM) to determine the value of valence, arousal, dominance, and liking. The final classification of the emotions in the model uses only valence and arousal ratings, ignoring dominance and liking. Table 18.1 shows the shape and format of the arrays used from the preprocessed DEAP data set. Before we used DEAP, we preprocessed the data by downsampling the signal to 128Hz, removing artefacts caused by eye movement using a bandpass filter (4.0–45.0Hz). Finally, we reordered the trials of each user to video order so that the trials of different users could be easily compared. The 3 s baseline for each trial was also removed before the extraction of features, bringing each video's size down to 60 seconds (7680 data points).

Table 18.1 EEG Data Format for Each Subject Before Removal of 3 Seconds Baseline [27]

Array	Array Shape	Array Content
Data	40 × 32 × 8064 (384 base + 7680 trial) for each subject	40: video/trial 32: EEG channels per video 8064: samples per channel
Labels	40 × 2	40: video/trial 2: labels (valence, arousal) per video (labels scale of 1–9)

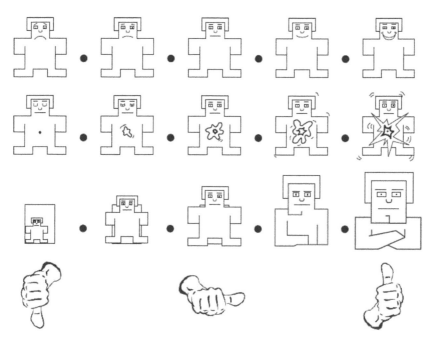

Figure 18.3 From the top: Images used to represent the scales of valence, arousal, dominance, and liking [5].

18.4.1.2 Class Formation

The SAM [28] gives a promising solution to the issues connected with measuring emotional response. SAM uses arousal, valence, liking, and dominance scales to assess emotional response, and the scales were visualised as shown in Figure 18.3. During the assessment, scales for arousal, valence and dominance represented by manikins were displayed on the screen, with the numbers 1 through 9 displayed underneath. To represent their self-assessment level, participants selected a point along the scale on the numbers or any point between them, making the scale continuous.

The valence scale measures how pleasant/positive or unpleasant/negative emotion is, and the arousal scale measures the emotion's intensity. The dominance level ranges from submissive to dominant. The liking scale was used to record participants' personal preferences with respect to the videos. Instead of focusing on the participants' feelings, this poll focuses on their preferences. It means that a participant can like a video that made them feel sad or negative. The participants also rate their familiarity with each of the songs.

We used the valence and arousal label arrays for classification purposes, leaving out the dominance and liking arrays as these two are the most commonly used labels.

Two-class classification: For the two-class classification, we mapped the ratings on the continuous scale of 1–9 (based on SAM ratings) into two labels for valence and arousal states. Ratings lower than 6 are mapped to label 0, and the rest are mapped to label 1.

Four-class classification: For the four-class classification, we mapped the emotions into four main classes based on the 2D VA space created using valence and arousal (see Figure 18.4).

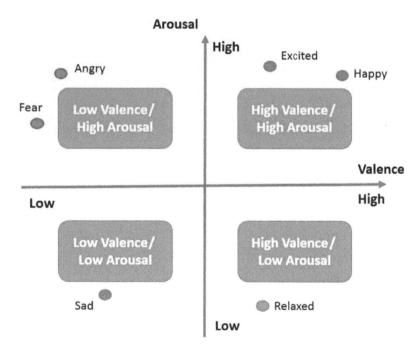

Figure 18.4 Four-class emotion model [11].

18.4.2 Selecting the Optimum Number of Channels

We conducted the experiments with varying numbers of channels (4 to 32) to test whether fewer channels can give accuracy comparable with that for the full set of 32 channels. The accuracy we obtained using fivefold cross-validation with the increasing number of channels is plotted in Figure 18.5. In this experiment, to prevent overfitting, we restricted the number of features to 367 (20% of the number of rows after using SMOTE on the data set) using PCA.

Figure 18.5 shows that taking into account fluctuations due to the random nature of sample selection in cross-validation; from 16 channels onward, the maximum of 69.9% occurs at 22 and 28 (with only 22 marked in the graph) which is 0.6% higher than the accuracy at 16. This can be attributed to the fact that at 16 channels, the number of features exceeds the threshold of 20% of the sample size, and all channel sets after that are restricted to the same number using PCA. Therefore, we chose 16 as the optimum number of channels as increasing channels only gave negligible increases in accuracy while increasing hardware cost. The selected 16 channels are shown in Table 18.6, along with their obtained accuracy with individual channels.

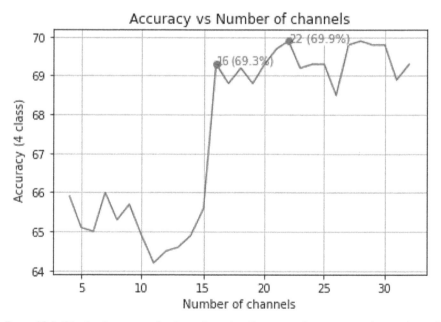

Figure 18.5 Obtained accuracy for four-class classification with respect to the number of channels used.

Table 18.2 The 16 Channels with the Highest Accuracy (sorted in descending order)

S. No.	1	2	3	4	5	6	7	8
Channel	T7	CP5	CP6	P4	F8	FP2	Pz	CP2
Accuracy	61.1%	61.0%	60.8%	60.4%	60.3%	59.7%	59.7%	59.7%
	9	10	11	12	13	14	15	16
	Cz	P7	FC2	FC6	Fz	AF4	FP1	O2
	59.7%	59.6%	59.4%	59.4%	59.2%	59.2%	59.1%	59.0%

Table 18.3 Results for Four-Class Classification with and without Using SMOTE

Classifier	With or without SMOTE	F1	Accuracy
Decision tree	without	25.0%	36.2%
	with	47.9%	48.1%
KNN	without	40.0%	44.1%
	with	70.3%	70.8%
SVM	without	39.6 %	42.2%
	with	**72.7%**	**72.7%**
Random forest	without	33.7%	40.7%
	with	71.3%	70.5%

18.4.3 Results Using SMOTE vs without SMOTE

This section demonstrates the impact of using SMOTE to address the class imbalance issue. The feature matrix here was the same as discussed in Section 18.4.1. However, the increase in the number of samples post-oversampling made it feasible to use more features without overfitting. Therefore, we used 256 features for non-oversampled and 367 for oversampled cases. We trained these feature matrices using fivefold cross-validation using SVM, KNN, decision tree, random forest, and hyperparameter tuning to get the best possible results.

The results show that the highest accuracy of 72.7% and F1 of 72.7% were obtained for SVM using SMOTE. The use of SMOTE improved the accuracy of all the classifiers significantly, mainly because of the increase in the number of samples due to oversampling of the minority class and also because the class imbalance present in the original data set was removed, thereby giving all the classes equal weight during classification. The increase in accuracy is due to the increase in samples, and the increase in F1 (a more useful metric for observing imbalance in classes) is due to both the increase in the number of samples and the mitigation of the class imbalance. Here it also needs to be noted that with SMOTE, the difference between accuracy and F1 is lower than that without SMOTE, indicating a more balanced distribution.

18.4.4 Results Obtained Using the Proposed Method for Two- and Four-Class Classification

This section gives the results for two- and four-class classification using 32 and 16 channels. In both cases, we performed SMOTE to balance class samples and then used PCA to restrict the features to 367.

Results for two-class classification: From Table 18.4, it is evident that in the case of valence, the 32- and 16-channel accuracies are very close to each other. In the case of arousal, 16 channels show marginally higher accuracy, which can be attributed to the randomness with which a k-fold cross-validation splits its folds. This indicates that 16 channels are sufficient for the two-class classification.

Figure 18.6(a) and Figure 18.6(b) show the confusion matrices obtained for the highest classification accuracies of 82.8% (KNN) and 82.3% (SVM) for valence and arousal, respectively. The hyperparameters obtained for KNN are the number of neighbours (k): 1, Distance metric: Correlation, Distance weight: Inverse.

Table 18.4 Results for Two-Class Classification

Label	Channels	Classifier	Precision	Recall	F1	Accuracy
Valence	32	**KNN**	82.9%	82.8%	82.7%	82.8%
	16	SVM	82.6%	82.6%	82.6%	82.6%
Arousal	32	KNN	82.2%	81.8%	81.8%	81.8%
	16	**SVM**	82.3%	82.3%	82.3%	82.3%

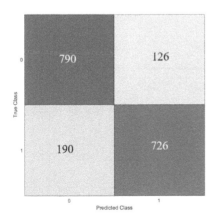 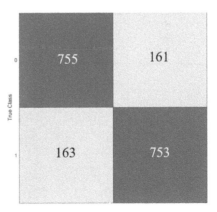

Figure 18.6 Confusion Matrix (a) 2 class classification (valence) using 32 channels (b) 2 class classification (arousal) using 16 channels and KNN as classifier and SVM as classifier.

The hyperparameters obtained for SVM are Kernel Function: Quadratic, Box Constraint Level: 0.0027, Multiclass Method: One vs All.

Results for four-class classifications: From Table 18.5, it is evident that 32- and 16-channel accuracy and recall are very close to each other with only marginal variation, the same as for two-class classification. At the same time, the precision and F1 are higher for 16 channels. This indicates that the 16-channel subset is a valid alternative to using all 32 channels. Figure 18.7 shows the confusion matrix obtained SVM's highest classification accuracy of 72.7%. The hyperparameters obtained for SVM are Kernel Function: Quadratic, Box Constraint Level: 0.0010, Multiclass Method: One vs One.

Table 18.5 Results for Four-Class Classification

Channels	Classifier	Precision	Recall	F1	Accuracy
32	SVM	**72.8%**	**72.7%**	**72.7%**	**72.7%**
16	SVM	76.3%	72.3%	73.2%	72.3%

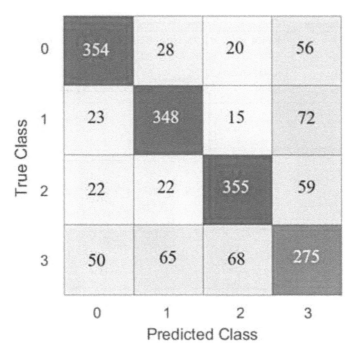

Figure 18.7 Confusion matrix for four-class classification using 32 channels and SVM as classifier.

18.4.5 Comparison with Other Methods

The comparison results with existing methods for two-class and four-class classification are provided in Tables 18.6 and 18.7, respectively. The tables show that the proposed model obtains better accuracy than all the existing methods. The method proposed by Xing et al. [29] for two-class classification shows accuracy close to the proposed model for valence labels. However, the accuracy for arousal is significantly lower than that for the proposed model (74.38% vs 82.3%).

Similarly, for the four-class classification, the accuracy of Zheng et al.'s method produced 69.67% accuracy, 3.03% lower than that for the proposed model. The results also demonstrate that using fewer channels, that is 16, shows no significant drop in accuracy. The two-class arousal classification shows marginally better accuracy than that obtained with 32 channels. This marginal improvement, however, is more likely due to the randomness with which k-fold cross-validation splits its folds. In conclusion, the general trend of results shows that this 16-channel subset can be a viable alternative to the entire 32-channel array.

Table 18.6 Comparison with Other Methods for Two-Class Classification

Method	Channels	Label	Classifier	Accuracy
Xing et al. [29]	32	Valence	LSTM	81.10%
		Arousal	LSTM	74.38%
Kusumaningrum et al. [30]	32	Valence	–	–
		Arousal	Random Forest	62.58%
Koelstra et al. [5]	40 (32 + 8)	Valence	Naive Bayes	57.6%
		Arousal	Naive Bayes	62.0%
Khateeb et al. [14]	4	Valence	SVM	60.3%
		Arousal	SVM	63.0%
Proposed method	32	**Valence**	**KNN**	**82.8%**
		Arousal	KNN	81.8%
	16	Valence	SVM	82.6%
		Arousal	**SVM**	**82.3%**

Table 18.7 Comparison with Other Methods for Four-Class Classification

Method	Channels	Classifier	Accuracy
Zheng et al. [16]	32	GELM	69.67%
Khateeb et al. [14]	4	SVM	40.3%
Proposed method	32	**SVM**	**72.7%**
	16	SVM	72.3%

18.5 CONCLUSION AND FUTURE WORKS

This section summarises the final results and their conclusions, along with a discussion about the scope of future works.

18.5.1 Conclusion

This study uses EEG data to propose an emotion recognition model for two and four discrete emotion states. The proposed model extracted and combined time and wavelet features to create a multidomain feature set. After that, the feature vector was reduced to 20% of the sample size to prevent overfitting using PCA. Then a study to find an optimal subset of channels was conducted to see if accuracy comparable with that achieved by using features from all 32 channels can be achieved. It is observed that 16 channels give accuracy results similar to the entire 32-channel feature set and sometimes even slightly better, as found in the case of two-class classifications of arousal. This, however, can mainly be attributed to the randomness of sample selection in k-fold cross-validation.

The stabilisation of accuracy can be attributed to the fact that 16 channels and beyond the feature vector exceeds the 20% threshold and hence is restricted to the same number of features, thereby giving similar accuracy with slight variations. A study was also conducted to see if minority class oversampling with SMOTE helps increase the accuracy and distribution of correctly classified samples. The results show that using SMOTE significantly increases the accuracy and F1 for all tested classifiers. During training, hyperparameter tuning using Bayesian optimisation was used to acquire the highest possible accuracy. The final results were obtained based on a fivefold cross-validation of the entire dataset, with the highest accuracy being 72.7% for four-class classifications using SVM and 82.8% and 82.3% for valence and arousal using KNN and SVM, respectively, for two-class classification.

18.5.2 Future Works

The DEAP data set contains eight additional peripheral physiological signal channels that can be used along with the 32 EEG signal channels to experiment and determine if their addition improves model performance. Furthermore, the samples can be further windowed to increase the number of samples, making it viable for classification with neural networks that need a large number of samples to work on. Subject-wise classification accuracy is a problem on which research is still ongoing since individual differences between the brain waves of two participants make it very difficult to predict the emotions of an individual based on data trained on other individuals, especially if the data set is as small as DEAP [17]. It is an area where further studies can be conducted to increase the accuracy of subject-wise classification to make the model more viable for real-time deployment. Other wavelet transforms like tunable Q-factor wavelet transform and wavelet scattering should be explored.

REFERENCES

[1] R. W. Picard, *Affective computing*. MIT press, 2000.

[2] A. Sano and R. W. Picard, "Stress recognition using wearable sensors and mobile phones," in *2013 Humaine association conference on affective computing and intelligent interaction*. IEEE, 2013, pp. 671–676.

[3] F. Al Machot, A. H. Mosa, K. Dabbour, A. Fasih, C. Schwarzlmu"ller, M. Ali, and K. Kyamakya, "A novel real-time emotion detection system from audio streams based on bayesian quadratic discriminate classifier for adas," in *Proceedings of the Joint INDS'11 & ISTET'11*. IEEE, 2011, pp. 1–5.

[4] A. Kolli, A. Fasih, F. Al Machot, and K. Kyamakya, "Non-intrusive car driver's emotion recognition using thermal camera," in *Proceedings of the Joint INDS'11 & ISTET'11*. IEEE, 2011, pp. 1–5.

[5] S. Koelstra, C. Muhl, M. Soleymani, J.-S. Lee, A. Yazdani, T. Ebrahimi, T. Pun, A. Nijholt, and I. Patras, "Deap: A database for emotion analysis; using physiological signals," *IEEE Transactions on Affective Computing*, vol. 3, no. 1, pp. 18–31, 2011.

[6] K. Guo, H. Candra, H. Yu, H. Li, H. T. Nguyen, and S. W. Su, "Eeg-based emotion classification using innovative features and combined svm and hmm classifier," in *2017 39th Annual International Conference of the IEEE Engineering in Medicine and Biology Society (EMBC)*. IEEE, 2017, pp. 489–492.

[7] R. W. Homan, J. Herman, and P. Purdy, "Cerebral location of international 10–20 system electrode placement," *Electroencephalography and Clinical Neurophysiology*, vol. 66, no. 4, pp. 376–382, 1987.

[8] E. Niedermeyer and F. L. da Silva, *Electroencephalography: basic principles, clinical applications, and related fields*. Lippincott Williams & Wilkins, 2005.

[9] W. Tatum IV, A. Hausain, S. Banbadis, and P. Kaplan, *Handbook of EEG interpretation*. Demos Medical Publishing, 2008.

[10] C. C. Chernecky and B. J. Berger, *Laboratory tests and diagnostic procedures*. Elsevier Health Sciences, 2012.

[11] M. Ali, A. H. Mosa, F. Al Machot, and K. Kyamakya, "Eeg-based emotion recognition approach for e-healthcare applications," in *2016 eighth international conference on ubiquitous and future networks (ICUFN)*. IEEE, 2016, pp. 946–950.

[12] N. V. Chawla, K. W. Bowyer, L. O. Hall, and W. P. Kegelmeyer, "Smote: synthetic minority over-sampling technique," *Journal of Artificial Intelligence Research*, vol. 16, pp. 321–357, 2002.

[13] B. Nakisa, M. N. Rastgoo, D. Tjondronegoro, and V. Chandran, "Evolutionary computation algorithms for feature selection of eeg-based emotion recognition using mobile sensors," *Expert Systems with Applications*, vol. 93, pp. 143–155, 2018.

[14] M. Khateeb, S. M. Anwar, and M. Alnowami, "Multi-domain feature fusion for emotion classification using deap dataset," *IEEE Access*, vol. 9, pp. 12 134–12 142, 2021.

[15] S. M. Alarcao and M. J. Fonseca, "Emotions recognition using EEG signals: A survey," *IEEE Transactions on Affective Computing*, vol. 10, no. 3, pp. 374–393, 2017.

[16] W.-L. Zheng, J.-Y. Zhu, and B.-L. Lu, "Identifying stable patterns over time for emotion recognition from eeg," *IEEE Transactions on Affective Computing*, vol. 10, no. 3, pp. 417–429, 2017.

[17] D. Nath, M. Singh, D. Sethia, D. Kalra, S. Indu *et al.*, "An efficient approach to eeg-based emotion recognition using lstm network," in *2020 16th IEEE international colloquium on signal processing & its applications (CSPA)*. IEEE, 2020, pp. 88–92.

[18] Z. Lan, O. Sourina, L. Wang, R. Scherer, and G. R. Mu¨ller-Putz, "Domain adaptation techniques for eeg-based emotion recognition: a comparative study on two public datasets," *IEEE Transactions on Cognitive and Developmental Systems*, vol. 11, no. 1, pp. 85–94, 2018.

[19] H. Adeli, Z. Zhou, and N. Dadmehr, "Analysis of eeg records in an epileptic patient using wavelet transform," *Journal of Neuroscience Methods*, vol. 123, no. 1, pp. 69–87, 2003.

[20] S. G. Mallat, "A theory for multiresolution signal decomposition: the wavelet representation," *IEEE Transactions on Pattern Analysis and Machine Intelligence*, vol. 11, no. 7, pp. 674–693, 1989.

[21] R. Polikar *et al.*, "The wavelet tutorial," 1996.

[22] L. E. Peterson, "K-nearest neighbor," *Scholarpedia*, vol. 4, no. 2, p. 1883, 2009.

[23] C. Cortes and V. Vapnik, "Support-vector networks," *Machine Learning*, vol. 20, no. 3, pp. 273–297, 1995.

[24] L. Breiman, J. Friedman, R. Olshen, and C. Stone, "Cart," *Classification and Regression Trees*, 1984.

[25] L. Breiman, "Random forests," *Machine learning*, vol. 45, no. 1, pp. 5–32, 2001.

[26] J. Mockus, "The bayesian approach to global optimisation," in *System Modeling and Optimization*. Springer, 1982, pp. 473–481.

[27] Y. Yang, Q. Wu, Y. Fu, and X. Chen, "Continuous convolutional neural network with 3d input for eeg-based emotion recognition," in *International Conference on Neural Information Processing*. Springer, 2018, pp. 433–443.

[28] J. D. Morris, "Observations: Sam: the self-assessment manikin; an efficient cross-cultural measurement of emotional response," *Journal of Advertising Research*, vol. 35, no. 6, pp. 63–68, 1995.

[29] X. Xing, Z. Li, T. Xu, L. Shu, B. Hu, and X. Xu, "Sae+ lstm: A new framework for emotion recognition from multi-channel EEG," *Frontiers in Neurorobotics*, vol. 13, p. 37, 2019.

[30] T. Kusumaningrum, A. Faqih, and B. Kusumoputro, "Emotion recognition based on deap database using EEG time–frequency features and machine learning methods," in *Journal of Physics: Conference Series*, vol. 1501, no. 1. IOP Publishing, 2020, p. 012020.

Chapter 19

Exploration of Impactful Brain Region and EEG Bands for Affective Computing**

Harsh Sonwani, Earu Banoth
and Puneet Kumar Jain

19.1 INTRODUCTION

Emotions have a significant role in human physiology and are influenced by both internal and external events. Accurately identifying emotions is essential for diagnosing mental disorders like schizophrenia and epilepsy, and EEG-based therapy offers critical advantages to patients and medical professionals. Aside from monitoring cerebral activity, EEG [1] is frequently employed in anxiety evaluation and military training because of its superior temporal resolution.

Different models, including dimensional and discrete models, are used for emotion representation. The three-dimensional model adds a dominant dimension, while the two-dimensional model uses a continuous two-dimensional space to represent arousal and valence. Valence assesses emotions from positive to negative, arousal assesses feelings on a spectrum from weak to vigorous, and dominance sets emotions on a range from calm to excited.

Since muscle movements can produce artefacts, recording EEG signals can be difficult. Advanced approaches like noise reduction and fast Fourier transform [2] are used to deal with artefacts. This enables the evaluation of various brainwave bands for emotion recognition using machine learning techniques.

Given the importance of emotions in daily life, more needs to be understood about them scientifically. The development of psychology and its applied fields need to progress in the affective sciences. Increased productivity and cost savings can result from incorporating machines into emotion recognition systems, particularly in the education and healthcare sectors.

An area of artificial intelligence called affective computing studies how to automatically recognize emotions by employing inexpensive sensors and EEG analysis. Emotional intelligence is increased, and personal and professional success is influenced by emotional awareness, which is essential for decision-making and problem-solving. EEG devices accurately identify emotional states by capturing and analysing electrical activity in the central nervous system. EEG-based brain–computer interface (BCI) technologies solve these issues with noninvasive and wearable solutions.

DOI: 10.1201/9781003486930-26

Decoding and attributing certain emotions to EEG data offer obstacles. Numerous studies on understanding emotions have been made possible by BCI technology, such as helmets and headbands. Complex emotions can be represented using dimensional models, such as valence-arousal (VA) and valence-arousal-dominance. The VA model employs valence and arousal axes to measure emotions on a scale of calm to agitated and joyful to miserable. In three-dimensional models, adding a dominant axis allows for evaluating feelings ranging from submissive to powerful. This illustration distinguishes between anger and fear on the VA plane. Arousal is represented on the vertical axis, whereas valence is represented on the horizontal axis.

Emotion recognition from EEG signals has been a topic of interest in recent research. Various feature extraction techniques and classification models have been proposed to improve the accuracy of emotion recognition systems. Subasi et al. [3] introduced an automated method that utilised a tunable Q wavelet transform (TQWT) as a feature extractor, followed by dimensionality reduction using statistical methods. The classification was performed using a rotating forest ensemble (RFE) algorithm and support vector machine (SVM), achieving 93% classification accuracy. This approach demonstrated the viability of TQWT and RFE for identifying emotions from EEG signals [3].

In the domain of driver distraction detection, Wang et al. [4] proposed a computational framework based on EEG-measured brain activity for the early identification of distractions during map viewing. Instead of focusing solely on classifying distracted and nondistracted periods, their framework aimed to predict the start and conclusion of a distraction period. The study achieved overall accuracies of 81% and 70% in predicting the beginning and conclusion of map viewing using continuous EEG signals collected from participants engaged in a simulated driving scenario.

Khateeb et al. [5] explored the use of multidomain characteristics (time, wavelet, and frequency) for emotion classification using the DEAP dataset. They employed an SVM classifier combined with 10-fold and leave-one-out cross-validation methods. Their proposed model achieved an average accuracy of 65.92% in recognising nine categories of emotions, showing promise for affective computing solutions capable of handling a broader range of emotional states. Amin et al. [6] focused on the classification of EEG signals using the DWT method and demonstrated 98% accuracy in distinguishing EEG signals recorded during a challenging cognitive task and those recorded during resting periods using distinct classifiers.

To address the complexity of EEG-based emotion identification systems caused by excessive channels and features, Zhang et al. [7] proposed a technique based on sample entropy and empirical mode decomposition (EMD). They utilised EMD to decompose EEG signals into intrinsic mode functions (IMFs) and calculated sample entropies for these IMFs. This method achieved an accuracy of 93.20% for multiclass tasks and an average accuracy of 94.98% for binary-class tasks on the DEAP database, demonstrating its effectiveness in emotion identification.

Feature extraction techniques in emotion recognition from EEG signals have included methods such as TQWT [3], PCA [8], DWT [6], and EMD [7]. These techniques enable extracting relevant information from EEG signals, aiding in identifying and characterising emotional states. In terms of classification models, studies have utilised RFE [3], k-nearest neighbor (KNN) [9], SVM [10], artificial neural network (ANN) [11], random forest [12], decision tree [3], and deep learning [13]. These models contribute to accurately classifying emotions based on EEG signals, with each approach offering its strengths and potential for improving emotion recognition systems.

This study conducts experiments to identify the prominent brain regions and EEG bands for the classification of valence and arousal. For this, a publicly available data set, DEAP, is used. First, the signals are denoised using multiscale principal component analysis (MSPCA) and then decomposed into five bands using DWT to produce separate frequency bands associated with EEG bands. Four features are extracted, including skewness, kurtosis, power spectral density (PSD), and standard deviation. These features are used to train the various classification models. Exploring the prominent brain regions and EEG bands for emotion classification will significantly enhance affective computing for various real-life applications.

The rest of this chapter is organised as follows. Section 2 describes the details about the method and material used in this study. The obtained results are presented and discussed in Section 3. Finally, Section 4 provides the conclusion of this study.

19.2 METHODS AND MATERIALS

A schematic diagram of the framework used in this study is presented in Figure 19.1. Specific channels are selected for each subject. After selecting useful channels, the signals are passed through MSPCA to remove unwanted frequency components. Once the denoised signal is obtained, required frequency bands are captured by decomposing EEG signals using DWT. From each frequency band, features are extracted and then used as input by different machine-learning models to classify emotions.

19.2.1 Channel Selection

In the DEAP data set, there are a total of 40 EEG channels present. Among these 40 channels, 32 are selected for this study based on the literature survey, including 'Fp1', 'AF3', 'F3', 'F7', 'FC5', 'FC1', 'C3', 'T7', 'CP5', 'CP1', 'P3', 'P7', 'PO3', 'O1', 'Oz', 'Pz', 'Fp2', 'AF4', 'Fz', 'F4', 'F8', 'FC6', 'FC2', 'Cz', 'C4', 'T8', 'CP6', 'CP2', 'P4', 'P8', 'PO4', and 'O2'. Figure 19.2 describes the location of each channel used for this study. These electrodes can be categorised into five brain regions: frontal, central, parietal, occipital, and temporal (left and right).

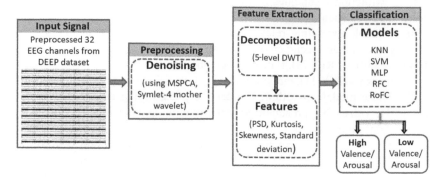

Figure 19.1 Proposed framework for classification of efficient EEG region and EEG bands.

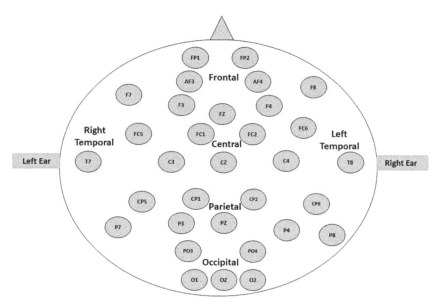

Figure 19.2 32 channels selected per the 10–20 electrode system.

19.2.2 Signal Denoising Using MSPCA

PCA and wavelets are combined to create multiscale PCA (MSPCA), which removes cross-correlation between each instance [14]. With the aid of wavelet analysis, the data is decomposed in approximation and detail coefficients representing various scales. Data analysis at different scales made it possible to capture both global and local trends. As part of the MSPCA architecture, the decomposed coefficients can be subjected to PCA at each scale.

PCA determines the primary components unique to each scale, which capture the most important differences in the data at that particular scale. The variables are combined through PCA as a linearly weighted sum of transformations. The vector on the hyperplane that, while maintaining orthonormality, yields the examined instance's maximum possible residual variance as measured by the principal components. Wavelet decomposition creates the multiscale representation, while PCA determines the most valuable features at each scale, allowing for a thorough investigation of the multiscale dynamics of the data. In this study, the Symlet-4 mother wavelet is used to decompose the signal up to five levels.

19.2.3 DWT Decomposition

The time-varying frequency content of EEG data can be examined and processed using the DWT. The DWT breaks down the EEG signal into five frequency bands or scales, revealing details about the underlying brain activity connected to various cognitive or affective processes. This decomposition is accomplished by applying several filtering and downsampling processes to the EEG signal. Using DWT, the EEG signal is divided into detail coefficients 'D' and approximation coefficients 'A' at various levels or scales. Each level represents a separate frequency band. The signal's broad trends are captured at the lowest level ($h = 1$), corresponding to the coarsest approximation. Higher levels offer finer details and higher-frequency components.

Filtering and downsampling: The DWT applies a high-pass filter (wavelet function) and a low-pass filter (scaling function) on the coefficients from the previous level at each decomposition level. While a high-pass filter pulls information at higher frequencies, a low-pass filter records information at lower frequencies. The downsampled coefficients reduce the quantity of the data and concentrate on the most important information. The approximation coefficients obtained at each level are iteratively applied to the filtering and downsampling phases. The wavelet decomposition tree, also called the wavelet pyramid, is produced by this recursive process. The highest level of the tree reflects the most general estimate, while the lower levels offer more precise information.

Analysis and feature extraction: Additional analysis can be performed on the DWT coefficients to identify and extract pertinent features. These qualities could be anything from the size of the wavelet coefficients, statistical measurements, the energy distribution across various frequency bands, or other traits. Further analysis, interpretation, and categorisation of cognitive or affective states are made possible by these features, which offer useful information about the EEG signal's frequency content and temporal dynamics.

A variety of filtering and downsampling processes can be used to calculate the DWT of an EEG signal. Assume we have an EEG signal x(n) with length n. The signal is divided by the DWT into D and A at various scales or levels. The DWT at a particular level h has the following formulas:

$$A_h(k) = \sum_n x(n) \cdot \phi_{k_2, k}(n)$$

(19.1)

$$D_h(k) = \sum_n x(n) \cdot \psi_{k_k, k}(n)$$

(19.2)

In this instance, $A_h(k)$ stands for the approximation coefficients at level h and position k, while $D_h(k)$ stands for the detail coefficients at level h and position k. The scaling and wavelet functions at level h and position k are represented by the functions $\phi_{h,k}(n)$ and $\psi_{h,k}(n)$. The obtained signals at each level are shown in Figure 19.3.

19.2.4 Feature Extraction

EEG signal analysis relies on feature extraction, which seeks to isolate the signals' most salient and instructive features. Certain elements can be retrieved from EEG

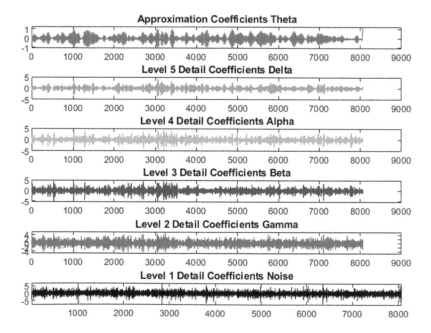

Figure 19.3 Obtained approximation and five detailed level coefficients.

across moods to capture various signal components. Features used in this study are as follows:

(1) **Power spectral density:** The EEG signal's PSD shows power distribution throughout various frequency bands [15]. The PSD can be calculated to extract properties like absolute or relative power in particular bands. These characteristics can shed light on the overall spectral makeup of the EEG signal, which may change based on one's mood.

Peter D. Welch's is a commonly used method to estimate spectral density [16]. It determines the strength of a signal at different frequencies. The method relies on periodogram spectrum estimates, which are generated via a time-to-frequency transformation of a signal. Although Welch's method reduces frequency resolution and increases power spectrum noise, it is superior to both Bartlett's and the traditional periodogram spectrum estimating method. Due to the presence of noise in limited and approximate data, Welch's approach is often required. By averaging, the Welch method lowers the periodogram method's variation.

By first applying a window to each sub-sequence and then averaging the periodogram of each sub-sequence, this technique separates a time series into overlapping sub-sequences, as shown in Figure 19.4. The applied window's length determines how bias and variance of the resulting PSD are traded off.

(2) **Standard deviation:** The standard deviation calculates the EEG signal's variability or dispersion. Finding the signal's standard deviation will show you how far the signal values stray from the mean. Higher standard deviations could signify more erratic or variation in the EEG signal, which might be connected to particular emotional states.

(3) **Skewness:** Skewness is a statistical feature that can show whether the distribution of EEG signal values is skewed towards positive or negative values. Skewness offers details about the signal's shape and aids in identifying various mood-related EEG patterns. Skewness produces values that are close to 0 for signals that are symmetrically distributed, values between 0 and 1 for signals that are right-skewed (also known as positively skewed), and values between 0 and −1 for signals that are right-skewed (also known as negatively skewed).

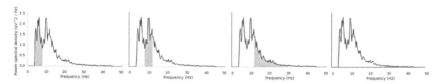

Figure 19.4 Welch's periodogram for power spectral density estimation: (a) theta band, (b) alpha band, (c) beta band, and (d) gamma band.

(4) **Kurtosis:** Kurtosis quantifies the pattern of the signal distribution while concentrating on the presence of outliers, or extremely high or low values. Low kurtosis values reflect a more Gaussian-like distribution, whereas high kurtosis values suggest a distribution with heavy tails or extreme values. By looking at kurtosis, you can tell if particular mood-related EEG patterns exhibit more extreme values or vary from a normal distribution.

19.2.5 Classification Models

The extracted features are used to classify the emotional states. For this purpose, the following five classification models are considered.

19.2.5.1 Support Vector Machine

SVM is a supervised machine-learning technique for regression and classification applications. It is frequently employed to resolve both linear and nonlinear issues. The primary objective of SVM is to identify an ideal hyperplane that divides several classes of data points. The margin, or the separation between the hyperplane and the nearest data points from each category, is what the hyperplane seeks to maximise in a binary classification task. Support vectors are the moniker for these nearby data points, therefore the name 'support vector machines'. This study uses a linear kernel function with a random parameter set to 42, and probability remains true.

19.2.5.2 K-Nearest Neighbour

KNN is also a supervised machine-learning algorithm used for classification and regression applications. The 'k' in KNN represents how many nearest neighbours should be considered when forecasting. The algorithm determines how far each new data point is from each other in the training set. The next step is to choose the k nearest neighbours based on the estimated distances. For classification tasks, the predicted class for the new data point is given as the majority class among the k neighbours. In regression problems, the expected value is frequently the weighted average of the k nearest neighbours' goal values. In the KNN model, we took the value of k as five and the Euclidean distance for measuring the distance between each nearest neighbour.

19.2.5.3 Multilayer Perceptron

Multilayer perceptron (MLP) is a feedforward ANN that comprises numerous layers of interconnected artificial neurons (perceptrons). An MLP typically has an input layer, one or more hidden layers, and an output layer in its network architecture. Weighted connections link neurons in one layer to neurons in the layer above it. During forward propagation, these links enable information to move through the network.

The weighted total of the inputs applied by each neuron in an MLP is activated. Standard activation functions include the sigmoid, hyperbolic tangent, and rectified linear unit. The model gains nonlinearity from the activation function, which enables it to understand intricate correlations between inputs and outputs. Adam optimiser is used with tanh as an activation function in parameter tuning while implementing MLP. In the MLP model, the Adam optimiser is used along with tanh as an activation function for 400 iterations. The L2 method is used for the regularisation with λ set as 0.3.

19.2.5.4 Random Forest Classifier

The random forest classifier (RFC) is an ensemble technique combining multiple decision trees to produce reliable and accurate caste polarisation. It tackles the limitations of individual trees by reducing overfitting, providing feature importance scores, and making predictions based on the consensus of numerous trees. It is a well-liked option for classification jobs, particularly when handling complicated data sets. Compared with individual decision trees, random forest can take categorical and numerical features, performs well with high-dimensional data, and is less prone to overfitting. Additionally, it offers feature importance scores that show how important each component is concerning the others during categorisation. In the RFC model, 100 decision trees are used, and the Gini index is calculated for measuring impurity.

19.2.5.5 Rotation Forest Classifier (RoFC)

The rotation forest classifier (RoFC) combines feature extraction with ensemble learning. Utilising the rotation of feature space seeks to improve the efficiency of categorisation jobs. Beginning with a random division of the initial feature space into several subsets or feature subsets, the RoFC algorithm first searches for patterns. Each feature subset embodies a distinct interpretation or angle of the data.

A primary classifier, such as a decision tree or SVM, is individually trained on each feature subset. The central concept underlying rotation forest is applying a rotation modification to each feature subset. This transformation seeks to align the features to maximise the distinction between classes. The approach improves the discriminative ability of each base classifier by rotating the feature space. In RoFC, a total of 90 decision trees are used. Here, decision trees rotate themselves to make different decision trees.

19.3 EXPERIMENTAL RESULTS

A publicly available DEAP data set is used for the experiment, as described in the following subsection. Experiments are conducted with different brain regions, EEG bands, and classification methods to explore the significant brain regions and EEG bands for the classification of emotional states. The obtained results and conclusion are provided in the following subsections.

19.3.1 Data Set Description

The DEAP data set was assembled in two stages [17]. The first stage consisted of an online self-assessment in which 14–16 participants rated 120 YouTube music videos, each of which had a 1 minute clip, according to the standards stated in the online ratings for valence, arousal, dominance, likeness, and familiarity. The second part contains physiological information and assessments from 32 subjects. The BioSemi. pdf format was used for these physiological clips, which were raw and unedited. Each participant viewed a total of 40 of the 120 videos.

The original 512 Hz sampling rate of the EEG signals was downsampled to 128 Hz. These signals were filtered and segmented, and artefacts like eye blinking and muscle movements were removed. There are two arrays, one for the data and one for the labels, present in each of the 32. dat files. In terms of channels, videos, and EEG signal data points, the data array had a size of 40 channels, 40 videos, and 8064 data points. Thus, there were 40 channels in each film and 8064 EEG signal data points. The labels array had valence, arousal, dominance, and liking dimensions, with a size of 40 by 4. Latin-1 encoding was used to encode the. dat files, and the cPickle library was used to read and write them.

19.3.2 Evaluation Metrics

In the context of classification tasks, accuracy, and F1 are methodical in evaluating the efficacy of a model or algorithm by contrasting the expected results with the 'ground truth' values.

(1) **Accuracy:** A model's accuracy is determined by comparing its proportion of accurate predictions to all other forecasts. Following is the formula used to compute it:

$$\text{Accuracy} = \frac{\text{Number of Correctly Classified EEG segment}}{\text{Total Number of EEG Segments}} \tag{19.3}$$

The 'Number of Correctly Classified EEG Segments' in this formula refers to the total number of EEG signal segments that were successfully predicted or categorised. The total number of EEG segments in the dataset that were utilised for categorisation is shown by the 'Total Number of EEG Segments' field.

(2) **F1:** F1 evaluates both precision and recall to determine how accurate a model is. While recall gauges a model's capacity to locate every good case, precision shows how well it can identify positive examples:

$$F1 \rightarrow Score = \frac{2 \times (\text{Precision} \times \text{Recall})}{\text{Precision} + \text{Recall}}$$ (19.4)

In conclusion, accuracy gives a broad measure of accurate predictions, while F1 takes into account both precision and recall to assess a model's performance, especially when dealing with unbalanced data sets or uneven costs due to various forms of errors.

19.3.3 Results

The experiments were conducted to separately classify the EEG emotions based on the valence and arousal score. For this, the valence and arousal score, which is ranged from 0–9, is categorised into two classes, high (>5) and low (≤5). These classifications were performed separately using different brain regions and EEG bands to identify their significance in classification.

19.3.3.1 Results for Brain Regions

Table 19.1 presents the obtained results for the valence classification using different brain regions with different classifiers used in this study. The table describes the top three regions achieving the highest accuracy and F1. The best accuracy of 64.8% is achieved for the frontal region using KNN. While the best F1 of 75.1%

Table 19.1 EEG Regions with the Three Highest Valence Scores

ML model	EEG regions	Accuracy (%)	F1 (%)
KNN	Frontal	**64.80**	70.70
	Right	62.01	68.22
	Central	62.01	67.92
SVM	Left	61.45	74.91
	Right	61.45	74.91
	Occipital	60.89	73.80
MLP	Left	63.13	**75.10**
	Perietal	61.45	72.87
	Central	59.78	72.22
RFC	Left	62.01	74.80
	Perietal	60.89	72.87
	Occipital	60.89	72.80
RoFC	Left	62.57	73.52
	Perietal	61.45	72.80
	Central	60.34	72.31

is achieved using the left region with MLP. From the table, it can be observed that the left region produces the best result with four classification methods. Although the highest accuracy is achieved using the frontal region, the F1 is lower compared to the F1s obtained using the left region. This indicates that the left region plays a substantial role in accurately predicting valence.

Table 19.2 presents the obtained results for the arousal classification using different brain regions with different classifiers used in this study. The table describes the top three regions achieving the highest accuracy and F1. Since different regions produced the highest accuracy and F1, the results are provided separately. The best accuracy of 68.16% and the best F1 of 68.51% were achieved for the frontal region using KNN. The regions with the highest accuracy and F1 with other classification methods are inconsistent. They obtained significantly higher accuracy for the frontal region using KNN and F1 using KNN and SVM, indicating that the frontal region dominantly affects arousal.

19.3.3.2 Results for EEG Bands

Similar to the experiments conducted to identify the prominent brain regions, experiments were conducted to identify prominent EEG bands for the classification of valence and arousal. EG bands are distinct frequency ranges observed within the EEG signal, including theta, alpha, beta, and gamma. Table 19.3 illustrates

Table 19.2 The Three EEG Regions with the Highest Arousal Accuracies and F1s

ML model	Top 3 regions based on the accuracy		Top 3 regions based on F1	
	EEG regions	Accuracy (%)	EEG regions	F1 (%)
KNN	Frontal	**68.16**	Frontal	**68.51**
	Occipital	64.80	Parietal	64.89
	Right	63.13	Occipital	64.80
SVM	Central	53.63	Frontal	64.57
	Left	53.07	Right	63.20
	Frontal	52.51	Left	51.06
MLP	Occipital	59.22	Left	50.00
	Central	57.54	Perietal	48.37
	Left	56.98	Right	47.13
RFC	Left	58.10	Central	57.44
	Central	56.98	Occipital	51.03
	Occipital	56.98	Left	49.33
RoFC	Occipital	59.78	Central	53.57
	Left	58.10	Left	50.33
	Frontal	57.54	Occipital	49.32

Table 19.3 The Two EEG Bands with the Highest Valence Accuracies and FIs

ML model	Top 2 bands for accuracy		Top 2 bands for FI	
	EEG band	Accuracy (%)	EEG band	FI (%)
KNN	Beta	**64.80**	Beta	70.70
	Gamma	63.69	Gamma	69.19
SVM	Gamma	61.45	Gamma	74.91
	Alpha	61.45	Alpha	74.16
MLP	Beta	63.13	Beta	73.23
	Theta	62.57	Gamma	**75.10**
RFC	Beta	62.01	Beta	73.44
	Gamma	61.45	Gamma	74.80
RoFC	Beta	62.57	Theta	73.52
	Theta	62.01	Gamma	73.08

Table 19.4 The Two EEG Bands with the Highest Arousal Accuracies and FIs

ML Model	Top 2 bands based on accuracy		Top 2 bands based on FI	
	EEG Band	Accuracy (%)	EEG Band	FI (%)
KNN	Theta	**68.16**	Beta	**70.70**
	Alpha	63.69	Gamma	69.19
SVM	Gamma	53.63	Theta	63.20
	Theta	52.51	Alpha	64.57
MLP	Gamma	59.22	Beta	48.37
	Beta	56.42	Gamma	50.00
RFC	Gamma	58.10	Theta	48.81
	Alpha	56.42	Gamma	57.44
RoFC	Gamma	59.78	Beta	53.57
	Alpha	57.54	Gamma	50.33

the EEG bands that demonstrated the highest accuracy and F1 for valence. The best accuracy of 64.8% is obtained using the beta band with KNN, and the best F1 of 75.10% is obtained using gamma. With other classifications, in most cases, gamma and beta produce the best results. Both gamma and beta belong to a higher frequency range, indicating that the higher frequencies play a vital role in valance classification.

Table 19.4 presents the two most prominent EEG bands for arousal classification. The best accuracy of 68.16% is obtained using theta with KNN and the best F1 of 70.70% is obtained using beta. The obtained results using KNN are significantly higher than those with the other classification methods. With other classifications, in most cases, gamma and beta produce the best results, while in two cases, theta produces the best results. This indicates that in addition to gamma and beta, theta also plays a vital role in classifying arousal, which belongs to the lower frequency range.

19.3.3.3 Results for EEG Bands Mapped with Brain Regions

Tables 19.5 and 19.6 provide information regarding the prominent EEG bands that exhibited good accuracy and F1 concerning the classification of valance and arousal within distinct brain regions. Tables show that the theta, beta, and gamma bands are prominent for emotion recognition. This data offers additional perspectives on the efficacy of various brain regions and EEG bands in classifying valence.

As presented in previous subsections, KNN produced the best results in most cases. Considering this fact and Table 19.5 and Table 19.6, it can be stated that the beta and theta are the prominent bands for valence and arousal classification, respectively. From these tables, it should also be observed that the prominent bands for specific regions are not consistent, indicating that the inclusion of each band with slightly higher weight to a higher-frequency band is required to classify the emotional states.

Table 19.5 EEG Bands with the Highest Valence Accuracy for Each EEG Region

EEG Regions	Classification Algorithms				
	KNN	SVM	MLP	RFC	RoFC
Left	Beta	Alpha	Beta	Beta	Beta
Frontal	Beta	Alpha	Theta	Alpha	Theta
Right	Gamma	Gamma	Theta	Theta	Theta
Central	Theta	Theta	Beta	Beta	Beta
Parietal	Beta	Alpha	Alpha	Theta	Theta
Occipital	Beta	Theta	Alpha	Beta	Alpha

Table 19.6 EEG Bands with the Highest Arousal Accuracy per Each EEG Region

EEG Regions	Classification Algorithms				
	KNN	SVM	MLP	RFC	RoFC
Left	Theta	Gamma	Gamma	Gamma	Gamma
Frontal	Theta	Beta	Gamma	Alpha	Alpha
Right	Theta	Gamma	Gamma	Alpha	Gamma
Central	Theta	Gamma	Gamma	Gamma	Beta
Parietal	Theta	Theta	Beta	Beta	Beta
Occipital	Theta	Beta	Gamma	Gamma	Gamma

19.4 CONCLUSION

Due to various factors, it might be challenging to decipher EEG data and link it to particular emotions; multiple emotions may simultaneously influence the same portions of the brain in various ways, involving distinct brain regions and EEG bands. Therefore, this study presented the significant brain regions and EEG bands for the classification of valence and arousal. The results show that the frontal and left regions play a crucial role in emotion classification, producing the best accuracy and F1. While the higher-frequency EEG bands, specifically gamma and beta, have a significant role in emotion classification, some experiments also indicated the prominent role of theta. These findings demonstrate the potential of EEG-based emotion detection and emphasise the significance of choosing the proper EEG areas and models for reliable outcomes in BCI applications. However, it's critical to keep in mind that emotion recognition from EEG data is still an intricate and active area of research, requiring additional improvements and adjustments to increase accuracy and applicability in real-world circumstances.

REFERENCES

[1] N. Kannathal, U. R. Acharya, C. M. Lim, and P. Sadasivan, "Characterisation of EEG—a comparative study," *Computer Methods and Programs in Biomedicine*, vol. 80, no. 1, pp. 17–23, 2005.

[2] W. T. Cochran, J. W. Cooley, D. L. Favin, H. D. Helms, R. A. Kaenel, W. W. Lang, G. C. Maling, D. E. Nelson, C. M. Rader, and P. D. Welch, "What is the fast Fourier transform?," *Proceedings of the IEEE*, vol. 55, no. 10, pp. 1664–1674, 1967.

[3] A. Subasi, T. Tuncer, S. Dogan, D. Tanko, and U. Sakoglu, "Eeg-based emotion recognition using tunable q wavelet transform and rotation forest ensemble classifier," *Biomedical Signal Processing and Control*, vol. 68, p. 102648, 2021.

[4] S. Wang, Y. Zhang, C. Wu, F. Darvas, and W. A. Chaovalitwongse, "Online prediction of driver distraction based on brain activity patterns," *IEEE Transactions on Intelligent Transportation Systems*, vol. 16, no. 1, pp. 136–150, 2014.

[5] M. Khateeb, S. M. Anwar, and M. Alnowami, "Multi-domain feature fusion for emotion classification using the deep dataset," *IEEE Access*, vol. 9, pp. 12134–12142, 2021.

[6] H. U. Amin, A. S. Malik, R. F. Ahmad, N. Badruddin, N. Kamel, M. Hussain, and W.-T. Chooi, "Feature extraction and classification for EEG signals using wavelet transform and machine learning techniques," *Australasian Physical & Engineering Sciences in Medicine*, vol. 38, no. 1, pp. 139–149, 2015.

[7] Y. Zhang, X. Ji, and S. Zhang, "An approach to EEG-based emotion recognition using combined feature extraction method," *Neuroscience Letters*, vol. 633, pp. 152–157, 2016.

[8] J. J. Rodriguez, L. I. Kuncheva, and C. J. Alonso, "Rotation forest: A new classifier ensemble method," *IEEE Transactions on Pattern Analysis and Machine Intelligence*, vol. 28, no. 10, pp. 1619–1630, 2006.

[9] S. A. Dudani, "The distance-weighted k-nearest-neighbor rule," *IEEE Transactions on Systems, Man, and Cybernetics*, no. 4, pp. 325–327, 1976.

[10] W. S. Noble, "What is a support vector machine?" *Nature Biotechnology*, vol. 24, no. 12, pp. 1565–1567, 2006.

[11] H. Kukreja, N. Bharath, C. Siddesh, and S. Kuldeep, "An introduction to an artificial neural network," *International Journal of Advance Research and Innovative Ideas in Education*, vol. 1, pp. 27–30, 2016.

[12] C. Lehmann, T. Koenig, V. Jelic, L. Prichep, R. E. John, L.-O. Wahlund, Y. Dodge, and T. Dierks, "Application and comparison of classification algorithms for recognition of Alzheimer's disease in electrical brain activity (EEG)," *Journal of Neuroscience Methods*, vol. 161, no. 2, pp. 342–350, 2007.

[13] J. Cheng, M. Chen, C. Li, Y. Liu, R. Song, A. Liu, and X. Chen, "Emotion recognition from multi-channel eeg via deep forest," *IEEE Journal of Biomedical and Health Informatics*, vol. 25, no. 2, pp. 453–464, 2020.

[14] A. A. Akinduko and A. N. Gorban, "Multiscale principal component analysis," in *Journal of Physics: Conference Series*, vol. 490, p. 012081, IOP Publishing, 2014.

[15] C. Kim, J. Sun, D. Liu, Q. Wang, and S. Paek, "An effective feature extraction method by power spectral density of EEG signal for 2-class motor imagery-based bci," *Medical & Biological Engineering & Computing*, vol. 56, pp. 1645–1658, 2018.

[16] R. N. Youngworth, B. B. Gallagher, and B. L. Stamper, "An overview of power spectral density (PSD) calculations," *Optical Manufacturing and Testing VI*, vol. 5869, pp. 206–216, 2005.

[17] S. Koelstra, C. Muhl, M. Soleymani, J.-S. Lee, A. Yazdani, T. Ebrahimi, T. Pun, A. Nijholt, and I. Patras, "Deap: A database for emotion analysis; using physiological signals," *IEEE Transactions on Affective Computing*, vol. 3, no. 1, pp. 18–31, 2012.

Index